Applied M

There is a growing theoretical and practical interest in the topic of meta-cognition: how we monitor and control our mental processes. *Applied Metacognition* provides a coherent and up-to-date overview of the relation between theories in metacognition and their application in real-world situations. As well as a theoretical overview, there are substantive chapters covering metacognition in three areas of application: metacognition in education, metacognition in everyday life memory, and metacognition in different populations. A diverse range of topics is covered such as how we judge our own learning, why we create false beliefs about our past, how children learn to monitor and control their memory, how well eyewitnesses can judge the accuracy of their own memories, and how memory judgments change across the lifespan. The book has contributions from many of the leading researchers in metacognition worldwide.

TIMOTHY J. PERFECT is Professor of Experimental Psychology at the University of Plymouth. He is on the editorial board of *Memory* and of *Applied Cognitive Psychology*, and has published numerous articles. He is co-editor with E. Maylor of *Models of Cognitive Aging* (2000).

BENNETT L. SCHWARTZ is Associate Professor of Psychology at Florida International University. His research interests include metacognition, memory accuracy, and memory in non-human primates. He has authored and co-authored over twenty papers, and published *Tip-of-the-Tongue States: Phenomenology, Mechanism and Lexical Retrieval* (2002).

Applied Metacognition

Edited by

Timothy J. Perfect
Bennett L. Schwartz

CAMBRIDGE
UNIVERSITY PRESS

PUBLISHED BY THE PRESS SYNDICATE OF THE UNIVERSITY OF CAMBRIDGE
The Pitt Building, Trumpington Street, Cambridge, CB2 1RP, United Kingdom

CAMBRIDGE UNIVERSITY PRESS
The Edinburgh Building, Cambridge CB2 2RU, UK
40 West 20th Street, New York, NY 10011-4211, USA
477 Williamstown Road, Port Melbourne, VIC 3207, Australia
Ruiz de Alarcón 13, 28014 Madrid, Spain
Dock House, The Waterfront, Cape Town 8001, South Africa

http://www.cambridge.org

First published 2002

Printed in the United Kingdom at the University Press, Cambridge

Typeface Plantin 10/12 pt   *System* LaTeX 2$_\varepsilon$ [TB]

A catalogue record for this book is available from the British Library

Library of Congress Cataloguing in Publication data

Applied metacognition / edited by Timothy J. Perfect, Bennett L. Schwartz.
    p.   cm.
Includes bibliographical references and index.
ISBN 0 521 80189 3 – ISBN 0 521 00037 8 (pbk.)
    1. Metacognition–Congresses. I. Perfect, Timothy J. II. Schwartz, Bennett L.
BF311 .A638 2002   153–dc21   2002024499

ISBN 0 521 80189 3 hardback
ISBN 0 521 00037 8 paperback

This book is dedicated to our wives,
Tara Hollins and Leslie Frazier

Contents

Contributors

BENNETT L. SCHWARTZ, Florida International University, USA

TIMOTHY J. PERFECT, University of Plymouth, UK

LISA K. SON, Barnard College, USA

RUTH H. MAKI, Texas Tech University, USA

MICHAEL J. McGUIRE, Texas Tech University, USA

JOHN DUNLOSKY, University of North Carolina at Greensboro, USA

KATHERINE A. RAWSON, University of Colorado at Boulder, USA

SUSAN L. McDONALD, University of North Carolina at Greensboro, USA

GIULIANA MAZZONI, Seton Hall University, USA

IRVING KIRSCH, University of Connecticut, USA

MARIE CARROLL, University of Canberra, Australia

CHRISTOPHER HERTZOG, Georgia Institute of Technology, USA

CHRIS MOULIN, University of Leeds, UK

WOLFGANG SCHNEIDER, University of Würzburg, Germany

KATHRIN LOCKL, University of Würzburg, Germany

ASHER KORIAT, University of Haifa, Israel

Preface

The seeds for this volume were planted prior to the Society for Applied Research in Memory and Cognition (SARMAC) conference in Boulder, Colorado. The editors of this volume planned to organize a symposium for the conference on applications of metacognition research. Within days of their initial emails to potential participants, the symposium had become symposia, and in the end, there were three separate sessions on metacognition at that conference. The enthusiasm of metacognition researchers, generally a theoretically oriented lot, for applications was palpable. Most of these chapters stem from discussions held at that conference.

During the conference barbecue, the editors began mapping out a volume to be called *Applied metacognition*, whilst simultaneously contemplating the Rocky Mountains in the distance, trying to eat a barbecue with a plastic knife while sitting on the grass, and helping themselves to the contents of a complimentary bar. The conversation and wine flowed freely, and eventually the current volume took shape. Our aim was a book that would cover as many potential applications of metacognitive research as possible and would be inclusive of different approaches within the field. To meet this aim, we decided to approach some of the foremost researchers in the area. Fortunately, many of them were at the same barbecue, and so the task was not as onerous as it might have been.

There are many people to thank who helped us prepare the book. We gratefully acknowledge all of the authors who contributed to this book. Others were instrumental to the book's genesis. Tom Nelson and Janet Metcalfe, although they did not contribute chapters, encouraged us and provided us with ideas and inspiration. We especially thank Chris Moulin for providing the cover photograph. We are immensely indebted to Sarah Caro at Cambridge University Press both for encouragement and for gently directing us towards completion.

1 Introduction: toward an applied metacognition

Bennett L. Schwartz and Timothy J. Perfect

Metacognition is traditionally defined as the experiences and knowledge we have about our own cognitive processes (e.g. Flavell, 1979). Although ripe for philosophers and cognitive psychologists (e.g. Nelson, 1996), this topic may not appear at a first glance to be one immediately applicable to everyday human life. However, we hope to show in this book that metacognition has broad applications across a number of different settings. Furthermore, we contend that, unlike some laboratory research, metacognitive data from the lab have parallels to real-world phenomena and therefore can be applied. The nature of metacognition is such that, in order to study it effectively in the lab, one must devise situations that mimic real life. The current volume will also attest to the ease with which metacognition research moves back and forth from theoretical questions to applied concerns, a situation we consider most desirable in any scientific endeavor.

Let us begin with examples from everyday life in which metacognition is important. Imagine a student studying for an exam. It is well past midnight, she has been studying for hours, and is exhausted. The decision that this student must make is whether she has studied the material for the exam sufficiently and can go to sleep, or whether she must brew another pot of coffee and keep studying. The student must decide whether the material is generally well-learned, and if not, what information necessitates further study. These decisions influence not only the student's caffeine intake but also her studying behavior and, ultimately, her test performance (see Nelson, 1993). In the lab, this situation has been modeled with judgments of learning and the control of study time (see Dunlosky, Rawson, and McDonald, this volume; Son and Schwartz, this volume). These studies reveal important and counterintuitive findings which can be applied in educational settings.

Now imagine a lawyer questioning a witness. The lawyer asks if the witness is confident that his memory of the events he saw at the scene of the crime are accurate. The witness replies, "Absolutely, I'll never forget that face as long as I live." We know, from decades of research, that eyewitness memory is not always accurate. However, it is also important to determine if the witness' confidence in the accuracy of his own memory predicts the actual accuracy of the memory. Indeed, there have been cases in which the witness declares something similar to the sentence above and then points to the lawyer rather than the defendant. Witness confidence is a metacognitive judgment, and recent progress in this area is reviewed in this volume as well (see Perfect, this volume).

In the course of this volume, we will touch on applications of metacognition to children's learning (Schneider and Lockl), to adult education (Carroll and Perfect; Maki and McGuire; Dunlosky et al.; Son and Schwartz), to eyewitness memory (Perfect; Mazzoni and Kirsch), and to neuropsychological patients and older adults (Moulin; Hertzog). Whereas the first two fields of application are already quite advanced, the second two areas are just beginning to gain momentum. In this chapter, we will briefly review the history of metacognition research, introduce the key concepts of monitoring and control, reflect on the importance of metacognition to consciousness, and then entice the reader to read the remaining chapters.

History of metacognition research

Modern research in metacognition has two parallel roots, one in the emerging cognitive psychology of the 1960s (e.g. Hart, 1965) and the other in the post-Piagetian developmental psychology of the 1970s (e.g. Flavell, 1979). To some extent, these two tracks have remained largely separate. Today, there are two parallel fields, each called metacognition (Kuhn, 2000; Schwartz, Benjamin, and Bjork, 1997). Recently, however, there has been a more concerted effort to bring these two tracks in metacognition closer together (e.g. Hacker, Dunlosky, and Graesser, 1998; Hertzog, this volume). It is our belief that each track has something to add to the advancement toward an applied metacognition.

Hart (1965, 1967) was interested in the accuracy of judgments people made about memory. Coming from an adult cognition tradition, Hart assumed that adults have conscious experiences such as "feelings of knowing." What was important to discover was whether they were valid predictors of behavior. He devised a paradigm, dubbed the RJR procedure, to test metamemory judgments. First, he gave people a recall test (R), of either newly learned information or general knowledge. For example, participants might have been asked, "What is the capital city of the Bahamas?" (Nassau). If the participant was unsuccessful at recall, the participant was asked to make a feeling-of-knowing judgment (J), predicting the answer would be recognized in a multiple-choice format. In Hart's (1965) first study, participants simply indicated yes – they had a feeling of knowing – or no – they did not. In the second experiment, Hart (1965) used a six-point scale for feeling of knowing, although this was dichotomized with points 1–3 corresponding to feeling of knowing, and 4–6 corresponding to feeling of not knowing. Subsequent studies introduced more conventional Likert-scale measurements (see Nelson, 1988). Finally, the participant received the recognition test (R). Hart (1965) showed that feeling-of-knowing judgments did indeed predict the likelihood of correct recognition for general knowledge materials, an observation replicated many times (see Nelson, 1988; Schwartz, 1994). Hart (1967) extended this technique to episodic memory, demonstrating that feeling-of-knowing judgments were above chance in predicting recognition of trigram materials in a paired-associate task. The RJR technique mostly lay dormant until the 1980s when it was revised by Thomas Nelson and his colleagues (e.g. Nelson and Narens, 1980, but see Gruneberg and Monks, 1974 for an exception).

Developmentalists were also interested in metacognition, but chose a different avenue of exploration. Flavell (1979) was interested in finding out if the improvement in children's memory abilities was a function of greater conscious understanding of the rules that govern memory and cognition (see Kuhn, 2000). Thus, his studies trace the development of metacognitive thinking, that is, the ability to reflect on one's cognitive processes. Unfortunately, not yet fully armed with the ideas of monitoring and control (Nelson and Narens, 1990), Flavell's research agenda did not show any strong correlations between metacognitive thinking and improvements in memory. Indeed, many developmentalists from this camp abandoned metacognition for the greener pastures of theory of mind (Wimmer and Perner, 1983). Nonetheless, Flavell's approach has had a strong influence on the development of metamemory in a number of domains (Hacker, 1998).

In recent years, there has been a impressive confluence of the two "schools" of metacognition. Developmentalists have begun to borrow the tools developed by Hart, Nelson, and others to investigate the questions that Flavell originally set out to answer. In this volume, Schneider and Lockl offer a more extensive history of this interaction and the many fruits it is now bearing. They focus on how this has led to new understanding of how metacognition develops in children. Also in this volume, Hertzog focuses on how metacognition changes in later adulthood.

In mainstream cognitive psychology, metacognition still lingered at the fringes. Indeed, at most conferences, metacognition researchers presented their papers in memory sessions not metacognition sessions. At the American Psychonomic Society meeting, a session on metacognition did not emerge until 1997. Metacognition did receive a significant boost from its endorsement by the "everyday memory" movement (e.g. Neisser, 1978). Early pioneers in the everyday memory movement studied meta-memory phenomena, particularly the feeling of knowing (e.g. Gruneberg and Monks, 1974). In 2002, although not quite as "hot" or "fashionable" an area as false memories or theories of word recognition, metacognition has emerged as an important sub-field of cognitive psychology. Perhaps in part, the emergence of metacognition into the mainstream reflects the greater focus of cognitive psychologists on the experiential aspects of memory (Tulving, 1985). The concept of a false memory brings with it the notions of *beliefs* in memory and *judgments* about the source, and veracity of memories. Thus, cognitive researchers focusing on false memory are led inevitably towards a consideration of metacognitive aspects of remembering (see Mazzoni and Kirsch, this volume).

Monitoring and control

Metacognition came into the "modern" era with the publication of Nelson and Narens' (1990; see Nelson, 1996) theory of monitoring and control. This theory was able to organize and integrate almost all of the extant research on metacognition. As the chapters in this volume show, it has also served as an effective model for applications of metacognition (see Son and Schwartz, this volume). The theory concentrates on the interaction between two metacognitive processes, monitoring and control.

Metacognitive monitoring is those processes that allow the individual to observe, reflect on, or experience his or her own cognitive processes. Thus, one may know that one has mastered his or her arithmetic tables, or one may feel that they have understood a text they have just read. In the laboratory, metacognitive monitoring is revealed by asking participants to make feeling-of-knowing judgments, judgments of learning, ease-of-learning judgments, warmth judgments, judgments of comprehension, etc. Monitoring informs the person of the state of their cognition relative to their current goal.

Metacognitive control is the conscious and non-conscious *decisions* that we make based on the output of our monitoring processes. Control processes are revealed by the behaviors a person engages in as a function of monitoring. Thus, if a person feels that an item is not adequately encoded, they may choose to continue studying that item. If a person feels that they have not understood a passage of text, they may re-read it. In the laboratory, we can observe control processes through such measures as response latency, allocation of study time, and decisions about which items to study (e.g. Son and Metcalfe, 2000; Thiede and Dunlosky, 1999).

The idea of control processes is crucial to the development of applied metacognition. If control processes exist and influence human behavior and cognition, it may be possible to improve or alter control processes in ways which will improve human learning. Consider the work of Thiede and Dunlosky, 1999 (see also Son and Schwartz, this volume). Thiede and Dunlosky asked students to make judgments of learning (JOLs) on paired-associate word pairs, that were either concrete nouns (e.g. dog–spoon) or abstract words (e.g. democracy–gravity). Later, they were given the option to chose items for re-study. When time pressure to learn was high, the students chose those that had been given high JOLs. When time pressure was low, the students chose the harder items to study, that is, those given low JOLs. Thus, depending on the context, the students made different control decisions. Although conducted in a lab under controlled settings, the applied value of this study is obvious: perhaps we can teach students to use adaptive and flexible control strategies. Thus, the introduction of the concept of control radically altered the kinds of questions that could be asked about how to apply metacognitive findings.

Metacognition and awareness

Flavell (1979) made the distinction between metacognitive knowledge and metacognitive awareness (see also Kuhn, 2000). Metacognitive knowledge refers to explicit knowledge about our own cognitive strengths and weaknesses. Thus, the authors of this chapter can confidently assert that they know most of the capitals of the nations of Western Europe, but very few of the capitals of the nations of Africa. This statement requires no conscious retrieval. Similarly, the first author would assert that he knows a great deal about the sport of basketball, but very little about cricket, with the reverse being true for the second author. Metacognitive awareness refers to the feelings and experiences we have when we engage in cognitive processes, such as retrieval. Thus, when asked about what happened during the last series played between the nations of the West Indies and England at cricket, the first author experiences a vague feeling of familiarity without being able to specify the when, the where, and the events associated with this story. He might make a judgment that he might recognize some of this information, but would also judge an inability to recall any specific information. The second author on the other hand recalls the events vividly, can give the exact score of the series, details of each match, and has clear recollections of a day spent pacing in front of the television set during a crucial match in the series.

Traditionally, developmentalists have been more interested in the first aspect of metacognition. Schneider and Lockl (this volume) and Hertzog (this volume) concentrate their chapters on the development of metacognitive knowledge and how it changes over the lifespan. Important here is the concept of memory self-efficacy, that is, how well people think they are going to learn new information. The very young tend to overestimate their self-efficacy, whereas older adults often underestimate theirs. Mazzoni and Kirsch (this volume) make some interesting applications about people's beliefs about their own memory to the development of false autobiographical memories. Cognitivists have been more interested in metacognitive experience, as reflected in their attention to feeling-of-knowing judgments, judgments of learning, etc. Of interest here are both the underlying processes and the extent to which these judgments predict actual performance. We see a focus on this issue in the work here of Dunlosky et al., Maki and McGuire, Perfect, and Son and Schwartz. Perfect, for example, examines how people's feelings of confidence for witnessed events predict the likelihood that their memories are indeed accurate.

Domains of application

Our goal in this volume is to establish the importance of metacognition to a variety of applied concerns, and specifically, to demonstrate how metacognition can inform these areas. It is our belief that metacognition has made a good start at being applied, as a number of researchers in the field are actively engaged in applying their results. In addition, many metacognition researchers ask questions that are applied in nature to begin with.

We consider that the following chapters will make important contributions to two applied domains, namely (a) education, specifically applications toward improving learning and training; and (b) legal contexts, specifically in the self-evaluation of eyewitness reports. The chapters here also touch on applications to other domains including counseling (self-evaluation of coping strategies, beliefs in recovered memories), human factors (self-monitoring of job performance), and recovery from brain injuries.

The current volume contains at least one chapter on each of these topics. Educational applications predominate, as most applied metacognition has had some form of learning as its focus. Maki and McGuire (this volume) discuss the growing literature on the monitoring of comprehension. Many studies find that students, even capable college students, do not always adequately monitor their understanding of texts that they have read. If they do not know that they do not understand what they have read, they cannot take steps to ensure learning and understanding. Maki and McGuire describe steps that can be taken to improve the accuracy of monitoring of comprehension.

In another chapter with important educational implications, Carroll and Perfect (this volume) discuss the metacognitive bases of unconscious plagiarism. As any professor knows, plagiarism occurs quite regularly among the students we teach. Some of it is largely unintentional and even unconscious. Nonetheless, such plagiarism can still have disastrous consequences for students. The ability to self-identify unconscious plagiarism, and the ability of teachers to distinguish intentional from unconscious plagiarism has the potential for far-reaching impact in our schools and universities.

Dunlosky et al. investigate how practicing can help improve metacognitive monitoring. They argue that encouraging people to take practice tests can improve their ability to predict how they will do on the actual tests. In this way, practice testing may help people to study more effectively. Schneider and Lockl write a review of the development of metacognitive knowledge and its implications for children's learning. Son and Schwartz review the theory of monitoring and control and discuss how this theory may be used to develop better educational techniques.

If we turn our attention to eyewitness memory and the psychology of memory that has become so important in court proceedings, we find that metacognitive issues have been at the forefront of this domain from almost the beginning. The confidence a witness displays in his or her testimony has a strong effect on juries, judges, and the general public. Unfortunately, and surprisingly, much of the research on this topic suggests that confidence and accuracy are very loosely correlated (e.g. Bothwell, Deffenbacher, and Brigham, 1987; Perfect, this volume). Does this research suggest that judges and juries should revise their opinion and attempt to discount variation among witnesses' confidence? Perfect (this volume) argues that it is too early to answer this question. He argues that, because this research examines a correlation between two psychological measures, problems inherent in correlational data, such as restricted range issues, must be addressed first. Instead, he proposes a research agenda that will assess if confidence–accuracy associations are driven by such features as level of performance, the details of interest, across personality types, and across people's metacognitive beliefs about their areas of expertise. Perfect finds that whereas personality types do not predict much about eyewitness accuracy, people who believe they have strong memories often express overconfidence leading to poor accuracy. These findings have important implications for both theoretical and applied research.

Mazzoni and Kirsch examine the role of metacognitive beliefs in the retrieval of autobiographical memories and discuss the implications in legal and clinical settings. In their model, people use metacognitive criteria to assess the veracity of retrieved memories. Furthermore, metacognitive beliefs are also used to assess if the inability to retrieve a memory implies that person did not witness or participate in an event. Mazzoni and Kirsch then discuss many studies that support this general system. For example, they point to research that suggests that misinformation is more likely to produce a false memory for a plausible than a non-plausible event (Pezdek, Finger, and Hodge, 1997), and that credible information indicating that an event did occur increases the rate that the person believes the event did occur (Mazzoni et al., in press).

For Mazzoni and Kirsch, metacognitive beliefs function similarly to Flavell's (1979) notion of metacognitive knowledge, that is, it is explicit reportable knowledge about how memory functions. As such, it is educable. Thus, the role of metacognitive beliefs in false memories is a correctable one. This has implications for both legal and clinical outcomes.

Hertzog is also concerned with memory beliefs, namely the changing beliefs about the efficacy of one's memory as one ages. Hertzog is concerned that many older adults may have internalized stereotypes of age-related memory declines, even when these beliefs are not necessarily accurate. These stereotypes create a self-fulfilling prophecy because the poor expectations may lead to anxiety and other negative effects. Again, as these beliefs are educable, it is possible that better education can reassure and provide a sense of confidence to older adults.

One of the new exciting areas of application of metacognitive theory is in the area of neuropsychological assessment. Although the role of the brain in metacognition has been occasionally the subject of inquiry (Shimamura and Squire, 1986; Metcalfe, 1993), application to patient groups is a very new area. Moulin (this volume) incorporates concepts of metacognition, particularly that of improved control, as a method for softening the loss of mnemonic ability associated with early Alzheimer's disease. This is based on his studies, which suggest that early Alzheimer's patients can still accurately monitor their memory abilities.

We suspect that metacognition will increasingly be applied in areas of psychology as diverse as educational psychology, neuropsychology, psychological gerontology, as well as other sub-fields. Although not represented here, Bjork and his colleagues have been applying metacognition research to a variety of training situations from the military to sports teams (see Bjork, 1994; 1999). Nelson and his colleagues have been applying metacognitive research to the learning of foreign language vocabulary (Nelson et al., 1994). Thus, we anticipate a bright future for metacognition research.

Conclusions

Hermann (1998) distinguished between four types of research methodologies, three of which were related to applied research. The first group are theory-based researchers, for whom application is not initially relevant. Rather, their goal is to understand basic processes. The second group of researchers are basic researchers who stress ecological validity, also known as the "everyday memory" movement, in memory research. These researchers are fundamentally interested in basic questions of theory, but wish to address them in a way that has direct validity to everyday life. The important point about "ecologically valid" research is that, although it tells us something about ordinary life, it may not be directly applicable.

The third type of research is labeled "applicable research" by Hermann (1998). Applicable research implies ecologically valid research, but research for which applications follow naturally. A typical example is that Loftus' misinformation-effect studies clearly suggest that investigators should avoid leading and misleading questions when questioning a witness or suspect. Finally, Hermann's fourth type of research is "application research." This involves research on specific instruments, products, or services which have been designed to work in specific domains. Thus, application research might involve experimenting on whether a specific form of therapy helps amnesic patients remember more of what they have been taught.

The chapters in this book are mostly of the "applicable research" variety. The researchers have not yet designed specific interventions to improve learning, to ameliorate Alzheimer's, or to assist judges and juries. However, because the research is ecologically valid and application is kept in mind, the potential application of much research on metacognition falls naturally out of the studies used to explore it. Thus, the schoolteacher looking for specific methods to improve metacognitive understanding may find these chapters premature, but the researcher looking to design specific application tools should find these chapters invaluable.

REFERENCES

Bjork, R. A. (1994). Memory and metamemory considerations in the training of human beings. In J. Metcalfe and A. P. Shimamura (eds.), *Metacognition: knowing about knowing*, pp. 185–205. Cambridge, MA: MIT Press.

(1999). Assessing our own competence: heuristics and illusions. In D. Gopher and A. Koriat (eds.), *Attention and performance XVII. Cognitive regulation of performance: interaction of theory and application*. Cambridge, MA: MIT Press.

Bothwell, R. K., Deffenbacher, K. A., and Brigham, J. C. (1987). Correlation of eyewitness accuracy and confidence: optimality hypothesis revisited. *Journal of Applied Psychology*, 72, 691–695.

Flavell, J. H. (1979). Metacognitive and cognitive monitoring: a new area of cognitive developmental inquiry. *American Psychologist*, 34, 906–911.

Gruneberg, M. M., and Monks, J. (1974). "Feeling of knowing" and cued recall. *Acta Psychologica*, 38, 257–265.

Hacker, D. J. (1998). Definitions and empirical foundations. In D. J. Hacker, J. Dunlosky, and A. C. Graesser (eds.), *Metacognition in educational theory and practice*, pp. 1–24. New Jersey: Lawrence Erlbaum Associates.

Hacker, D. J., Dunlosky, J., and Graesser, A. C. (1998). *Metacognition in educational theory and practice*. New Jersey: Lawrence Erlbaum Associates.

Hart, J. T. (1965). Memory and the feeling-of-knowing experience. *Journal of Educational Psychology*, 56, 208–216.

(1967). Memory and the memory-monitoring process. *Journal of Verbal Learning and Verbal Behavior*, 6, 685–691.

Herrmann, D. J. (1998). The relationship between basic research and applied research in memory and cognition. In C. P. Thompson, D. J. Hermann, D. Bruce, J. D. Read, D. G. Payne, and M. P. Toglia (eds.), *Autobiographical memory: theoretical and applied perspectives*, pp. 13–27. New Jersey: Lawrence Erlbaum Associates.

Kuhn, D. (2000). Metacognitive development. *Current Directions in Psychological Science*, 9, 178–181.

Metcalfe, J. (1993). Novelty monitoring, metacognition, and control in a composite holographic associative recall model: interpretations for Korsakoff amnesia. *Psychological Review*, 100, 3–22.

Neisser, U. (1978). Memory: what are the important questions? In M. M. Gruneberg, P. Morris, and R. L. Sykes (eds.), *Practical aspects of memory*, pp. 3–24. London: Academic Press.

Nelson, T. O. (1988). Predictive accuracy of feeling of knowing across different criterion tasks and across different subject populations and individuals. In M. Gruneberg, P. Morris, and R. Sykes (eds.), *Practical aspects of memory: current research and issues, Volume 1*, pp. 190–196. New York: Wiley.

(1993). Judgments of learning and the allocation of study time. *Journal of Experimental Psychology: General*, 122, 269–273.

(1996). Consciousness and metacognition. *American Psychologist*, 51, 102–116.

Nelson, T. O., Dunlosky, J., Graf, A., and Narens, L. (1994). Utilization of metacognitive judgments in the allocation of study during multitrial learning. *Psychological Science*, 5, 207–213.

Nelson, T. O., and Narens, L. (1980). Norms of 300 general-information questions: accuracy of recall, latency of recall, and feeling-of-knowing ratings. *Journal of Verbal Learning and Verbal Behavior*, 19, 338–368.

(1990). Metamemory: a theoretical framework and new findings. In G. Bower (ed.), *The psychology of learning and motivation, Volume 26*, pp. 125–141. San Diego, CA: Academic Press.

Pezdek, K., Finger, K., and Hodge, D. (1997). Planting false childhood memories: the role of event plausibility. *Psychological Science*, 8, 437–441.

Schwartz, B. L. (1994). Sources of information in metamemory: judgments of learning and feelings of knowing. *Psychonomic Bulletin and Review*, 1, 357–375.

Schwartz, B. L., Benjamin, A. S., and Bjork, R. A. (1997). The inferential and experiential basis of metamemory. *Current Directions in Psychological Science*, 6, 132–137.

Shimamura, A. P., and Squire, L. R. (1986). Memory and metamemory: a study of the feeling-of-knowing phenomenon in amnesic patients. *Journal of Experimental Psychology: Learning, Memory, and Cognition*, 12, 452–460.

Son, L. K., and Metcalfe, J. (2000). Metacognitive and control strategies in study-time allocation. *Journal of Experimental Psychology: Learning, Memory, and Cognition*, 26, 204–221.

Thiede, K. W., and Dunlosky, J. (1999). Toward a general model of self-regulated study: an analysis of selection of items for study and self-paced study time. *Journal of Experimental Psychology: Learning, Memory, and Cognition*, 25, 1024–1037.

Tulving, E. (1985). Memory and consciousness. *Canadian Psychologist*, 26, 1–12.

Wimmer, H., and Perner, J. (1983). Beliefs about beliefs: representation and constraining function of wrong beliefs in young children's understanding of deception. *Cognition*, 13, 103–128.

Part 1

Metacognition in learning and education

2 The relation between metacognitive monitoring and control

Lisa K. Son and Bennett L. Schwartz

> Introspective observation is what we have to rely on first and foremost and always.
>
> William James (*Principles of psychology*, p. 185)

William James' (1890) quote foreshadowed the current focus in the field of metacognition, the relation between monitoring and control. Monitoring means the ability to judge successfully one's own cognitive processes, and control means the ability to use those judgments to alter behavior. This chapter, like much of current metacognition research, concerns how we apply our judgments to alter our behavior, both during learning and during remembering.

About twenty years ago, Cavanaugh and Perlmutter (1982) wrote that the "present state of metamemory is not good..." (p. 22), and Flavell (1982) wrote that "none of us has yet come up with deeply insightful, detailed proposals about what metacognition is, how it operates, and how it develops" (p. 28). Some thought that metacognition was no longer a worthwhile topic (see Marshall and Morton, 1978; Wellman, 1983). However, starting with the seminal work of Thomas Nelson and his colleagues (e.g. Nelson, 1984; Nelson et al., 1982; Nelson et al., 1986), metacognition made a strong comeback. Whereas the research on metacognition prior to the 1980s was dominated by research directed at developmental processes (e.g. Flavell, 1979), research in the 1980s and 1990s was dominated by cognitive psychologists interested in already-developed processes in adults. It seems, though, that in order to maximize the knowledge gained from both lines of research, a marriage between the two is needed. This combination will be especially important for the applied standpoint taken here, where we attempt to understand how metacognitive strategies are put to use in everyday learning situations.

Within the adult tradition, much of the research in the 1980s concerned whether metacognitive judgments were, indeed, accurate (see Nelson, 1988 for a review). This was followed by a brief spurt of research concerned with the cognitive mechanisms underlying metacognitive

15

judgments (see Schwartz, 1994 for a review). Nowadays, many researchers in metacognition have switched their focus to issues of metacognitive control, or how people use metacognitive judgments to adjust, strategize, and maximize learning (e.g. Dunlosky and Hertzog, 1998; Nelson et al., 1994; Schwartz, 2001; Son and Metcalfe, 2000; Thiede and Dunlosky, 1999). Consistent with this trend, this chapter reviews the current data regarding the interaction between monitoring and control during learning and remembering. However, it is important first to investigate the accuracies of metacognitive judgments and how they are made. Only then is it worthwhile to investigate how these metacognitions are used to control behavior.

Is there a relation between monitoring and control?

Flavell (1976) first coined the term metacognition as "one's knowledge concerning one's own cognitive processes and products or anything related to them, e.g. the learning-relevant properties of information and data" (p. 232). He further described metacognition as that which "refers among other things, to the active monitoring and consequent regulation and orchestration of these processes in relation to the cognitive objects or data on which they bear, usually in the service of some concrete goal or objective" (p. 232). Along similar lines, Kluwe (1982) summarized two general attributes of metacognition: (a) the thinking subject has some knowledge about his own thinking and that of other persons; and (b) the thinking subject may monitor and regulate the course of his own thinking. A third theorist, Brown (1987), referred to metacognition as the state of one's knowledge and the control of one's own cognitive system. Based on these definitions, many researchers agreed that there were two distinct processes taking place: monitoring and control. However, at the time that these ideas were advanced, there was little direct evidence to suggest that people did use the output of their monitoring to control their behavior.

In contrast, it was possible to think of metacognitive judgments as being mere epiphenomena. Individuals experience feelings, which can be stated as judgments, but they have no influence on the cognitive processes that we use to encode, retrieve, calculate, and solve problems. Indeed, some have speculated, these ephemeral feelings and judgments may not even accurately reflect those cognitive processes. Nelson and Narens (1990) feared, early in their research, that participants' judgments resembled a funhouse mirror, by which they meant that the judgments may be reliable, but consistently distorted. They also wondered if an individual's own metacognition was any better than the judgments of an outside observer

(Nelson et al., 1982). If monitoring is completely inaccurate, the issue of control becomes moot; why investigate whether metacognition has a causal role in cognition, if it cannot reflect ongoing cognition?

If, under certain conditions, judgments are accurate in predicting learning, then the nature of the relation between judgments and the control of behavior is important both theoretically and in applied settings. There is also a remarkable consensus on the heuristic value of an important process theory developed by Nelson and Narens (1990, 1994). The theory consists of a basic structure containing two interrelated levels: a metalevel and an object-level. The metalevel is dynamic in that it works by assessing the present situation state by state, and is guided by introspection. The object-level includes an individual's actions and behaviors, and describes the external state of the present situation. During metacognitive monitoring, the metalevel is informed by the object-level of the present state, and, in turn, during metacognitive control, the metalevel modifies the object-level. An overview of the two separate, but influencing, processes during learning illustrated by Nelson and Narens is shown in Figure 2.1 (1990, 1994). Monitoring occurs before retrieval, either in advance of learning, or during ongoing learning and retention. This includes ease-of-learning judgments, judgments of learning, and feeling-of-knowing judgments. Feeling-of-knowing judgments may also take place during retrieval. Confidence judgments may occur after retrieval has taken place. Conversely, control comes into play during ongoing learning, as in the allocation of study time, and during retrieval, specifically for search strategy and termination of search.

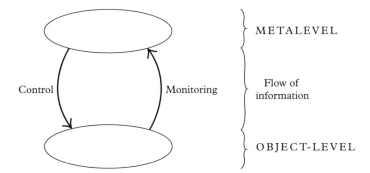

Figure 2.1 An overview of the two separate, but influencing, processes during learning as illustrated by Nelson and Narens (1990, 1994). During metacognitive monitoring, the metalevel is informed by the object-level of the present state, and, in turn, during metacognitive control, the metalevel modifies the object-level.

Metacognitive monitoring

The first studies investigating the accuracy of metacognitive monitoring judgments were published in the 1960s by Hart (1965), Underwood (1966), and Arbuckle and Cuddy (1969). Hart (1965) was the first person to investigate feeling-of-knowing judgments. He asked participants general-information questions in a recall test, then asked for feeling-of-knowing judgments for those questions that were unanswered, and finally gave a recognition test. His results showed that subjects' feeling-of-knowing judgments were accurate at predicting which items would be correctly recognized. Underwood (1966), the first to investigate ease-of-learning judgments, presented subjects with three-letter trigrams. The trigrams varied from common three-letter words to difficult consonant syllables. Participants had to rate the difficulty of learning the items either by drawing a line with a length corresponding to the rate of learning that particular trigram or by giving a numerical rating for how difficult the item seemed relative to an average. Finally, the participants were all given a recall test. Results showed that individuals predicted their own learning with high success (correlations approximately 0.90). Arbuckle and Cuddy (1969) were the first to study what would later be called judgments of learning (e.g. Nelson and Narens, 1994). They presented participants with lists of paired associates, and participants were asked to predict if they could recall each pair. After giving a rating of how sure they were that they would remember the pair, the participants were then given a memory test. Results showed that the predictions were significantly accurate for each individual – those paired associates given lower, or more difficult, ratings were recalled less well than those given higher, or easier, ratings. The main finding from these early studies was that people could reliably predict at the time of presentation if they would be able to recall that item later.

Although there have been a number of experiments demonstrating the accuracy of people's monitoring judgments before, or during, ongoing study (Brown, 1978; Dunlosky and Nelson, 1992, 1994, 1997; Gruneberg and Monks, 1974; Jacoby, Bjork, and Kelley, 1993; Johnson, 1988; Johnson and Raye, 1981; King, Zechmeister, and Shaughnessy, 1980; Leonesio and Nelson, 1990; Lovelace, 1984; Mazzoni et al., 1997; Mazzoni and Nelson, 1995; Metcalfe, 1986a, 1986b; Metcalfe, Schwartz, and Joaquim, 1993; Metcalfe and Weibe, 1987; Nelson, 1988; Nelson and Dunlosky, 1991, 1994; Nelson et al., 1986; Schwartz and Metcalfe, 1994; Thiede and Dunlosky, 1994; Vesonder and Voss, 1985; Widner and Smith, 1996; Widner, Smith, and Graziano, 1996), most researchers in metacognition today would agree with Blake's (1973) early statement concluding that judgments are *intermediate* in accuracy, being reliably above chance, but far from perfect. Furthermore, there have been a few circumstances under which people are not always accurate and indeed sometimes inaccurate (see Koriat, 1995 for a description of these exceptions). People were found to be consistently overconfident in their judgments (Fischhoff, Slovic, and Lichtenstein, 1977; Lichtenstein and Fischhoff, 1977), inaccurate in eyewitness testimony (Loftus and Zanni, 1975; Siegel and Loftus, 1978), and both overconfident and inaccurate in predicting future memory performance (Benjamin, Bjork, and Schwartz, 1998). Still, there was hope in the notion that metacognitions might be improved under certain conditions. In fact, it has been shown that predictive accuracy of metacognitive judgments can be improved upon by presenting a delay after presentation of a new item, and before making the judgment – this is known as the delayed-judgment-of-learning effect (Nelson and Dunlosky, 1991; Weaver and Keleman, 1997). Nelson and Dunlosky (1991) presented participants with lists of cue-target pairs, and, rather than asking for metacognitive judgment immediately after study, they put in a delay of at least ten intervening items between study and judgment. With the introduction of that delay, predictive correlations between the judgments and later performance became close to great (jumping from about 0.4 to 0.9!). In general, researchers have held the notion that people do have an ability to look at their cognitions and make somewhat accurate assessments about them.

Mechanisms of metacognition

What is the basis for the judgments? Given that people have the ability to make fairly accurate metacognitive judgments, the next question was how? Two fundamental hypotheses have dominated the discussion concerning the mechanisms underlying metacognitive judgments. Two views are commonly called the direct access and inferential views (Nelson, Gerler, and Narens, 1984; Schwartz, 1994). Direct access states that people are able to make a metacognitive judgment based on features of the target that they can access or retrieve. With respect to feeling-of-knowing (FOK) and tip-of-the-tongue (TOT) states, this means that rememberers have metacognitive access to information they cannot fully retrieve. This direct mechanism states that if an individual can access features of a searched-for target, then a strong and positive metacognitive judgment would be given to that particular item. If, on the other hand, only a few features of the target were accessible, a weaker metacognitive judgment would be recorded. In contrast, the inferential view states that people base their metacognitive judgment on a host of clues and cues. One variant of the inferential view, the cue familiarity hypothesis, states that metacognitive judgments are based on the level of recognition of the cue at the time the judgments are made (Metcalfe, 1993a). For example, a person may give a high feeling-of-knowing judgment for the question "Who won the 100 meter dash in 1992?" (Linford Christie) because of the high familiarity in the subject of athletics and not because of any actual information that they had on the target answer. Cue familiarity has had success in predicting experimental results (Glenberg et al., 1987; Metcalfe, 1993a, 1993b; Metcalfe, Schwartz, and Joaquim, 1993; Miner and Reder, 1994; Reder, 1987; Reder and Ritter, 1992; Schwartz and Metcalfe, 1992).

A second inferential mechanism is a hybrid of direct access and inferential theory in that it relies on retrieved information, but it treats that information as a potential clue for the determination of an inferential judgment. The accessibility mechanism, proposed by Koriat (1993, 1994, 1995), states that metacognitive judgments are based on all information that is retrieved, regardless of whether the information is correct or incorrect. In this account, the quantity of information that is retrieved when given a question or cue is used as a clue to determine the metacognitive judgment. For example, if an individual were in a TOT state when searching for the answer to the question, "Who wrote the novel *Little Women?*" and was able to access the name "Charlotte Brontë," he or she would assign a high metacognitive judgment for this item simply because an entire name had been accessed. In this case, retrieving *incorrect* information (the correct answer is Louisa May Alcott) is used as a clue and boosts the judgment.

Evidence exists to support both the direct access and inferential views, and it is highly likely that both contribute to our metacognitive judgments (Metcalfe, 1999). Certainly, the two views are not mutually exclusive (Schwartz and Metcalfe, 1992). Rather, the process of metacognitive monitoring is complex and a moving assessment of an unstable object-level framework. Although much research has been conducted investigating the direct versus the indirect accounts of metacognitions, no strong conclusion has been made.

The relation between monitoring and control

Perhaps the dominant trend in metacognition research today is the search for the relations between monitoring and control. In the applied sense, researchers are interested in understanding people's study strategies, and how these strategies might be improved. This research agenda has strong implications for theories of metacognition and obvious applications in educational practice. For the rest of this chapter, we focus on theoretical issues, but will touch upon a few of the findings in the educational literature. We have subdivided the issue of the relation between monitoring and control into their interaction at encoding and their interaction at retrieval. Following Nelson and Narens (1990, 1994), we consider encoding first.

Control at encoding

Not too long ago, before the current boom in the American economy and the current bust in the Japanese economy, many Americans viewed with horror the different amount of time that American and Japanese schoolchildren spent doing homework and watching TV. The American children spent much more time watching TV and much less time doing homework than their Japanese counterparts, leading to poorer test scores on the whole (Stevenson, Lee, and Stigler, 1986; Travers et al., 1985). This was cause for much concern about the future of American education, particularly because several studies in the USA showed that increasing homework time or improving homework strategies could improve students' grades (Balli, Demo, and Wedman, 1998; Mau and Lynn, 1999; Olympia et al., 1994; Openshaw, 1998; Tymms and Fitz-Gibbon, 1992). But, does time alone measure the effectiveness of learning or can learners use less time more efficiently by employing a variety of metacognitive strategies? Furthermore, are all people aware of their own metacognitions? It has been stated that academically successful students are those who are aware of their own studying strategies whereas unsuccessful students are unaware of their own learning strategies (McWhirter et al., 1998). Furthermore, the more knowledge one has about different strategies and their potential applications, the easier it will be to select the optimal strategy and modify it to meet the demands of a particular task, and monitor performance, changing the strategy if necessary (Pressley, Borkowski, and O'Sullivan, 1985). The first question, then, is to ask what strategies the good learners are using when they study.

Although to most laypeople the answer to this question is that there is an obvious relation between study time and performance, the psychological evidence supporting the validity of this idea has been ambiguous, in both educational research and cognitive research. If the relation is not a strict one, is it possible that metacognition can aid in the development of more efficient study regimens? The two main questions with respect to the metacognition of encoding have been: (a) Do people choose to self-regulate so that they spend more time on topics that they do not know? (b) Does learning always increase with time spent studying?

Dunlosky and Hertzog (1998) advanced one important theory, the discrepancy-reduction hypothesis, delineating how learners use metacognition. This hypothesis focuses on the mechanism of study-time-allocation strategies. In this model, individual learners compare the degree to which they have learned certain material to a hypothetical desired level of learning (i.e., good enough to pass an exam). This desired level of learning is known as the "norm of study" (Dunlosky and Hertzog, 1998, p. 252). Therefore, learners continually restudy items or select items for study until they have met the criteria necessary to meet the norm of study. Once that criterion is met, no future study is considered to be necessary. Metacognition plays the important role of assessing how well information has been learned and then comparing that to the norm of study.

A number of investigators in metacognitive research have tested the discrepancy-reduction hypothesis in a study-time-allocation paradigm. Typically, participants initially rate the ease of learning particular items, and thereafter have time to study each item individually, for as long as they wish, for a later memory test. Results have shown that people tend to allocate more study time to the judged-difficult-to-learn materials than to the judged-easy-to-learn materials (Cull and Zechmeister, 1994; Mazzoni and Cornoldi, 1993, Experiments 1, 4, 5; Mazzoni, Cornoldi, and Marchitelli, 1990, Experiments 2, 3; Nelson et al., 1994; Nelson and Leonesio, 1988; Thiede and Dunlosky, 1999; for a review see Son and Metcalfe, 2000). Presumably, the reason for this finding is that it takes more time for people to master the materials that are difficult or are judged to be difficult than it does to master the easy materials, and, hence, people must and do spend more time studying the difficult materials. This supports the discrepancy-reduction model, and the idea that educators should teach children to spend more time studying.

There have been recent challenges to the discrepancy-reduction model by suggesting greater complexity to the relation between monitoring and control during learning. Two studies, in particular, emphasize this point. The first, Thiede and Dunlosky (1999), examined how learners allocate study time and select items for restudy under different norms of study. The second, Son and Metcalfe (2000), showed the importance of several non-mnemonic factors in determining study time. Thiede and Dunlosky (1999) asked participants to study new paired associates, such as "dog–spoon." They then employed the basic study-time-allocation paradigm, allowing the participants to decide how much time to study each item. However, they also examined the selection of items for re-study. This meant that some items could be skipped and not studied again while other items would be presented to them again. They called this a strategy of item selection during encoding.

Thiede and Dunlosky found that, under some circumstances, people chose to study the easier items first and the difficult items later. Thus, rather than focusing on what they were have problems learning, the participants tried to ensure that they knew the easier items. This is not simple discrepancy reduction because that view suggests that people will always choose items they know less well for more study, whereas Thiede and Dunlosky's study suggests a more complex strategy was employed by participants. It seems that a different model – one that includes different factors, not just item difficulty – may fit the data better. Thiede and Dunlosky proposed a model in which there is a higher order strategy-selection stage, which allows the person to focus on whether it is more worthwhile to consolidate knowledge by focusing on easy items or to attempt new knowledge by focusing on difficult items.

Son and Metcalfe (2000) extended this logic by showing that people did not allocate more study time to the judged-difficult items in all situations. In three experiments, they investigated studying strategies using a more naturalistic, but still tightly experimental, paradigm. In a typical paradigm, individuals are shown each item one at a time in an experimenter-controlled order (e.g. Mazzoni, Cornoldi, and Marchitelli, 1990). The problem in assessing study time in this way is that there is no opportunity to go back to a particular item once it has been studied in a manner in which people normally do while studying. So, presumably, what people do is study each item until they think it has been learned. Thus, the difficult items would need to have more study time allocated to them than to the easier items. In real-life study situations, however, people usually have the opportunity to go back to materials that had previously been studied. Furthermore, time pressure is one of the factors that learners face during study. These factors motivated the experimental design in Son and Metcalfe's studies.

In Experiment 1, items could be restudied whenever the participant thought it was necessary, although the total study time was limited. Participants could return to any item whenever they wanted to. Moreover, more naturalistic stimuli, biographical essays of famous people, were used. In the study, participants ranked eight biographical figures in terms of perceived difficulty of learning and perceived interest based on one-paragraph excerpts. These ranks were used as judgments of learning, and judgments of interest. Then, all eight biographical figures appeared on a circular menu on the computer as shown in Figure 2.2. A total of 30 minutes – about only half the time needed to read through all eight biographies – was given during which participants could pick and choose the biography that they wanted for however long they wanted to study it. Once a particular item had been studied, they could return to the

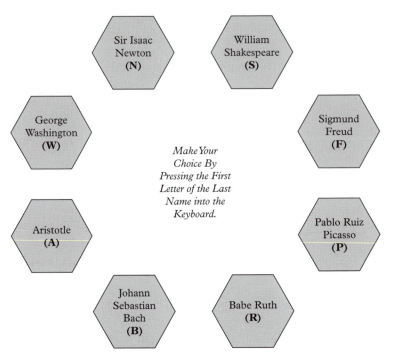

Figure 2.2 The menu presented to participants during the study phase of Son and Metcalfe's (2000) study-time allocation procedure. Unlike other procedures, all of the to-be-learned items were presented simultaneously so that people's choices for study, as well as study times, could be measured.

main circular menu and choose another item, or go back to a previously studied item. At the end of 30 minutes a final test was given on all eight biographies. Results on study time showed that people allocated more study time to the judged-easy and judged-interesting biographies. This contradicts the previous wisdom that participants choose the most difficult item. Son and Metcalfe suspected that the choice of easy items was influenced by the restricted study time allowed in this experiment.

In a second experiment, the stimulus materials were changed to seven Japanese haiku poems. Participants rated the haikus in terms of judgments of learning and of interest by reading through each one for 3 seconds. Then, they were given a study phase in which they were told to learn as many of the seven haikus as possible. Time pressure was not high – participants were given a total study time of 2 minutes when it took only an average 50 seconds to read through the seven haikus. Results showed that people allocated more study time to the judged-difficult poems – contradicting the results in Experiment 1, although people also spent more time on the judged-interesting poems.

In order to resolve the discrepancy between Experiments 1 and 2, in Experiment 3 time pressure was manipulated so that some people were under high time pressure, and others were under medium time pressure. Every participant studied the same materials – eight medium-length Elizabethan sonnets. The procedure was exactly the same as for Experiments 1 and 2. However, each participant was first given a pre-test in which they had to study one sonnet until at least 50 percent of that sonnet could be written down from memory. Study times were recorded. If a participant was randomly assigned to the High-Time-Pressure group, then the total study time allowed later in the study phase of the experiment was found by multiplying time needed to memorize half of the sonnet by a factor of three. In this condition, participants were under extremely strong time pressures because they now had to learn not one, but eight sonnets. Individuals assigned to the Moderate-Time-Pressure group were given a total study time of the recorded time multiplied by ten. All participants made judgments of learning and of interest prior to the study phase based on two lines of each of the sonnets. Finally, they were tested. Results replicated the first two experiments in that when people were under high time pressure, they allocated more study time to materials that were judged as easy and interesting. When the time pressure was not so great, however, people were able to focus on the difficult items.

The studies conducted on time pressure influencing control strategies suggest that there is an adaptive basis for focusing on less difficult items when time pressure is high. Allocating more study time to those extremely difficult materials would be a "waste of time" and might also divert the person's efforts from easier items that could benefit from the study time available. It has, in fact, been shown that, at times, study does not result in better learning, known as the labor-in-vain effect (Mazzoni et al., 1990; Mazzoni and Cornoldi, 1993; Nelson and Leonesio, 1988). Nelson and Leonesio described situations in which difficult items were studied for longer times than easy items but performance on the difficult items was not better than performance for the easier items. Furthermore, items studied for a longer time did not have any greater probability of being recalled than items studied for a shorter time. In this situation, then, it would be more beneficial for the learner to allocate study time to the easier, or perhaps to the moderately easy, items. Atkinson (1972), in a classic paper, discussed a three-stage Markov model of an optimal control strategy in which the most study time is allocated to items that are in an intermediate state of learning – not fully learned but also not totally unlearned. In his investigation, the allocation of study time to items that were neither too difficult nor too easy was found to be the most effective strategy. The recent data, as well as the Atkinson model, suggest that a simple learning model, such as the discrepancy-reduction model, will not suffice for study control strategies. Rather, metacognitive control seems to encompass several different factors – such as the difficulty level of the items, the total time available, and judgments of interest – in different situations. In the following paragraphs, other models that have incorporated various factors for metacognitive control are discussed.

Winne and Hadwin (1998) proposed that studying should be considered in terms of two main factors. The first factor is the student's expertise in the subject matter. The second factor to be considered is the degree to which the student is metacognitively active. In the first stage of the sequence, a student forms a perception of what the task is. Goals are then created, followed by enacting study tactics that the student predicts can achieve those goals. As operations are performed in each of these stages, evaluations are generated that the students may metacognitively monitor. Metacognitive monitoring can also occur at the end of a study session. When a student metacogntively examines studying, metacognitive control can be exercised to toggle study tactics on and off, or editing may be done to adapt the conditions, operations, or standards in cognitive structure that describe studying. Finally, a "Grounded theory" approach has been proposed by Pressley et al. (1998) which assumes that regulation of learning may be influenced not only by knowledge of the to-be-learned materials, but by many other factors as well such as motivation and reward benefits. Furthermore, strategies will be affected by the tactics used: the amount of organization, note-taking, rehearsing, and asking for assistance (Zimmerman and Martin-Pons, 1986, 1988, 1990).

Some of these ideas have been applied to educational settings. In general, the research has also shown results contradicting the discrepancy-reduction hypothesis, suggesting that in the real world, people maybe should not and do not allocate most of their study time to the difficult materials. With regard to the relationship between study time and achievement, Keith (1982) found that time spent on homework was positively related to students' grades in high school ($r = 0.32$). In contrast, Schumann et al. (1985) found a correlation of only 0.11 between hours studied and achievement, suggesting that the total hours studied accounts for less than 1 percent of the variance in grade-point average (GPA). When conducting analyses on single courses, the investigators found similarly weak relationships. Delucchi, Rohwer, and Thomas (1987) reported total study time, their allocation of that time to specific study activities, and relationships between such allocations and achievement across three grade levels, junior high, senior high, and college. Their results, like Schumann et al.'s (1985), provide no evidence for recommendations that increasing the number of hours that students engage in homework will improve achievement. Again, this refutes the discrepancy-reduction hypothesis. Interestingly, Carroll (1963) was credited with identifying three time variables that are believed to affect the time–achievement relationship. According to Carroll, learning is a function of the time allocated to learning, but more importantly, one must also consider the amount of time a student is actively engaged in learning as well as the amount of time needed for learning given the ability level of the student.

To summarize, the educational data seem to suggest study time is not the only factor in increasing learning. This accords with the recent experimental work of Thiede and Dunlosky (1999) and Son and Metcalfe (2000), both of whom found that factors other than difficulty were important during studying for participants. Rather, awareness of self-regulation and competent metacognitive control seems to be the important factor when attempting to improve learning performance.

Control at retrieval

Recent studies also suggest that control influences decisions at the time of retrieval (e.g. Barnes et al., 1999; Reder, 1987, 1988; Reder and Schunn, 1996; Schwartz, 2001). Monitoring information can help people to determine if particular information is accessible in memory. If the monitoring information is positive, participants may spend more time attempting retrieval and may try other retrieval strategies to recall the information. This topic has received less attention from researchers than the topic of control at encoding, but there have been a few relevant studies. Rememberers must decide at the time of retrieval how to recall difficult items, whether it is worth the effort, and whether to admit that one does not know.

Reder and colleagues (Reder 1987, 1988; Reder and Schunn, 1996) were interested in how metacognition affected strategic decisions in the regulation of recall. In particular, Reder was interested in whether people relied on memory search or opted for other strategies such as calculation (in math problems) or inference (in general-information problems). For example, some questions may be so difficult ("How many minutes have passed since the Big Bang?") that most people will quickly respond "I don't know." The answers to other questions ("How many legs do wildebeests have?") may not be stored in memory, but may be easily inferred once the question is posed. Similarly, questions such as "How many windows does your current home have?" may not be stored in memory and hence immediately retrievable, but may be easily determined by mental counting. Other questions ("What is the largest ocean in the world?") elicit a quick and definitive response, easily drawn from memory. One of the functions of metacognition, according to Reder and Schunn, is that it allows us to make rapid decisions about our state of knowledge. For Reder and Schunn, metacognition directs the strategies that people use to solve problems or answer questions.

Barnes et al. (1999) designed an experiment to test the strategic regulation or control of memory retrieval. They presented participants with general-information questions for retrieval (e.g. "Who was the first person to walk on the moon?" [Armstrong]). They provided penalties for lack of speed, and rewards for numbers of correct answers. Participants were penalized for each second that the question was on the screen, but were rewarded when they gave a correct answer. They compared conditions in which either the penalty for slowness or the reward for correctness was large or small. These incentives affected the metacognitive control processes.

Barnes et al. found that when incentives for speed were great, the rememberers spent less time at retrieval, and the number of correct answers decreased. However, when incentives for correct answers was high, the rememberers spent more time attempting retrieval and generated more correct answers as a consequence. In a second experiment, Barnes et al. found that when accuracy incentives were high, participants spent less time attempting retrieval, but there were also fewer errors of commission. These findings suggest that rememberers are capable of using sophisticated control processes at retrieval (see Koriat and Goldsmith, 1996, for a similar theory and analysis).

In the Barnes et al. (1999) study, explicit measures of metacognition were not made. However, other research has demonstrated correlations between the magnitude of feeling of knowing and retrieval latency. Nelson et al. (1984) and Nelson, Kruglanski, and Jost (1998) showed that FOK judgments were positively correlated with retrieval latency for omission errors, that is, the longer the response time to recall, the higher the FOK judgment would be. These results were replicated by Costermans, Lories, and Ansay (1992). Recently, Schwartz (2001) also observed an association between tip-of-the-tongue states and retrieval time as well. Following failure to retrieve the general-information question, participants were asked whether they were experiencing a TOT. TOTs were also collected if the recall response was incorrect (i.e., an error of commission). Finally an eight-alternative forced-choice recognition test was presented. The critical variable was the amount of time participants spent attempting retrieval during TOTs and during n-TOTs (not TOTs). Four studies showed a clear association between retrieval time and the likelihood of a TOT (Schwartz, 2001). This suggests that the TOT experience serves as a trigger to continue the search for the missing target word.

Other studies also address issues of control processes and metacognition. One study (Koriat and Goldsmith, 1996) differs from the others reviewed here because it concerns retrospective monitoring and its effect on control rather than prospective monitoring. Retrospective monitoring refers to judgments about the correctness of an already-retrieved target. These judgments are often called simply confidence judgments and have been studied heavily in the eyewitness memory area (e.g. Loftus et al., 1989). Confidence in a retrieved answer can affect control decisions. Koriat and Goldsmith were interested in whether these confidence judgments would affect decisions to output answers when the situation called for different criteria of correctness.

Consider a question such as "What is the capital of California?" (Sacramento). There are three possible categories or answers, a correct one, an incorrect one, and a "don't know" response. A "don't know" response is not incorrect, and therefore does not count as an "inaccurate" memory. On the other hand, if one says "San Francisco," one has committed a commission error, which does count against the accuracy score. Now consider the person who, when asked this question, originally thinks of San Francisco, and then realizes that the capital is a smaller, less well-known city, but is not sure of its name. If forced to guess, the person may say "San Francisco," even though the confidence is weak for that name. Thus, Koriat and Goldsmith's (1996) interest was in how participants withhold low-confidence answers. The withholding of answers is defined as the control operation, whereas the confidence judgment is the monitoring process that informs the control process.

In their experiment, Koriat and Goldsmith presented participants with general-information questions. They were required to answer all questions and then were asked to make a confidence judgment (on a 0 to 100 percent scale) for each question. Thus, even if they had no idea what the answer was, they were forced to make a guess. Presumably, such guesses elicited low-confidence judgments. After they answered all of the questions, the instructions switched to free-report conditions. The questions were shown again, and now the participants were free to answer only those questions that they were sure were correct. Koriat and Goldsmith could then examine the relation between the original confidence judgments and the subsequent decision to report and withhold. To make matters more interesting, in one condition, the participants were offered a financial incentive to answer correctly, but an equal disincentive for wrong answers (moderate-incentive condition). In a second condition, the disincentive was much larger than the incentive (high-incentive).

The results were quite striking. First, the participants were quite accurate with their confidence judgments. Those given high confidence were much more likely to be correct than those given lower confidence. Indeed, the gamma correlation was 0.87 for recall. There was also a strong positive correlation between confidence and whether the answer would be volunteered in the second phase. Moreover, in the high-incentive condition, the participants screened out more of their incorrect answers, resulting in an increase in overall accuracy. This came at a cost of a decrease in quantity, but it does show that the participants were able to monitor their output (via confidence) and control their accuracy (via volunteering or withholding answers).

Koriat and Goldsmith (1996) argued that these data are consistent with a metacognitive model. Rememberers monitor the accuracy of their answers, reflected in their confidence judgments. Then, depending on the incentives, they can use their confidence judgments to alter which answers they will output and which they will withhold. Control is represented by the volunteering or withholding of answers. Therefore, we see the usefulness of the metacognitive model of monitoring and control in both prospective judgments (feelings of knowing and judgments of learning) and retrospective judgments (post-answer confidence).

Earlier, in the late 1970s, John Flavell and his colleagues conducted several studies assessing a child's ability to use different retrieval cues to assist his or her performance on a retrieval task (Flavell, 1978; Keniston and Flavell, 1979; Salatas and Flavell, 1976). Similar to Reder's regulation of search at retrieval, they suggested that very young children are not perfect at regulating their retrieval searches. Rather, metacognitive control at retrieval must be formally learned. Flavell (1978) presented several ideas that were important in regulation during retrieval, especially for children. First, children should know how to perform a systematic and exhaustive search through an entire memory space. Second, when trying to retrieve an as-of-yet unretrieved target word, related words should be retrieved deliberately because they may cue recall of the target. Finally, and perhaps most importantly, people should know that there may be, and usually is, more than one retrieval strategy applicable to a given retrieval problem.

Keniston and Flavell (1979) put the above ideas into tests for participants in grades 1, 3, and 7, as well as college students. All participants were read a list of twenty-seven nonsense characters consisting of letters and numbers. As each character was read, participants wrote them down one at a time on separate notecards. The task was an incidental task in that participants did not expect a memory test and were never told how many letters and numbers were initially written. After taking down the list, participants were divided into two groups and given a memory test. In one group, the task was *uninstructed* in that they were asked to figure out and write down all and only the letters they had previously written on the cards. In the *instructed* group, participants were given hints that a "really good trick" would help – going through the alphabet and numbers 1 through 10 subvocally, asking themselves if they had previously written down each character. They were never told the exact trick, however, until the end of the session. This latter search strategy would make the task much easier in that "figuring out" all the characters that one has not written seems like a more difficult problem than "figuring out" those that one has written – a not-so-obvious metacognitive control strategy. While the memory test was transpiring, participants' responses of strategy were recorded. Results showed that the older students were, the more spontaneously they used the "really good trick" as opposed to the rote-learning method, and the more easily, completely, and accurately, they could report the retrieval method that they had used. Furthermore, although children in the younger grades spontaneously used rote-retrieval strategies, when instructed to do so they abandoned their strategies for those used by the older children, leading to better recall. Thus, if monitoring and control are not an automatic process during learning, retrieval knowledge and strategies may be taught successfully to children at younger ages, improving performance.

Whether retrieving an answer to a school-examination question, the name of a person on the street, or a trivia question on a game show, metacognitive strategies during retrieval seem to be vital for individuals at any stage of learning. Furthermore, some strategies may not be automatic, but, rather, a learned skill. Knowledge of such control strategies and short-cuts could improve performance, while decreasing the amount of time and cost for retrieving the correct answer. Specifically during test-taking, metacognitive cues inform the individual of how close they are to retrieving the target answer to a particular question. With such information, the person can then decide whether to continue searching for the answer or to move on to another question. If these cues were not available, or if a student were unaware of them, considerable time could be wasted attempting to retrieve a target that might never be retrieved.

Conclusion

In this chapter, we have outlined the important issues in metacognitive research, starting with monitoring and mechanisms, and then focusing on the relation between monitoring and control, which is currently the most studied issue in metacognition. During encoding, it was once thought that simple models may describe human study behavior, in terms of allocation of study time. However, we now realize that the relation between monitoring and control is influenced by several different factors that we know of – such as interest and study time – and possibly many other unknown factors. We have also discussed research that suggests the importance of metacognitive control of factors at the time of retrieval, such as the decision criterion and how long to engage in retrieval.

We see one of the important issues for the future will be the use of metacognition to optimize learning and retrieval. Can adults and children use metacognition to optimize their learning under varying contextual conditions? This issue remains largely unstudied (but see Nelson et al., 1994). It is possible that adults can be trained to use their metacognitive introspections better to improve their learning in college and in on-the-job training. However, if children do not intuitively develop optimal strategies, we wonder if these are skills that can be taught. Vygotsky wrote that "in order to subject a function to intellectual and volitional control, we must first possess it" (1986, p. 168), suggesting that children may not yet be ready to employ metacognition in the control of memory. Vygotsky's hypothesis has yet to be put to rigorous empirical test, and we suspect that the delineation of the nature of the role of metacognitive control in children could have important theoretical and educational implications.

ACKNOWLEDGMENTS

The research was supported by the National Institute of Mental Health grant number 48066 to Janet Metcalfe. We would like to thank Janet Metcalfe and Timothy Perfect for comments on earlier drafts.

REFERENCES

Arbuckle, T. Y., and Cuddy, L. L. (1969). Discrimination of item strength at time of presentation. *Journal of Experimental Psychology*, 81, 126–131.

Atkinson, R. C. (1972). Optimizing the learning of a second-language vocabulary. *Journal of Experimental Psychology*, 96, 124–129.

Balli, S. J., Demo, D. H., and Wedman, J. F. (1998). Family involvement with children's homework: an intervention in the middle grades. *Family Relations: Interdisciplinary Journal of Applied Family Studies*, 47, 149–157.

Barnes, A. E., Nelson, T. O., Dunlosky, J., Mazzoni, G., and Narens, L. (1999). An integrative system of metamemory components involved in retrieval. In D. Gopher and A. Koriat (eds.), *Attention and performance XVII: cognitive regulation of performance: interaction of theory and application*, pp. 287–313. Cambridge, MA: MIT Press.

Benjamin, A. S., Bjork, R. A., and Schwartz, B. L. (1998) The mismeasure of memory: when retrieval fluency is misleading as a metamnemonic index. *Journal of Experimental Psychology: General*, 127, 55–68.

Blake, M. (1973). Prediction of recognition when recall fails: exploring the feeling-of-knowing phenomenon. *Journal of Verbal Learning and Verbal Behavior*, 12, 311–319.

Brown, A. L. (1978). Knowing when, where, and how to remember: a problem of metacognition. In R. Glaser (ed.), *Advances in instructional psychology, Volume 1*, pp. 77–165. Hillsdale, NJ: Lawrence Erlbaum Associates.

Brown, A. L. (1987). Metacognition, executive control, self-regulation, and other more mysterious mechanisms. In F. E. Weinert and R. H. Kluwe (eds.), *Metacognition, motivation, and understanding*, pp. 65–116. Hillsdale, NJ: Lawrence Erlbaum Associates.

Carroll, J. B. (1963). A model of school learning. *Teachers College Record*, 64, 723–733.

Cavanaugh, J. C., and Perlmutter, M. (1982). Metamemory: a critical examination. *Child Development*, 53, 11–28.

Costermans, J., Lories, G., and Ansay, C. (1992). Confidence level and feeling of knowing in question answering. *Journal of Experimental Psychology: Learning, Memory, and Cognition*, 18, 142–150.

Cull, W. L., and Zechmeister, E. B. (1994). The learning ability paradox in adult metamemory research: where are the metamemory differences between good and poor learners? *Memory and Cognition*, 22, 249–257.

Delucchi, J. J., Rohwer, W. D., and Thomas, J. W. (1987). Study time allocation as a function of grade level and course characteristics. *Contemporary Educational Psychology*, 12, 365–380.

Dunlosky, J., and Hertzog, C. (1998). Training programs to improve learning in later adulthood: helping older adults educate themselves. In D. J. Hacker, J. Dunlosky, and A. C. Graesser (eds.), *Metacognition in educational theory and practice*, pp. 249–276. Mahwah, NJ: Lawrence Erlbaum Associates.

Dunlosky, J., and Nelson, T. O. (1992). Importance of the kind of cue for judgments of learning (JOL) and the delayed-JOL effect. *Memory and Cognition*, 20, 374–380.

(1994). Does the sensitivity of judgments of learning (JOLs) to the effects of various study activities depend on when the JOLs occur? *Journal of Memory and Language*, 33, 545–565.

(1997). Similarity between the cue for judgments of learning (JOL) and the cue for test is not the primary determinant of JOL accuracy. *Journal of Memory and Language*, 36, 34–49.

Fischhoff, B., Slovic, P., and Lichtenstein, S. (1977). Knowing with certainty: the appropriateness of extreme confidence. *Journal of Experimental Psychology: Human Perception and Performance*, 3, 552–564.

Flavell, J. H. (1976). Metacognitive aspects of problem solving. In L. B. Resnick (ed.), *The nature of intelligence*, pp. 231–235. Hillsdale, NJ: Lawrence Erlbaum Associates.

(1978). Metacognitive development. In J. M Scandura and C. J. Brainerd (eds.), *Structural-process theories of complex human behavior*. Leyden: Sijthoff and Noordhoff.

(1979). Metacognitive and cognitive monitoring: a new area of cognitive developmental inquiry. *American Psychologist*, 34, 906–911.

(1982). On cognitive development. *Child Development*, 53, 1–10.

Glenberg, A. M., Sanocki, T., Epstein, W., and Morris, C. (1987). Enhancing calibration of comprehension. *Journal of Experimental Psychology: General*, 116, 119–136.

Gruneberg, M. M., and Monks, J. (1974). "Feeling of knowing" and cued recall. *Acta Psychologica*, 38, 257–265.

Hart, J. T. (1965). Memory and the feeling-of-knowing experience. *Journal of Educational Psychology*, 56, 208–216.

Jacoby, L. L., Bjork, R. A., and Kelley, C. M. (1993). Illusions of comprehension and competence. In D. Druckman and R. A. Bjork (eds.), *Learning, remembering, believing: enhancing team and individual performance*, pp. 57–80. Washington, DC: National Academy Press.

Johnson, M. K. (1988). Reality monitoring: an experimental phenomenological approach. *Journal of Experimental Psychology: General*, 117, 390–394.

Johnson, M. K., and Raye, C. L. (1981). Reality monitoring. *Psychological Review*, 88, 67–85.

Keith, T. Z. (1982). Time spent on homework and high school grades: a large sample-path analysis. *Journal of Educational Psychology*, 74, 248–253.

Keniston, A. H., and Flavell, J. H. (1979). A developmental study of intelligent retrieval. *Child Development*, 50, 1144–1152.

King, J. F., Zechmeister, E. B., and Shaughnessy, J. J. (1980). Judgments of knowing: the influence of retrieval practice. *American Journal of Psychology*, 93, 329–343.

Kluwe, R. H. (1982). Cognitive knowledge and executive control. In D. Griffin (ed.), *Human mind – animal mind*, pp. 201–224. New York: Springer.

Koriat, A. (1993). How do we know what we know? The accessibility model of the feeling of knowing. *Psychological Review*, 100, 609–639.

(1994). Memory's knowledge of its own knowledge: the accessibility account of the feeling of knowing. In J. Metcalfe and A. P. Shimamura (eds.), *Metacognition: knowing about knowing*, pp. 115–135. Cambridge, MA: MIT Press.

(1995). Dissociating knowing and the feeling of knowing: further evidence for the accessibility model. *Journal of Experimental Psychology: General*, 124, 311–333.

Koriat, A., and Goldsmith, M. (1996). Monitoring and control processes in the strategic regulation of memory accuracy. *Psychological Review*, 103, 490–517.

Leonesio, R. J., and Nelson, T. O. (1990). Do different metamemory judgments tap the same underlying aspects of memory? *Journal of Experimental Psychology: Learning, Memory, and Cognition*, 16, 464–470.

Lichtenstein, S., and Fischhoff, B. (1977). Do those who know more also know more about how much they know? *Organizational Behavior and Human Decision Processes*, 20, 159–183.

Loftus, E. F., and Zanni, G. (1975). Eyewitness testimony: the influence of the wording of a question. *Bulletin of the Psychonomic Society*, 5, 86–88.

Loftus, E. F., Donders, K., Hoffman, H. G., and Schooler, J. W. (1989). Creating new memories that are quickly accessed and confidently held. *Memory and Cognition*, 17, 607–616.

Lovelace, E. A. (1984). Metamemory: monitoring future recallability during study. *Journal of Experimental Psychology: Learning, Memory, and Cognition*, 10, 756–766.

Marshall, J. C., and Morton, J. (1978). On the mechanics of EMMA. In A. Sinclair, R. J. Jarvella, and W. J. M. Levelt (eds.), *The child's conception of language*. Berlin: Springer.

Mau, W. C., and Lynn, R. (1999). Racial and ethnic differences in motivation for educational achievement in the United States. *Personality and Individual Differences*, 27, 1091–1096.

Mazzoni, G., and Cornoldi, C. (1993). Strategies in study-time allocation: why is study time sometimes not effective? *Journal of Experimental Psychology: General*, 122, 47–60.

Mazzoni, G., Cornoldi, C., and Marchitelli, G. (1990). Do memorability ratings affect study-time allocation? *Memory and Cognition*, 18, 196–204.

Mazzoni, G., Cornoldi, C., Tomat, L., and Vecchi, T. (1997). Remembering the grocery shopping list: a study on metacognitive biases. *Applied Cognitive Psychology*, 11, 253–267.

Mazzoni, G., and Nelson, T. O. (1995). Judgments of learning are affected by the kind of encoding in ways that cannot be attributed to the level of recall. *Journal of Experimental Psychology: Learning, Memory, and Cognition*, 21, 1263–1274.

McWhirter, J. J., McWhirter, B. T., McWhirter, A. M., and McWhirter, E. H. (1998). Educational interventions. In J. J. McWhirter, B. T. McWhirter, A. M. McWhirter, and E. H. McWhirter (eds.), *At-risk youth*, pp. 280–299. Pacific Grove, CA: Brooks/Cole.

Metcalfe, J. (1986a). Premonitions of insight impending error. *Journal of Experimental Psychology: Learning, Memory, and Cognition*, 12, 623–634.

   (1986b). Feeling of knowing in memory and problem solving. *Journal of Experimental Psychology: Learning, Memory, and Cognition*, 12, 288–294.

   (1993a). Novelty monitoring, metacognition, and control in a composite holographic associative recall model: implications for Korsakoff amnesia. *Psychological Review*, 100, 3–22.

   (1993b). Monitoring and gain control in an episodic memory model: relation to the P300 event-related potential. In A. F. Collins and S. E. Gathercole (eds.), *Theories of memory*, pp. 327–353. Hove, UK: Erlbaum.

   (1999). Metamemory: theory and data. In E. Tulving and F. I. M. Craik (eds.), *Oxford handbook of memory*. Oxford: Oxford University Press.

Metcalfe, J., Schwartz, B. L., and Joaquim, S. G. (1993). The cue-familiarity heuristic in metacognition. *Journal of Experimental Psychology: Learning, Memory, and Cognition*, 19, 851–864.

Metcalfe, J., and Weibe, D. (1987). Intuition in insight and noninsight problem solving. *Memory and Cognition*, 15, 238–246.

Miner, A. C., and Reder, L. M. (1994). A new look at feeling of knowing: its metacognitive role in regulating question answering. In J. Metcalfe and

A. P. Shimamura (eds.), *Metacognition: knowing about knowing*, pp. 47–70. Cambridge, MA: MIT Press.

Nelson, T. O. (1984). A comparison of current measures of the accuracy of feeling-of-knowing predictions. *Psychological Bulletin*, 95, 109–133.

(1988). Predictive accuracy of the feeling of knowing across different criterion tasks and across different subject populations and individuals. In M. M. Gruneberg, P. E. Morris, and R. N. Sykes (eds.), *Practical aspects of memory: current research and issues*, pp. 190–196. Chichester, UK: Wiley.

Nelson, T. O., and Dunlosky, J. (1991). When people's judgments of learning (JOL) are extremely accurate at predicting subsequent recall: the delayed-JOL effect. *Psychological Science*, 2, 267–270.

(1994). How shall we explain the delayed-judgment-of-learning effect? *Psychological Science*, 3, 317–318.

Nelson, T. O., Dunlosky, J., Graf, A., and Narens, L. (1994). Utilization of metacognitive judgments in the allocation of study during multitrial learning. *Psychological Science*, 5, 207–213.

Nelson, T. O., Gerler, D., and Narens, L. (1984). Accuracy of feeling-of-knowing judgments for predicting perceptual identification and relearning. *Journal of Experimental Psychology: General*, 113, 282–300.

Nelson, T. O., Kruglanski, A. W., and Jost, J. T. (1998). Knowing thyself and others: progress in metacognitive social psychology. In V. Y. Yzerbyt and G. Lories (eds.), *Metacognition: cognitive and social dimensions*, pp. 69–89. Thousand Oaks, CA: Sage Publications.

Nelson, T. O., and Leonesio, R. J. (1988). Allocation of self-paced study time and the "labor-in-vain effect." *Journal of Experimental Psychology: Learning, Memory, and Cognition*, 14, 676–686.

Nelson, T. O., Leonesio, R. J., Landwehr, R. S., and Narens, L. (1986). A comparison of three predictors of an individual's memory performance: the individual's feeling of knowing versus the normative feeling of knowing versus base-rate item difficulty. *Journal of Experimental Psychology: Learning, Memory, and Cognition*, 12, 279–287.

Nelson, T. O., Leonesio, R. J., Shimamura, A. P., Landwehr, R. S., and Narens, L. (1982). Overlearning and the feeling of knowing. *Journal of Experimental Psychology: Learning, Memory, and Cognition*, 8, 279–288.

Nelson, T. O., and Narens, L. (1990). Metamemory: a theoretical framework and new findings. In G. H. Bower (ed.), *The psychology of learning and motivation, Volume 26*, pp. 125–141. New York: Academic Press.

(1994). Why investigate metacognition? In J. Metcalfe, and A. P. Shimamura (eds.), *Metacognition: knowing about knowing*, pp. 1–25. Cambridge, MA: MIT Press.

Olympia, D. E., Sheridan, S. M., Jenson, W. R., and Andrews, D. (1994). Using student-managed interventions to increase homework completion and accuracy. *Journal of Applied Behavior Analysis*, 27, 85–99.

Openshaw, D. K. (1998). Increasing homework compliance: the SEA method. *Journal of Family Psychotherapy*, 9, 21–29.

Pressley, M., Borkowski, J. G., and O'Sullivan, J. T. (1985). Children's metamemory and the teaching of memory strategies. In D. L. Forrest-Pressley,

G. E. MacKinnon, and T. G. Waller (eds.), *Metacognition, cognition, and human performance, Volume I*, pp. 111–149. New York: Academic Press.

Pressley, M., Van Etten, S., Yokoi, L., Freeburn, G., and Meter, P. V. (1998). The metacognition of college studentship: a grounded theory approach. In D. J. Hacker and J. Dunlosky (eds.), *Metacognition in educational theory and practice. The educational psychology series*, pp. 347–363. Mahwah, NJ: Lawrence Erlbaum Associates.

Reder, L. M. (1987). Strategy selection in question answering. *Cognitive Psychology*, 19, 90–138.

(1988). Strategic control of retrieval strategies. In G. H. Bower (ed.), *The psychology of learning and motivation: advances in research and theory*, Vol. 22, pp. 227–259. San Diego, CA: Academic Press.

Reder, L. M., and Ritter, F. E. (1992). What determines initial feeling of knowing? Familiarity with question terms, not with the answer. *Journal of Experimental Psychology: Learning, Memory, and Cognition*, 18, 435–451.

Reder, L. M., and Schunn, C. (1996). Metacognition does not imply awareness: strategy choice is governed by implicit learning and memory. In L. M. Reder (ed.), *Implicit memory and metacognition*, pp. 45–77. Mahwah, NJ: Lawrence Erlbaum Associates.

Salatas, H., and Flavell, J. H. (1976). Retrieval of recently learned information: development of strategies and control skills. *Child Development*, 47, 941–948.

Schumann, H., Walsh, E., Olsen, C., and Etheridge, B. (1985). Effort and reward: the assumption that college grades are affected by quantity of study. *Social Forces*, 63, 945–966.

Schwartz, B. L. (1994). Sources of information in metamemory: judgments of learning and feelings of knowing. *Psychonomic Bulletin and Review*, 1, 357–375.

(2001). The relation of tip-of-the-tongue states and retrieval time. *Memory and Cognition*, 29, 117–126.

Schwartz, B. L., and Metcalfe, J. (1994). Methodological problems and pitfalls in the study of human metacognition. In J. Metcalfe and A. P. Shimamura (eds.), *Metacognition: knowing about knowing*, pp. 93–113. Cambridge, MA: MIT Press.

(1992). Cue familiarity but not target retrievability enhances feeling-of-knowing judgments. *Journal of Experimental Psychology: Learning, Memory, and Cognition*, 18, 1074–1083.

Siegel, J. M., and Loftus, E. F. (1978). Impact of anxiety and life stress upon eyewitness testimony. *Bulletin of the Psychonomic Society*, 12, 479–480.

Son, L. K., and Metcalfe, J. (2000). Metacognitive and control strategies in study-time allocation. *Journal of Experimental Psychology: Learning, Memory, and Cognition*, 26, 204–221.

Stevenson, H. W., Lee, S. Y., and Stigler, J. W. (1986). Mathematics achievement of Chinese, Japanese, and American children. *Science*, 231, 693–699.

Thiede, K. W., and Dunlosky, J. (1994). Delaying students' metacognitive monitoring improves their accuracy in predicting their recognition performance. *Journal of Educational Psychology*, 86, 290–302.

(1999). Toward a general model of self-regulated study: an analysis of selection of items for study and self-paced study time. *Journal of Experimental Psychology: Learning, Memory, and Cognition*, 25, 1024–1037.

Travers, K. J., Crosswhite, F. J., Dossey, J. A., Swafford, J. O., McKnight, C. C., and Cooney, T. J. (1985). *Second international mathematics study summary report for the United States*. Champaign, IL: Stipes.

Tymms, P. B., and Fitz-Gibbon, C. T. (1992). The relationship of homework to A-level results. *Educational Research*, 34, 3–10.

Underwood, B. J. (1966). Individual and group predictions of item difficulty for free-recall learning. *Journal of Experimental Psychology*, 71, 673–679.

Vesonder, G., and Voss, J. (1985). On the ability to predict one's own responses while learning. *Journal of Memory and Language*, 24, 363–376.

Vygotsky, L. (1986). *Thought and language*. Cambridge, MA: MIT Press.

Weaver, C. A. III, and Kelemen, W. L. (1997). Judgments of learning at delays: shifts in response patterns or increased metamemory accuracy? *Psychological Science*, 8, 318–321.

Wellman, H. M. (1983). Metamemory revisited. *Contribution to Human Development*, 9, 31–51.

Widner, R. L., and Smith, S. M. (1996). Feeling-of-knowing judgments from the subject's perspective. *American Journal of Psychology*, 109, 373–387.

Widner, R. L., Smith, S. M., and Graziano, W. G. (1996). The effects of demand characteristics on the reporting of tip-of-the-tongue and feeling-of-knowing states. *American Journal of Psychology*, 109, 525–538.

Winne, P. H., and Hadwin, A. F. (1998). Studying as self-regulated learning. In D. J. Hacker, J. Dunlosky, and A. C. Graesser (eds.), *Metacognition in educational theory and practice*, pp. 277–304. Mahwah, NJ: Lawrence Erlbaum Associates.

Zimmerman, B. J., and Martin-Pons, M. (1986). Development of a structured interview for assessing student use of self-regulated learning strategies. *American Educational Research Journal*, 23, 614–628.

(1988). Construct validation of a strategy model of student self-regulated learning. *Journal of Educational Psychology*, 80, 284–290.

(1990). Perceptions of efficacy and strategy use in self-regulation of learning. In D. H. Schunk and J. L. Meece (eds.), *Student perceptions in the classroom*, pp. 185–207. Hillsdale, NJ: Lawrence Erlbaum Associates.

3   Metacognition for text: findings and implications for education

Ruth H. Maki and Michael J. McGuire

Reading and learning from text is a fundamental part of the life of college students. More than likely, a student's academic welfare will depend on how well he or she retains information from reading. One aspect of reading that has become the focus of study for cognitive psychologists and educators alike is self-assessment of comprehension. Assessing or monitoring of reading falls under the category of metacognition (Flavell, 1979), a person's cognitions about their own cognitive phenomena. For text material, metacognition includes judgments about levels of comprehension and learning of the text, and predictions about future memory for the material. Because of the importance of comprehension in learning from text, Maki and Berry (1984) used the term metacomprehension to refer to metacognition involving text material. We will use the terms metacomprehension and metacognition for text synonymously in this chapter.

Metacomprehension ability should be important for a college student's academic success. The first theme of this chapter is the relevance of theoretically motivated research to classroom settings because it is in classroom settings that students must use their abilities to judge learning from text material. We will describe studies that have been conducted in classroom settings and then discuss differences between these studies and those conducted in the laboratory. To preview our discussion, we will show that studies in classroom settings have differed from laboratory studies in many ways. We suggest that the major reason for different conclusions is the use of different measures of metacomprehension in the two settings. As will be seen, research examining students' overconfidence and underconfidence produces quite different conclusions from research investigating students' predictions of future performance on specific parts of a text relative to other parts.

A second theme of the chapter is the role of individual differences in metacomprehension ability. If accurate metacomprehension is important for control of studying in classroom settings, then academically stronger students should make more accurate predictions of their future performance on text. As will be seen, this relationship is often not observed, either because of the measures that have been used or because measures of metacomprehension (and of metacognition in general) may not be reliable and valid (Kelemen, Frost, and Weaver, 2000). We will discuss the implications of the evidence for unreliability in the context of metacomprehension research.

Metacomprehension in classroom environments

The testing environment (e.g. classroom versus laboratory) may be an important factor in determining the accuracy of metacognition for text. Most of the metacomprehension studies conducted in the laboratory have asked participants to read short texts and make predictions about future performance. Other studies have focused on postdiction, i.e., post-test estimates of the accuracy of prior-test performance. Both types of judgments are theoretically important in metacomprehension, but predictions are most important in educational settings because students need to be able to predict future performance if they are to control their study effectively.

The few classroom studies (Grabe, Bordages, and Petros, 1990; Hacker et al., 2000; Jacobson, 1990; Leal, 1987; Shaugnessy, 1979; Sinkavich, 1995) that have been conducted uniformly show better-than-chance prediction and postdiction accuracy, but laboratory studies have shown both accurate predictions (Maki and Serra, 1992a; Weaver, 1990) and predictions that are not more accurate than chance (Glenberg and Epstein, 1985; Glenberg et al., 1987; Pressley et al., 1990). In contrast, both laboratory (e.g. Maki, 1998a) and classroom studies (Shaughnessy, 1979; Sinkavich, 1995) have typically produced accurate postdiction ratings. The difference in classroom and laboratory results for predictions may have occurred because there are a number of differences between tests given in classroom settings and tests given in the laboratory. The material for classroom tests was probably presented in multiple ways, including reading text, hearing lectures, and participating in discussion; whereas, in laboratory studies, the material was probably studied by reading text alone. In addition, students should be more motivated for classroom tests; more material has typically been studied for classroom than for laboratory tests, the retention interval between reading and the test is typically longer in the classroom. Each of these factors may contribute to more consistently accurate metacognition in classroom than in laboratory settings.

Most studies conducted in classroom settings have asked students to make a single prediction or postdiction for actual examinations given as part of a course. Researchers have then used between-subject correlations to show whether students who have high average ratings also have high average performance and vice versa. Leal (1987) conducted a study as part of a college course. She was mainly interested in whether knowledge about memory processes related to classroom examination performance, and she found that scores on her memory questionnaire related positively to examination scores. In addition, Leal asked students to predict examination performance, and then she correlated each participant's single estimate with their actual performance on each examination. She found that these between-subjects correlations were significantly greater than zero for all examinations. Jacobson (1990) also asked students to make predictions about examination performance, but she asked for specific predictions for short-answer and essay portions of an examination. Jacobson's correlations between actual grades and predictions across students were significantly greater than chance and similar for each type of test. Postdiction confidence judgments were more highly correlated with short-answer test grades than with essay test grades.

In another classroom study by Grabe et al. (1990), students made predictions about performance on each of three chapters covered on three multiple-choice exams. Between-subjects correlations between predictions for each chapter and performance on questions related to the chapter were significantly greater than chance. However, a regression analysis indicated that when grade-point average (GPA) and previous test performance were statistically controlled, the correlations between prediction and examination performance generally become nonsignificant. Thus, students apparently used past performance to predict accurate future performance.

More recently, Hacker et al. (2000) asked students in an educational psychology course to predict the percentage they would get correct on three multiple-choice examinations. Immediately after each examination, they estimated their actual percentage correct. Hacker et al. calculated correlations between predictions and performance across students and found a significant relationship that increased with test experience, especially for students who performed well on the examinations. Postdictions were also accurate, but that accuracy remained fairly consistent across examinations.

In addition to calculating correlations across students, Hacker et al. found the difference between predictions and mean performance on each test. Such a signed difference is called bias, with a positive value showing overconfidence and a negative value showing underconfidence (Yates, 1990). Hacker et al. compared bias for students who did well and those who did poorly on examinations. Higher examination performance was associated with more accurate predictions. Students who performed more poorly tended to be overconfident, especially on pre-test predictions.

Other classroom studies have focused exclusively on postdictions made following examinations. Sinkavich (1995) asked students to make confidence judgments after answering multiple-choice questions covering textbook and lecture material on three exams. Between-subjects correlations between confidence judgments and exam performance ranged between 0.35 and 0.65. Shaughnessy (1979) asked students to make post-test confidence judgments on each multiple-choice item on a test in introductory psychology. He subtracted the mean rating for incorrect items from the mean rating for correct items and divided this difference by the standard deviation of the ratings. Shaughnessy called this measure a confidence accuracy quotient (CAQ; Shaughnessy, 1979). He found that the mean CAQ was significantly greater than zero, showing greater-than-chance prediction accuracy.

Differences between classroom and laboratory studies

Measures of prediction and postdiction accuracy

Almost all classroom studies have used correlations across participants between overall predictions (or postdictions) and overall performance. Many laboratory studies have used accuracy within participants as the measure of metacomprehension. This may be the reason for stronger evidence for accurate metacomprehension in classroom than in laboratory studies.

Between-subjects correlations Overall correlations require a single rating and single measure of performance for each participant. These global values are correlated across participants. Such correlations have usually been significant, both in the classroom studies described above (e.g. Grabe et al., 1990; Hacker et al., 2000; Jacobson, 1990; Leal, 1987) and in laboratory settings (e.g. Glover, 1989; Gillström and Rönnberg, 1995; Magliano, Little, and Graesser, 1993). These between-subjects correlations show whether students who have high average ratings also have high average performance and vice versa. They tell us whether an individual's scores fall close to a regression line defined by all the participants in a sample. Thus, all the scores in the sample determine overall metacognitive accuracy; there is no way to assess an individual's accuracy. In addition, such scores are sensitive to how individuals use the rating scale. Two individuals giving the same rating or estimate may actually have different levels of confidence and vice versa, but the ratings are taken at face value. Because there is no correction for the overall level of ratings given by an individual, such between-subjects differences in use of the scale influence the overall correlation.

Relative within-subjects measures For within-subjects measures, a rating and test score are obtained for each section of text or for each of several texts, so that each participant has multiple ratings and test scores. These values are correlated individually for each participant to determine metacomprehension accuracy. Multiple measures for each individual indicate whether participants can predict their performance on some texts relative to other texts. This type of measure has been used in laboratory studies, but not in classroom studies. Early researchers reported Pearson r correlations (Glenberg and Epstein, 1985; Glenberg et al., 1987), but more recent researchers (e.g. Maki and Serra, 1992a, 1992b; Rawson, Dunlosky, and Thiede, 2000; Weaver and Bryant, 1995) have used nonparametric gamma correlations. Nelson (1984) suggested that gamma is the most appropriate measure, in part because rating scales cannot be assumed to be interval in nature. These relative measures are unaffected by the specific levels of the ratings; instead they ask whether high ratings given by a student to certain units correspond to high performance by the student on those units.

Other measures that show within-subjects discrimination among texts or sections of texts involve calculating mean ratings for material related to test items that are answered correctly and subtracting the mean rating for material related to test items that are answered incorrectly. Some laboratory studies (Maki and Berry, 1984; Pressley et al., 1990) have used this difference as the dependent variable. In a classroom study, Shaughnessy (1979) divided this difference by the standard deviation of the ratings to create the CAQ measure for postdictions. Generally, however, such within-participant measures have not been used in classroom studies.

Measures such as within-subjects correlations and confidence accuracy quotients seem to have the most utility for education because they require that individuals judge comprehension and/or learning of different sections of the study material. Such monitoring allows the most control, in that students can then study sections that are less well learned and not continue to study better-learned material. However, these types of measures have rarely been used in classroom environments. The most commonly used measure in classroom studies has been between-subjects correlations which tell us nothing about individuals' abilities to discriminate what they know well from what they know less well. Within-subjects correlations to show students' abilities to discriminate what they know from what they don't know, along with bias to show overconfidence and underconfidence, would be most useful for understanding metacognition for text in classroom settings. Unfortunately, there are almost no studies in the literature that use both measures.

Although the use of different measures in classroom settings (usually between-subjects correlations) and laboratory settings (within-subjects correlations and bias) may explain different conclusions, other differences may also be responsible. Variables such as the level of processing of the text, text length and difficulty, and the nature of the test may be crucial. Each of these differences is discussed below.

Level of processing for text

Presumably students process text more deeply in classroom than in laboratory settings. In addition, they are exposed to material in multiple ways, by hearing it and possibly discussing it in class, and reading it in the text. In the laboratory, manipulations that increase the level of processing of text have produced greater metacomprehension accuracy. Level of processing has been manipulated by varying the goals in reading (Schommer and Surber, 1986), increasing the effort needed to read text (Maki et al. 1990), varying the strategies used during reading (Magliano et al., 1993), and rereading of text (Rawson et al., 2000). In two recent reviews of the literature, Maki (1998a) concluded that deeper processing generally leads to more accurate metacomprehension and Lin and Zabrucky (1998, p. 379) reached a stronger conclusion, that "the processing demands placed on learners during reading seem to have striking effects on calibration levels." This statement is stronger than warranted by our reading of the literature, but we do agree that processing variables have produced reliable effects in the metacomprehension literature. As can be seen below, researchers have used very different ways of influencing text processing and very different measures of metacomprehension accuracy.

Schommer and Surber (1986) asked students to judge comprehensibility of passages (shallow processing) or to read with the goal of teaching the main points to another student (deep processing). Students rated their comprehension and made post-test confidence ratings. Schommer and Surber's measure of metacomprehension was illusion of knowing, defined as poor performance and a high rating. For both pre-test and post-test ratings, illusions were more frequent with the shallow processing goal than with the deep processing goal, but only for difficult passages; this pattern was reversed for easy passages. Maki et al. (1990) manipulated level of processing by having students read text with deleted letters as compared to intact text. Within-subjects correlations of both predictions and postdictions and performance were higher for text with deleted letters, suggesting that students could better discriminate sections of text they knew from sections they didn't know when they had put more effort into processing the text. Magliano et al. (1993) found similar effects. They instructed students to read two sets of texts using conceptual or superficial processing strategies, and they measured metacomprehension with a correlation between overall test scores and mean prediction ratings. Correlations were significant in all conditions except for the first set of texts in the superficial instructions condition. Magliano et al. concluded that the superficial instructions interfered with metacomprehension accuracy, but this interference could be overcome with practice.

Related to level of processing, Rawson et al. (2000) manipulated whether students reread texts or read texts once. Within-subjects correlations were used as the measure of metacomprehension accuracy. Prediction accuracy was significantly better for the reread group (mean gamma = 0.57) than for the control group (mean gamma = 0.24). Postdiction accuracy, however, was approximately the same (mean gammas = 0.47 and 0.50) for the reread and the control groups. The difference in prediction accuracy is one of the largest effects in the literature.

Level of processing could be the reason why classroom studies show accurate metacognition for text if it is assumed that students process text fairly deeply when they read for a test that will partially determine a course grade. Laboratory studies probably lead to more superficial processing of text unless specific instructions and tasks to promote deep processing are used.

Characteristics of the studied text

Text difficulty Texts used in the laboratory have varied in difficulty so that some are probably harder than texts that students read in the classroom and some are easier. Indeed, texts used in the classroom may be of medium difficulty, which might explain consistent metacomprehension accuracy in naturalistic settings. Weaver and Bryant (1995) reported that medium difficulty texts produced higher metacomprehension accuracy than difficult or easy texts. This was a very large effect, with gamma correlations approaching 0.70 for the medium difficulty texts as compared to gammas of about 0.30 for other texts. Weaver and Bryant (1995) proposed an optimum effort hypothesis that predicts that metacomprehension accuracy will be highest when text readability levels are ideally matched to readers' ability levels. Weaver and Bryant's assumption was that college students' reading levels were closest to the levels of the medium difficulty texts; the easy texts were too far beneath the readers' levels and the difficult texts were too far above their levels. However, Weaver and Bryant did not test actual reading levels of the students, so it is unknown whether any group of participants would do best on the easy or difficult texts. Rather than the match between text difficulty and student reading level, it may be that the eight texts used in the medium condition by Weaver and Bryant were particularly discriminable, producing high within-subjects correlations. An experiment using several sets of texts at each level of difficulty and participants of different abilities is needed to support Weaver and Bryant's optimum effort hypothesis.

Other studies have shown variable effects of text difficulty. Schommer and Surber (1986) varied text difficulty along with processing instructions. With their illusion-of-knowing measure, text difficulty interacted with level of processing, but there were no main effects of difficulty on either prediction or postdiction illusions of knowing (a failure to identify inconsistency and high comprehension). Maki (1998b) studied several measures of metacomprehension for easier and more difficult expository texts, and found that the conclusions depended upon the measure. Not surprisingly, there was more negative bias (underconfidence) for the easy texts and very little bias for the difficult texts, especially for predictions as compared to postdictions. There was also some suggestion that within-subjects correlations were higher for easier texts, showing that the two measures produced opposite results; difficult texts produced less bias but also poorer prediction accuracy than did easier texts.

The conclusions about text difficulty are consistent for the Weaver and Bryant (1995) and Maki (1998b) studies because Maki's easy texts were at about the same reading level as Weaver and Bryant's medium difficulty texts. If it turns out that matching text difficulty and student reading level produces optimal metacomprehension accuracy, this might explain better metacomprehension in classroom as opposed to laboratory settings assuming that texts read in classroom settings are well-matched to student reading levels.

Text length The texts over which students are tested in classroom examinations are usually much longer then texts used in laboratory studies, suggesting text length as a possible reason for different findings in the two settings. Commander and Stanwyck (1997) examined whether reading skill and passage length influenced postdiction accuracy. They found more accurate postdiction judgments in the longer passage condition (twenty-nine sentences) relative to the shorter passage condition (thirteen sentences). The increase in postdiction accuracy was attributed to additional elaborating information and contextual cues in the longer passage condition. However, Glenberg, Wilkinson, and Epstein (1982) found just the opposite effect in an error-detection task in which students identified inconsistencies in text and rated comprehension. Illusions of knowing were more frequent when several paragraphs preceded the error-containing paragraph than when only one paragraph preceded it. They attributed this length effect to the presence of more potential conflicting information with more context.

Although not investigating length per se, Maki (1998a) reported a higher metacomprehension accuracy using many short texts as compared to using sections of one long text. The longer text did not allow students to use differences in domain familiarity for predictions, but predictions about shorter texts on different topics allowed for the use of domain familiarity. Domain familiarity is not a primary basis for predictions (Lin, Zabrucky, and Moore, 1997; Maki and Serra, 1992a), but differences in familiarity with text topics may provide some cues to increase the accuracy of predictions. At the extreme, experts in an area predict better performance on texts related to their domain of expertise than on texts from other domains; in fact, experts perform better on those texts (Glenberg and Epstein, 1987).

Thus, text length per se does not appear to be an important variable in metacomprehension accuracy; however, it may produce various effects depending on the role played by the added context. Students may predict performance better in classroom than in laboratory settings because there is more textual context for each examination question. Examinations may also cover several different domains allowing students to use domain familiarity in making their predictions and postdictions for different topics covered in classes.

Characteristics of the test

Retention interval The naturalistic studies have used undetermined retention intervals because students study material at unknown intervals before the tests. However, intervals between study and classroom tests have probably been several hours at least. In contrast, laboratory studies usually use minimal intervals with reading, predictions, and testing all completed in one session lasting less than 2 hours. An exception is a study by Maki and Berry (1984) that was conducted in the laboratory, but was designed to be similar to studying in a classroom setting. Participants read a chapter from a textbook, made predictions for each section, and then were tested either immediately, after 24 hours, or after 72 hours. Prediction ratings given to material related to incorrect test answers were subtracted from ratings given to material related to correct test answers. On Maki and Berry's (1984) immediate test, predictions were higher for material related to correctly answered questions independent of test performance; on the delayed tests, however, only those students who scored above the median on the test showed accuracy in their predictions. Maki (1998c), in a laboratory experiment using within-subjects correlations, also found that prediction accuracy was highest when reading, predictions, and the test were close together in time; adding a delay between reading and the test reduced prediction accuracy. Although these findings suggest that the longer retention intervals used in classroom settings may pose difficulty for students, all of the naturalistic classroom studies showed that students make prediction and postdiction judgments that are more accurate than chance.

Number of test items Classroom examinations usually have many test items. In contrast, laboratory studies use very few test items per text. The first laboratory studies of test predictions with college students used only one test item per prediction (e.g. Glenberg and Epstein, 1985, 1987; Glenberg et al., 1987). Metacomprehension accuracy was very poor. Weaver (1990) demonstrated that the number of test questions per text could dramatically increase metacomprehension accuracy, as measured by within-subjects correlations. Corroborating Weaver's earlier finding, Kelemen et al. (2000) found better monitoring accuracy in their Experiment 1 with ten questions per text relative to Experiment 2 with only one question per text. Using multiple test items per prediction or postdiction seems to be the key to obtaining accurate metacomprehension, apparently because this increases the reliability of the test. The use of many test items may help to explain the prediction accuracy seen in classroom studies.

Type of test The majority of studies investigating metacomprehension accuracy have employed multiple-choice tests both in the classroom (e.g. Grabe et al., 1990; Hacker et al., 2000; Shaughnessy, 1979; Sinkavich, 1995) and in the laboratory (Maki and Berry, 1984; Maki and Serra, 1992a; Rawson et al., 2000; Weaver and Bryant, 1995). An exception is the classroom study by Jacobson (1990) who reported a higher between-subjects correlation for postdictions on short-answer tests relative to essay tests. There was no difference due to type of test for predictions.

The earliest studies of metacognition of text by Glenberg and Epstein and colleagues (Glenberg and Epstein, 1985, 1987; Glenberg et al., 1987) used true–false inference verification questions. Metacomprehension accuracy was very low. More recently, Morris (1995) used four inference questions per text (the true and false version of two different questions) and found zero correlation between predictions and performance. He argued, in opposition to Weaver (1990), that his result shows that Glenberg and Epstein's earlier negative results were not an artifact of number of questions. However, Morris used the same inference questions as in the earlier Glenberg and Epstein studies, so his result may provide more evidence that true–false inference questions are particularly difficult for students to predict. In recent reviews of the metacomprehension literature, Lin and Zabrucky (1998) and Maki (1998a) agreed that true–false inference questions result in particularly poor within-subjects prediction accuracy.

Maki et al. (1990) and Magliano et al. (1993) used cued recall tests and found evidence for prediction accuracy. Gillström and Rönnberg (1995) used both recall and multiple-choice tests. They found somewhat higher between-subjects correlations between predictions and recall performance than between predictions and multiple-choice test performance, although they did not test for statistical differences as a function of type of test.

Lin and Zabrucky (1998) concluded that number of test questions is much more important than type of test, but few studies have directly investigated type of tests. One can look across experiments, but then the differences in measures loom larger than the differences in test format.

Although there are many differences between classroom and laboratory studies of metacognition for text, the most plausible reason for more accurate metacomprehension in the classroom is the type of measures used to assess accuracy. In classroom studies, correlations have usually been computed across students. This measure consistently shows accurate metacomprehension for various levels of processing and text difficulty, and for different types of tests.

Verbal ability and metacomprehension accuracy

There are a number of studies asking the basic question of whether individuals with stronger verbal skills predict future test performance and postdict past test performance better than individuals with weaker skills. If metacomprehension is an important mediator in learning from text, then better learners should produce greater metacomprehension accuracy. Studies investigating the link between metacomprehension accuracy and verbal ability have varied in the measures used for both concepts. One method of defining ability level is to use performance on the criterion test. Hasselhorn and Hager (1989) have criticized this method of defining ability because the measure of ability (the criterion test) and the measure of metacognitive accuracy (a relationship between predictions and the criterion test) are not independent. A second, and preferable, method of defining ability uses independent comprehension or verbal tests. Although both methods of defining ability have been used, different ways of defining ability do not seem to be the key to understanding why some studies show relationships between metacomprehension and comprehension ability and other studies do not. In Lin and Zabrucky's (1998) review of the literature relating general reading ability to metacomprehension, they concluded that the relationship is generally positive. However, their review did not distinguish between predictions and postdictions or between different measures of metacomprehension. Maki (1998a) concluded that there is little evidence for a relationship between verbal ability and prediction accuracy, but that there is a positive relation between verbal ability and postdiction accuracy.

Prediction accuracy and verbal abilities

The studies investigating the relationship between the accuracy of test predictions and verbal or comprehension abilities have used several different measures of prediction accuracy. These studies are summarized in Table 3.1. As can be seen in the table, different measures have produced different results.

Within-subjects discrimination among sections of text As described earlier, Maki and Berry (1984) conducted one of the earliest studies to investigate individual differences in metacomprehension ability. When tests were delayed, they found that students who scored above the median on tests could predict future performance with some accuracy, but students who scored below the median on tests could not. By comparing ratings on material related to correct and incorrect test questions, Maki and Berry were asking whether students could discriminate portions of text that they had learned better from portions that they learned less well. That is, they used a within-subjects measure that asks individuals to discriminate their relative strength on different parts of the text.

Other studies investigating the relationship between prediction ability and verbal ability have also used relative within-subjects measures, but they have generally not shown a relationship between prediction accuracy and verbal/comprehension ability. Maki, Jonas, and Kallod (1994) defined verbal ability both by the multimedia comprehension battery (Gernsbacher and Varner, 1988; Gernsbacher, Varner, and Faust, 1990) that tests students' memory for narratives presented in written, auditory, and pictorial form; and by the Nelson–Denny Reading Test (Brown, Nelson, and Denny, 1973). Students read texts having twelve sections,

Table 3.1. *Summary of studies investigating pre-test prediction accuracy and verbal/comprehension abilities.*

Authors (year)	Metacomprehension measure	Verbal ability measure	Verbal ability/metacomprehension relationship
Maki and Berry (1984)	Difference in ratings for correct/ incorrect answers (relative within-subjects)	Performance on criterion test (college)	Yes; significantly different for above median, not below
Maki et al. (1994)	Gamma correlation (relative within-subjects)	Nelson–Denny, multimedia comprehension battery (college)	No; although positive for auditory comprehension, not for five other measures
Maki (1998b)	Gamma correlation (relative within-subjects)	Performance on criterion test (college)	No
Maki and Swett (1987)	Prediction accuracy quotient (relative within-subjects)	Performance on criterion test (college)	No
Hacker et al. (2000)	Bias (signed overall difference)	Performance on criterion test (college)	Yes; higher performance related to less overconfidence
Maki (1998b)	Bias (signed overall difference)	Performance on criterion test (college)	Yes; higher performance related to less overconfidence
Grabe et al. (1990)	Bias (signed overall difference)	Grade-point average (GPA)	Yes; higher GPAs related to less overconfidence
Jacobson (1990)	Bias (signed overall difference)	Performance on criterion test (college)	Yes; high performers more likely to underrate; low performers more likely to overrate
Glover (1989)	Bias (signed overall difference)	Nelson–Denny (college and high school)	Yes; good readers smaller error than poor readers
Jacobson (1990)	Absolute global difference	Performance on criterion test (college)	No
Commander and Stanwyck (1997)	Absolute global difference	Nelson–Denny (college)	No
Pressley et al. (1987)	Absolute global difference	Comprehension from scholastic aptitude test (SAT) (college)	No
Gillström and Rönnberg (1995)	Absolute global difference	Verbal skills	No
Gillström and Rönnberg (1995)	Across-participant correlation	Verbal skills	Yes; medium and low skill show correlation; high does not

predicted performance for each section, and answered multiple-choice questions. Correlations were computed for each participant between the predictions and the performance on the twelve sections. Overall, students were not very accurate at making predictions, although the mean gamma correlation ($G = 0.114$) was significantly greater than chance. Gamma correlations were then correlated with verbal ability measures. Correlations were not significant for most of the measures of comprehension ability, including scores on the written and pictorial narratives, the Nelson–Denny comprehension score, and scores on the criterion tests. However, there was a significant positive correlation between performance on the auditory narratives and prediction accuracy, and the correlation between the amount read in one minute on the Nelson–Denny test and metacomprehension accuracy approached significance. Overall, the evidence for a positive relationship between verbal ability and test prediction accuracy was not very compelling, but the evidence for accurate test predictions was also quite weak in this study.

Maki (1998b) examined the effects of text difficulty and participant expectations on a number of measures of metacomprehension. She correlated each measure with performance on the criterion test. Within-subjects measures that required discrimination of texts that would lead to good performance from texts that would lead to poorer performance were not related to test performance. Maki and Swett (1987) also correlated criterion-test performance with their within-subjects measure of metacomprehension accuracy, prediction accuracy quotients (PAQs) (which are the same as Shaughnessy's [1979] CAQs except PAQs involve predictions and CAQs involve post-test confidence). Maki and Swett found no relationship between PAQs and criterion-test performance.

Overall, studies requiring participants to discriminate sections or texts that they learned well from those they learned less well have not consistently produced correlations with comprehension ability. However, this may be because metacomprehension accuracy was rather poor in all the studies and was not significantly better than chance in several of the Maki (1998b) conditions. Accuracy was significantly greater than chance in the Maki and Berry (1984), Maki et al. (1994), and Maki and Swett (1987) studies, but the level was not impressive.

Bias in predictions Bias (the signed difference between performance judgments and actual performance) has consistently shown a relationship between prediction accuracy and verbal skills. Maki (1998b) found a negative correlation between bias and criterion test performance. Students whose performance was poorer gave more overestimates of performance, whereas students whose performance was higher gave more

underestimates of performance. Grabe et al. (1990) also found a negative relationship between GPA and bias in a classroom setting. Jacobson
(1990) found the same thing when she asked students to make a prediction in terms of expected grade on tests in an actual class setting. Students
who performed better on the test were more likely to give predictions that
were congruent with or lower than their performance. Students who performed poorly were more likely to make predictions that were higher
than their performance. Hacker et al. (2000) found a similar result. In
addition, they found that absolute accuracy in predictions improved with
increasing test experience, especially for students who scored higher on
examinations. Glover (1989) found that students who did poorly on the
Nelson–Denny Reading Test overestimated their text comprehension performance whereas students who did better on the Nelson–Denny gave
estimates that were much closer to their actual scores.

Each of these studies using bias shows that poorer performers and those
with weaker verbal skills perform more poorly on criterion comprehension tests, and they overestimate their performance. Students rarely give
low values in making their estimates, so low performers show overconfidence on the bias measure. Students with better verbal skills tend to
underpredict their performance.

Congruence between predictions and performance Another type of
measure used in laboratory studies is the absolute (i.e., unsigned) difference between predictions and performance. Commander and Stanwyck
(1997) used this measure with a particular interest in illusions of knowing
(Glenberg et al., 1982), that is, high predictions and low performance.
College students were classified as high or low in verbal skill as measured by the Nelson–Denny Reading Test. Students were further divided
into high or low on multiple-choice test performance and high or low
on comprehension ratings taken immediately after reading. Commander
and Stanwyck classified students into congruent (match between rating and performance classification) and incongruent (mismatch between
rating and performance classification) monitors. Congruent comprehension monitors did not differ from incongruent comprehension monitors
on the Nelson–Denny Reading Test, showing that measures of metacomprehension ability using absolute difference scores are not related to
comprehension ability.

Although Jacobson (1990) did not analyze her data in this way, one can
combine her overraters and underraters into an incongruent category and
then compare congruent versus incongruent raters, high versus low performers. A chi-square on these data shows no relationship between congruent rating and criterion test performance. Other studies using absolute

differences between judgments and performance also show no significant relations between metacomprehension accuracy and verbal skill. Pressley et al. (1987) had students predict their future performance on a test either before reading, after reading, or after the test. Prediction accuracy was defined as the absolute difference between a global recall prediction and number of items answered correctly. Ability was determined from the comprehension passages and test items on the Scholastic Aptitude Test and the Graduate Record Exam. Students' comprehension ability was not related to the accuracy of their predictions.

Gillström and Rönnberg (1995) used a number of measures in their study, two of which were absolute differences. Students were classified on verbal ability based on an analogy test and a synonym–antonym test. Gillström and Rönnberg investigated the match between judgments of comprehension and multiple-choice performance, and between predictions of recall and free recall performance. For their difference scores, a match was defined as within 20 percent of the actual score. Although they did not report the statistics, chi-square tests showed no relation between the number of accurate and inaccurate predictors in high, medium, and low verbal ability groups for either multiple-choice or recall predictions.

Studies using absolute differences between predictions and performance consistently show that students who are high and low in verbal skills do not differ in their ability to predict their performance. This can be reconciled with the findings using bias (the signed difference) because those studies generally show that high performers are underconfident and low performers are overconfident. Thus, when the sign is removed from the bias scores and absolute accuracy is assessed, the differences cancel and both high and low performers are equally accurate.

Between-subjects correlations between estimates and performance
Between-subjects correlations calculated across participants for overall judgments and mean performance have also been used in studies of verbal ability and metacognition for text. Correlations have produced mixed results. Gillström and Rönnberg (1995) calculated correlations between predictions and multiple-choice test performance separately for high, medium, and low verbal ability groups. The only correlation that was significantly greater than chance was that for medium verbal skill participants. Similarly, the correlations between performance and predicted performance for recall tests were significant only for groups of low verbal skill students and for one group of students with medium-level verbal skills. Because lower verbal skill students were more likely to show significant correlations, the authors concluded that reading is less automatized in students with lower verbal skills than in students with higher verbal

skills. Lower correlations in the high verbal skill group may have been due to lower standard deviations (i.e., less variance to explain). Thus, the evidence that individuals with lower verbal skills have better metacomprehension skills was not strong in this study.

Conclusions about prediction accuracy and verbal ability In summary, studies that have used bias have shown consistently that students with lower comprehension and verbal skills are more likely to be overconfident and students with higher skills are more likely to be underconfident. Studies using relative within-subjects measures, such as gamma correlations, have sometimes, but not always, shown weak relationships between verbal ability and metacomprehension ability. One difficulty with these studies is that the accuracy of metacomprehension has been quite low, making it difficult to find individual differences when the phenomenon itself is either nonsignificant (Pressley et al., 1987) or very small (Maki et al., 1994). Studies using absolute differences between predictions and performance have uniformly shown no relationship between metacomprehension ability and verbal/comprehension ability.

Postdiction accuracy and verbal abilities

As with prediction accuracy, there are mixed conclusions in the literature about whether there is a positive relationship between postdiction accuracy and verbal abilities. Again, however, the measures of both variables vary widely across studies. These studies are summarized in Table 3.2.

Relative, within-subjects measures of metacomprehension accuracy The studies that show a positive relationship between postdiction accuracy and verbal/comprehension abilities all used relative, within-subjects measures of accuracy. The best studies used an independent measure of verbal abilities. For example, Maki et al. (1994) used both the Nelson–Denny Reading Test (Brown et al., 1973) and the multimedia comprehension battery (Gernsbacher and Varner, 1988) to define verbal ability. Their measure of postdiction accuracy was gamma correlations between test performance on questions related to sections of text and confidence in performance on those questions. Maki et al. found a positive relationship between these gamma correlations and all measures of verbal abilities except for the pictorial comprehension measure from the multimedia comprehension battery. Maki (1998b) used a similar measure of postdiction accuracy, but test performance itself was used as the measure of comprehension ability. She also found a positive relationship between postdiction gammas and test performance.

Table 3.2. *Summary of studies investigating post-test confidence judgment accuracy and verbal/comprehension abilities*

Authors (year)	Metacomprehension measure	Verbal ability measure	Verbal ability/metacomprehension relationship
Maki et al. (1994)	Gamma correlation (relative within-subjects)	Nelson–Denny, multimedia comprehension battery	Yes; higher gammas with better performance on all except pictorial comprehension
Maki (1998b)	Gamma correlation (relative within-subjects)	Performance on criterion test	Yes; higher gammas with better performance
Shaughnessy (1979)	Confidence accuracy quotient (relative within-subjects)	Performance on criterion test	Yes; higher CAQs with better test performance
Hacker et al. (2000)	Bias (signed overall difference)	Performance on criterion test (college)	Yes; higher performance related to less overconfidence
Sinkavich (1995)	Performance increases across judgment values (relative within-subjects)	Performance on final examination	Yes; performance increases with judgments for students in upper third, not lower third
Pressley et al. (1990)	Judgments differ between correct and incorrect answers (relative within-subjects)	Verbal SAT	No
Jacobson (1990)	Absolute global difference	Performance on criterion test	No
Commander and Stanwyck (1997)	Absolute global difference	Nelson–Denny	No
Pressley et al. (1987)	Absolute global difference	Comprehension from SAT	No
Schraw (1994)	Absolute global difference	Performance on criterion test	Yes; high performers made more accurate estimates
Gillström and Rönnberg (1995)	Absolute global difference	Verbal skills	Yes, *but negative*, low verbal ability gave more accurate recall postdictions

Studies conducted in classrooms have also shown positive relationships between ability and postdiction accuracy. Hacker et al. (2000) found that students who performed well on examinations showed less postdiction bias than those who performed less well. Similarly, Shaughnessy (1979) had students make confidence judgments for each item on a multiple-choice test. His within-subjects measure of discriminability, the CAQ, increased across quartiles of test performance with higher CAQs for students who performed better on the test. Sinkavich (1995) asked students to made judgments about the correctness of their answers on classroom tests. He defined good and poor students by final exam performance with the top 33 percent identified as good students and the bottom 33 percent identified as poor students. Sinkavich found that students' performance increased as rating values increased for good students, but there was no similar increase for poor students.

There is one exception to the conclusion that students who are higher in verbal ability are more accurate when measures are based on relative, within-subjects judgments. Pressley et al. (1990) defined verbal competence with the verbal section of the scholastic aptitude test (SAT). Using a measure similar to the CAQ, they subtracted the mean rating for incorrectly answered questions from the mean rating for correctly answered questions. They then correlated this difference with the verbal skill measure. Correlations in the two experimental conditions were both less than 0.20. With only twenty participants per condition, these correlations were not significant. However, other studies (e.g. Maki et al., 1994) showing significant effects have used more participants, but the other studies have also yielded somewhat higher correlations (i.e., in the 0.30 to 0.40 range). The Pressley et al. study may represent a statistical Type II error because there was too little power.

Global measures of accuracy There are also a number of studies in the literature that show no relationship between the accuracy of postdictions and verbal abilities. Each of these studies uses a global difference measure between overall test performance and overall ratings. In Jacobson's (1990) classroom study, she asked students to give themselves grades on short-answer and essay tests after writing their answers. Although she reports that better students were more likely to be congruent raters (i.e., their estimated grades were within two levels of their actual grades) than were poorer students, she did not do appropriate statistics to show this. For both the short-answer test and the essay test, students fell into the four categories of high and low performers by congruent and incongruent raters about as expected by chance (as judged by a chi-square). Thus, there was no evidence that better performers gave estimated grades that were closer to what they actually received than did low performers. Other studies using global judgments of test performance also showed no difference in accuracy for high- versus low-skill students. Commander and Stanwyck (1997) defined congruent raters in a way similar to that of Jacobson and they also found no relationship between congruence and scores on the Nelson–Denny Reading Test. Pressley et al. (1987) used the absolute difference between global predictions and overall performance. They found that this difference did not vary with ability as measured by comprehension items from the SAT.

There are two exceptions to the conclusion that the accuracy of global post-test estimates does not relate to individual differences in comprehension or verbal abilities. One of these studies shows a positive relationship and the other shows a negative relationship. Schraw (1994) found a positive correlation between the absolute difference between post-test estimated scores and actual scores and criterion test performance. Schraw's study differs from other studies in which no individual differences were found in that Schraw's participants also made immediate judgments after answering questions for each text, as is required for within-subjects measures. As Schraw discusses, those earlier judgments may have benefited better performers more than poorer performers, thus resulting in a correlation between final global prediction accuracy and overall performance.

The other study showing a relationship between verbal ability and absolute prediction error is by Gillström and Rönnberg (1995) for postdictions on recall tests. Verbal ability was defined by an analogy and a synonym–antonym test. Recall was scored in terms of the percent of correct propositions recalled. Postdictions were given as the estimated percent propositions recalled. The absolute difference between actual performance and estimates was averaged across three texts. Congruent raters were defined as those who were within 20 percent of their actual score. Although Gillström and Rönnberg did not conduct any statistics on the number of congruent and incongruent raters at each ability level, we calculated a chi-square from the data that were presented. This analysis showed that students with *low* verbal skills actually were more congruent in their overall ratings than students with high verbal skills. Recall may produce a different pattern than other types of tests because it is obvious that little was recalled in cases where little was written. That is, with recall, students may be able to judge their performance by the amount written and students with weaker verbal skills may be more likely than students with more verbal skills to write very little for some texts.

Overall, the literature shows a relationship between comprehension and verbal ability and the accuracy of judgments on post-tests when accuracy is defined by within-subjects relative measures. That is, people with higher verbal skill appear to be better able to discriminate correct from incorrect answers on tests than do people with lower verbal skill. However, there does not appear to be verbal skill differences in students' abilities to estimate their overall level of performance on tests. Both good and poor performers and students with higher and lower verbal skills are fairly accurate at judging overall performance.

Is there a general metacomprehension ability?

The studies that ask whether metacomprehension ability is related to comprehension or verbal ability presume that there is such a thing as general metacomprehension ability. This presumption might be extended to ask whether there is a stable and general metacognitive ability. Several studies have examined this question.

Generalization across metacognitive tasks If there is a general metacognitive ability, then individuals should show similar levels of metacognitive accuracy across tasks. Schraw (Schraw, 1997; Schraw et al. 1995; Schraw and Nietfeld, 1998) and West and Stanovich (1997) have reported evidence for such a general ability, but Kelemen et al. (2000) found no support for a general metacognitive ability.

Schraw et al. (1995) tested a domain-general hypothesis of metacognition versus a domain-specific hypothesis. If metacognitive awareness is domain general, then monitoring ability should be similar across many domains. They measured the accuracy of post-test confidence judgments by finding the difference between correct and incorrect answers, and they also calculated bias (the signed difference between mean estimates and mean performance). Students answered questions in seven very different domains, including general knowledge, computing probabilities, and spatial judgments. Intercorrelations among the domains for confidence judgments were quite high, as were the intercorrelations among bias on the different tests. The correlations across domains for the within-subjects relative measure (correct minus incorrect ratings) were generally small and nonsignificant. That relative measure was related to level of performance, with higher performance being related to larger correct–incorrect differences in confidence. Schraw (1997) conducted a similar study with different materials and found consistency in bias across various domains. Schraw and Nietfeld (1998) investigated domains that could be classified as fluid (e.g. Raven's matrices, probabilistic reasoning) and crystallized abilities (e.g. reading comprehension, vocabulary, geographical distances). Metacognitive ability was measured by bias and by accuracy that they defined as the absolute difference between confidence and performance averaged across items. Bias scores in all domains were correlated fairly strongly, but the relative accuracy scores showed more correlations within type of knowledge (fluid versus crystallized) than across types. Thus, the Schraw et al. (1995) and Schraw and Nietfeld (1998) studies suggest that bias may represent a general metacognitive characteristic but the ability to discriminate which answers are correct from which are incorrect may be more domain specific.

West and Stanovich (1997) also found support for bias being a general characteristic. They looked specifically at overconfidence in two tasks, a general knowledge task and a motor task. For the general-knowledge task, participants selected an answer and then made a probability estimate about the likelihood that the answer was correct. In the motor task (the penny-slide task), participants were instructed that they were to slide pennies onto a strip on the table. There was a scoring system based on where pennies landed in a block of thirty trials. Before each block, participants were to predict their score for the block. The primary measure used was bias because West and Stanovich were particularly interested in overconfidence in the two tasks. They split the sample at the median bias on the general-knowledge test. Next, they looked at differences of the two groups on the penny-slide task. They found the knowledge overconfident group gave higher predictions on the penny-slide task, especially for the second block. Participants who were overconfident on the knowledge assessment task thought that they would improve much more than less confident participants on the second block of the penny-slide task relative to the first block. Thus, West and Stanovich provided evidence for generalized overconfidence. This is interesting because the overconfidence generalized across very different tasks and from item-by-item postdictions about responses to a global prediction about performance. These results, along with those of Schraw (Schraw et al., 1995; Schraw and Nietfeld, 1998), suggest that bias is a stable individual difference. Bias is also the one measure that consistently showed individual ability differences in prediction judgments.

The existence of a general metacognitive ability presumes that both performance and judgments are reliable. Furthermore, the accuracy of judgments relative to performance must also be reliable. Thompson and Mason (1996) investigated split-half reliability by calculating gamma correlations separately for odd and even items, and test–retest reliability by testing individuals in two sessions. Participants judged their confidence in recognition of different types of materials, i.e., general knowledge question, faces, and words. Neither the split-half nor the test–retest gammas were reliable. Thus, Thompson and Mason (1996) concluded that present methods do not produce stable metacognitive accuracy. Leonesio and Nelson (1990) investigated across-task reliability. They found that different types of metamemory judgments (ease of learning, predictions about future memory, and predictions about recognition following recall) were not highly correlated, suggesting that there is no general metamemory ability.

Kelemen et al. (2000) also sought evidence for a general metacognitive ability in memory-related tasks by testing reliability both within and across tasks. They used four different metamemory tasks involving pre-test predictions, and they investigated both test–retest reliability and inter-task reliability. They had students judge the ease of learning of word pairs, predict future recall of word pairs, judge the likelihood of future recognition for general knowledge questions for which they could not recall the answer, and predict their future memory performance on text. Participants completed each task twice so that test–retest reliability could be assessed. Kelemen et al. found that the levels of the judgments and performance were both fairly reliable across time. Furthermore, there were a number of significant correlations among the different types of judgments and among the measures of memory. However, the gamma correlations used to assess metacognitive accuracy did not correlate either across time or across tasks. This suggests that metamemory accuracy is not a stable individual difference. In spite of this absence of reliability in metamemory accuracy, like West and Stanovich (1997), Kelemen et al. found that bias scores were reliable across time and across tasks.

The lack of evidence for reliability of metacognitive accuracy within tasks is troubling. If the same individual produces varying levels of accuracy within the same task, that would explain why it has been so difficult to find stable relations between metacomprehension ability and verbal abilities. The metacognitive measure that has shown good reliability both within (Kelemen et al., 2000) and between tasks (Kelemen et al., 2000; West and Stanovich, 1997) is bias. This is also the measure that consistently correlated with the accuracy of text predictions (Glover, 1989; Jacobson, 1990; Maki, 1998b). Thus, there is evidence that people are generally overconfident or underconfident, but there is no evidence that some people can consistently predict their performance accurately.

Metacognitive ability as a predictor of comprehension Although the evidence for a generalized metacognitive ability is weak, some researchers have included metacognitive ability as an important variable in predicting comprehension. Britton et al. (1998) developed an individual differences model of learning from text in which they argued that making connections among ideas in text depends upon four variables. Metacognition is the trigger for other processes that are necessary for understanding. Students must first sense that a connection between concepts needs to be made; that is, that there is a gap in their understanding. Then they can use working memory, their domain knowledge, and inference-making to understand text. Poor metacognitive ability would interfere with the triggering of other important comprehension processes, making metacognitive ability a primary ability in comprehension. Using structural equation modeling, Britton et al. found support for their proposed linear model in which metacognitive monitoring plays a primary role in comprehension by triggering the action of the other processes.

Stimson (1998) tested the role of metacognitive ability in the comprehension of standard linear text and hypertext. The hypertext used in his study consisted of text presented on a computer with links to definitions of words. The text was relatively impoverished compared to most hypertext because there were few links among concepts in the text. Learning from text was measured by performance on multiple-choice questions. Stimson used a number of measures of metacognitive ability, including the metacognition questionnaire (Schraw and Dennison, 1994), predictions of future performance on just-studied word pairs (immediate judgments of learning, Nelson and Dunlosky, 1991), and postdictions on recalled words. Overall, the questionnaire was not correlated with learning from text, but when specific questions related to online metacognitive skills were selected, there was a positive correlation between questionnaire answers and learning for hypertext but not for linear text. Prediction accuracy for the word pairs (measured by gamma correlations between predictions and performance) did not relate to learning from either hypertext or linear text. However, bias for word pair recall correlated with learning from hypertext with more underconfident students learning better. Bias did not relate to learning from linear text. For postdictions, accuracy (as measured by gammas relating confidence and recall accuracy of the word pairs) related to learning from hypertext but not from linear text. Postdiction bias also related to learning from hypertext with more underconfidence related to better learning. Thus, these data suggest that metacognitive ability may be particularly important in learning from hypertext where participants must decide what links to follow during learning.

Implications for education

The most important variables determining prediction accuracy are level of processing (Maki et al., 1990), especially rereading (Rawson et al., in press); text difficulty (Weaver and Bryant, 1995) (although this may actually be an effect of specific texts used in different conditions); and number of questions associated with each prediction (Weaver, 1990). None of these variables has been studied in actual classroom settings, although it may be assumed that classroom texts are processed deeply, they are of medium difficulty, and that there are multiple test questions. Studies conducted in classrooms generally show that students can predict performance, but those studies have mostly used between-subjects correlations. Thus, we do not know if individuals can discriminate which parts of material they know well from which parts they know less well when they study material for real-world tests.

Due to the inherent importance of metacomprehension, it is surprising that there are not more classroom studies. On the other hand, though, metacomprehension researchers may be overestimating the benefits of improving metacomprehension accuracy. We know a fair amount about monitoring of comprehension, but little about control, the second component of metacognition described by Nelson and Narens (1990). Using the outcome of monitoring is essential for controlling study. However, there is no evidence that students actually use monitoring to control learning from text. Furthermore, there is little evidence that improved metacomprehension accuracy results in better understanding of material. If that were the case, then students with higher GPAs and those with higher test scores should show better metacomprehension. There is some evidence that students who perform better in college and on tests are less likely to be overconfident than students who perform more poorly (Grabe et al., 1990; Jacobson, 1990; Maki, 1998b), but those who do better on tests and in classes do not appear to predict performance more accurately (Jacobson, 1990; Maki, 1998b). The primary problem in detecting individual differences in metacomprehension may be that stable individual differences have not been demonstrated across metacognitive tasks (Kelemen et al., 2000). Thus, at present, using the laboratory results showing variables that improve metacomprehension accuracy to make recommendations about education is not justified. We have little evidence that improving metacomprehension accuracy would actually improve learning in classroom settings.

Although the relationship between individual differences in verbal and academic ability and metacomprehension accuracy is not strong in the metacomprehension literature, Britton et al. (1998) place metacognitive ability as a triggering variable for comprehension strategies in their model of comprehension, and they have some evidence to support this. Furthermore, Stimson (1998) found a weak relationship between metacognitive ability and learning from hypertext, but not from linear text. With more and more material presented as hypertext on the World Wide Web, it might be constructive to investigate metacomprehension in that setting where more decisions about reading are made necessary by the medium. Stronger and more consistent relationships between metacomprehension ability and performance from text may show up in the context of hypermedia. If so, then training in metacognition may become particularly important as hypermedia becomes a more primary source of information. A review of the metacomprehension literature in ten years' time may show many more strong relationships between metacomprehension and other variables if more studies are conducted using hypertext and if more studies use real-world acquisition of knowledge in classrooms. If future research shows these trends, then recommendations to improve metacomprehension might be relevant to improving learning.

REFERENCES

Britton, B. K., Stimson, M., Stennett, B., and Gülgöz, S. (1998). Learning from instructional text: test of an individual difference model. *Journal of Educational Psychology*, 90, 476–491.
Brown, J. L., Nelson, M. J., and Denny, E. C. (1973). *The Nelson–Denny Reading Test*. Chicago: Riverside.
Commander, N. E., and Stanwyck, D. J. (1997). Illusion of knowing in adult readers: effects of reading skill and passage length. *Contemporary Educational Psychology*, 22, 39–52.
Flavell, J. H. (1979). Metacognition and cognitive monitoring: a new area of cognitive developmental inquiry. *American Psychologist*, 34, 906–911.
Gernsbacher, M. A., and Varner, K. R. (1988). *The multi-media comprehension battery* (Tech. Rep. No 88–07). Eugene, OR: Institute of Cognitive and Decision Studies.
Gernsbacher, M. A., Varner, K. R., and Faust, M. E. (1990). Investigating differences in general comprehension. *Journal of Experimental Psychology: Learning, Memory, and Cognition*, 16, 430–445.
Gillström, A., and Rönnberg, J. (1995). Comprehension calibration and recall prediction accuracy of texts: reading skill, reading strategies, and effort. *Journal of Educational Psychology*, 87, 545–558.
Glenberg, A. M., and Epstein, W. (1985). Calibration of comprehension. *Journal of Experimental Psychology: Learning, Memory, and Cognition*, 11, 702–718.
    (1987) Inexpert calibration of comprehension. *Memory and Cognition*, 15, 84–93.
Glenberg, A. M., Sanocki, T., Epstein, W., and Morris, C. (1987). Enhancing calibration of comprehension. *Journal of Experimental Psychology: General*, 116, 119–136.
Glenberg, A. M., Wilkinson, A. C., and Epstein, W. (1982). The illusion of knowing: failure in the self-assessment of comprehension. *Memory and Cognition*, 10, 597–602.
Glover, J. (1989). Reading ability and the calibrator of comprehension. *Educational Research Quarterly*, 13, 7–11.

Grabe, M., Bordages, W., and Petros, T. (1990). The impact of computer-supported study on student awareness of examination preparation and on examination performance. *Journal of Computer-Based Instruction*, 17, 113–119.

Hacker, D. J., Bol, L., Horgan, D. D., and Rakow, E. A. (2000). Test prediction and performance in a classroom context. *Journal of Educational Psychology*, 92, 160–170.

Hasselhorn, M., and Hager, W. (1989) Prediction accuracy and memory performance: correlational and experimental tests of a metamemory hypothesis. *Psychological Research*, 51, 147–152.

Jacobson, J. M. (1990). Congruence of pre-test predictions and post-test estimations with grades on short answer and essay tests. *Educational Research Quarterly*, 14, 41–47.

Kelemen, W. L., Frost, P. J., and Weaver, C. A. III (2000). Individual differences in metacognition: evidence against a general metacognitive ability. *Memory and Cognition*, 28, 92–107.

Leal, L. (1987). Investigation of the relation between metamemory and university students' examination performance. *Journal of Educational Psychology*, 79, 35–40.

Leonesio, R. J., and Nelson, T. O. (1990). Do different metamemory judgments tap the same underlying aspects of memory? *Journal of Experimental Psychology: Learning, Memory, and Cognition*, 16, 464–470.

Lin, L.-M., and Zabrucky, K. M. (1998). Calibration of comprehension: research and implications for education and instruction. *Contemporary Educational Psychology*, 23, 345–391.

Lin, L.-M., Zabrucky, K., and Moore, D. (1997). The relations among interest, self-assessed comprehension, and comprehension performance in young adults. *Reading Research and Instruction*, 36, 127–139.

Magliano, J. P., Little, L. D., and Graesser, A. C. (1993). The impact of comprehension instruction on the calibration of comprehension. *Reading Research and Instruction*, 32, 49–63.

Maki, R. H. (1998a). Test predictions over test material. In D. J. Hacker, J. Dunlosky, and A. C. Graesser (eds.), *Metacognition in educational theory and practice*. Mahwah, NJ: Lawrence Erlbaum Associates.

(1998b). Metacomprehension of text: influence of absolute confidence level on bias and accuracy. In D. L. Medin (ed.), *The psychology of learning and motivation, Volume 38*, pp. 223–248. San Diego, CA: Academic Press.

(1998c). Predicting performance on text: delayed versus immediate predictions and tests. *Memory and Cognition*, 26, 959–964.

Maki, R. H., and Berry, S. L. (1984). Metacomprehension of text material. *Journal of Experimental Psychology: Learning, Memory, and Cognition*, 10, 663–679.

Maki, R. H., Foley, J. M., Kajer, W. K., Thompson, R. C., and Willert, M. G. (1990). Increased processing enhances calibration of comprehension. *Journal of Experimental Psychology: Learning, Memory and Cognition*, 16, 609–616.

Maki, R. H., Jonas, D., and Kallod, M. (1994). The relationship between comprehension and metacomprehension ability. *Psychonomic Bulletin and Review*, 1, 126–129.

Maki, R. H., and Serra, M. (1992a). The basis of test predictions for test material. *Journal of Experimental Psychology: Learning, Memory, and Cognition*, 18, 116–126.

(1992b). Role of practice tests on the accuracy of test predictions on text material. *Journal of Educational Psychology*, 84, 200–210.

Maki, R. H., and Swett, S. (1987). Metamemory for narrative text. *Memory and Cognition*, 15, 72–83.

Morris, C. C. (1995). Poor discourse comprehension monitoring is no methodological artifact. *The Psychological Record*, 45, 655–668.

Nelson, T. O. (1984). A comparison of current measures of the accuracy of feeling-of-knowing predictions. *Psychological Bulletin*, 95, 109–133.

Nelson, T. O., and Dunlosky, J. (1991). When people's judgments of learning (JOLs) are extremely accurate at predicting subsequent recall: the "delayed JOL effect." *Psychological Science*, 2, 267–270.

Nelson, T. O., and Narens, L. (1990). Metamemory: a theoretical framework and new findings. *The Psychology of Learning and Motivation*, 26, 125–141.

Pressley, M., Ghatala, E., Pirie, J., and Woloshyn, V. E. (1990). Being really, really certain you know the main idea doesn't mean you do. *National Reading Conference Yearbook*, 39, 249–256.

Pressley, M., Snyder, B. L., Levin, J. R., Murray, H. G., and Ghatala, E. S. (1987). Perceived readiness for examination performance (PREP) produced by initial reading of text and text containing adjunct questions. *Reading Research Quarterly*, 22, 219–236.

Rawson, K. A., Dunlosky, J., and Thiede, K. W. (2000). The rereading effect: metacomprehension accuracy improves across reading trials. *Memory and Cognition*, 28, 1004–1010.

Schommer, M., and Surber, J. R. (1986). Comprehension-monitoring failure in skilled adult readers. *Journal of Educational Psychology*, 78, 353–357.

Schraw, G. (1994). The effect of metacognitive knowledge on local and global monitoring. *Contemporary Educational Psychology*, 19, 143–154.

(1997). The effect of generalized metacognitive knowledge on test performance and confidence judgments. *The Journal of Experimental Education*, 65, 135–146.

Schraw, G., and Dennison, R. S. (1994). Assessing metacognitive awareness. *Contemporary Educational Psychology*, 19, 460–475.

Schraw, G., Dunkle, M. E., Roedel, T. D., and Bendixen, L. D. (1995). Does a general monitoring skill exist? *Journal of Educational Psychology*, 87, 433–444.

Schraw, G. and Nietfeld, J. (1998). A further test of the general monitoring skill hypothesis. *Journal of Educational Psychology*, 90, 236–248.

Shaughnessy, J. J. (1979). Confidence-judgment accuracy as a predictor of test performance. *Journal of Research in Personality*, 13, 505–514.

Sinkavich, F. J. (1995). Performance and metamemory: do students know what they don't know? *Journal of Instructional Psychology*, 22, 77–87.

Stimson, J. J. (1998). Learning from hypertext depends on metacognition. Dissertation: University of Georgia, 1–114.

Thompson, W. B., and Mason, S. E. (1996). Instability of individual differences. *Memory and Cognition*, 24, 226–234.

Weaver, C. A. III (1990). Constraining factors in calibration of comprehension. *Journal of Experimental Psychology: Learning, Memory, and Cognition*, 16, 214–222.

Weaver, C. A. III, and Bryant, D. S. (1995). Monitoring of comprehension: the role of text difficulty in metamemory for narrative and expository text. *Memory and Cognition*, 23, 12–22.

West, R. F., and Stanovich, K. E. (1997). The domain specificity and generality of overconfidence: individual differences in performance estimation bias. *Psychonomic Bulletin and Review*, 4, 387–392.

Yates, J. F. (1990). *Judgment and decision making*. Englewood Cliffs, NJ: Prentice-Hall.

4 Influence of practice tests on the accuracy of predicting memory performance for paired associates, sentences, and text material

John Dunlosky, Katherine A. Rawson and Susan L. McDonald

Learning and retaining class material is not only the primary goal in many class exercises (e.g. from learning the ABC to the periodic table of the elements) but may be essential for successfully mastering more complex lessons (e.g. reading, and developing chemical compounds). Accordingly, many researchers and educators have devoted their careers to engineering techniques that will improve learning. In the present chapter, we discuss the utility of one technique for improving individuals' ability to master new materials: practice tests or self-testing. A practice test involves an individual testing their memory or comprehension of class material to evaluate whether they will succeed on a subsequent test and, as such, can be considered a metacognitive activity. That is, practice testing may inform the learner about the degree to which to-be-learned materials have been stored in memory (or have been comprehended) so that they can accurately predict future test performance. In this way, practice tests may help students to regulate their study more effectively. For instance, a student may devise a test to evaluate whether to-be-learned material can be retrieved. If the material is retrieved during the test, they can move on to study other less well-learned materials. If the material is not successfully retrieved, then more study time should be allocated. The idea is that self-testing will improve the efficiency of self-regulated learning by helping students isolate poorly learned material for restudy. This simple strategy has been included in popular learning techniques and is undoubtedly used by many students.

Even so, the presumed effectiveness of this simple strategy relies upon an implicit (albeit straightforward) assumption, which we refer to as the *diagnosticity* assumption. If this assumption is invalid, practice tests may actually reduce the effectiveness of students' learning. This assumption is that for a practice test to benefit learning, the outcomes of the test need to be highly diagnostic of criterion performance, whether the criterion test is answering questions on an exam, reciting poetry in front of a classroom, and so on. To understand why high diagnosticity is essential, consider a student studying a verse for an upcoming recital. Immediately after studying it, the student may correctly recite the verse during a self-test, predict that the upcoming recital will be a success, and hence not study it any longer. Unfortunately, correctly reciting a verse immediately after studying it does not necessarily mean it will be remembered later during the recital. If substantial forgetting occurs, the recital may be a flop; or they may incorrectly retrieve the verse and fail to realize it, which may prove even more embarrassing.

Although somewhat counterintuitive, practice tests may not always be highly diagnostic of criterion performance, which leads to the question "What circumstances ensure that testing will be highly diagnostic of criterion performance?" In this chapter, we provide some preliminary answers to this question. Note that the experiments described herein do not address the issue of whether accurately predicting performance can support effective self-regulated learning, although we discuss this intuitive assumption further in the General discussion. Instead, our specific goal was to discuss techniques that prompt students to test their memory of various materials – including paired-associate items (Introduction), simple sentences (Experiment 1), and key vocabulary embedded in text (Experiment 2) – in service of predicting criterion test performance. For each kind of material, we present evidence relevant to how accurately students predict criterion test performance after they have tested their memory.

But why focus on predictive accuracy instead of on the diagnosticity assumption itself? Although they can be evaluated jointly (e.g. Maki and Serra, 1992; McDonald, 1997), one reason to focus initially on the former is that the accuracy of a student's predictions – that is, his or her perceptions about the diagnosticity of the outcomes of a practice test – are more central to the regulation of learning. For instance, the student may incorrectly retrieve a response during a practice test, which itself may be objectively predictive of (incorrect) performance on the criterion test. More important, after retrieving an incorrect response, the individual may believe that it was correctly retrieved and predict that it will be remembered on the criterion test. In this case, the material may not be restudied, even though test performance would be poor. Thus, learning is regulated by a student's subjective perception about the outcomes of practice tests (which are tapped by a student's predictions) and not by the objective outcome of the practice tests. Accordingly, our interest lies in the accuracy of people's subjective predictions.

Delaying practice tests can yield high levels of predictive accuracy

To assess the degree to which practice tests support predictions that are highly predictive of criterion performance, we need procedures to evaluate the accuracy of students' predictions. Methodological and statistical advances in the area of metamemory have provided tools for this endeavor (e.g. Hart, 1965; Nelson, 1984). Consider a method used to investigate the accuracy of predictions for associative memory. College students begin by studying paired-associate items (e.g. doctor–lobster), which are presented individually at a fixed rate. Sometime after a given item had been presented for study, the stimulus of the pair is presented again (i.e., doctor–?), and the students predict the likelihood of recalling the response term (i.e., lobster) when shown the stimulus on an upcoming test.[1] Finally, after all items have been studied and judged, the criterion test occurs, which is often paired-associate recall (i.e., each stimulus is presented and the student attempts to recall the corresponding response). This procedure for collecting predictions presumably elicits a test of memory. By presenting the stimulus alone, an individual attempts to retrieve the response and uses the outcome of this practice test to predict criterion performance (Nelson and Dunlosky, 1991, 1996). If the outcomes of the tests are highly diagnostic of criterion performance, the accuracy of an individual's predictions are expected to be high (but see the General discussion for a caveat).

To measure predictive accuracy using this procedure, one computes a Goodman–Kruskal gamma correlation between an individual's predictions and criterion test performance (Nelson, 1984). Accuracy as measured by gamma is called *relative* accuracy because it indicates the degree to which an individual correctly predicts performance for one item relative to another. A correlation of 0 indicates that an individual's judgments have no predictive accuracy, and a correlation of 1.0 indicates perfect accuracy.[2] The level of predictive accuracy that is sufficient to produce

---

[1] In the context of learning paired-associate items, these predictions have typically been called judgments of learning. In the context of learning text material, such predictions have been called text predictions or metacomprehension judgments. Given that we discuss outcomes from experiments involving various kinds of materials, we have decided to keep the terminology consistent throughout this chapter by using the term "prediction."

[2] Another measure of predictive accuracy is *absolute* accuracy, which is the degree to which the magnitude of predictions for a set of items matches the actual level of test performance for those items. Obtaining high levels of absolute accuracy is also valuable for effective learning. For instance, if a student consistently overestimates learning (e.g. predicts that 80 percent of class material has been learned even though subsequent test performance would be only 40 percent), he or she may terminate study before the material had been adequately learned. In the present chapter, however, we focus solely on relative accuracy and leave a detailed analysis of practice tests and absolute accuracy for future enquiry.

effective self-regulated learning has not yet been established. Certainly, however, students' predictions tend to be more effective in the regulation of learning when they are more, rather than less, accurate (e.g. Thiede, 1999), and hence developing practice tests that yield close-to-perfect levels of accuracy (i.e., correlations near 1.0) is arguably an important research agenda. Note that in the present chapter, we occasionally state that some levels of accuracy are "relatively high," which literally means that they are high relative to corresponding control conditions or relative to the levels of accuracy that are reported in the corresponding literature. Even so, at least in some cases, the techniques that support these "relatively high" levels of accuracy will require further refinement to achieve perfect accuracy.

How accurate are students at predicting performance on tests of paired-associate recall? The answer to this question partly depends upon when the predictions occur. In particular, in the majority of experiments reported in the 1980s, individuals predicted performance for each item immediately after the item had been studied, so that the interval between study and prediction was minimal. Accuracy of these immediate predictions has usually been low, and although some exceptions exist, correlations from numerous studies typically have been close to 0. Accuracy of immediate predictions is often constrained because a test that follows immediately after studying a paired-associate item would not be highly diagnostic of performance on a criterion test that is administered at a delay. One reason for the low diagnosticity is that almost every response would be correctly recalled prior to these immediate predictions, whereas many of the responses would be forgotten prior to the criterion test.

Accordingly, Nelson and Dunlosky (1991) had individuals make delayed predictions (see also Begg et al., 1989). Between the study and delayed prediction for a given item, an individual studied other items for at least 30 seconds. In their experiment, the mean accuracy of delayed predictions across individuals was substantial (0.90), far exceeding the accuracy of immediate predictions. One explanation for this outcome is that the products of delayed practice tests for paired-associate items are highly diagnostic of criterion performance (for debate concerning why such practice tests are diagnostic, see Nelson and Dunlosky, 1992; Spellman and Bjork, 1992).

The high level of accuracy for these delayed predictions has been obtained across a wide variety of paired-associate materials, for younger and older adults, and even when adults are under the influence of alcohol or nitrous oxide. Across twenty-five different conditions reported in ten articles (Connor, Dunlosky, and Hertzog, 1997; Dunlosky et al., 1998; Dunlosky and Nelson, 1992; 1994; 1997; Kelemen and Weaver, 1997;

Nelson and Dunlosky, 1991; Nelson et al., 1998; Thiede and Dunlosky, 1994; Weaver and Kelemen, 1997), high levels of accuracy for delayed predictions have been demonstrated, with the median level of accuracy being 0.83 ($M = 0.82$, $SD = 0.09$; some values were estimated from figures). The educational implications are straightforward: if students are trained to assess memory with delayed tests of to-be-remembered paired associates, they presumably will be able to utilize the outcome of these tests to regulate study effectively. Consistent with this possibility, adults in their twenties and older adults in their sixties and seventies appear to spontaneously utilize the delayed predictions in regulating self-paced study (Dunlosky and Hertzog, 1997; Nelson et al., 1994). Based on such evidence, Dunlosky and Hertzog (1998) proposed that training adults to self-test would improve their self-regulated learning, which has led to the development of a memory intervention program that is currently under way (Kubat, 2000).

Is delaying practice tests sufficient for obtaining high levels of predictive accuracy?

Even with these encouraging outcomes in mind, it is important to stress that delayed practice tests may not always support high levels of predictive accuracy. That is, in at least three situations, the accuracy of delayed predictions has been closer to chance than to perfect. First, delayed predictions are typically no more accurate than are immediate predictions when the entire stimulus–response pairs are used to prompt predictions. A possible difficulty here is that when the entire item is presented, students do not have a chance to evaluate whether the response can be recalled from long-term memory (for detailed discussion, see Dunlosky and Nelson, 1997). Second, even when people assess their memory with delayed predictions that are cued by only the stimulus, high levels of predictive accuracy are not ensured. Kelemen and Weaver (1997) reported that the duration of the lag between study and prediction is critical: as compared to immediate predictions, which have a minimal study–prediction (SP) lag, accuracy of delayed predictions improves somewhat, even when the SP lag is only a few seconds. However, not until the SP lag exceeds several minutes are the highest levels of accuracy obtained. These empirical generalizations provide some recommendations for maximizing predictive accuracy through practice tests. In particular, students should make sure: (a) that the practice tests are based on the recall of to-be-remembered materials from memory; and (b) that these practice tests are delayed after the to-be-remembered materials are studied, with an SP lag of several minutes or more.

Finally, and most pertinent to the remainder of this chapter, the conclusions based on paired associates described above may not entirely generalize to other materials that students need to learn, such as individual words, sentences, and texts. For instance, students often need to memorize lists of related terms, such as lobes of the brain, founders of impressionism, and leaders of the federalist party. To investigate predictive accuracy for these materials, Kelemen (2000) had undergraduates study categories of related terms (e.g. kinds of fuel: petroleum, alcohol, butane, etc.). During study, the category heading (type of fuel) remained on the screen as the exemplars were presented for study. After twenty-four categories had been studied, delayed predictions were made by representing each category heading (e.g. type of fuel) individually and asking the participants to predict the likelihood of recalling the exemplars. In the first experiment, participants made the prediction on a 6-point scale ranging from 0 to 100 in 20-point increments; 0 meant they definitely would not recall the members of the category, 20 meant they were 20 percent sure, and so on. The SP lag was at least one minute (average lag = 5 minutes) and afforded a practice recall attempt of the exemplars because they were not presented with the prompt. The criterion test was cued recall in which the category headings were used to cue the recall of the exemplars. According to the rationale provided above, this preparation was expected to yield levels of predictive accuracy that approached the levels obtained when students made delayed predictions for paired associates. By contrast, the relative accuracy of the delayed predictions made for these lists of items was only 0.48, which was not even reliably greater than a control group that made immediate predictions.

Why might practice tests for sets of related words not support high levels of accuracy? When studying paired associates, the stimulus-alone prompt (i.e., doctor–?) elicits a practice test for the response term. By contrast, even though the students' predictions were prompted with only the category heading, these prompts apparently did not elicit a self-test of the entire set of exemplars (Kelemen, 2000). Thus, when the technique afforded self-testing, the students failed to test themselves prior to predicting criterion performance. Consistent with this interpretation, in a condition in which students apparently attempted to covertly recall the exemplars of each category prior to making delayed predictions, accuracy was elevated to nearly 0.80.

An important point here is that the relatively simple practice tests that support high levels of accuracy for predicting associative memory may not necessarily produce high levels of predictive accuracy for other materials. In the remainder of this chapter, we present results from two experiments that describe the levels of accuracy produced by self-tests that occur prior to students' predictions of recall performance for sentences (Experiment 1) and text material (Experiment 2).

Experiment 1: predicting memory for simple sentences

Although some research has been conducted on predictions for sentence memory, previous research has exclusively evaluated the accuracy of people's immediate predictions. Not surprisingly, the level of accuracy for predicting future memory performance of sentences is above chance but quite unremarkable. Based on the recommendations above, attaining high levels of accuracy will require a technique to prompt a prediction that elicits a delayed test of the to-be-learned sentence. Using the entire sentence as a prompt for the predictions is akin to cueing predictions for paired associates with the stimulus–response pair, which presumably would not support high levels of predictive accuracy. Accordingly, to prompt predictions for sentence memory, McDonald (1997) developed two techniques that do not rely on re-presenting the entire sentence. For a *subject* prompt, the prediction for a sentence was cued by the subject of the sentence (Lovelace, 1984): If "The fisherman chased the whale" was studied, "fisherman" would be the cue for the prediction. Namely, the participant would be presented with the subject alone and would be asked to predict future recall of the sentence. For a *generated* prompt, the individual would first generate a one-word prompt for the sentence immediately after the presentation of the sentence for study. For instance, the participant might generate the word "Moby" for "The fisherman chased the whale."

In Experiment 1, we present accuracy with respect to these two prompts for predicting the free recall of thirty-two sentences. For half the sentences, participants made immediate predictions, and for the remaining sentences, they made delayed predictions, which had an average SP lag that exceeded 90 seconds. To foreshadow, although we expected a high level of accuracy for the delayed predictions (e.g. in the 0.80 range often found for paired associates), the outcomes defied this expectation.

Method overview

Design, participants, and materials Eighty-five students from The University of North Carolina at Greensboro participated to partially fulfill a requirement for an introductory psychology course. Two variables were manipulated: delay between study and prediction (immediate versus delayed) was manipulated within each participant, and kind of prompt (subject- versus self-generated) was manipulated between participants.

Participants were randomly assigned to groups by order of appearance. Forty-three participants received subject prompts, and forty-two generated their own prompts.

Thirty-two sentences of the form subject-verb-object were used as stimuli (e.g. "The fisherman chased the whale"). Macintosh computers displayed instructions and sentences and recorded all responses.

Procedure Before beginning the task, participants were told that they would be presented with sentences that they were to study for a subsequent memory test. They were instructed that after studying each sentence they would be asked to type in a word that would serve as a prompt for the sentence. Participants in the subject group typed in the subject of the sentence. Participants in the generated group were to generate a single word that would help them recall the sentence later. They were also instructed not to use any word that appeared in the sentence. All subjects were instructed that sometime after typing in the word they would be prompted to make a prediction.

Two blocks of sixteen sentences were presented, with sentences in each block presented in random order for study at a rate of 14 seconds/ sentence. Eight items from each block were randomly selected to receive an immediate prediction in which the prompt (either the subject of the sentence or the generated word) was presented above the question: "What is the likelihood that you will recall this sentence in about 10 minutes from now? 0%, 20%, 40%, 60%, 80%, 100%," where 0% indicates definitely will not recall, 20% indicates 20 percent certain will recall, etc. After the prediction was made, the next sentence was presented for study. After all sixteen sentences had been studied, the order of the prompts for the eight sentences scheduled to receive delayed predictions was randomized and each prompt was presented individually with the prompt question given above. When all judgments had been made for the first block of sixteen items, the second block was presented identically to the first block.

Finally, participants engaged in an unrelated filler task for 5 minutes, after which they were given a free recall test for the studied sentences. Participants were instructed to recall as many of the sentences as they could remember. No time limit was imposed.

Results

Recall performance was scored in two ways. Gist scoring allowed for synonym substitutions for one or more words; sentences were scored as correct if the original meaning of the sentence was preserved (as in Lovelace, 1984). For verbatim scoring, sentences were scored as correct if

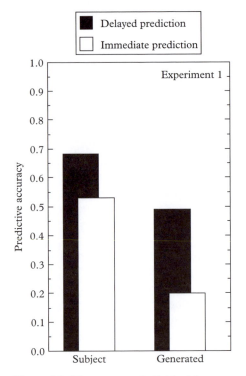

Figure 4.1 Means across individuals' gammas between predictions and recall performance as a function of timing of predictions (immediate or delayed) and the kind of prompt for predictions (either the subject of a sentence or an individual's self-generated word about a sentence)

the participant's response identically matched a studied sentence. Because the qualitative pattern of results did not differ substantively across the two scoring methods, we report analyses based on gist scoring. Finally, for both experiments, all differences reported as statistically reliable have $p < 0.05$.

Predictive accuracy Goodman–Kruskal gamma (G) correlations were computed between predictions and recall, which refers to the degree to which participants accurately predicted recall of one sentence relative to another. Means across individuals' Gs are presented in Figure 4.1.

A 2 (time of prediction: immediate or delayed) × 2 (kind of prompt: subject or generated) mixed factor analysis of variance (ANOVA) revealed a main effect for the kind of prompt, $F(1,66) = 6.80$, $MSe = 0.30$, indicating that accuracy was greater for subject prompts than for generated prompts. This effect was unexpected and has since been replicated.

Although intriguing, given that it is less relevant to our present aims, we leave solution of this particular mystery for future research. Most important, a main effect occurred for the time of predictions, $F(1,66) = 7.42$, $MSe = 0.22$. The interaction was not reliable. These results demonstrate that the *delayed judgment-of-learning* effect (in which accuracy is higher for delayed than immediate predictions) observed for paired associates (Nelson and Dunlosky, 1991) generalizes to predicting memory for sentences, regardless of whether the prompt for the prediction is the subject of a sentence or is a self-generated term. However, the relative accuracy of delayed predictions for sentences was far from the high levels of accuracy described in the paired-associate literature. Perhaps most surprising was the extremely low accuracy of delayed predictions prompted by generated words, which fell three *SD*s below the accuracy typically demonstrated in the paired-associate literature.

Recall performance For the group which had subject prompts, mean recall was 0.22 after immediate predictions and was 0.41 after delayed predictions; for the group which had generated prompts, mean recall was 0.29 after immediate and 0.48 after delayed predictions, all *SEM*s ≤ 0.04. A 2 × 2 mixed-factor ANOVA revealed a main effect of time of predictions, with higher recall after delayed compared with immediate predictions, $F(1,78) = 122.03$, $MSe = 0.01$. The effect of prompt, $F(1,78) = 2.8$, $MSe = 0.08$, $p = 0.12$, and the interaction were not reliable.

Discussion

Two outcomes from this experiment are relevant to the role of practice tests in informing people's predictions about criterion test performance. First, accuracy was higher for delayed than immediate predictions. This effect was presumably due to a self-administered practice test: when the prompt for a sentence was presented at a delay, students presumably tested themselves by covertly attempting to recall the sentence. The prediction was then based on the outcome of this test. In particular, if a sentence was recalled, the individual made a higher prediction than if one was not recalled. McDonald (1997) confirmed this speculation by forcing individuals to overtly attempt recall immediately prior to making each prediction; that is, she administered a mandatory test prior to each prediction (as in Nelson and Dunlosky, 1996). As expected, the outcome of these overt tests correlated highly with the subsequent predictions.

The second outcome of interest is that the accuracy of the delayed predictions was relatively low, compared to the high levels of accuracy typically demonstrated with the same kind of prediction for paired-associate memory. Was this outcome a function of using sentence materials, suggesting that techniques that are highly effective for paired associates will not fully generalize to more complex materials? In two follow-up experiments, McDonald discovered that the sentence materials were not the constraining factor. Instead, the mismatch between the prompt for the predictions (a single-word cue) and the form of the criterion test (free recall) was responsible. Once the criterion test was changed to cued recall – in which the subject of each sentence was presented at test – the accuracy of the delayed predictions rose dramatically and was well within the range typically found for paired associates (for details, see McDonald, 1997). In Experiment 2, we utilize the cueing techniques developed by McDonald in an attempt to help students predict performance for sentences embedded within texts.

Experiment 2: predicting memory for sentences embedded within texts

In contrast to the high levels of predictive accuracy that has been demonstrated for associative memory and sentence memory, students' accuracy for predicting performance on tests over text material has been quite low (for reviews, see Lin and Zabrucky, 1998, and Maki, 1998b; for two exceptions, see Rawson, Dunlosky, and Thiede, 2000, and Weaver and Bryant, 1995).[3] The two investigations in the metacomprehension literature that have examined practice tests have also yielded less than promising results. In a study by Glenberg et al. (1987), students read sixteen texts. After reading each, they received a practice test consisting of one idea-recognition question in which participants chose between which of two ideas had been presented in the text. They then predicted how well they would perform on a criterion test for that text, which again consisted of idea-recognition questions. For the criterion test, three different kinds of questions were used: one was identical to the practice question, one was a paraphrase of the practice question, and the content of one was unrelated to the content of the practice question.

Perhaps most surprising, predictive accuracy when the practice question and criterion question were identical (same condition) was not close to perfect (gammas of 0.10, 0.40, and 0.35, for Experiments 6, 7, and 8,

---

[3] In this and many other metacomprehension studies, individuals were not forced to test themselves prior to predicting performance, even though self-testing in principle is afforded by the prompts to make the predictions. Thus, students may not typically test themselves prior to making metacomprehension judgments (cf. Morris, 1990), which reduces the relevance of outcomes from this research to our present aims of understanding how practice tests influence predictive accuracy.

respectively), although it was typically greater than the predictive accuracy for the related condition. Accuracy for predicting performance for the unrelated test questions was also consistently low. To follow up this research, Maki and Serra (1992) dealt with some potential methodological problems that may have constrained predictive accuracy in Glenberg et al.'s (1987) study. Across three experiments, however, they again found that even when the practice test and the criterion test were identical, predictive accuracy was only 0.32 (Experiment 2).

One reason why accuracy may have been poor can be derived from theory of memory monitoring for paired associates. In particular, the transfer-appropriate monitoring (TAM) hypothesis is that predictive accuracy increases as the similarity increases between the context of monitoring (in this case, the practice test) and the context of the criterion test (Dunlosky and Nelson, 1992). According to the TAM hypothesis, Maki and Serra (1992) may have found relatively low accuracy because the contextual similarity between practice tests and criterion tests was not high. For instance, even in their "identical" condition, participants had three practice questions for each text followed by only one prediction, which reduces contextual similarity by posing a many-to-one mapping: perhaps participants had difficulty translating the outcomes of three questions into one predictive judgment.

Based on the rationale and findings described above, we sought to develop a technique that would support high levels of accuracy for predicting the memory of main ideas within text. Our initial aim was not to evaluate specifically why accuracy had been low in previous research, but instead to demonstrate high levels of accuracy, which then could motivate theoretical research that has more relevance to education. We had college students read six expository texts that each contained definitions for four key terms (see Appendix for an example text). Immediately after studying each text, a student predicted how well he or she would perform on "a test over the text material." We refer to these as *global* predictions because they refer to an individual's beliefs in performance for an entire text and not specific items (e.g. words or sentences) within a text. Global predictions are standard in the metacomprehension literature. Next, we had individuals make judgments for specific terms, called *term-specific* predictions, to contrast them with the global judgments. To obtain these predictions, we represented each of the four terms from a text individually, and participants were asked to predict the likelihood of recalling the definition of the term on the criterion test. We used a subject prompt to cue the term-specific predictions because they supported the highest levels of accuracy in the sentence-memory experiment (see subject-prompted, delayed predictions in Figure 4.1). Most important, the SP lag was greater than zero and was filled with reading, so the prompt would afford a delayed practice test.

Finally, the criterion test for a given text, which consisted of cued recall for the four definitions, occurred immediately after all four terms had been judged. The rationale was motivated more by theory than by application. In particular, although exams typically occur well after studying, we wanted to increase the match between the practice tests and the criterion tests as much as possible – a methodological decision recommended by the TAM hypothesis. Moreover, Maki (1998a) found that for predictions involving text material, accuracy was greater when criterion tests were immediate than when they were delayed. Given the evidence from the present experiment using sentences and from Maki (1998a), we expected that the accuracy for term-specific predictions made for individual key terms would be quite high and would be considerably higher than the accuracy for the standard global predictions.

Method overview

Participants, design, and materials Participants included twenty-seven undergraduates, nineteen from University of Colorado and eight from The University of North Carolina at Greensboro. Kind of judgment (global or term-specific) was a within-participant manipulation.

Seven expository texts (one sample and six critical) were developed from introductory-level textbooks from various undergraduate courses (e.g. American government, economics, nutrition). Texts were between 271 and 281 words long, with Flesch–Kincaid scores ranging from grade level 10 to 12. Each text contained four key terms (presented in capital letters), each accompanied by a one-sentence definition. Key terms were also used as cues for recall. Macintosh computers presented all experimental materials and recorded responses.

Procedure Participants were told that they were to read several texts, to make predictions about subsequent test performance, and then to complete a cued-recall test of their memory for the information in the texts. Participants practiced each of these tasks with a sample text and test questions.

The critical texts were presented in random order for each participant. Each text was presented individually for self-paced study. When participants terminated study of a text with a key-press, they were presented with the following prompt for a global prediction: "How well will you be able to complete a test over this material? 0 = definitely won't be able, 20 = 20% sure I will be able, 40 = 40% sure ..., 100 = definitely will be able." After making the global judgment, they made four specific predictions, one for each of the key terms in that text. For each, they were asked, "How well do you think you will be able to define—?" These prompts were presented one at a time in random order, along with the rating scale described above. After the four term-specific predictions were collected, participants answered the four cued-recall questions. For each, a key term appeared individually along with a field in which participants were to type in their recall of the definition of that term. After each question, participants were presented with the following prompt for a postdiction: "How confident are you that you answered correctly?" Participants used a rating scale similar to the one provided for predictions.

Results

As in Experiment 1, the analyses reported below were based on gist scoring, unless otherwise noted. Mean percentage of recall performance was 72 percent.

Predictive accuracy We examined the accuracy of both kinds of prediction. For global predictions, we first computed mean recall performance for each text, and then computed an intra-individual *G* between the predictions and mean recall across the six texts. For the term-specific predictions, we computed two correlations. The first involved computing a *G* across all twenty-four term-specific predictions. The second involved computing the mean term-specific prediction for each text, and then computing an intra-individual *G* between these mean predictions and mean recall across the six texts. This particular technique allows a more appropriate comparison across the two kinds of prediction because the number of observations (i.e., six prediction–recall pairs) that are the basis of each *G* are identical. Means across individuals' *G*s are reported in Figure 4.2.

Two outcomes are noteworthy. First, all gamma correlations were reliably greater than 0, indicating above-chance accuracy at predicting performance for the key terms across the texts. Second, and most important, accuracy was not reliably greater for term-specific predictions than for global predictions, regardless of how accuracy was computed. Note that when accuracy was based on verbatim recall performance, the apparent trend for better accuracy of term-specific predictions over global predictions vanished (means of 0.38 versus 0.37, respectively). These outcomes were quite surprising, because theory and evidence from previous research described above led us to expect substantial levels of accuracy for the term-specific predictions.

Why might accuracy of the term-specific predictions be so low? One possibility is that the students were poor at accurately judging the

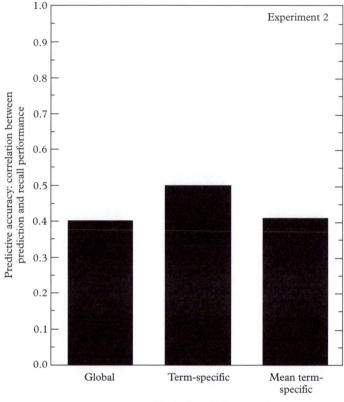

Figure 4.2 Means across individuals' gammas between the twenty-four term-specific predictions and recall performance, the six global predictions and mean recall performance for each text, and the six mean term-specific predictions and mean recall performance.

outcomes of the practice tests. That is, students presumably attempted to retrieve the definitions of each term prior to predicting performance but were not good at discriminating between correctly (versus incorrectly) recalled definitions. In partial support of this possibility, the mean gamma correlation between recall performance and term-specific *post*dictions was 0.72 (*SEM* = 0.06). This value provides a kind of upper bound on predictive accuracy, assuming students based their predictions on their confidence about recall outcomes during the practice tests. The idea here is that monitoring performance during the practice test was not perfectly accurate and hence constrained the accuracy of the subsequent term-specific predictions. Even so, postdictive accuracy was still greater than predictive accuracy, suggesting some other factor(s) also constrained predictive accuracy.

Another possibility is that the SP lag was not long enough, so that any retrieval attempt elicited by the practice tests (i.e., prompts for the predictions) did not involve retrieval solely from long-term memory. That is, although the term-specific predictions were delayed (SP lag greater than zero), these predictions may have been functionally related to immediate predictions for paired associates. Evidence pertaining to the distributions of the term-specific predictions is indirectly consistent with this interpretation. In particular, immediate predictions for paired associates are distributed across the rating scale in an inverted U-shaped pattern (e.g. Dunlosky and Nelson, 1994), with middle ratings (i.e., 40 and 60) typically being used the most often and extreme ratings (i.e., 0 and 100) rarely being used. By contrast, delayed predictions for paired associates are distributed in a U-shaped pattern, with the extreme ratings being used most often. The term-specific predictions manifested the former inverted U-shaped pattern. The mean proportion of term-specific predictions made for each point of the rating scale (in parentheses) was 0.08 (0), 0.14 (20), 0.15 (40), 0.21 (60), 0.24 (80), and 0.18 (100).

Even so, another outcome appears to vindicate the short SP lag as a major constraint on accuracy. In particular, recall performance was only 72 percent. Given that the criterion tests occurred soon after the predictions, practice test performance was also probably not perfect. If so, some definitions were recalled whereas others were not, and it is exactly this kind of information that substantially boosts the accuracy of delayed predictions for paired associates and is not available for immediate predictions (in which nearly every one of the target responses is correctly recalled). Thus, although both poor performance monitoring and short SP lags may constrain predictive accuracy, neither currently appears to provide a sufficient explanation for the present outcomes.

General discussion

Benefits of practice tests: predictive accuracy versus criterion performance

Two questions about the rationale for improving predictive accuracy often arise. Why does it matter if you can improve predictive accuracy if criterion test performance itself is not improved? In some cases, for instance, having students use delayed practice tests for paired associates yields high predictive accuracy but does not improve memory performance beyond conditions in which no practice tests are made. So, why should a student care about taking practice tests when their goal is to perform well? Of course, one reason is that practice tests often do improve performance, both for learning relatively simple materials such as paired associates and for learning more complex text materials.

More important for the present purposes is that improving predictive accuracy is not considered an end in itself. Instead, the benefits of predictions are manifest when they are utilized to regulate *extra* study. Put differently, a key point, which is often not appreciated, is that highly accurate predictions can be used to improve performance if and only if students have time to restudy. If students cannot restudy, such as if they decide to cram the night before a test, the benefits of using practice tests to improve predictive accuracy are lost (cf. Begg, Martin, and Needham, 1992). For those students who do allow time for restudying, practice tests may benefit their regulation of study. Consistent with this idea, Thiede (1999) reported that individuals with higher levels of predictive accuracy (versus those with worse predictive accuracy) performed better across multiple study-test trials. In this case, accurate feedback about learning on one trial presumably was used to allocate the most study to the least-well learned items on the subsequent study trial, which is an effective way to regulate learning when individuals are attempting to master class materials (Nelson et al., 1994). Given that predictive accuracy is related to the effectiveness of self-regulated learning, the remainder of our discussion focuses on the influence of practice tests on accuracy.

When will practice tests improve predictive accuracy?

What is evident from the extant research is that the efficacy of practice tests for improving predictive accuracy is both straightforward and not well understood. This apparent paradox results from the differential efficacy of practice tests across materials. For associative memory and list learning, the recommendation for students is straightforward. For instance, when students are learning translation equivalents (e.g. pombe – beer), practice tests that are delayed several minutes after study and are prompted by the stimulus alone have almost universally supported high levels of predictive accuracy (see also King, Zechmeister, and Shaughnessy, 1980; Lovelace, 1984). Such delayed practice tests are even effective when students are learning lists of related terms (e.g. branches of the government), given that they attempt to retrieve the list prior to predicting performance (Kelemen, 2000). Although the 5- to 10-minute retention intervals that are often used in this research are substantially shorter than those often faced by students (e.g. days or weeks), results from one study suggest the outcomes from laboratory experiments will generalize to more naturalistic settings. In particular, Hall and Bahrick (1998) found that predictions which were delayed only a few minutes after a final study-test session of foreign-language vocabulary had a moderate level of accuracy ($M = 0.63$) for predicting performance on tests that occurred up to five years after learning.

For predicting sentence memory, results reported here are promising but are also preliminary. Although McDonald (1997) found that using the subject of a sentence to prompt a delayed test yielded relatively high accuracy for predicting performance on a cued-recall test, accuracy was substantially lower when the criterion test was free recall. Research aimed at developing effective practice tests for predicting performance on criterion tests that provide minimal cues (e.g. free recall, essay tests, etc.) is essential. Moreover, the sentences used in Experiment 1 above were short, being comprised of a subject, verb, and object (e.g. "The fisherman chased the whale"), which poses two potential problems. First, sentences of this length are adequate for tests of memory (e.g. recall) but are too simple to support reasonable tests of comprehension (e.g. inference questions). Criterion tests in educational settings typically require that students not only remember relevant information, but that they understand it as well (see Kintsch, 1994, for explication of differences between these types of learning). Thus, students need to assess both their comprehension and anticipated memory for text material when predicting future performance. Constructing slightly longer and more technical sentences (e.g. Rawson, Dunlosky, and McDonald, 2002) will likely afford the exploration of this key issue.

Second, we initially believed the results from the sentence research provided a no-fail technique for boosting students' accuracy for predicting memory for sentences embedded within texts. Presenting the subject of a to-be-remembered sentence for delayed predictions yielded relatively high levels of accuracy when the criterion test comprised cued recall using the subject of each sentence as the cues. Thus, we reasoned that if key sentences in text were prompted in the same way and the criterion test was also cued recall, accuracy would be near perfect. Quite to our surprise, results from Experiment 2 were not encouraging. Term-specific predictions, which were based on delayed tests prompted by only the term of each definition, produced only a moderate level of accuracy. The level of accuracy was not higher than the accuracy of the global predictions and was substantially lower than the accuracy demonstrated for delayed subject-cued predictions for sentences (compare Figure 4.1 with Figure 4.2). Given the number of differences between Experiments 1 and 2, conclusions based on comparisons across them should be made cautiously. Nevertheless, the different methods suggest several avenues for future research aimed at identifying factors that moderate the accuracy of predicting sentence memory. For instance, given the length and difficulty of the definitions used in Experiment 2 versus the simple sentences used in Experiment 1, the participants may not have attempted to covertly retrieve a definition prior to making a term-specific prediction. That is, although the prompts for these predictions afforded practice tests, the students may not have utilized them (Kelemen, 2000; Morris, 1990). This possibility could be evaluated by having students attempt to overtly recall each definition prior to predicting performance, which presumably would yield higher levels of accuracy.

In contrast to the research on paired associates and sentences, the role practice tests may play in boosting metacomprehension accuracy is not well understood (for insights into other issues in metacomprehension, see Lin and Zabrucky, 1998; Maki, 1998b). Thus, in the remainder of this discussion, we consider why practice tests have been relatively ineffective at yielding high levels of accuracy for predicting test performance across text materials (e.g. Glenberg et al., 1987; Maki and Serra, 1992; Experiment 2, above). Comprehending and remembering text is central to almost all student scholarship, so advances in this area provide a major challenge for theoretical and applied research. To guide such endeavors, we couch our discussion in terms of theory that has been largely informed by research on associative memory, and we also discuss implications for guiding both student learning and future research on metacomprehension.

For each material (i.e., paired associates, sentences, and texts), the kind of practice test and the kind of criterion test have been shown to influence predictive accuracy. To provide a unified account of these effects, some researchers have invoked hypotheses based on the notion of transfer-appropriate monitoring (TAM), which implicate the match between the practice test and the criterion test. The outcomes from the sentence research described above are consistent with this hypothesis, given that accuracy was higher when the practice test (cued recall) matched the criterion test (cued recall) than when it did not (free recall). However, not all results are consistent with this hypothesis. Dunlosky and Nelson (1997, Experiment 3) emphasized the importance of the match between the *context* of the two tests (i.e., objective characteristics of the display for the test itself) and empirically evaluated this TAM hypothesis by having individuals study paired associates and make delayed predictions for a future test of associative recognition. For the criterion test, participants made old/new responses for old items (e.g. if dog–spoon and tick–maid were studied, these items would be represented) and for new items that were composed by repairing each stimulus with a randomly chosen response (e.g. dog–maid and tick–spoon). The prompt for the practice test was either the stimulus alone (e.g. dog – ?) or the stimulus–response pair (i.e., dog–spoon). Based on the TAM hypothesis, the prediction was that accuracy would be greater when the judgments were prompted by the stimulus–response pair than by the stimulus alone because the context of the former more closely matched the context of the criterion test. Results disconfirmed this hypothesis, with accuracy being reliably less when practice tests were prompted by the stimulus–response pair (mean gamma = 0.51) than by the stimulus alone (mean gamma = 0.63).

Although these data are inconsistent with the contextually-based TAM hypothesis, another version of TAM provides a plausible account. In particular, Glenberg et al. (1987) developed the modified feedback hypothesis: "feedback from a [practice test] can be used to [accurately] predict performance on a post-test to the extent that the processes and knowledge required on the post-test are similar to the processes that generated the feedback." In contrast to the contextually based TAM hypothesis, the modified feedback hypothesis implicates the match between the underlying *processes* (and not the context) of the practice and criterion test. This version can account for the effect from Dunlosky and Nelson (1997) because performance on a criterion test of associative recognition is based on retrieval of associations from long-term memory (Clark, Hori, and Callan, 1993), which is more similar to the retrieval processes elicited by a practice test based on presenting only the stimulus than those elicited by presenting both the stimulus and response.

Given the modified feedback hypothesis, a question arises: "Can the match between processes completely account for predictive accuracy?" The answer is definitely "No." For instance, regardless of the match, reliability of the practice test, reliability of the criterion test, or correct guessing may reduce predictive accuracy (Schwartz and Metcalfe, 1994; Thiede and Dunlosky, 1994). A more subtle issue is highlighted by general assumptions about predictive accuracy. The diagnosticity assumption mentioned earlier is that for accuracy to be high, the outcome of practice tests must be highly predictive of the criterion tests. Both TAM and the modified feedback hypothesis pertain specifically to this assumption by providing explanations for when practice tests will be highly diagnostic. *Bases assumptions* refer to the nature of how predictions are made; that is, they describe the psychological bases of predictions.[4] A major limitation

---

[4] These assumptions appear in hypotheses of various kinds of metacognitive judgments and hence are not novel to the present discussion. For instance, Nelson (1996, Figure 3) provides a general description of how an external stimulus may influence the magnitude of metacognitive judgments (bases assumption), and Koriat's (1993) accessibility hypothesis highlights the importance of both the diagnosticity and bases assumptions.

of the TAM and modified feedback hypotheses is that they do not adequately specify the bases assumption. For instance, these hypotheses do not account for the possibility that students may not always correctly interpret or utilize the outcomes of practice tests when predicting future performance, which may constrain predictive accuracy even if a practice test is *perfectly* diagnostic. This point is illustrated by outcomes from Maki and Serra (1992). For one group, the practice tests were identical to the criterion tests. As expected, the correlation between performance on practice and criterion tests was quite high (*M* intra-individual gamma = 0.85), with ten of the seventeen participants having correlations of 1.0. However, predictive accuracy was only 0.32. These outcomes are less surprising when one considers that the mean correlation between performance on the practice test and the predictions was 0.31. Thus, even though the diagnosticity assumption was met, participants apparently failed to utilize the (accurate) outcome from the practice tests when predicting performance.

So why might accuracy be low even when the practice test and criterion test are identical? Results from Maki and Serra indicate that one reason is that students fail to utilize the outcome of the practice tests. One explanation for this particular failure is that the predictions were not made immediately after the practice tests were administered, so students may have forgotten the outcomes of those tests. Another reason is that students may not correctly interpret their performance on a practice test (Koriat, 1993). For instance, people tend to perceive commission errors as correct, or at least as more likely to be correct than omission errors (Krinsky and Nelson, 1985). If a particular practice test produces many commission errors, students may (falsely) believe they know some material and hence predict success on the criterion test. In this case, the diagnosticity assumption would likely be met, yet predictive accuracy would suffer. This unfortunate circumstance may arise most frequently when recognition tests are used as practice tests because they typically force (or at least encourage) a student to respond and hence increase the likelihood of commission errors. Although speculative, the hypothesis that commission errors reduce predictive accuracy can be systematically evaluated using techniques developed by Koriat and Goldsmith (1994). If this hypothesis survives empirical evaluation, it may provide a partial explanation for the small gains in metacomprehension accuracy after practice tests because recognition-based practice tests have been used almost exclusively.

This hypothesis also suggests that to benefit fully from practice tests, students may need instructions on how to interpret outcomes from those tests. One alternative is to make sure that students always have access to the correct responses on practice tests, so that their own self-generated feedback can be supplemented with perfectly accurate feedback (for one investigation involving experimenter-generated feedback, see Maki and Serra, 1992). To make matters more complex, however, practice tests have yielded the best accuracy when they were identical to the criterion test (in accord with the modified feedback hypothesis). That is, although identical practice tests have yielded quite low levels of metacomprehension accuracy, it is even lower when the practice tests are merely similar to the criterion tests, such as when both tests cover the same material but in different ways (Glenberg et al., 1987; Maki and Serra, 1992). These kinds of practice test (i.e., similar but not identical to the class exam) are primarily used by students because they rarely have access to the actual class exams. Accordingly, developing similar practice tests that will yield highly accurate predictions provides a major challenge for future research.

In summary, we have reviewed evidence that indicates practice tests can support high levels of accuracy for predicting memory performance for paired associates and for individual sentences. Although the techniques used in this research are applicable to predicting performance for text material, a preliminary experiment that used them demonstrated only a moderate level of predictive accuracy. Other research on metacomprehension has also yielded relatively low levels of predictive accuracy, even when the practice tests were identical to the eventual criterion tests. We offered several testable hypotheses for why practice tests may not always be highly informative and remain optimistic that systematic research will foster the development of practice tests that ensure high levels of accuracy across a wide variety of materials and criterion tests.

APPENDIX: EXAMPLE TEXT FOR EXPERIMENT 2

The body uses energy for three major purposes, basal metabolism, physical activity, and the thermic effects of food. To a lesser extent, it also uses energy for adaptive thermogenesis. BASAL METABOLISM is the minimal energy required for a resting, awake body to stay alive. This requires about 60 percent to 70 percent of total energy use by the body, and includes maintaining a heartbeat, respiration, and temperature. The amount of energy used for basal metabolism depends primarily on lean body mass. Physical activity increases energy expenditure beyond our basal energy needs by as much as 25 percent to 40 percent. Unlike basal metabolism, energy expenditure from physical activity varies widely among people. The THERMIC EFFECT OF FOOD refers to the fact that the body uses energy to digest, absorb, and further process food nutrients. The energy cost of this thermic effect is analogous to a sales tax, in which you are taxed about 5 percent to 10 percent for the total energy you eat. Finally,

ADAPTIVE THERMOGENESIS is when the body expends energy to produce heat in response to a cold environment or as a result of overfeeding. Though adaptive thermogenesis probably does not play a major role in weight regulation, it appears to represent a small portion of energy use. The amount of energy a body uses can be measured by direct calorimetry. DIRECT CALORIMETRY measures the amount of heat that emanates from a body. Usually, a person is put into an insulated chamber, and body heat released raises the temperature of a layer of water surrounding the chamber. The difference in the temperature of the water before and after the person entered the chamber indicates the number of calories expended.

ACKNOWLEDGMENTS

Thanks to Greg Matvey for comments on an earlier version of this chapter. Please send correspondence to John Dunlosky, PO Box 26170, UNCG, Psychology Department, Greensboro, NC 27402-6170; dunlosky@uncg.edu.

REFERENCES

Begg, I., Duft, S., Lalonde, P., Melnick, R., and Sanvito, J. (1989). Memory predictions are based on ease of processing. *Journal of Memory and Language*, 28, 610–632.

Begg, I. M., Martin, L. A., and Needham, D. R. (1992). Memory monitoring: how useful is self-knowledge about memory? *European Journal of Cognitive Psychology*, 4, 195–218.

Connor, L. T., Dunlosky, J., and Hertzog, C. (1997). Age-related differences in absolute but not relative metamemory accuracy. *Psychology and Aging*, 12, 50–71.

Clark, S. E., Hori, A., and Callan, D. E. (1993). Forced-choice associative recognition: implications for global-memory models. *Journal of Experimental Psychology: Learning, Memory, and Cognition*, 19, 871–881.

Dunlosky, J., Domoto, P. K., Wang, M., Ishikawa, T., Roberson, I., Nelson, T. O., and Ramsay, D. (1998). Inhalation of 30% nitrous oxide impairs people's learning without impairing people's judgments of what will be remembered. *Experimental and Clinical Psychopharmacology*, 6, 77–86.

Dunlosky, J., and Hertzog, C. (1997). Older and younger adults use a functionally identical algorithm to select items for restudy during multitrial learning. *Journal of Gerontology: Psychological Science*, 52, 178–186.

(1998). Aging and deficits in associative memory: What is the role of strategy production? *Psychology and Aging*, 13, 597–607.

Dunlosky, J. and Nelson, T. O. (1992). Importance of the kind of cue for judgments of learning (JOLs) and the delayed-JOL effect. *Memory and Cognition*, 20, 373–380.

(1994). Does the sensitivity of judgments of learning (JOLs) to the effects of various study activities depend on when the JOLs occur? *Journal of Memory and Language*, 33, 545–565.

(1997). Similarity between the cue for judgments of learning (JOL) and the cue for test is not the primary determinant of JOL accuracy. *Journal of Memory and Language*, 36, 34–49.

Glenberg, A., Sanocki, T., Epstein, W., and Morris, C. (1987). Enhancing calibration of comprehension. *Journal of Experimental Psychology: General*, 116, 119–136.

Hart, J. T. (1965). Memory and the feeling-of-knowing experience. *Journal of Educational Psychology*, 56, 208–216.

Hall, L. K., and Bahrick, H. P. (1998). The validity of metacognitive predictions of widespread learning and long-term retention. In G. Mazzoni and T. O. Nelson (eds.), *Metacognition and cognitive neuropsychology: monitoring and control processes*, pp. 23–36. Hillsdale, NJ: Lawrence Erlbaum Associates.

Kelemen, W. L. (2000). Metamemory cues and monitoring accuracy: judging what you know and what you will know. *Journal of Educational Psychology*, 92, 800–810.

Kelemen, W. L., and Weaver, C. A. III (1997). Enhanced metamemory at delays: why do judgments of learning improve over time? *Journal of Experimental Psychology: Learning, Memory, and Cognition*, 23, 1394–1409.

King, J. F., Zechmeister, E. B., and Shaughnessy, J. J. (1980). Judgments of knowing: the influence of retrieval practice. *American Journal of Psychology*, 93, 329–343.

Kintsch, W. (1994). Text comprehension, memory, and learning. *American Psychologist*, 49, 294–303.

Koriat, A. (1993). How do we know that we know? The accessibility model of the feeling of knowing. *Psychological Review*, 100, 609–639.

Koriat, A., and Goldsmith, M. (1994). Memory in naturalistic and laboratory contexts: distinguishing the accuracy-oriented and quantity-oriented approaches to memory assessment. *Journal of Experimental Psychology: General*, 123, 297–315.

Krinsky, R., and Nelson, T. O. (1985). The feeling of knowing for different types of retrieval failure. *Acta Psychologica*, 58, 141–158.

Kubat, A. K. (2000). Training older adults' self-regulation skills to improve learning. Paper presented at the 46th Annual Meeting of the Southeastern Psychological Association, New Orleans, LA.

Lin, L. M., and Zabrucky, K. M. (1998). Calibration of comprehension: research and implications for education and instruction. *Contemporary Educational Psychology*, 23, 345–391.

Lovelace, E. A. (1984). Metamemory: Monitoring future recallability during study. *Journal of Experimental Psychology: Learning, Memory, and Cognition*, 10, 756–766.

Maki, R. H. (1998a). Predicting performance on text: delayed versus immediate predictions and tests. *Memory and Cognition*, 26, 959–964.

(1998b). Test predictions over text material. In D. J. Hacker, J. Dunlosky, and A. C. Graesser (eds.), *Metacognition in educational theory and practice*, pp. 117–144. Hillsdale, NJ: Lawrence Erlbaum Associates.

Maki, R. H., and Serra, M. (1992). The basis of test predictions for text material. *Journal of Experimental Psychology: Learning, Memory, and Cognition*, 18, 116–126.

McDonald, S. L. (1997). *What underlies the accuracy of predictions of recall for sentences? A competitive evaluation of two hypotheses.* Master's thesis, UNCG.

Morris, C. (1990). Retrieval processes underlying confidence in comprehension judgments. *Journal of Experimental Psychology: Learning, Memory, and Cognition,* 16, 223–232.

Nelson, T. O. (1984). A comparison of current measures of the accuracy of feeling-of-knowing predictions. *Psychological Bulletin,* 95, 109–133.

——— (1996). Consciousness and metacognition. *American Psychologist,* 51, 102–116.

Nelson, T. O., and Dunlosky, J. (1991). When people's judgments of learning (JOLs) are extremely accurate at predicting subsequent recall: the "delayed-JOL effect." *Psychological Science,* 2, 267–270.

——— (1992). How shall we explain the delayed-judgment-of-learning effect? *Psychological Science,* 3, 317–318.

——— (1996). Toward the theoretical mechanisms underlying immediate versus delayed judgments of learning. Paper presented at the 37th Annual Meeting of the Psychonomic Society, Chicago, IL.

Nelson, T. O., Dunlosky, J., Graf, A., and Narens, L. (1994). Utilization of metacognitive judgments in the allocation of study during multitrial learning. *Psychological Science,* 5, 207–213.

Nelson, T. O., Graf, A., Dunlosky, J., Marlatt, A., Walker, D., and Luce, K. (1998). Effect of acute alcohol intoxication on recall and on judgments of learning during the acquisition of new material. G. Mazzoni, and T. O. Nelson (eds.), *Metacognition and neuropsychology,* pp. 161–180. Mahwah, NJ: Lawrence Erlbaum Associates.

Rawson, K., Dunlosky, J., and McDonald, S. (2002). Influences of metamemory on performance predictions for text. *The Quarterly Journal of Experimental Psychology,* 55A, 505–524.

Rawson, K., Dunlosky, J., and Thiede, K. W. (2000). The rereading effect: metacomprehension accuracy improves across reading trials. *Memory and Cognition,* 28, 1004–1010.

Schwartz, B. L., and Metcalfe, J. (1994). Methodological problems and pitfalls in the study of human metacognition. In J. Metcalfe and A. P. Shimamura (eds.), *Metacognition: knowing about knowing,* pp. 93–114. Cambridge, MA: MIT Press.

Spellman, B. A., and Bjork, R. A. (1992). When predictions create reality: judgments of learning may alter what they are intended to assess. *Psychological Science,* 3, 315–316.

Thiede, K. W. (1999). The importance of monitoring and self-regulation during multi-trial learning. *Psychonomic Bulletin and Review,* 6, 662–667.

Thiede, K. W., and Dunlosky, J. (1994). Delaying students' metacognitive monitoring improves their accuracy in predicting their recognition performance. *Journal of Educational Psychology,* 86, 290–302.

Weaver, C. A. III, and Bryant, D. S. (1995). Monitoring of comprehension: the role of text difficulty in metamemory for narrative and expository text. *Memory and Cognition,* 23, 12–22.

Weaver, C. A. III, and Kelemen, W. L. (1997). Judgments of learning at delays: shifts in response patterns or increased metamemory accuracy? *Psychological Science,* 8, 318–321.

Part 2

Metacognition in everyday memory

5 When does eyewitness confidence predict performance?

Timothy J. Perfect

Imagine the following scenario. A thief throws a brick through a shop window, grabs the merchandise on display, and runs off before the shop-keeper sees anything. The only two witnesses to the crime were standing in the street at the time, and they come forward to help the police. One witness – let's call him Jake – says that he is very confident that the thief was dark-haired, whilst another witness – Sam – is fairly confident that the thief had blonde hair. Clearly there is a discrepancy in the descriptions, and in the confidence that the witnesses espouse in their descriptions. Should the police (and later the courts) have greater faith in the witness with the most confidence? Whilst the majority of members of the public might say "yes," the psychological literature does not warrant such a clear-cut and positive response.

Expert psychologists were asked a generalized version of this question, over ten years ago, in a survey of expert opinion by Kassin, Ellsworth, and Smith (1989). Kassin et al. asked sixty-three experts in the area whether they felt that various forensic psychology findings were reliable enough for psychologists to present in courtroom testimony. One such issue was the weak relationship between confidence and accuracy. An overwhelming majority of experts in the area (87 percent) agreed that the effect (i.e., the *lack* of relationship between confidence and accuracy) was reliable enough to present as testimony, and a similar figure (83 percent) reported that they would be prepared to testify themselves (37 percent already having done so). Thus, in the late 1980s the overwhelming belief of psychological experts was that the answer to the question posed in the previous paragraph was "no." However, as we shall see, it is unclear whether there would be such a strong degree of support for this conclusion today.

However, before I describe the evidence that led to the negative conclusion, and the later evidence that questions it, let me muddy the waters a little. Would the counterintuitive conclusion reached in the psychological research seem so counterintuitive if you were told that Jake was an outgoing, confident individual whilst Sam was more reserved? Could

95

their personalities have more to do with their expressed confidence than their actual abilities as witnesses? Alternatively, what if you learned that Jake believed himself to have an excellent memory for faces, whilst Sam thought himself about average at remembering faces? Could their beliefs about their general abilities impact more on their confidence than their actual ability to identify this particular individual? I turn to these questions after a brief review of previous work in the area.

Previous reviews of the confidence–accuracy relation in eyewitness memory

The reason that the expert psychologists were prepared to support such a counterintuitive conclusion about confidence and accuracy in eyewitness memory is that that is what the overwhelming number of studies showed at the time. Rather than detail the individual studies here, I will give a metareview, by reviewing the reviews of the area that have been carried out. However, before I do so, one issue needs to be explained, because this turns out to be crucial when dealing with the confidence–accuracy relation in eyewitness memory.

There are two ways of calculating the relation between confidence and accuracy. The conventional approach in eyewitness research – used in the meta-analyses reviewed below – is to compare the accuracy of individuals who differ in confidence. That is, to ask the question whether a more confident witness is likely to be a more accurate witness. Typically, such studies usually examine many witnesses for a single eyewitness event and the correlation between confidence and accuracy is calculated across the witnesses. However, there is an alternative question that can be asked – is a witness more accurate about the material for which they show the greatest confidence. To answer this question requires that the confidence–accuracy relation be calculated across items for the same individual. This approach therefore requires each witness to be asked multiple questions, rather than a single question as in the previous approach. I return to the implications of the two methods later in the chapter.

The early (negative) meta-analyses

One of the first quantitative summaries of the literature was carried out in a 1980 Ph.D. thesis by Penrod. Because this is a Ph.D. thesis, it has only entered the literature through later secondary citation. Penrod and Cutler (1995) report that Penrod (1980) found that the weighted average correlation between confidence and accuracy across sixteen published studies of lineup performance was $r = 0.23$.

Wells and Murray (1984) reviewed thirty-one studies that had been published that reported the relationship between confidence and accuracy in eyewitnesses. The studies they included were somewhat heterogeneous, with the majority (twenty-two) using recognition of perpetrators from lineups, but with a minority testing memory for other details of the events witnessed. They reported an average correlation between confidence and accuracy of $r = 0.07$. (In my classes when I discuss this paper, I always take pains to ensure the students appreciate where the decimal point goes.) Few would cavil with their conclusion that "a correlation of such magnitude is relatively useless in any applied sense" (p. 162).

Bothwell, Deffenbacher, and Brigham (1987) conducted a meta-analysis of the confidence–accuracy literature review, this time restricting their analysis to studies that used staged incidents, followed by recognition tested by a lineup. Their review consisted of thirty-five studies. The weighted average correlation was remarkably close to the figure reported by Penrod in his thesis, at $r = 0.25$. They went further, and looked for moderator variables within the set of studies they examined. They found that longer exposure durations were associated with stronger confidence–accuracy relations, a finding in line with the expectations of Deffenbacher's (1980) optimality hypothesis. For the seventeen studies with the shortest exposure duration, the mean correlation was $r = 0.19$, whilst the seventeen studies with the longest exposure duration produced a mean correlation of $r = 0.31$. However, the moderating variables of retention interval, lineup size, and target presence/absence were not significant. The authors also make the point that the overall effect size ($r = 0.25$), appears small, but actually converts to an effect size (d) of 0.52, which in Cohen's (1977) terminology is a moderate effect in the behavioral sciences. Nevertheless, it is still a debatable point whether a correlation of $r = 0.25$ (which equates to 6.25 percent of the variance explained) constitutes a level of association that has forensic utility. Such a correlation would be of little use in discriminating between two hypothetical witnesses.

Challenges to the negative conclusion

Sporer et al. (1995) reviewed thirty studies that had used staged incidents followed by lineups with perpetrators present and perpetrators absent. Overall they reported a weighted average correlation between confidence and accuracy of $r = 0.28$. This is remarkably consistent with the figures reported above, with the exception of Wells and Murray's (1984) review. However, Sporer et al. went further with their meta-analysis. They examined the correlation between confidence and accuracy separately for those who had selected a lineup member (choosers) and those who had declined to choose a lineup member (non-choosers). For the choosers, a response is accurate only if the perpetrator is chosen from a perpetrator-present lineup. Choosing a foil from a perpetrator-present lineup, or anyone from the perpetrator-absent lineup constitutes an error. For the non-choosers, a negative response is correct in a perpetrator-absent lineup, but constitutes an error in a perpetrator-present lineup. There was a marked difference between the two kinds of responders. For choosers (i.e., those who make an identification, and so might end up in court as a witness) there was a weighted average correlation between confidence and accuracy of $r = 0.37$, whilst the figure for non-choosers was $r = 0.12$. Thus, as Sporer et al. conclude, their data offer the first challenge to the previously negative conclusions about confidence and accuracy:

> Thus, it appears that the counterintuitive finding – confidence is not a good predictor of accuracy – stressed by many researchers and psychological experts in their courtroom testimony may only characterize broad comparisons of witnesses (i.e., including witnesses who make positive identifications as well as witnesses who reject lineups). These present findings indicate that when limited to witnesses who make positive identifications under laboratory conditions, confidence appears to be a somewhat stronger predictor of accuracy. (p. 322)

Recent studies by Read, Lindsay, and Nicholls (1998), and Lindsay, Read, and Sharma (1998) argue even more strongly than Sporer et al. (1995) that the previous conclusions about the confidence–accuracy relation in eyewitness memory may be mistaken. They argued that the low levels of relation reported between confidence and accuracy may stem from the low level of variability between witnesses in traditional experimental studies. For example, Read et al. (1998) reported a naturalistic study that demonstrated markedly higher confidence–accuracy levels than previously reported. Retail clerks interacted with male targets in an "interview." Halfway through the interview half the clerks were warned that they would later be tested for their ability to identify the interviewer. Three, six, or nine months later, participants were given a lineup that was either target present or absent. Recognition was better for the warned group than for the group not given the prior warning of the test. At three months, the pre-warned group showed a confidence–accuracy correlation of $r = 0.18$, in line with previous studies. However, the no-warning group showed a correlation of $r = 0.69$, which is markedly higher than reported previously, and is at a level that might have some forensic utility. By nine months, the equivalent correlations were $r = 0.72$ and $r = 0.26$ for the same two groups, thus showing the reverse pattern. Read et al. argue that this is because the pre-warned group are initially homogenous (at ceiling) at three months, but by nine months show considerable variability. Conversely, the non-warned group initially show variability in performance, but become homogenous (at floor) by nine months. It can be noted in passing that the reversal of the pattern of confidence–accuracy relations is incompatible with any account based on encoding effects, such as the optimality hypothesis, or based on chooser–non-chooser differences between witnesses.

Thus Read et al. (1998) argue that conditions that produce homogeneity amongst witnesses will produce low correlations. The ironic corollary of this is that experimental methods may be exactly the ones likely to produce low correlations. In most experiments, participants witness the same event, under the same conditions, with the same instructions. Level of attention and motivation will be relatively homogenous across participants, who often come from the ubiquitous homogenous population of psychology undergraduates. Inter-individual variation is thus minimised, and so, following the logic of Read et al., correlations are low.

Let us return for a moment to our original example. Jake is more confident than Sam. Do we expect Jake to be more accurate? We have already raised the questions of personality and beliefs (which we will address later) which might cause us to question the intuitive expectation that confidence should predict accuracy. However, what if we were to learn that Jake had been looking into the shop window that was burgled, whilst Sam was standing 50 meters away? Or what if Jake had seen the thief for 30 seconds before the crime, whilst Sam only glimpsed him as he ran past? With such variation in the encoding conditions, we expect confidence to relate to accuracy quite closely.

What advice can an expert witness give, in light of the above?

It cannot be stressed too strongly that what we are discussing is correlational data, and is therefore subject to all the shortcomings associated with correlations. In order to find a reliable correlation, one needs variation, in both accuracy and confidence. Correlations will tend towards zero if performance is too low, or too high, to afford variation. There have been concerns that many of the studies that report low confidence–accuracy relations are doing so because performance is so poor, or because confidence has been measured in an insensitive way (Stephenson, 1984). Failing to find a correlation between confidence and accuracy is rather like failing to provide satisfactory bed and breakfast for Goldilocks. The bed (aka the test materials) mustn't be too hard or too soft, and the porridge (aka confidence) mustn't be too hot or too cold. Getting the right conditions for a confidence–accuracy relation to emerge requires both measures to be just right in terms of mean performance and variability. With injudicious choice of materials, conditions, or participants one can all too easily find no association between confidence and accuracy in a particular study.

Conversely, it is also possible to arrange studies so as to demonstrate high correlations. By contrasting witnesses with considerable exposure to the target with witnesses with very little exposure one is almost guaranteed to get a correlation between confidence and accuracy across people. As an example try to answer this question (without looking): "what is the exact title of this chapter?" How confident are you? I am prepared to say that I am very confident that I know the title (after all I wrote it!), and expect that my memory is more accurate than the average reader of this chapter. Thus, contrasting my memory with the average reader's would produce a robust positive association. Of course there are other ways of increasing variability amongst people, other than exposure to the target material. One could contrast individuals of widely differing ability – such as children versus high ability undergraduates. Similarly, one can demonstrate high correlations across items by asking for recall and confidence judgments for central versus peripheral details. Encouraging responses to all items will help in this regard, since this will elicit low-confidence responses that might otherwise be withheld (Koriat and Goldsmith, 1996).

This is a profoundly unsatisfactory state of affairs. By manipulating the variability amongst individuals, either naturally occurring or through differential exposure, and by judicious selection of test materials one can demonstrate either no association between confidence and accuracy, or a robust association. What advice should an expert witness give under such circumstances? At present, I doubt that psychologists can offer any definitive advice, until we can provide answers to the following thorny questions.

What levels of performance do we get in real cases?

At present we can get a wide range of confidence–accuracy associations in part driven by the difficulty of the material under focus. How does memory for our laboratory material – however well staged and unexpected – compare with memory for cases investigated by the police? Even cursory consideration of this question makes plain that this question is unanswerable. How can one generalize about level of performance of witnesses across the wide range of events of concern to the police and courts? Crimes vary and so, correspondingly, does the memory of the witnesses who see those crimes. Witnesses vary in how well they witnessed the event, from those who were right at the heart of the event, to those standing some way off as bystanders. Events can be brief or drawn out over time. Witnesses can be paying attention, or witness something incidentally. Witnesses might be familiar with the environment and with the relevant people in the event, or the event and the environment may be entirely new to them. They may be young or old, drunk or sober, visually impaired or have perfect vision, and so on. There is no standard level of performance we can expect. If level of performance is a determining factor in the strength of the confidence–accuracy relation, it therefore follows that our conclusions about the likely confidence–accuracy relation will not hold across all crimes.

Does this mean that we should endeavor to assess the relation between performance and the level of the confidence–accuracy relation? For example, should we strive to find out the average confidence–accuracy correlation when recall is 25 percent, 50 percent, or 75 percent? Unfortunately, even if this did produce a lawful relationship that applied across conditions (and I doubt that it would) this would not help the expert witness testify usefully in court. For the court to make use of such information would require that the accuracy of a particular witness in a particular case be known. Of course, there is no way to determine this.

What variations in performance and confidence do we get in real cases?

In our studies we use standardized events (staged crimes/films) in front of relatively homogenous sets of (usually undergraduate) volunteers. As discussed earlier, such arrangements are essential for tight experimental studies, but will tend to produce low variation across witnesses, in both performance and confidence, and hence low confidence–accuracy correlations. How does this compare with real cases? Do real-world witnesses vary more widely in ability, and opportunity to witness the event? One might expect that initially this might be the case. Some witnesses might have had an excellent opportunity to witness the crime and others less so. Motivation and attention might reasonably be expected to vary more widely in the real world than in our studies. Delays in real cases are longer than the typical experimental paradigm, and so differential forgetting is likely to occur, and hence introduce greater variability. All such factors are likely to increase variability, and so one might expect the confidence–accuracy relation to be greater in the real world.

However, what happens once the police interview each witness? Those witnesses who have an extremely poor memory for the event (due to poor encoding) are unlikely to volunteer themselves as witnesses. Those who do, but can only give a poor account of the event are likely to be dropped from the investigation, and are certainly unlikely to appear in court. The prosecution barristers are unlikely to call a witness to trial who has only the haziest memory of the event, or can recall only few details, with no knowledge of key aspects of the case. They are also unlikely to bring to court those witnesses rating their confidence as low. (One can imagine the defence barrister rubbing their hands with glee as the witness says "I picked the defendant out of the lineup, but really I wasn't very sure.") Thus, the forensic process is likely to restrict the range of performance across which a confidence–accuracy relation applies in the real world. Whilst the population of *possible* witnesses might hypothetically be expected to generate a robust confidence–accuracy relation, it is not so clear that in the real world the population of *forensically relevant* witnesses would lead to the same robust association. In fact, it is not at all clear how much variability there is likely to be in witnesses that the police and courts would actually be interested in. Thus, as before, given the unknown range of variability between witnesses in real cases, it is impossible to generalize the population of events that are of forensic interest. My strong suspicion, however, is that restriction of range is likely to be a serious concern.

There are other questions that follow consideration of the variability across witnesses. Correlations are sample coefficients. That is, they tell us something about the relationship between two variables in a sample. Thus, they do not tell us about the strength of a relationship in a subset of that sample. A robust correlation of $r = 0.50$ may stem from a small sample of very highly confident individuals being correct, with a few other individuals of low confidence being incorrect. That level of association will have very little utility in deciding between two individuals, one of whom is "fairly certain," and another who is "moderately sure."

What kinds of details are of interest in real cases?

The majority of the meta-analytic reviews have focused on identification of a stranger from a lineup. How typical is this kind of evidence, and how well do conclusions drawn from such research generalize to other forms of memory pertinent to a crime? Whilst identification is an important aspect of testimony, it is by no means the only evidence of interest in a trial. For example, what about remembering what was said, or a descriptive detail, or establishing criminal intent? The ability of a witness to judge the confidence in an identification may not generalize to other tests such as these. A person may be "very sure" in a lineup identification and yet be in error. This does not necessarily mean that when they are "very sure" that Person A intended to harm Person B, or that when they are "very sure" a gun was brandished, that their confidence has no validity. A general conclusion about the confidence–accuracy relation for "eyewitness memory" is not warranted from the data collected.

Whilst my own research focusing on this question (e.g. Hollins and Perfect, 1997; Perfect and Hollins, 1996; Perfect, Watson, and Wagstaff, 1993) suggests that the conclusion for event memory is similar to the work on stranger identification, I am aware of its ecological shortcomings. The questions we have asked about the events have been driven by experimental considerations. We have sought to use "memory pointers" (Koriat and Lieblich, 1977) because these have specific answers rather than estimates that are difficult for experimenters to evaluate. The generation of these questions has been entirely driven by the materials we have been using, and the number of details we, as experimenters, can identify. They have *not* been driven by a consideration of the forensic importance of each detail. We have asked many questions about objects, colors of clothing, and words spoken, all of which are easy to score as correct or incorrect and so allow for easy calculation of the confidence–accuracy relation. We have not asked about durations of events ("How long were you able to see the accused?"), distances ("How far away was the gunman?"), speed ("How fast was the car travelling?"), age, weight, or height of the actors, the time of day, the emotional responses of the actors (e.g. "Did A appear frightened?"), attributions of intent behind actions of actors (e.g. "Did A deliberately hit B, or act in self-defence?"), and so forth. In each of these important aspects it is less easy to define what is a correct answer. Estimates can be compared to the true value, but errors can only be defined relatively (i.e., within 5 percent, 10 percent, etc. of the true score). Judgments of intentionality, emotion, and so forth are problematic for different reasons because such details are often matters of interpretation or opinion. The extent to which confidence judgments made for our questions generalize to forensically relevant questions of these kinds is unknown.

To what extent are confidence judgments for isolated "memories" typical of real world judgments?

Another aspect of the kind of event that people witness in a typical experimental study is that it is an isolated episode rather than a firsthand experience that is integrated into their lives. In such studies, the only basis for recollection and confidence is the episodic memory trace. This makes for interesting psychology, and useful information about metacognitive ability, but limits the ecological validity. Gruneberg and Sykes (1993) give a telling example. Two witnesses see a car accident. One reports it occurring at 4.45pm with some confidence, whilst another witness is fairly sure it happened at 6.15pm. However, the first witness is confident about the time because they saw the accident on their way home from a football match that finished at 4.40pm. The second witness has no such corroboration. Thus, in the real world, where events are not isolated from the rest of a person's life, there may be corroborative factors that underpin confidence in an entirely appropriate way. A witness may be sure how far they were from the perpetrator because they know the layout of the crime scene very well. Another witness may be sure of the identity of a perpetrator because they have seen them often in the neighborhood. Of course, it may be possible to construct contrary examples. Hence our isolated experiments testing stranger identification, and event memory for novel material, do not match the conditions under which all witnesses experience events they later make confidence judgments about in the real world.

How can we interpret an isolated individual's confidence for a particular event?

This issue has previously been discussed by Luus and Wells (1994) as the "confidence-main effect issue" (Luus and Wells, 1994, p. 351). Here is the problem. Assessment of the relationship between confidence and accuracy by means of between-subject correlations can only tell us about relative performance. If we find an association, it tells us that, in that sample, those who are more confident on the scale used are more accurate on the test taken. This is impossible to compare in any meaningful way to different samples, who have witnessed a different event, and used a different confidence scale. So, as Luus and Wells cogently argue, it is impossible to interpret a particular confidence rating (say 5 on a 7-point scale), since on one occasion a rating of 5 might reflect relatively high confidence, and on another it may reflect relatively low confidence. A particular confidence rating can only be interpreted relative to other ratings made under the same conditions. What then can we advise the police and courts about a single witness who gives a rating of 5/7 on a scale? Are they likely to be accurate? We simply cannot know.

Perhaps numerical scales are relative, but what of verbally anchored scales? Perhaps we might be able to deduce something about a witness who declares themselves to be "very" or "highly" confident. Such terms are well understood by the general public, and are commonly used descriptors. Are such terms transferable across witnesses? Do they have absolute value? Unfortunately they do not. Wright, Gaskell, and

O'Muircheartaigh (1995) examined the relationship between numerical estimates and vague quantifiers. They varied the format of a life-satisfaction survey. The question of interest asked how many days in the past week people had felt either satisfied with their life, very satisfied, or extremely satisfied. This manipulation was carried out both within subjects (by repeated questioning) and between subjects. There was a clear effect of the modifying adjectives within subjects, such that people rated themselves more frequently satisfied than they did very satisfied, which in turn was more frequent than extremely satisfied. However, when comparing across individuals on the first question they were asked, there was no difference in rated frequency between people who reported how often they were satisfied, and those who reported how often they were very satisfied. To turn this round, for between-person comparisons, one person's rating of satisfied was equivalent to another person's very satisfied. The modifier "very" conveyed no information whatsoever. Thus, one person's "confident" may be equivalent to another person's "very confident."

Summary so far

Much of the early forensic research on the relation between confidence and accuracy has addressed the issue of the absolute magnitude of the relation for eyewitness memory. The early research made much of the counterintuitive finding that confidence did not predict performance. More recently there has been a move toward research demonstrating a stronger confidence–accuracy relation than the earlier work suggested.

However, I have argued here that the forensic research so far does not generalize well. Real-life witnesses do not always identify strangers, do not only make lineup decisions, do not always view the crime from a homogenous viewpoint, do not all have the same degree of motivation, do not all have the same degree of prior familiarity with the environment, do not all have the same level of ability, and so on. The influence of these factors, and many others not discussed, means that it is impossible to draw firm conclusions about the absolute magnitude of the confidence–accuracy relation. Some of the factors might be expected to increase the confidence–accuracy relation, others reduce it. But the net effect cannot be known. Whilst much of the previous research was explicitly directed at the forensically important issue of confidence in lineup performance for stranger identification, the result is a literature that is limited in application, despite its apparent applied focus. Without answers to the difficult questions posed above, the data on eyewitness confidence may be theoretically important, but have little definitive to say about application.

An alternative approach, with some alternative questions

My interest in the confidence judgments of eyewitnesses started in 1992. A student of mine at the time – Emma Watson – wanted to do an undergraduate research project on eyewitness confidence. For my Ph.D. a few years previously I had researched confidence judgments and feeling-of-knowing judgments for general knowledge items in younger and older adults. In all my studies there were robust relations between confidence and accuracy of performance. My initial expectation was that there would be no difference for eyewitness memory. I was therefore intrigued when I began to read the literature described above. My revised expectation – that underpinned the project that Emma and I carried out (subsequently published as Perfect, Watson, and Wagstaff, 1993) – was that eyewitness confidence was inaccurate because it was based on a single item test. Participants in the majority of eyewitness studies witness a single event, and select a single item from a single lineup. Whilst such a form of testing has a sound ecological basis, it means that the psychometric properties of the tests are suspect. I strongly expected that if multiple items were used a robust association would be found.

It was because of this background that the study we designed contrasted a participant's ability to make accurate confidence judgments for eyewitness memory with the ability to judge their accuracy in general knowledge. Because we wanted multiple items in eyewitness memory, we chose to study memory for details of the event, rather than ability to identify strangers from a lineup. I have continued in the same vein because this comparison has proven to have some utility. It enables me to ask whether there is anything special about eyewitness confidence judgments compared to judgments for general knowledge. The data from that first study suggested that perhaps there could be. The confidence–accuracy relation for general knowledge was robust, whether calculated across items or individuals (i.e., within- or between-subjects). However, for eyewitness memory, the confidence–accuracy relation was robust across items but not across people (i.e., within-subjects only).

The comparison between general knowledge and eyewitness memory is useful also because it allows one to rule out statistical artifacts. The pattern reported above holds true even when the two tests are matched for mean level of performance, and range of performance. Subsequent studies have shown that the same pattern pertains when the same individuals do both tests (Hollins and Perfect, 1997; Perfect and Hollins, 1996), thus ruling out simple personality differences as an explanatory factor. Thus, the focus of our research has not been so much on the absolute ability of eyewitnesses to judge the veracity of their memories, as the relative ability of people to judge their memories in different domains of knowledge. Rather than ask whether witnesses are accurate, we ask whether people are as accurate when judging event-based memories as they are when judging general-knowledge memory. This focus on relative ability to judge memory accuracy allows us to escape from the sterility of the debate that has focused on the absolute level of the confidence–accuracy relationship.

Thus, in our research we have been able to match the tests of two domains of knowledge in terms of both overall level of accuracy and variability, and yet still demonstrate that between-subjects correlations between confidence and accuracy are lower for event memory than general knowledge. At the same time, we have shown repeatedly that the across-item confidence–accuracy relation is robust and equivalent across domains. This has led us to explore the reasons why such a pattern should occur. It has moved us away from the ecologically important question of whether eyewitness' confidence is "accurate," but with the benefit that we are able to address a different question: is there something different about judging memory from different domains of knowledge? In any case, as argued above, the generalized version of the ecological question is not a sensible question to ask.

In the research that my colleagues and I have conducted since that first study, I have come to be haunted by a pattern of data that I have repeatedly observed in many studies, some published, some not. I have been trying to work out what this pattern means for some time. There is considerable regularity in the data, and I have long believed that it must be telling me something, possibly something important, about the nature of confidence judgments, and why they are (in our studies at least) not predictive of performance. I finally believe I am beginning to understand what it means. However, I don't want to give away the ending of my story; instead I shall begin at the beginning with the data.

Table 5.1 reports the data from twelve experiments that have measured performance and confidence on tests of both general knowledge and eyewitness memory (ten from our laboratory, and two from a recently published paper). In each there are the same number of items for each kind of test. The first two columns of data report the relation between mean confidence and proportion correct on each test. As you can see, for general knowledge there are robust associations between confidence and performance on virtually all studies. The mean correlation, weighted by degrees of freedom, across the ten studies is $r = 0.51$. In contrast, the association is generally weak (with one notable exception) for eyewitness memory, giving a weighted mean correlation across the same ten studies of $r = 0.21$. Despite my concerns about the generalization of

Table 5.1. *Pearson correlation coefficients between confidence and accuracy, accuracy across domains, and confidence across domains*

Study	Number of participants	Test format	Confidence–accuracy relation		Correlations between GK and EM	
			General knowledge	Eyewitness memory	Accuracy	Confidence
Hollins (1998) Experiment 5	57	Recall	—	—	0.09	0.48
Hollins (1998) Experiment 6	38	Recall	0.36	0.08	0.14	0.58
Hollins and Perfect (1997)	24	Recall	0.46	0.19	−0.04	0.50
Hollins and Perfect (1997)	25	Recog.	0.67	0.19	0.36	0.70
Perfect (2001) Experiment 1	63	Recog.	0.76	0.18	0.18	0.08
Perfect (2001) Experiment 2	39	Recog.	0.41	0.28	0.29	0.74
Perfect and Hollins (1996) Experiment 1	48	Recall	0.42	0.18	0.10	0.58
Perfect and Hollins (1996) Experiment 2	46	Recall	0.28	0.06	0.23	0.52
Perfect and West (unpublished)	12	Recog.	0.66	0.11	0.24	0.81
Perfect and Webber (unpublished)	30	Recall	0.66	0.70	0.38	0.51
Bornstein and Zickafoose (1999) Experiment 1	117	Recog.	—	—	0.09	0.36
Bornstein and Zickafoose (1999) Experiment 2	96	Recog.	—	—	0.16	0.49
Unweighted mean			0.52	0.21	0.19	0.53
Weighted mean			0.51	0.21	0.16	0.47
Median			0.46	0.18	0.17	0.52

Notes: Several of these studies involved multiple conditions. Where no between-condition differences were observed, the data were collapsed across conditions for the purposes of this summary.

face-identification studies, this latter figure is close to that reported in the literature. However, this datum is *not* the aspect of the data that has haunted me. It is the data in the next two columns that have exercised my mind.

The third column shows the relationship between mean performance on the general knowledge test and mean performance on the eyewitness memory test. Generally, there is at best a weak association between the two, with an overall weighted mean correlation across the twelve studies of $r = 0.16$. This is consistent with the idea that the two tests are tapping different aspects of cognition. People who are good eyewitnesses are not necessarily good at general knowledge, and vice versa.

Contrast this with the data in column four. Here there is a robust association across all studies between the mean confidence on each kind of test. The weighted mean correlation across the same twelve studies is $r = 0.47$. People who are sure of their answers in general knowledge are generally sure of their answers in eyewitness memory. Conversely, those unsure in eyewitness memory are unsure in general knowledge. But their performance does not warrant such generalization. Thus, it appears that there is some stable individual characteristic that is being tapped by the measures of confidence that is independent of changes in performance across domains. Clearly it is not totally independent of performance, because confidence does predict performance for general knowledge. Nonetheless, across the studies there is clearly something stable in the way people rate confidence.

In an attempt to understand how such a pattern of findings might arise, I decided to generate some data that demonstrate all the properties I have been observing in my real data. Table 5.2 contains this model data, and shows two distributions of responses for our hypothetical witnesses Jake and Sam. This data set models every aspect of the experimental data observed to date.

Feature 1: *Robust within-subject correlations that are equivalent across domains of knowledge* (e.g. Perfect et al., 1993)

On both tests both witnesses are able to discriminate across items. For eyewitness memory, such data produce a gamma correlation of $G = 0.80$ for Jake and $G = 0.79$ for Sam. The equivalent figures for the general knowledge tests are $G = 0.77$ and $G = 0.77$. Thus, there are no domain (eyewitness memory versus general knowledge) or person (Jake versus Sam) differences in within-subject confidence–accuracy relations.

Table 5.2. *Hypothetical response distributions for Jake (confident witness) and Sam (a more cautious witness) in (a) eyewitness memory, and (b) general knowledge*

(a) Eyewitness memory

	Confidence rating				
	1 Low	2	3	4 High	Total
Jake					
Correct	0	4	8	10	22
Incorrect	2	6	6	0	14
Sam					
Correct	6	6	10	0	22
Incorrect	10	4	0	0	14
Total	18	20	24	10	72

(b) General knowledge

	Confidence rating				
	1 Low	2	3	4 High	Total
Jake					
Correct	1	2	14	7	24
Incorrect	4	5	2	1	12
Sam					
Correct	4	6	8	2	20
Incorrect	9	7	0	0	16
Total	18	20	24	10	72

Feature 2: *A between-subject correlation between confidence and accuracy for general knowledge, but not eyewitness memory* (e.g. Perfect et al., 1993)

On general knowledge, Jake scores 67 percent to Sam's 56 percent. He is also more confident. Thus, there is a positive association between confidence and performance across people for general knowledge. However, for eyewitness memory, Jake is again more confident, but both Jake and Sam score 61 percent. Hence, there is no confidence–accuracy relation for eyewitness memory in this example.

Feature 3: *A lack of correlation between performance across the two domains* (see Table 5.1)

It follows from the above that since Jake outscores Sam in general knowledge, but does not differ from him on eyewitness memory, then the correlation between performance on both tests would be zero.

Feature 4: *A positive correlation between confidence on both tests* (see Table 5.1, final column)

Jake has more of a tendency to use the higher end of the confidence scale than Sam. His mean (or median or mode) confidence is higher on both tests. Thus, for this sample, there is a correlation between the confidence-levels across the tests.

Feature 5: *The above pattern remains true even when mean performance and mean confidence are matched*

All the above remain true, even though absolute level of difficulty of performance across tests remains identical. Across the two participants, the total number of correct responses on each test is 44 out of 72. Likewise, collapsed across participants, the distribution of confidence judgments is identical, with the same number of responses at each level of confidence for each test. Thus, the problematic issues of level of performance, and variability (at least in the confidence data) are not an issue here.

This demonstration shows that it is possible to generate a data set that simultaneously models the robust and within-subject correlations observed across domains, while at the same time showing an interaction between domain and confidence–accuracy relations calculated across individuals. However, it does not explain, psychologically, why such a pattern of data should repeatedly arise.

Could such a pattern arise as a consequence of the personality attributes of our two witnesses, Jake and Sam? Would it arise if there were a stable personality trait that underpins use of the confidence scale? One aspect of the data is certainly consistent with such a view, namely the differential bias towards one end of the confidence scale. If Jake is a generally confident person, then it is plausible that he would tend to use the higher end of the confidence scale to describe his memory state more than the more cautious Sam. This would explain why there is a cross-domain confidence correlation. However, it cannot readily explain why the between-subjects confidence–accuracy relation is higher for general knowledge than for eyewitness memory.

You might think that the example above *does* explain this aspect of the data. After all, I made up the data to do just this. However, everything I argued above merely applies to two different tests. I could equally have re-labeled the tests in Table 5.2 the other way around, so that eyewitness memory showed the robust confidence–accuracy relation and general knowledge did not. The argument would still hold, but the conclusion would be psychologically wrong. Thus, the hypothetical data above only show that it is possible to obtain such a pattern, not why the pattern is always in the same direction. Why is it, in psychological terms, that eyewitness memory shows the lack of confidence–accuracy relation? If a personality factor is the answer, why does it have a detrimental effect on the accuracy of confidence judgments for eyewitness memory but not for general knowledge?

This is the question that Tara Hollins worked on for her thesis (Hollins, 1998). In a series of studies she examined the confidence of participants in both general knowledge and eyewitness memory tests, and tested various aspects of personality and self-belief. Our expectation was that personality would play a greater role in confidence judgments for eyewitness memory. We reasoned that people have insight into their relative expertise in areas of general knowledge, and this expertise heuristic might provide an anchor point for their relative judgments of confidence within that domain. However, we thought that people might lack this insight into their ability at eyewitnessing, and so individual differences that are unrelated to ability might play more of a role. So, for an eyewitness event, a self-assured individual might tend to use the high end of the confidence scale, whilst a less self-assured person might use the lower end. Thus we expected that personality measures would correlate more with confidence in eyewitness memory than they do with confidence in general knowledge. Building on this we reasoned that statistical control of individual differences would lead to a strengthening of the confidence–accuracy relation for eyewitness memory (because personality factors were acting as suppresser variables), but less so for general knowledge. For her thesis, Hollins (1998) investigated a number of personality correlates of confidence in this manner. The scales she investigated are described below.

Snyder's self-monitoring scale   This personality variable was selected because it was one of the few that had previously been studied in the literature. Hosch and colleagues (Hosch, 1994; Hosch et al., 1984; Hosch and Platz, 1984) tested the hypothesis that people high in self-monitoring would make better witnesses. Self-monitoring was measured using Snyder's self-monitoring questionnaire (Snyder, 1979, 1987).

The Eysenck personality inventory Bothwell, Brigham, and Pigott (1987) investigated the relation between face identification performance and the personality measures tapped by the EPI. They found that extraverts tended to be more confident in their responses than introverts and that neuroticism was negatively correlated with confidence. They did not report data on the lie scale. However, since Bothwell et al. only looked at eyewitness performance, we cannot know whether these correlations reflect factors unique to confidence judgments in eyewitness memory, or apply to all confidence judgments. Nor do we know whether controlling the personality variables would increase the confidence–accuracy relation for eyewitness memory.

The cognitive failures questionnaire The pattern of data in Table 5.1 is consistent with another pattern of data on memory – the relation (or rather lack of it) between objective laboratory measures of memory and self-reports of memory function (see Hertzog, this volume). Because confidence ratings are subjective judgments of memory function, it was hypothesized that they might correlate better with other subjective judgments about cognitive function. That is, there may be a bias in cognition-related self-assessments that would be tapped by both confidence judgments and self-rating scales. For this reason we adopted the cognitive failures questionnaire (CFQ; Broadbent et al., 1982).

Social desirability Confidence in one's self, and in one's memory reports can be thought of in terms of making a judgment that has social worth. In the courtroom a memory reported with very low confidence is likely to have very low utility, being unlikely to withstand cross-examination, and unlikely to convince a jury. The intention behind measuring social desirability was therefore to see whether there is a propensity amongst some witnesses to ascribe high confidence inappropriately because of a desire to give a response that is socially more acceptable. In fact, we measured social desirability using two separate scales. The first – the Balanced Inventory of Desirable Responding (BIDR; Paulhus, 1988) – has been developed to measure both conscious image management and self-deception. However, since these two scales showed the same pattern, we merely report total scale score data here. The second scale we used was the Marlowe–Crowne Social Desirability scale (MCSD; Crowne and Marlowe, 1960), which measures need to avoid social disapproval. This scale correlated at $r = 0.38$ with the BIDR scale in our sample.

Table 5.3. *Pearson correlation coefficients between individual difference measures and confidence in eyewitness memory and general knowledge tests*

Study	Number of participants	Individual difference measure	Eyewitness memory	General knowledge
Perfect and Hollins (1996) Experiment 1	48	Self-monitoring	-0.16	-0.06
Perfect and Hollins (1996) Experiment 2	46	Self-monitoring	-0.17	-0.19
		Neuroticism	**-0.30**	**-0.52**
Hollins and Perfect (1997) Experiment 1	48	Extraversion	-0.14	**-0.29**
		Lie scale	**0.47**	**0.38**
Hollins and Perfect (1997) Experiment 2	40	CFQ	0.00	-0.01
		BIDR	-0.24	–
Perfect, Hollins, and Hunt (2000)	57	MCSD	-0.21	–
Experiment 1		Self-esteem	0.15	–
		Inadequacy	0.14	–

Notes: Data for Hollins and Perfect (1997) are collapsed across test format (recall versus recognition). Data for Perfect et al. (2000) are collapsed across three conditions. Significant correlation coefficients are in **bold**.

Self-esteem/inadequacy An alternative to an inappropriate concern with social approval is an inappropriate view of one's own abilities. That is, it may be that certain witnesses have inappropriately low opinions of themselves and their abilities as a witness, and so are lower in confidence than their ability merits. In order to test this idea we used two personality scales designed to tap self-valuations. The first was Rosenberg's self-esteem scale (Rosenberg, 1965) which measures self-approval, and the second was Fleming and Courtney's (1984) revised version of the Feeling of Inadequacy scale, designed to measure feelings of inferiority, social anxiety, and self-consciousness. These two scales correlated at $r = 0.77$ in our sample.

Table 5.3 contains the correlations for each of the personality measures with the mean confidence of participants in each study. There are a number of points to note in this data set. The first prediction – that personality would correlate with confidence – received only limited support. There were suggestions in Hollins and Perfect (1997) Experiment 1 that anxious individuals tended to have less confidence in their memories, and also that those who respond in a socially desirable way (on the lie scale) were more confident. However, the subsequent study which examined related concepts of self-esteem and social-desirability (Perfect, Hollins, and Hunt, 2000) did not show the same pattern.

The second prediction was that personality would play a greater role in eyewitness confidence judgments. This was clearly not the case. Personality was related to confidence in general knowledge as often as it was in eyewitness memory. The final prediction was also not borne out. Controlling for the various personality measures did not increase the confidence–accuracy relation across the studies in any systematic manner.

These data therefore do not support the idea that a personality factor underpins the relation between confidence in eyewitness memory and confidence in general knowledge. Nor do they support the idea that the confidence–accuracy relation in eyewitness memory could be strengthened by statistical control of a personality factor. However, we face the perennial problem of accepting the null hypothesis. The difficulty in drawing firm conclusions from such an exercise is that we have not conducted an exhaustive search through all possible personality measures searching for the critical measure. However, the start we have made does not encourage us that it is worth continuing to mine this particular seam. So far, the returns for our considerable effort have been disappointing. Our options for this line of research are to keep trying different personality measures in the hope that we might strike lucky one day, or to try a new approach. We have chosen the latter.

Fortunately, the new approach that we have taken to the question of confidence and accuracy does appear to be a more fruitful avenue. Rather than focus on personality measures, we have begun to investigate people's beliefs about their memory abilities. In one of these studies (Perfect, 2001), we asked participants to judge their ability in two domains, relative to their peers. Participants were asked to rate how good they were (compared to others) at recognising faces, and at answering questions about sport. We then tested the participants on three lineups, and three sports questions, asking for confidence ratings for each item selected in the recognition test. As before, we found that these postdictive confidence ratings were predictive for the general knowledge test ($r = 0.76$) but not for the lineups ($r = 0.18$), replicating once again the pattern we have observed many times. For the sports questions, we found that pre-test beliefs about ability in a domain predicted both actual performance ($r = 0.48$) and postdictive confidence ($r = 0.70$). For the lineups, pre-test beliefs did not correlate with performance ($r = 0.06$) but they did correlate with postdictive confidence ($r = 0.31$). Thus, for general knowledge, people know how good they are going to be, but for lineups they do not. For lineups, confidence in a choice is predicted better by pre-existing beliefs about ability than actual performance on the test.

Thus, the suggestion that comes from this study is that beliefs about expertise may underpin the confidence–accuracy relation in general knowledge, and undermine it in eyewitness memory, at least for face recognition. This idea is consistent with Wells, Lindsay, and Ferguson's (1979) calibration hypothesis. They argued that eyewitnesses may not receive feedback in their daily lives about the veracity of their recall, and so do not develop accurate calibration of confidence for memory for past events. Thus, they literally do not know how good they are at eyewitness memory. In contrast, such calibration is clearly present for general knowledge. Participants knew how much they knew about sport in this study (and we have since replicated this pattern for other domains of knowledge in a separate study). Our culture and education systems put a lot of store by accumulated knowledge, and many opportunities exist for people to develop a sense of their expertise in different domains of knowledge. Anyone who has played the game "Trivial Pursuit" will have a sense of their strongest and weakest categories.

This idea is consistent with a number of lines of research suggesting that expertise in a domain is a common heuristic in metacognitive judgments. For example, Glenberg and Epstein (1987) showed that judgments of comprehension were closely related to beliefs about what ought to be known (based on prior experience) rather than actual comprehension of presented texts that were being judged. They had students of music and physics read texts in both domains, and judge their comprehension of each. Whilst calibration was good across domains (i.e., musicians rated their comprehension as better for the music texts than the physics texts, and vice versa for the physicists), it was poor within domains. Musicians were poor judges of their relative performance across the music texts, and the same was true for the physicists with the physics texts. They concluded that confidence judgments are based on "self-classification as an expert or non-expert in the domain of the text, rather than an assessment of the degree to which the text was comprehended" (p. 84). This conclusion is essentially the same argument as I have sought to make for confidence judgments in eyewitness memory.

Thus, the suggestion from our recent research is that people's confidence in a particular memory decision is in part based on an expertise heuristic. Whilst this has some utility in general knowledge, in eyewitness memory it does not. People just don't know how good they are at eyewitnessing, and so an expertise heuristic has no value. Unfortunately, this does not appear to stop people using such a heuristic. There is a clear prediction from this idea. Giving people feedback as to how they perform on eyewitness tests, compared to others, should increase the confidence–accuracy relation for eyewitness memory. This is precisely what we recently reported (Perfect et al., 2000). Giving participants feedback on how they compared to others following a lineup choice increased the confidence–accuracy correlation from $r = -0.02$ on Trial 1 to $r = 0.55$ on Trial 3. Practice alone had no impact, with the corresponding correlations being $r = 0.10$ and $r = 0.07$. Interestingly, receiving feedback on the accuracy of one's own responses (but not those of the comparison group) also had no effect (Trial 1, $r = 0.04$: Trial 3, $r = 0.19$). Thus, learning how one compares to others in the group improves the confidence–accuracy relation for the group as a whole, but mere exposure to the kind of test, or even learning that one has succeeded or failed, does not. We argue that this pattern emerges because without a comparison group, there is no way to interpret one's success or failure. Failure might reflect one's inability, or the fact that the test was difficult. Only when a person learns that they have failed where most others succeeded, or vice versa, will they learn something about their relative ability.

Summary

In the past three decades, considerable effort has been dedicated to answering the question of whether eyewitness confidence is predictive of performance. Whilst early research suggested a negative conclusion, more recent research has challenged this view. The confidence–accuracy relation tends to be weak when conditions are homogeneous (as in the early experimental studies), and to be stronger when performance and confidence vary more widely. The consequence of this is that it is hard to establish a single estimate of the confidence–accuracy relation in eyewitness memory. Furthermore, I have argued that until we know a good deal more about the conditions under which confidence–accuracy relations apply in the real world, there is little we can conclude about the absolute level of association between confidence and accuracy.

There are useful and interesting questions that can be asked, however, if one is less concerned with answering the question about the absolute level of association. In the second half of this chapter I have focused on the pattern of association between confidence and performance in eyewitness memory and general knowledge. Across a number of studies a stable pattern has emerged. Within-subject confidence accuracy relations are robust and equal in both domains of knowledge. Between-subject confidence accuracy relations are higher for general knowledge than eyewitness memory, even when variability is controlled for. Whilst performance in the two domains is not related, mean confidence is. I have tried to argue that this pattern is not the result of a personality factor that underpins confidence in the two domains, but that it may be related to erroneous beliefs about memory ability. Whilst people seem to appreciate how good they are at general knowledge, they do not know how good they are at recognising faces. This pattern emerges because whilst people learn, through feedback, of their relative ability in general knowledge, this does not happen for eyewitness memory since events cannot be revisited, and people cannot make inferences from the comparison of their memories with other people's accounts of an event. Thus, whilst we cannot put an absolute figure on the confidence–accuracy relation in eyewitness memory, the suggestion of this latter work is that confidence and accuracy are always likely to be less strongly associated in eyewitness memory than for general knowledge. This is because an expertise-based heuristic will be useful for general knowledge, but not for eyewitness memory.

REFERENCES

Bornstein, B. H., and Zickafoose, D. J. (1999). "I know I know it, I know I saw it": the stability of the confidence–accuracy relationship across domains. *Journal of Experimental Psychology: Applied*, 5, 76–88.
Bothwell, R. K., Brigham, J. C., and Pigott, M. A. (1987). An exploratory study of personality differences in eyewitness memory. *Journal of Social Behavior and Personality*, 2, 335–343.

Bothwell, R. K., Deffenbacher, K. A., and Brigham, J. C. (1987). Correlations of eyewitness accuracy and confidence: optimality hypothesis revisited. *Journal of Applied Psychology*, 72, 691–695.

Broadbent, D. E., Cooper, P. F., Fitzgerald, P., and Parkes, K. R. (1982). The cognitive failures questionnaire (CFQ) and its correlates. *British Journal of Clinical Psychology*, 21, 1–16.

Cohen, J. (1977). *Statistical power analysis for the behavioral sciences*. New York: Academic Press.

Crowne, D. P., and Marlowe, D. (1960). A new scale of social desirability independent of psychopathology. *Journal of Consulting Psychology*, 24, 349–354.

Deffenbacher, K. A. (1980). Eyewitness accuracy and confidence: can we infer anything about their relationship? *Law and Human Behavior*, 4, 243–260.

Fleming, J. S., and Courtney, B. E. (1984). The dimensionality of self-esteem II: hierarchical facet model for revised measurement scales. *Journal of Personality and Social Psychology*, 46, 404–421.

Glenberg, A. M., and Epstein, W. (1987). Inexpert calibration of comprehension. *Memory and Cognition*, 15, 84–93.

Gruneberg, M., and Sykes, R. N. (1993). The generalizability of confidence–accuracy studies in eyewitnessing. *Memory*, 1, 185–189.

Hollins, T. S. (1998). *What influences the relation between memory and metamemory in eyewitnesses?* Unpublished Ph.D. thesis, University of Bristol.

Hollins, T. S., and Perfect, T. J. (1997). The confidence–accuracy relation in eyewitness memory: the mixed question type effect. *Legal and Criminological Psychology*, 2, 205–218.

Hosch, H. (1994). Individual differences in personality and eyewitness identification. In D. F. Ross, J. D. Read, and M. P. Toglia (eds.), *Adult eyewitness testimony: current trends and developments*, pp. 328–347. New York: Cambridge University Press.

Hosch, H., Leippe, M. R., Marchioni, P. M., and Cooper, D. S. (1984). Victimization, self-monitoring and eyewitness identification. *Journal of Applied Psychology*, 69, 280–288.

Hosch, H., and Platz, S. J. (1984). Self-monitoring and eyewitness accuracy. *Personality and Social Psychology Bulletin*, 10, 283–289.

Kassin, S. M., Ellsworth, P. C., and Smith, V. L. (1989). The general acceptance of psychological research on eyewitness testimony: a survey of the experts. *American Psychologist*, 44, 1089–1098.

Koriat, A., and Goldsmith, M. (1996). Memory metaphors and the real-life/laboratory controversy: correspondence versus storehouse conceptions of memory. *Behavioral and Brain Sciences*, 19, 167–228.

Koriat, A., and Lieblich, I. (1977). A study of memory pointers. *Acta Psychologica*, 41, 151–164.

Lindsay, D. S., Read, D. J., and Sharma, K. (1998). Accuracy and confidence in person identification: the relationship is strong when witnessing conditions vary widely. *Psychological Science*, 9, 215–218.

Luus, C. A. E., and Wells, G. L. (1994). Eyewitness identification confidence. In D. F. Ross, J. D. Read, and M. P. Toglia (eds.), *Adult eyewitness testimony:*

current trends and developments, pp. 348–361. New York: Cambridge University Press.

Paulhus, D. L. (1988). Assessing self-deception and impression management in self-reports: the balanced inventory of desirable responding. (Manual available from the author at University of British Columbia.)

Penrod, S. (1980). *Confidence, accuracy and the eyewitness.* Unpublished Ph.D. thesis, University of Wisconsin.

Penrod, S., and Cutler, B. (1995). Witness confidence and witness accuracy: assessing their forensic relation. *Psychology, Public Policy and Law*, 1, 817–845.

Perfect, T. J. (2001). The role of perceived ability in confidence judgements for eyewitness memory and general knowledge. Manuscript under review.

Perfect, T. J., and Hollins, T. S. (1996). Predictive feeling of knowing judgments and postdictive confidence judgments in eyewitness memory and general knowledge. *Applied Cognitive Psychology*, 10, 371–382.

Perfect, T. J., Hollins, T. S., and Hunt, A. L. R. (2000). Practice and feedback effects on the confidence–accuracy relation in eyewitness memory. *Memory*, 8, 235–244.

Perfect, T. J., Watson, E. L., and Wagstaff, G. F. (1993). Accuracy of confidence ratings associated with general knowledge and eyewitness memory. *Journal of Applied Psychology*, 78, 144–147.

Read, J. D., Lindsay, D. S., and Nicholls, T. (1998). The relationship between accuracy and confidence in eyewitness identification studies: is the conclusion changing? In C. P. Thompson, D. J. Herrman, J. D. Read, D. Bruce, D. G. Payne, and M. P. Toglia (eds.), *Eyewitness memory: theoretical and applied aspects*, pp. 107–130. Hillsdale, NJ: Lawrence Erlbaum Associates.

Rosenberg, M. (1965). *Society and the adolescent self-image.* Princeton, NJ: Princeton University Press.

Snyder, M. (1979). Self-monitoring processes. In L. Berkowitz (ed.), *Advances in experimental social psychology, volume 12* (pp. 85–128). New York: Academic Press.

Snyder, M. (1987). *Public appearances / private realities.* New York: W. H. Freeman.

Sporer, S. L., Penrod, S., Read, D., and Cutler, B. (1995). Choosing, confidence, and accuracy: a meta-analysis of the confidence–accuracy relation in eyewitness identification studies. *Psychological Bulletin*, 118, 315–327.

Stephenson, G. (1984). Accuracy and confidence in testimony. A critical review and some fresh evidence. In D. J. Muller, D. E. Blackman and A. J. Chapman (eds.), *Psychology and law: topics from an international conference*, pp. 229–248. Chichester: Wiley.

Wells, G. L., Lindsay, R. C. L., and Ferguson, T. J. (1979). Accuracy, confidence, and juror perceptions in eyewitness identification. *Journal of Applied Psychology*, 64, 440–448.

Wells, G. L., and Murray, D. M. (1984). Eyewitness confidence. In G. L. Wells and E. F. Loftus, (eds.), *Eyewitness testimony: psychological perspectives*, pp. 155–170. New York: Cambridge University Press.

Wright, D. B., Gaskell, G. D., and O'Muircheartaigh, C. A. (1995). Testing the multiplicative hypothesis of intensifiers. *Applied Cognitive Psychology*, 9, 167–177.

6 Autobiographical memories and beliefs: a preliminary metacognitive model

Giuliana Mazzoni and Irving Kirsch

Returning a rented car, the authors of this chapter tried to remember whose credit card had been imprinted when the car had been picked up. After some thought, the senior author reported a clear memory of giving the rental agent her card, and the junior author concurred that this had happened. Despite this clear shared memory, it was the junior author's card that had been imprinted.

People's memories and beliefs about events that may have happened to them can be true or false, and the consequences of being wrong are often more severe than those in the incident described above. Married couples argue about their divergent memories of past events, politicians are embarrassed when they misremember events that are a matter of popular record, and families can be destroyed when psychotherapy clients develop false memories of childhood abuse.

The central thesis of this chapter is that the answers people give to questions regarding the occurrence of events in their life are based on metacognitive decisional mechanisms. These mechanisms take two factors into account: (a) the information that is available about the event at the moment of the decision; and (b) the metacognitive beliefs that people hold. We maintain that the same decisional mechanisms and metacognitive beliefs that play a role when people have to answer questions about the occurrence of events that actually happened are also involved when people develop false beliefs and memories for events that did not happen to them.

We begin by drawing a distinction between false autobiographical beliefs and false autobiographical memories. Next, the role of metacognitive beliefs and inferential mechanisms in memory are discussed, and Koriat and Goldsmith's (1996) metacognitive model of the strategic regulation of memory accuracy is described. In the third section of this chapter, the Koriat and Goldsmith model is used as an exemplar for the development of a new metacognitive model of autobiographical memory and belief, and a large body of data supporting this model is summarized. The new model illustrates the mechanisms at play when answering questions like "Did event X happen to you at age Y?"

Our model is consistent with Hyman and Kleinknecht's (1999) theoretical explanation of false memory creation. Hyman and Kleinknecht list three conditions that are necessary for the creation of a false memory. First, the content of the memory must be plausible to the person; second, the person must construct an image and/or narrative of the event; and third, there must be an error in source-monitoring, such that the image or narrative is thought of as a memory. Each of these conditions is also contained in our theory. However, our model differs from the Hyman and Kleinknecht proposal in a number of ways. First, we explicate the steps involved in the creation of a false memory in detail. Second, we view the process by which false memories are created as consistent with the process by which accurate memories are produced. Therefore, our model describes the construction of both true and false autobiographical memories. Third, in addition to considering the creation of memories, we describe the process involved in the formation of accurate and inaccurate autobiographical beliefs, a process that is ignored in Hyman and Kleinknecht's theory. Finally, our theoretical proposal considers the reciprocal interplay between memory and belief.

Distinguishing autobiographical memories from autobiographical beliefs

The literature on false memories contains two types of studies that can be differentiated on the basis of the type of questions that participants are asked about autobiographical events. In some studies, people are asked to state whether they can remember the occurrence of a critical event, and they may also be asked to describe their memory of the event in some detail. These are studies of false memories. In other studies, people are asked to state how certain they are that a critical event has happened to them (i.e., to rate the likelihood that the event occurred), with no mention of whether they can actually remember it occurring. These are studies of autobiographical beliefs. Until recently, results of both kinds of studies were interpreted as evidence of false memories for autobiographical events. It is our contention that the two types of studies should be considered separately.

The distinction we are making between autobiographical beliefs and autobiographical memories is somewhat similar to the distinction between autobiographical knowledge and autobiographical memories proposed by Conway and Pleydell-Pearce (2000). According to their model, autobiographical memories are "transitory dynamic mental constructions generated from an underlying knowledge base" (Conway and Pleydell-Pearce, 2000, p. 261) that are characterized by different levels of specificity.

We share the view that autobiographical memories are based on the retrieval of autobiographical knowledge, but we also think an important distinction can be made between knowledge and belief. An autobiographical belief involves a judgment about a specific event that may be partly based on more general autobiographical knowledge. It is a conviction, derived from experience and/or suggestion, that guides the search for a memory and is generally biased toward selecting confirmatory information. A belief can be held with varying degrees of conviction, and it can be accurate or inaccurate. Reciprocally, general beliefs can shape the content of autobiographical knowledge and consequently change autobiographical memories (Barclay, 1996; Conway et al., 1996; Hirt, 1990). Conway and Pleydell-Pearce recognize that "beliefs and attitudes... play an important part in understanding autobiographical memory," but maintain that "currently there is insufficient research to develop these domains, in terms of autobiographical memory" (Conway and Pleydell-Pearce, 2000, p. 265). In this section, we review recent research that bears on the role of belief in autobiographical memory.

To some extent, the distinction we propose is also similar to the distinction between knowing and remembering that has been useful in research on recognition and recall (Gardiner, 1988; Gardiner and Java, 1993; Tulving, 1985). In this area of research, participants are sometimes asked to render "remember/know" judgments on items that are recalled. Remembering involves not just having a sense of knowing that an element was part of the to-be-remembered material, but also having a recollective experience of having seen the item on the list of elements to be recognized or recalled. Conversely, a "know" judgment indicates that the person's memory of the event does not have this recollective quality.

Despite the similarities, our distinction between beliefs and memories differs from the know/remember distinction in two ways. First, the know/remember distinction is a differentiation between two manners in which people remember information. Thus, it refers to something that is understood to be a memory (e.g. the items one recalls being on a list). In contrast, beliefs, as we define them, are not memories at all. Second, as noted above, belief is different from knowledge, in that it is a judgment or conviction and therefore need not be accurate.

In some instances, a person knows that an event has happened because they remember it happening. Because of this, there is considerable overlap between autobiographical memories and beliefs. However, there are many situations in which beliefs about the occurrence of an event are completely independent of the retrieval of an autobiographical memory of it. Consider, for example, the question "Were you fed when you were six months old?" Without doubt, all readers of this chapter would answer it affirmatively, despite the impossibility of retrieving any memory of being fed (or of anything else) at such an early age. In cases like this, the answer would be positive because people make inferences about the occurrence of the event using the knowledge and the information they have. They know that feeding is necessary to stay alive and that even a temporary lack of food at that age can be harmful and leave permanent traces. People know how infants in general are treated. They also know the habits and customs of their own families. In other words, a positive answer to questions of this sort can be based entirely on inferences drawn from information available to the person, without their use of any memory for the event.

The above example concerns an event that actually happened, but the distinction is equally important in considering questions about events that have not happened. For example, consider the question "Did you hear classical music in the hospital nursery during the first days of life?" Mazzoni and Vannucci (1999) elicited positive answers to this question after providing participants with misinformation about its likelihood (e.g. that most hospital nurseries in Italy aired classical music during a period of years including those in which the participants were born). The participants in this study did not develop memories of having heard the music, but they did acquire a false autobiographical belief.

In most studies addressing the false memory issue, participants are asked either about their autobiographical memories or about their autobiographical beliefs, but rarely about both. In at least one study (Mazzoni, Loftus, Seitz, and Lynn, 1999), however, both types of question were asked. The results of this study demonstrate the importance of the distinction between autobiographical memory and autobiographical belief. Specifically, they indicate that it is possible to increase people's beliefs about the occurrence of an event without creating any specific memory of it. After a bogus dream interpretation, most participants increased their ratings of how likely it was that a false event had occurred, and a substantial minority came to believe that it had probably happened. Very few participants, however, reported any memory of the event. Thus, the Mazzoni et al. (1999) study provides empirical support for the distinction between autobiographical belief and autobiographical memory.

Distinguishing between autobiographical beliefs and autobiographical memories makes it possible to discriminate between the processes involved in answering questions about autobiographical beliefs and those responsible for the report of autobiographical memories. In the model presented below, we claim that the mechanism by which autobiographical memories are produced involves a combination of recollective experiences and inferential processes. Autobiographical memories are reported when people access information that is retrievable from memory and construct a mental experience that has a recollective quality. Thus, memories are mental events that have enough of a recollective quality for the person to judge them to be memories.

In contrast, the process by which autobiographical beliefs are formed is inferential, rather than experiential. Although the experience of retrieved memories can be part of the information on the basis of which people decide whether an event has occurred, the autobiographical belief per se does not have a recollective quality. Instead, people decide whether an event has occurred to them on the basis of a decisional process that need not involve any recollective experience at all. It is possible, for example, to infer the occurrence of an event from the general and specific information people have about it. Thus, autobiographical beliefs are inferences or judgments that are in some cases based on autobiographical memories and in other cases based on other sources of information.

Metacognition plays a central role in our model of autobiographical memory and belief. Therefore, in the next section, we present an overview of the role of metacognition in memory. We also describe Koriat and Goldsmith's (1996) model of the metacognitive processes involved in deciding whether to report a mental content produced by a memory search, a model which partially inspired the model of autobiographical memory and belief presented in this chapter.

Metacognition and memory

Metacognition has two major components. The first consists of people's knowledge and beliefs about their cognitive processes and cognitive states. It is a "naive theory" of the functioning of human cognition. The second is an online control process that monitors and guides underlying cognitive processes (Nelson and Narens, 1990; Schneider, 1985).

Metacognition as a set of beliefs

The first component of metacognitive knowledge concerns the theory that individuals have about the way cognitive processes work and about what cognitive states are. The theory can be either explicit or implicit. It consists of a set of beliefs that people hold about cognition. Examples of common beliefs about cognition include the belief that it requires more effort to study difficult material than easy material and the belief that it is easier to remember an item if one pays attention to it than if one does not pay attention. Included in this component of metacognition is a set of beliefs that are held about various aspects of memory. Most of these beliefs are widely shared. For example, it is commonly believed that memory is a sort of storage of data that are encoded through experience. When the data are stored, then they can subsequently be accessed. The wide dissemination of information about psychoanalysis has added the common metacognitive belief that we can repress (i.e., store in a sort of hidden area) memories that would raise strong negative emotions (e.g. memories for traumatic events), but even these negative memories cannot be erased from memory.

The set of beliefs that people hold about memory includes convictions about encoding and retrieval processes. For example, people believe that items can vary in difficulty and that such difficulty influences encoding processes. It includes convictions about the factors that can help or interfere with encoding, and beliefs about the potential duration of encoded information in memory. It has been shown (Cornoldi, Gobbo, and Mazzoni, 1990) that even young children possess a clear set of beliefs about what helps and hinders memory. For example, even at age six they state that the length of the time interval between encoding and retrieval affects the number of items recalled. They also know that people can use strategies to enhance memory, and that some strategies are more effective than others. People commonly believe that, once stored in memory, encoded information can be retrieved, that retrieval requires effort, and that cues can be of help.

Metacognitive beliefs about memory and how memory works can play an important role not only in determining the result of memory tasks (see for example Strack and Bless, 1994), but also in the process of answering questions about autobiographical beliefs that are not memory-based (e.g. "Were you fed when you were six months old?"). This is because metacognitive beliefs about memory mediate the way lack of memory for such events is interpreted. Most people, for example, believe that it is impossible to retrieve memories from the first days of life, and because of that belief they do not use the lack of memory as a certain indication that the unretrieved event did not happen. Their metacognitive belief is that the absence of memories for events that might have happened very early in life does not imply that the events did not occur.

Metacognition as monitoring and control

The second component of metacognition consists of a set of monitoring and control processes that are assumed to regulate more basic cognitive processes. This component is dynamic, in that it actively guides the processes that occur in cognition. In a seminal paper on the topic, Brown (1975) described the following four functions of this dynamic component: (a) becoming aware of the existence of a cognitive problem; (b) planning and activating the appropriate strategies to address it; (c) predicting one's performance; and (d) monitoring and regulating the ongoing cognitive activity. Similarly, Nelson and Narens (1990) described metacognition as a supervisory or executive system. The executive system is responsible for assessing the current cognitive state, initiating and assessing the functioning of cognitive processes, and directing and modifying (i.e., redirecting, inhibiting, and coordinating) them. Mechanisms in this dynamic component of metacognition serve two main functions, assessment (or monitoring) and regulation (or control). The two mechanisms are thought to interact at any given moment (Nelson and Narens, 1990).

A number of models of metacognitive monitoring and control of memory have been proposed (e.g. Barnes et al., 1998; Koriat and Goldsmith, 1996; Metcalfe, 1993). Of these, the Koriat and Goldsmith model of the strategic regulation of memory accuracy is particularly relevant to the topic of true and false autobiographical beliefs and memories. The model is based on data showing that output from memory is under the direct control of the subject, who can decide whether to volunteer or withhold information retrieved from memory. The decision is based on the evaluation of the accuracy of the information retrieved (see Figure 6.1).

In the Koriat and Goldsmith model, asking a question triggers a search in long-term memory that leads to the retrieval of a candidate response and activates a monitoring process that assesses the correctness of the retrieved candidate. Good candidate answers will be output; poor candidate answers will not. However, the decision to withhold or output the retrieved candidate is based not just on the initial assessed probability

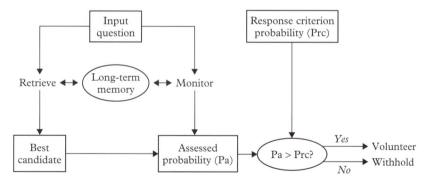

Figure 6.1 Koriat and Goldsmith's (1996) model of the strategic regulation of memory accuracy.

of its correctness, but on the comparison between the assessed probability of the response being accurate and a pre-set probability criterion that is required for a response to be output. The setting of this criterion depends on situational demands and the consequences of accurate and inaccurate reporting and withholding. Retrieved candidates will be output when the assessed probability of correctness is equal to or higher than the set probability criterion. Otherwise, retrieved candidates will be withheld. The assessment of the probability of accuracy of the retrieved response is a metacognitive monitoring function, whereas the comparison between assessed probability and criterion probability, which leads to the decision to volunteer or withhold the retrieved candidate, is a control function.

The model has been assessed on tests of general knowledge. The independent variable was the degree of freedom subjects were given in reporting what they retrieved from memory. In some cases, report from memory was forced (they had to say what they remembered); in other cases, report from memory was optional (they could withhold the response if they thought it was not the correct one). For example, in one experiment (Koriat and Goldsmith, 1996, Experiment 1), participants were presented with a general-knowledge test (e.g. "What is the capital of Australia?"), and their memory was tested either via recall or via recognition. Forced reports were considered to represent the best candidates found during retrieval; conversely, free reports were considered to represent the result of the decisional process of volunteering versus witholding the retrieved candidate. Participants also had to give a confidence judgment for each of the responses output in either the forced or the free conditions. The judgments were considered to represent monitoring, i.e., the assessed probability associated to each best candidate retrieved from memory. The results turned out to be consistent with the model. During forced reports people volunteered low-confidence responses, whereas during free reporting low-confidence responses were withheld.

In the Koriat and Goldsmith (1996) model, answers to questions are considered to be based only on memory. For many situations, the search for a memory and the evaluation of its accuracy may be sufficient for the individual to determine how a question should be answered. In many other situations, however, the answer to a question about memory must be based on other factors. For example, questions about events that happened in early childhood or other events for which there may be no specific memory (e.g. "Did you go to church on the fourth Sunday in November 1999?") are not likely to be answerable by means of an episodic memory search. In many cases, however, they can be answered on the basis of an inferential process. Very devoted churchgoers, for example, might quickly answer "Yes" because they have not missed a Sunday service in many years.

Inferential processes are particularly important when dealing with autobiographical beliefs. In the next section, we present a two-stage model of the metacognitive monitoring and control processes that govern people's responses to questions concerning the occurrence of autobiographical events, questions like "Did event X happen to you when you were Y years old?" We also explicate the role of metacognitive beliefs about memory in these processes.

Did it happen to you? A metacognitive model of autobiographical memory and belief

Consider the question "Did you spill punch on the bride's dress when you were eight?" This question concerns a belief about the occurrence of an event at a certain age. Next consider the question "Do you remember spilling punch on the bride's dress when you were eight?" This question concerns the possibility of retrieving a memory of the event. What mechanisms are activated in answering these two questions?

Autobiographical memory

A model of this first part of the process of answering a question about autobiographical belief is displayed in Figure 6.2. This model is a modification of the model proposed by Koriat and Goldsmith (1996) and represents the first part of our two-stage model of autobiographical belief. It is also a model of how people respond to questions about autobiographical memory.

As in the Koriat and Goldsmith (1996) model, a question about an event triggers a memory search and activates monitoring processes. The first part of our model is concerned with the evaluation of whether one can remember the target event. Whether the event occurred is not determined until after the presence or absence of a memory is established. Accordingly, when "best candidate" mental contents are retrieved, monitoring processes are used to determine whether they are memories and, if so, whether those memories are sufficient to provide an answer to the question that was asked. One difference between our model and that proposed by Koriat and Goldsmith is that we are not concerned with the decision of whether to disclose or withhold an answer. Instead, our interest is in whether people conclude that they can remember the event being asked about. As a result, we do not consider demand characteristics

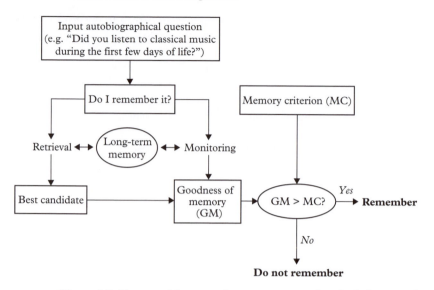

Figure 6.2 Metacognitive control processes governing the judgment of whether one remembers an event.

or response costs. This is not because they are unimportant, but merely because these concerns are beyond the scope of what we are attempting to model.

Koriat and Goldsmith (1996) assume that the "best candidate" that results from a memory search will be either an accurate memory, an inaccurate memory, or a "wild guess." This assumption works well enough for the task used in their validating studies (a general-knowledge test), but it presents problems when the task involves searching for an episodic memory. A long tradition of memory research, beginning with Bartlett (1932; see also Koriat and Goldsmith, 1996), suggests that memory is not a storage container, in which a search either does or does not produce an accurate memory. Instead, what is generally called memory retrieval can be viewed as a constructive process, in which a variety of mental contents (e.g. memories, thoughts, imaginings, confabulations, memories of dreams rather than events, etc.) are mingled together in ways that may be difficult to untangle. Thus, studies have shown that the provision of new information can modify what people remember about something they heard, knew, or experienced before (e.g. Conway and Ross, 1984; Hirt, 1990; Ross, 1989; Snyder and Uranowitz, 1978). These data show that the search for an episodic memory can yield mental contents that are not autobiographical memories.

Accordingly, the first monitoring task in answering an autobiographical question is to evaluate whether the best candidate resulting from the search is actually a memory. Suppose, for example, that the question is "Did you listen to classical music in the hospital nursery during the first days of life?" Although there can be no retrievable episodic memories of this event, the question is likely to stimulate some mental contents – images of hospital rooms and memories of the sound of classical music, for example. In most circumstances, people will correctly evaluate these as not being memories of the event being asked about.

The thoughts and images produced by a memory search are evaluated along dimensions that are relevant to the person's metacognitive beliefs. People believe that mental contents are more likely to be memories if they are vivid and clear, fluent, and easy to access; and each of these characteristics contributes to the person's evaluation of the goodness of the memory. Other metacognitive beliefs that contribute to the evaluation of a memory candidate are those proposed by Johnson and collaborators as important for reality or source monitoring (Johnson, Hashtroudi, and Lindsay, 1993). Thus, compared to fantasies, memories are believed to be richer in perceptual, contextual, semantic, and affective information.

The evaluated mental content is compared to an implicit criterion that establishes how good (i.e., how fluid, vivid, clear, detailed, plausible, etc.) a mental content must be in order to be judged a memory. The result of this comparison is a decision as to whether the mental content produced by the memory search constitutes an autobiographical memory. The threshold for this decision is fluid, rather than fixed. Thus, a particular degree of vividness will be sufficient to qualify a mental content as a memory in some circumstances but not in others. Metacognitive beliefs are one of the factors affecting the criterion threshold. For example, people believe that memories fade over time (Cornoldi, 1998), so that memories of the distant past are more vague then memories of events that happened recently. Similarly, actual events are believed to be more detailed than imagined or dreamed events (Johnson et al., 1993). Thus, to be accepted as a memory, the image of an event that one witnessed yesterday will require a mental content that is relatively detailed, clear, vivid, and compelling. In contrast, a much more impoverished image might be accepted as a memory of a dream that one had years ago.

This process also explains what happens when people create false memories. If, in response to an autobiographical question, a person has a very clear, vivid, and fluent image of an event that has never happened, and if the image is easily accessed and does not conflict with various metacognitive beliefs, its evaluated goodness may exceed the memory criterion, and it may therefore be labeled as a memory. This may explain what happens when people are asked to repeatedly imagine an event that never occurred. Repeated imagining should result in clearer, more vivid, and more easily accessed images that could then be mistaken for memories (Loftus, 1997).

There is a substantial body of research (reviewed in Kelley and Jacoby, 1996) indicating that the ease and fluency with which mental contents are generated are an important basis for the subjective experience of memory. In one study (Jacoby and Whitehouse, 1989), participants were given the task of determining whether each of a set of words had been on a previously studied list. A subset of the words were presented briefly just prior to participants having to judge which of the words had been on the list they had studied. Words that were presented just prior to the judgment were more likely to be "recognized" as having been on the list, regardless of whether they actually had been on the list.

The Jacoby and Whitehouse (1989) study also contained a condition in which the previewed test words were present for a long enough time to be seen clearly. Under these circumstances, previewing did not increase the probability of remembering seeing the word on the study list. Kelley and Jacoby's (1996, p. 288) explanation of this inhibition of the perceptual fluency effect is consistent with the criterion-matching step of our model: "Presumably, participants correctly interpreted the familiarity of the recognition test word as stemming from the preview." Thus, knowledge that they had seen the item in a context other than the study list may have raised their implicit criterion for judging the word as an earlier memory. The authors also noted that this "fits with the notion that the subjective experience of memory is an attribution or inference" (Kelley and Jacoby, 1996, p. 289).

The fluency or ease of access with which a mental content comes to mind can also be manipulated indirectly, by presenting participants with associates of a lure word that is excluded from the studied list, a procedure that creates false memories within recall and recognition task paradigms (Deese, 1959; Roediger and McDermott, 1995). A striking feature of these data is that false recalls and recognitions are characterized by a strong recollective experience. Subjects were asked to judge whether the critical lure was remembered vividly or whether it was just accompanied by a strong sense of familiarity, leading them to "know" that it had been on the list, without really remembering seeing it on the list. Most subjects said that they had a vivid memory of the lure's presentation among the other words in the list. This result is particularly important. Consistent with our model, it shows that a manipulation that enhances ease of access to a mental content increases the likelihood that it will be judged to be a memory.

A large body of data suggests that the effect of fluency on recognition memory can be extended to autobiographical memory. Studies have shown that simply imagining a false autobiographical event, without any other experimental manipulation, can increase people's ratings of how clearly they can remember it (Chiesi and Mazzoni, 1996) and also their belief that the event has happened (Garry et al., 1996). In addition, virtually all of the studies in which false autobiographical memories (as distinct from autobiographical beliefs that are not accompanied by actual memory reports) have been created have involved experimental manipulations in which mental contents are rehearsed, thereby making them more vivid and fluent (Hyman, Husband, and Billings, 1995; Hyman and Pentland, 1996; Loftus, Coan, and Pickrell, 1996; Scoboria et al., 2000; Spanos, 1996; Spanos et al., 1999).

Being evaluated as a memory is not in itself sufficient to determine the answer to an autobiographical memory question. If the best candidate is evaluated to be an autobiographical memory, the next monitoring task is to determine how well it fits the question that has been asked. The "spilling punch at a wedding" question, for example, may elicit an autobiographical memory of being at a wedding, and the evoked mental content may be accurately identified as a memory. The question, however, requires the event to include spilling a beverage and being eight years old. If the retrieved memory includes these two elements, the person will conclude that he or she remembers the event being asked about. Suppose, however, that the wedding is remembered to have occurred at a different age or that it does not include spilling a beverage. In this case, the person's answer about whether they can remember the event will depend on the goodness of the memory as an answer to the specific question asked and the memory criterion set for that question.

One way in which false autobiographical beliefs and memories can be created is when people have set a very low criterion of goodness of fit for determining that they remember the event referred to in the question. For example, they may overlook the importance of the age constraint or of the action of spilling punch, and they may thus accept events that had happened when they were older or when something else was poured. In this case, incorrect events would lead to a false "Yes, it happened to me" response.

One of the factors affecting the criterion for judging a mental content to be a memory is the plausibility of the event. A mental content for a relatively implausible event (e.g. witnessing a demonic possession) would have to be very compelling to be accepted as a memory rather than a fantasy. Thus, Pezdek, Finger, and Hodge (1997) showed that it was easier to lead people to report a false memory of a relatively plausible event than of a less plausible event. Catholic and Jewish children were read descriptions of two false events and were told that these events had been reported by their mothers. A Catholic mass was the setting for one of the false events, and a Jewish Shabbat was the setting for the other. None of the Jewish participants developed a false memory for the Catholic false event, but 14 percent of them created a false memory for a Jewish false event. Similarly, only 10 percent of the Catholic participants reported a false memory for the Jewish false event, compared with 31 percent of them for a Catholic event.

Note, however, that plausibility is malleable. Mazzoni, Loftus, and Kirsch (2001, Experiments 2 and 3) provided participants with printed information suggesting that two relatively implausible events (witnessing demonic possession and being threatened with kidnapping) were more common than is generally supposed in the population from which the sample was drawn. A number of steps were taken to minimize the effects of demand characteristics in this study. There was a three-month interval between the two assessments of plausibility, the plausibility measures were administered in a context that was separate from that of the experimental manipulation (i.e., they were presented as unrelated studies), and the critical events were embedded within a long list of other events. Nevertheless, this brief intervention produced significant increases in the plausibility of the events.

Autobiographical belief

To this point, we have modeled the process by which people respond to questions about autobiographical memories (e.g. "Do you remember the first time you took a train?"). We have also proposed that this process is the first stage in answering questions about autobiographical beliefs (e.g. "Did you take a train when you were a young child?"). In both cases, a search is undertaken for a memory of the event. If the result of this search is a mental content that (a) is judged to be a memory, and (b) corresponds to the event being asked about, then the person will conclude that the event happened. In cases of this sort, beliefs and memories are difficult to distinguish, and the distinction between them is relatively unimportant.

But what if no memory for the event is found (i.e., if the best candidate is judged not to be a memory of the event being asked about)? There are many autobiographical questions that can be answered affirmatively despite the absence of a memory for the event (e.g. "Where were you born?", "Did you go to the beach when you were less than three years old?", "Did you drink milk during the first year of life?").

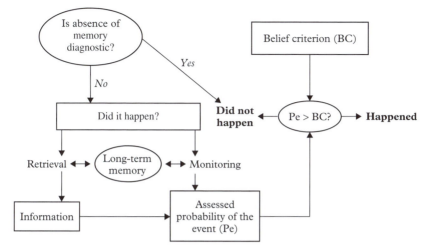

Figure 6.3 Metacognitive processes governing autobiographical belief in the absence of an autobiographical memory.

How are answers to questions about past events for which there are no autobiographical memories produced? The second stage of our model is illustrated in Figure 6.3. It portrays the process that is activated when people cannot retrieve a good enough candidate from memory.

As shown in Figure 6.3, the first step in deciding whether an unremembered event has happened is assessing whether the absence of a memory is diagnostic (Forster and Strack, 1998). This decision is taken on the basis of three metacognitive beliefs. First, people believe that the more time has elapsed between the event and the attempt to retrieve it, the greater the likelihood of forgetting. Events that occurred a long time ago are very likely to be forgotten. Therefore, the lack of memory cannot be taken as an indication that the event did not occur. Second, forgetting is also considered likely for events that happened during the first period of life. Most people believe in infantile amnesia and judge that a lack of memory cannot be taken as evidence for the nonoccurrence of events very early in life. The third type of metacognitive belief at play for this decision concerns the distinctiveness of the event. People generally believe that they would have remembered a rare or striking event (e.g. undergoing surgery), if it had occurred. Therefore, the lack of memory for an event of this sort will be interpreted as an indication that the event did not occur. Conversely, failing to remember a common event (e.g. having potatoes for dinner on a particular evening) would not be likely to lead to the conclusion that the event did not happen.

Empirical support for this step in the model was reported by Strack and Bless (1994). Participants were presented with a list comprising two categories of items: tools and non-tools. Tool items were presented more frequently on the list than non-tool items, the assumption being that the low frequency of occurrence of the non-tool items would make them more salient than the others. The results showed more false recognitions of tools that were not on the list than of non-tools that had not been on the list.

In a later study, Forster and Strack (1998) manipulated participants' metacognitive beliefs about the diagnostic value of the absence of an episodic memory. Half the participants were told that music enhanced learning and half were told that it inhibited learning. Participants then learned lists of words with and without music. When tested, false recognition of items that had been learned with music was more common among participants who had been led to believe that it would facilitate learning than among those led to believe that it would inhibit learning. These data were interpreted as indicating that the manipulated metacognitive belief altered participants' interpretations of the absence of a memory of having seen an item on the list. However, participants were not asked to distinguish between knowing something was on the list (an episodic belief) and remembering seeing it on the list (an episodic memory). Thus, the manipulations might also have affected the criterion for judging a mental content to be a memory. Thus, replication of these studies with both know and remember judgments distinguished would provide useful data.

The Strack and Bless (1994) and Forster and Strack (1998) data concern false recognition of items on a list. Mazzoni, Chiesi, and Primi (2000) reported data indicating that their findings should also apply to autobiographical events. Participants were asked to indicate the basis for their belief that an event had or had not occurred. Autobiographical beliefs about events that were considered rare or infrequent for that age (such as going to an emergency room at night) were more likely to be based on the presence or absence of a memory, whereas beliefs about events that were considered to be common (e.g. playing with sand) were more likely to be based on the inferential processes described below.

If lack of memory is considered to be diagnostic of nonoccurrence, then the response to the question "Did it happen to you?" (i.e., the autobiographical belief) will be negative. This decision can be made without having to take into account any additional information, and it therefore bypasses other steps in the model. However, if lack of memory is not considered to be diagnostic, then the decision about the occurrence of the event is based on inferential processes that determine the likelihood that the event happened. As shown in Figure 6.3, this begins with another memory search. In this case, however, the search is for various types of information, other than autobiographical memories of the event itself.

These inferential processes are based on several types of information and belief, including information that people already have and also newly provided information. They may include information about how common the event is, how plausible it is that the event happened to the individual, whether there are any objective signs or traces of the event having happened, whether they have been told that the event happened to them, and if so, by whom and with what degree of certainty. Consideration of newly acquired information, existing knowledge, and beliefs lead to an assessment of the likelihood of occurrence of the event. In answering the question "Did the event occur?" the assessed probability of occurrence is then compared with a criterion for concluding that the event occurred. If the assessed probability is higher than the criterion probability, then the answer is that the event occurred. If the assessed probability is lower than the criterion probability, then the answer is that the event did not occur.

The role of inferential processes in deciding whether an event has or has not happened has been demonstrated in a recent study (Mazzoni et al., 2000). The authors showed that in answering questions about the occurrence of autobiographical events, people realize that they make inferences using various types of information. For example, people said that they were certain that they played or that they did not play with sand before the age of three on three grounds: (a) because they remembered their playing with sand (approx. 33 percent); (b) because they were told by their parents (or others) that it occurred (approx. 27 percent); or (c) because they were making inferences taking into account where they lived, the way their parents raised them, their typical vacations, etc. (approx. 41 percent).

The inferential processes in the second stage include evaluation of newly acquired information, such as that which might be provided by an experimenter, a family member, or a therapist. Thus, in addition to altering the way an event is remembered, new information can affect the person's final decision about the occurrence of the event. This characteristic of the model is particularly important in the creation of false autobiographical beliefs. If people know that the event is extremely rare or impossible, then the rated subjective likelihood of occurrence is very low or nil. If the same people are then convincingly told that the event is plausible or more common than they had thought, the rated subjective likelihood of the event having occurred should also increase.

The hypothesis that increases in plausibility or perceived frequency of an event are associated with increases in belief has been tested in a number of studies (Mazzoni, 1999; Mazzoni and Vannucci, 1999; Mazzoni et al., 2001). In the Mazzoni and Vannucci (1999) experiments, participants were asked to read short texts reporting (inaccurately) that Italian nurseries aired classical music in a range of years that included their date of birth. This newly provided information had the effect of increasing significantly the confidence with which people reported having listened to classical music during the first days of life. A second set of studies (Mazzoni, 1999) indicated greater belief change when people are led to believe that an event has a high base rate of occurrence than when they are told that the rate of occurrence is relatively low. The third set of studies (Mazzoni et al., 2001, Experiments 2 and 3) showed that simply reading new information about the plausibility of initially implausible events (witnessing demonic possession and being threatened with kidnapping) significantly increased the confidence that they had happened.

Finally, in one of their experiments in which plausibility was enhanced by normative information on the frequency of an event, Mazzoni et al. (2001, Experiment 1) added personalized feedback falsely indicating that the event was likely to have happened to the participant. When compelling personalized misinformation was added, 18 percent of the participants came to believe that the event had happened to them. The results of these studies confirm the hypothesis that in absence of memory, people rely on inferential processes to decide if an event has happened to them or not; they support the contention that these inferential processes are applied to newly presented information, as well as to pre-existing information; and they indicate that the effect can be large enough to lead a substantial minority of people to develop false autobiographical beliefs.

From false beliefs to false memories

Because of the immaturity of the central nervous system, memories for the first day of life are nonexistent. Nevertheless, several studies have shown that after being exposed to various suggestive procedures, some people claim to remember events that happened in that period. They can be led to remember that a mobile was hanging on their crib (Spanos et al., 1999) and that classical music was played in the hospital nursery (Mazzoni and Vannucci, 1999). They can also generate their own novel events that they report experiencing as memories of the period of infantile amnesia (Malinowski and Lynn, 1999). In these studies, participants not only concluded that the events had happened, but also that they could remember them happening.

As described to this point, our model has shown how true and false autobiographical beliefs can be acquired. The question remains, how are false memories created? How is it possible that people come up with

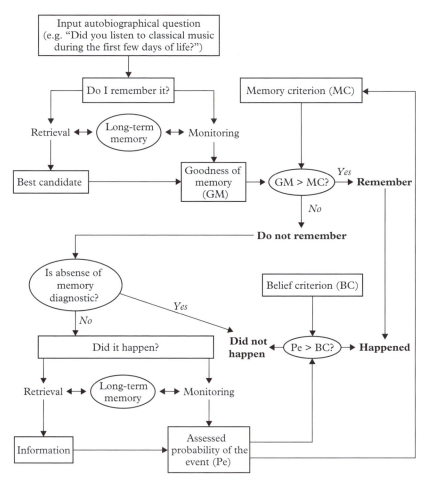

Figure 6.4 Metacognitive control processes governing autobiographical memory and belief.

autobiographical memories for events that did not happen to them? We hypothesize that two factors interact to influence the development of false memories from false autobiographical beliefs. These are (a) changes in the memory criterion; and (b) subsequent enhancement of the quality of the mental content corresponding to the event.

Figure 6.4 presents the full metacognitive model of autobiographical memories and beliefs. It is basically a synthesis of the partial models presented in Figures 6.2 and 6.3. Note, however, that an arrow has been added from the inferential conclusion that an event has occurred to the criterion for determining that a mental content corresponding to that event is a memory. Recall that the conclusion that one remembers an event depends not only on the quality of the "best candidate" mental content, but also on the person's criterion for judging the candidate to be a memory. We hypothesize that autobiographical beliefs affect this criterion. Specifically, the more likely the event is to have happened, the easier it is to conclude that a corresponding mental content is a memory, rather than merely a fantasy, imagining, etc. This is the first factor involved in converting a false belief into a false memory.

The second factor involved in the generation of false memories is enhancement of the memory content that is evaluated as a possible memory of the event. This can take many forms, all of which have in common the repeated elicitation of the content. Among the methods that can be used for this are requests to imagine the event, hypnotic and nonhypnotic age regression, and instructions to think and try to remember better.

These hypotheses are supported by two sets of findings. First, it has been found that manipulations aimed at inferentially altering autobiographical beliefs (Mazzoni and Vannucci, 1999) or imagination manipulation alone (Chiesi and Mazzoni, 1996) can also enhance memory ratings, although the increase in memory in this and similar studies is relatively low.

However, a large body of data indicates that when mental rehearsal of a false event is added to belief-enhancing information, the effect on memory can be substantial. For example, Loftus, Coan, and Pickrell (1996) reported a series of cases in which parents and siblings succeeded in persuading research participants that they could remember an event that never happened. They did this by telling the participants that the event had happened and inducing them to think about the events repeatedly.

Combining inferential belief manipulations with memory rehearsal manipulations is typical of studies in which high rates of false memories have been produced. In a series of studies conducted by Ira Hyman and his collaborators (Hyman et al., 1995; Hyman and Pentland, 1996), autobiographical beliefs were manipulated by (falsely) telling participants that their parents remembered an event to have happened. Memory was then enhanced by asking participants to repeatedly imagine the event. After this procedure 20 to 25 percent of participants were able to remember the event. In a recent extension of these studies, people were asked to imagine an equal number of false events and unremembered true events (Scoboria et al., 2000). The results indicated that participants developed new memories for the same number of false events as they did of true events.

In another series of studies, on remembering a mobile hanging over the eyes during the first days of life (Spanos, 1996; Spanos et al., 1999), beliefs were manipulated by giving participants false feedback about their visual skills and by telling them that their high visual ability was connected to looking at a colored mobile hanging on their cribs. Memory for the mobile was then enhanced by hypnosis or age regression. High percentages (46 to 56 percent) of participants in both conditions reported remembering the hanging mobile. These studies demonstrate that the combination of belief manipulations and memory enhancement manipulations can produce false memories in a substantial minority of people.

Conclusions

We have presented a two-part model of the process by which people come to report true and false autobiographical beliefs and memories. The first part of the model describes processes by which people determine whether they remember a particular autobiographical event. If they do remember it, their memory is sufficient basis for them to conclude that the event occurred. When they do not remember an event, they must first determine whether the absence of a memory can be interpreted as an indication that the event did not occur. This is done on the basis of a number of metacognitive beliefs about memory. If the absence of memory is not deemed to be indicative of nonoccurrence, a set of processes described in the second part of our model is initiated.

Many parts of the model are supported by existing research. Consistent with our model are the following findings:

- Information about a past event can modify how people remember the event (e.g. Hirt, 1990; Conway and Ross, 1984; Ross, 1989; Snyder and Uranowitz, 1978);
- Simply imagining an event can increase people's ratings of how clearly they can remember it (Chiesi and Mazzoni, 1996);
- Misinformation is more likely to produce a false memory for plausible events than for implausible events (Pezdek et al., 1997);
- Information suggesting that an event is likely to have happened can create the belief that it happened, without creating a memory of it having happened (Mazzoni, Loftus, Seitz, and Lynn, 1999);
- People have metacognitive beliefs, developed at an early age, about the way memory functions (Cornoldi et al., 1990);
- Inferentially based beliefs in the occurrence of unremembered events are very common (Mazzoni et al., in press);
- Inferential beliefs are a more frequent basis for autobiographical beliefs about common events than for beliefs about uncommon events (Mazzoni et al., 2001);

- People make use of base-rate information in deciding whether an un-remembered event occurred (Mazzoni, 1999; Mazzoni and Vannucci, 1999; Mazzoni et al., 2001);
- Credible information indicating that an event is likely to have happened to the particular individual can create relatively high rates of false autobiographical beliefs (Mazzoni et al., 2001, Experiment 1);
- A combination of misinformation indicating that an event has occurred and cognitive rehearsal of the memory candidate produces high rates of false memories (Hyman et al., 1995; Hyman and Pentland, 1996; Hyman and Billings, 1998; Loftus, Coan, and Pickrell, 1996; Scoboria et al., 2000; Spanos, 1996; Spanos et al., 1999).

Our model is based on a distinction between autobiographical memories and autobiographical beliefs. In addition to inspiring additional tests of the model, we hope that this chapter will lead researchers to take this distinction into account in future studies in the false memory domain.

NOTE

Address email correspondence to Giuliana Mazzoni at gium@att.net or mazzongi@shu.edu. Address mail to Giuliana Mazzoni, Dept of Psychology, Seton Hall University, S. Orange, NJ, 07079, USA. Preparation of this chapter has been supported by a grant from Seton Hall University.

REFERENCES

Barnes, A. E., Dunlosky, J., Mazzoni, G., Narens, L., and Nelson, T. O. (1998). An integrative system of metamemory components involved in retrieval. In D. Gopher and A. Koriat (eds.), *Attention and performance, cognitive regulation of performance: interaction of theory and application, Volume XVII*. Cambridge, MA: MIT Press.

Bartlett, F. C. (1932). *Remembering: a study in experimental and social psychology*. Cambridge, UK: Cambridge University Press.

Barclay, C. R. (1996). Autobiographical remembering: narrative constraints on objectified selves. In D. C. Rubin (ed.), *Remembering our past: studies in autobiographical memory*, pp. 94–128. Cambridge, UK: Cambridge University Press.

Brown, A. L. (1975). The development of memory: knowing, knowing about knowing and knowing how to know. In W. Reese (ed.), *Advances in child development and behavior, Volume 10*. New York: Academic Press.

Chiesi, F., and Mazzoni, G. (1996). *Alcune variabili che influenzano i falsi ricordi*. Paper presented at the meeting of Associazione Italia Psicologia, Capri.

Conway, M. A., Collins, A. F., Gathercole, S. E., and Anderson, S. J. (1996). Recollections of true and false autobiographical memories. *Journal of Experimental Psychology: General*, 125, 69–95.

Conway, M. A., and Pleydell-Pearce, C. W. (2000). The construction of auto-biographical memories in the self-memory system. *Psychological Review*, 107, 261–288.

Conway, M. A., and Ross, M. (1984). Getting what you want by revising what you had. *Journal of Personality and Social Psychology*, 47, 738–748.

Cornoldi, C. (1998). The impact of metacognitive reflection on cognitive control. In G. Mazzoni and T. Nelson (eds.), *Metacognition and cognitive neuropsychology: monitoring and control processes*, pp. 139–159. Hillsdale, NJ: Lawrence Erlbaum Associates.

Cornoldi, C., Gobbo, C., and Mazzoni, G. (1990). On metamemory–memory relationship: strategy availability and training. *International Journal of Behavioral Development*, 15, 46–58.

Deese, J. (1959). On the prediction of occurrence of particular verbal intrusions in immediate recall. *Journal of Experimental Psychology*, 58, 17–22.

Forster, F., and Strack, J. (1998). Self-reflection and recognition: the role of metacognitive knowledge in the attribution of recollective experience. *Personality and Social Psychology Review*, 2, 111–123.

Gardiner, J. M. (1988). Functional aspects of recollective experience. *Memory and Cognition*, 16, 309–313.

Gardiner, J. M., and Java, R. I. (1993). Recognizing and remembering. In A. Collins, M. A. Conway, S. E. Gathercole, and P. E. Morris (eds.), *Theories of memory*, pp. 163–168. Hillsdale, NJ: Lawrence Erlbaum Associates.

Garry, M., Manning, C., Loftus, E. F., and Sherman, S. J. (1996). Imagination inflation. *Psychonomic Bulletin and Review*, 3, 208–214.

Hirt, E. R. (1990). Do I see what I expect? Evidence for an expectancy-guided retrieval model. *Journal of Personality and Social Psychology*, 58, 937–951.

Hyman, I. E., and Billings, F. J. (1998). Individual differences and the creation of false childhood memories. *Memory*, 6, 1–20.

Hyman, I. E., Husband, T. H., and Billings, F. J. (1995). False memories of childhood experiences. *Applied Cognitive Psychology*, 9, 181–197.

Hyman, I. E., and Kleinknecht, E. E. (1999). False childhood memories: re-search, theory and applications. In L. Williams and V. Banyard (eds.), *Trauma and memory*. Thousand Oaks, CA: Sage Publications.

Hyman, I. E., and Pentland, J. (1996). The role of mental imagery in the creation of false childhood memories. *Journal of Memory and Language*, 35, 101–117.

Jacoby, J. J., and Whitehouse, K. (1996). Remembering, knowing, and feel-ing of knowing. In L. M. Reder (ed.), *Implicit memory and metacognition*, pp. 287–307. Mahwah, NJ: Lawrence Erlbaum Associates.

Johnson, M. K., Hashtroudi, S., and Lindsay, D. S. (1993). Source monitoring. *Psychological Bulletin*, 114, 3–28.

Kelley, C. M., and Jacoby, L. L. (1996). Memory attributions: remembering, knowing, and feeling of knowing. In L. M. Reder (ed.), *Implicit memory and metacognition*, pp. 287–307. Mahwah, NJ, Lawrence Erlbaum Associates.

Koriat, A., and Goldsmith, M. (1996). Monitoring and control processes in the strategic regulation of memory accuracy. *Psychological Review*, 103, 490–517.

Loftus, E. F. (1997). Creating false memories. *Scientific American*, September 1997, 72–77.

Loftus, E. F., Coan, J. A., and Pickrell, J. E. (1996). Manufacturing false memories with bits of reality. In L. M. Reder (ed.), *Implicit memory and metacognition*, pp. 195–220. Mahwah, NJ: Lawrence Erlbaum Associates.

Malinowski, P. T., and Lynn, S. J. (1999). The plasticity of very early memory reports: social pressure, hypnotizability, compliance and interrogative suggestibility. *International Journal of Clinical and Experimental Hypnosis*, 47, 320–345.

Mazzoni, G. (1999). When events become autobiographical: the role of metacognitive judgments. Paper presented at the meeting of the Society of Applied Research in Memory and Cognition, Boulder, CO.

Mazzoni, G., Chiesi, F., and Primi, C. (2000). Conoscenze autobiografiche dell'infanzia. *Giornale Italiano di Psicologia*, 27, 701–718.

Mazzoni, G. A. L., Loftus, E. F., and Kirsch, I. (2001). Changing beliefs about implausible autobiographical events: a little plausibility goes a long way. *Journal of Experimental Psychology: Applied*, 7, 51–59.

Mazzoni, G. A. L., Loftus, E. F., Seitz, A., and Lynn, S. J. (1999). Changing beliefs and memories through dream interpretation. *Applied Cognitive Psychology*, 13, 125–144.

Mazzoni, G., and Vannucci, M. (1999). The provision of new information can change beliefs and memories about autobiographical events. Paper presented at the meeting of the Society of Applied Research in Memory and Cognition, Boulder, CO.

Metcalfe, J. (1993). Novelty monitoring, metacognition and control in a composite holographic associative recall model: implication for Korsakoff amnesia. *Psychological Review*, 100, 3–22.

Nelson, T. O., and Narens, L. (1990). Metamemory: a theoretical framework and new findings. In G. H. Bower (ed.), *The psychology of learning and motivation, Volume 26*, pp. 125–173. New York: Academic Press.

Pezdek, K., Finger, K., and Hodge, D. (1997). Planting false childhood memories: the role of event plausibility. *Psychological Science*, 8, 437–441.

Roediger, H. L., and McDermott, K. B. (1995). Creating false memories: remembering words not presented in lists. *Journal of Experimental Psychology: Learning, Memory, and Cognition*, 21, 803–814.

Ross, M. (1989). Relation of implicit theories to the construction of personal histories. *Psychological Review*, 96, 341–357.

Schneider, W. (1985). Developmental trends in metamemory–memory relationship: an integrative review. In D. L. Forrest-Pressley, G. E. McKinnon, and T. G. Waller (eds.), *Cognition, metacognition and human performance*, pp. 57–109. New York: Academic Press.

Scoboria, A., Mazzoni, G., Kirsch, I., and Dugan, M. T. (2000, October). Rates of retrieval for true versus fabrication of false childhood events. Paper presented at the meeting of the Society for Clinical and Experimental Hypnosis, Seattle.

Snyder, M., and Uranowitz, S. W. (1978). Reconstructing the past: some cognitive consequences of person perception. *Journal of Personality and Social Psychology*, 36, 941–950.

Spanos, N. P. (1996). *Multiple identities and false memories*. Washington, DC: APA.

Spanos, N. P., Burgess, C. A., Burgess, M. F., Samuels, C., and Blois, W. O. (1999). Creating false memories of infancy with hypnotic and nonhypnotic procedures. *Applied Cognitive Psychology*, 13, 201–218.

Strack, F., and Bless, H. (1994). Memory for non-occurrence. Metacognitive and presuppositional strategies. *Journal of Memory and Language*, 33, 203–217.

Tulving, E. (1985). Memory and consciousness. *Canadian Psychologist*, 26, 1–12.

7 Students' experiences of unconscious plagiarism: did I beget or forget?

Marie Carroll and Timothy J. Perfect

As is often the case with research projects, what sparked our interest in the subject of this chapter – unconscious plagiarism – was a personal experience described to us by colleagues, which appears to be quite common. The experience is this: our colleagues' students believe that their supervisors have stolen their research ideas, while our colleagues believe that the idea was originally theirs, and can provide strong supporting evidence for their beliefs. The prime example we were made aware of involved a postgraduate student who accused his supervisor of having published a paper which appropriated the entire research plan for his Ph.D. The supervisor was justly outraged and amazed at this accusation. She attributed this to unconscious plagiarism of an idea that she first suggested to the student during an initial meeting at which she offered a number of suggestions to assist the student in implementing a research idea. The student was equally convinced that the paradigm he eventually adopted arose from his own intensive reading of the literature and problem-solving skills. The student conceded that at an initial meeting a number of ideas were bandied back and forth; however, he also claimed to remember the process by which he discovered how to apply a particular psychological paradigm to answer a research question in a novel way. This occurred at a date well after the initial discussion with the supervisor, and the novelty of the approach particularly impressed itself on the student's mind. He remembered the sense of pride and accomplishment he felt at having been so clever. Other feelings, such as excitement and skepticism also clearly stood out as markers of the uniqueness of this event. On the other hand, the supervisor believed that the student was an unconscious plagiarist because of the temporal sequence of events; the student had no knowledge of the paradigm in question, and its potential application, before his contact with the supervisor. At the time of first meeting the supervisor was already working on the paper that was eventually published.

While we make no judgment as to which party is more accurate in this instance, the experience will no doubt strike a chord with our readers. (And, of course, it is possible that the student independently developed

146

the idea later.) The circumstance is more or less serious, depending on the level of seniority of the student, and more or less visible and discussed, depending on his boldness. However, our reading of the existing literature on unconscious plagiarism did not appear to offer a full account of the experiences described to us. As academics and supervisors ourselves, we sought to find out why this relatively common occurrence, which can be distressing for all concerned, should give rise to such different and compelling memories.

In quite different settings, such as the commercial world of entertainment, there have also been numerous well-documented cases of plagiarism that most likely have not been deliberate (see Brown and Murphy, 1989, for a review of some of these). George Harrison was found guilty of copyright infringement for his song "My Sweet Lord" which bore too close a resemblance to the Chiffons' hit "He's So Fine" for the court's liking. Harrison admitted in court that he had heard the Chiffons' hit, but denied that he had copied it deliberately. Interestingly, the court agreed, in that they regarded his infringement as "unintentional copying of what was in (his) subconscious memory" (Dannay, 1980, cited in Brown and Murphy, 1989). Thus, the view of the court was that human creative output can be influenced by prior experience without conscious awareness. With one slight alteration, this view is close to the view of unconscious plagiarism that cognitive psychologists hold today. Instead of arguing that Harrison might have had a *sub*conscious representation of the previous hit song (which carries overtones of Freudian suppression or denial), cognitive psychologists would argue that Harrison's memory was *un*conscious. That is, Harrison may well have heard the previous hit, and stored the experience in memory. However, at the time of writing his own tune, he failed to bring this prior experience into consciousness, and so was unaware of the influence of the prior hit. Because the prior event was not remembered, Harrison might reasonably have concluded that his tune was entirely novel.

The obvious point made by both of the examples above – the Ph.D. student and George Harrison – is that a product or idea thought to be relatively novel and internally generated was in fact derived from an external source. There are explicit adverse consequences for deliberate plagiarists, but what are we to make of unconscious plagiarism? We are constantly made aware of the fact that in formal educational settings, as in the commercial world, institutional and legal sanctions against plagiarism are indicative of the fervent conviction that authorship is inherently *individual*. Critical thinking skills, such as note-taking, reading, paraphrasing, writing, and summarizing skills, have been used successfully in classrooms to decrease instances of plagiarism. In modern authorship and scholarship, the writer or researcher is deemed to be capable of working alone, autonomously, without being influenced by others. If the writer or researcher is a "true" author or scholar, the text should be an "original" text and the writer is accorded ownership of the text and ideas. In this continuum of authorship, at one extreme is the true author, recognized by their autonomy and originality. At the other extreme is the reviled plagiarist.

What follows in this chapter will, we hope, make it clear that plagiarism is not a sharply defined concept with clear-cut boundaries, but a continuum of states of belief about the source of our ideas. As Stein (1986) acknowledges: "it is interesting to note that historically, attitudes towards plagiarism have not always been negative. The problem of plagiarism may really be the problem of finding a proper mix between the ideas of the speaker and the ideas of those that have preceded the speaker." The same fuzziness of the concept is correctly noted by Roen and McNenny (1992), who state that, due to the interweaving of conscious and unconscious ideas, all writers are plagiarists to some degree. Teachers of language and culture also recognize the ambiguity of the concept of plagiarism and the complexity of relationships between texts and learning (Pennycook, 1998). Borrowing among texts necessarily invokes for them too, as well as for psychologists, concepts such as the nature of memory, the nature of language learning, the ownership of texts, the concepts of the author, authority, and authenticity, and the cross-cultural relations that emerge in educational contexts.

Despite the acceptance of such views by some, academics in general are wedded to the view that their ideas are intellectual private property which they alone own, and they often evade references to collaboration (since even collaborative writing can be seen as plagiarism in some contexts) by writing without a sense of location, as if their assumptions were self-evident. Yet these assumptions are often based on the theoretical formulations of others, or arise from lengthy discussions with colleagues.

Roen and McNenny suggest that part of the solution to these problems is a stronger sense of true collaboration, in which ideas are everyone's, not just one person's. Such liberalistic views would clearly not sit well with an academic promotion committee considering appointment on original contributions to knowledge.

Consider the task facing a student writing an assignment, a Ph.D. student writing a thesis, or an academic writing a paper: they must integrate a wide body of knowledge, and yet produce a novel, creative output. This is a difficult task, even for an experienced writer. There is evidence that students are not even clear what constitutes deliberate plagiarism anyway. Roig (1997) showed that students who are explicitly told that some material is plagiarized are sometimes unable to tell the difference between plagiarism and paraphrase. Undergraduate participants in this study were given an original paragraph and several rewritten versions of the paragraph, some of which were plagiarized (e.g. without a citation, superficially modified from the original) and some correctly paraphrased. Nearly half the students believed that the plagiarized versions were correctly paraphrased.

Leaving aside the issue of ignorance, and of deliberate plagiarism – where the author knowingly claims the work of others as their own – how can the creative writer know that what they are writing is truly their own idea? How can they know that an idea they are proposing is not one they have previously come across, but forgotten? The answer to this question, we suggest, is that they often cannot know this, due to the nature of human cognition. Not only are they apt to appropriate unconsciously the ideas of previous writers, but, we will argue here, *they have a strong sense of conviction of the originality of these ideas*. It is this conviction that we are particularly interested in. The example of the Ph.D. student accusing the supervisor of stealing an original idea emphasizes how firmly this conviction can be held. By contrast, in many laboratory studies of unconscious plagiarism, this firm conviction is an absent feature of the plagiarist's experience. Indeed the plagiarist, if pressed, might be willing to concede that an earlier (laboratory-induced) experience could possibly have been influential.

Before considering our own studies on circumstances that lead to this conviction, however, we need to look at common theoretical explanations and laboratory studies of unconscious plagiarism.

Review of previous work

Theoretical explanations: source monitoring/reality monitoring theory

Source monitoring refers to the way we make attributions about the origins of memories, knowledge, and beliefs (Johnson, Hashtroudi, and Lindsay, 1993). For example, sometimes we need to distinguish between something we have read and something we have seen, in which case we are distinguishing between two external sources. External source monitoring refers to the process of discriminating between two external sources of information such as between two utterances by different speakers. A different kind of decision – given the label of "reality monitoring" – is the distinction between something we have genuinely experienced (a "real" event), and something that we have merely imagined. Johnson and Raye (1981) proposed a reality monitoring model to account for the decision processes that people employ in deciding whether a previously experienced stimulus was "real" or "imagined"; i.e., whether information originally had an external source (obtained through perceptual processing) or an internal source (obtained through imagination and thought). They proposed that there exist differences in the relative amounts of various types of information "real" or "imagined" stimuli include, and that these differences are used to decide the source of a memory. Memories for real events tend to contain more perceptual detail (e.g. colour, sound), contextual information (e.g. temporal, spatial), and affective and semantic information, and fewer cognitive details. In contrast, memories for imagined events tend to contain less perceptual and contextual detail and more information about the reasoning, or the internal cognitive operations through which the memory was created, such as the logical process that led to the thought, or recall of the effort that went into generating it. "Compared with memories for imagined events, memories for perceived events have more sensory and contextual information, and they are more likely to give rise to supporting memories" (Johnson, 1988, p. 390).

Research on reality monitoring has shown that individuals can make striking reality monitoring errors, such as remembering the content of a dream, but attributing it to a real situation (Mazzoni and Loftus, 1996). Similarly, several studies have shown the imagination inflation effect, whereby repeatedly imagining an event increases the likelihood that a person will believe it really happened (e.g. Garry et al., 1996; Hyman and Pentland, 1996). Interestingly, in some of these studies, participants can become convinced that the imagined event really did happen, and resist suggestions to the contrary. Thus, unlike the laboratory studies of unconscious plagiarism – but like the real-world cases – there is an element of belief in these studies.

The usual investigations of memory illusions using the source monitoring framework (Johnson et al., 1993) have concentrated on the possibility of internally generated events being misattributed to external events, or confusion between two external events. Clearly there is a degree of symmetry about these studies and those on unconscious plagiarism. Unconscious plagiarism involves the misattribution of *external* to *internal* sources. Very little attention has been given to the possibility that external sources can be misattributed to internal sources, other than the small literature on unconscious plagiarism which we review below (Brown and Murphy, 1989; Landau and Marsh, 1997). Yet we believe that this is an appropriate theoretical framework for the phenomenon of unconscious plagiarism. Of course, unlike more usual situations in which source monitoring is a conscious process, in unconscious plagiarism people are not aware that they have confused two sources. They genuinely believe that they have a veridical self-generated memory.

An implication that follows from the reality monitoring framework is that unconsciously plagiarized ideas should have the characteristics of imagined memories. When people are asked to justify the origin of their plagiarized ideas (and in these studies they are often asked to say how they know that event X actually happened, or that it was imagined), the memory descriptions they give should involve reasoning responses and cognitive operations characteristic of imaginings, rather than the sensory qualities characteristic of external events. And this is indeed consistent with the explanations the graduate students have given our colleagues. The justification for knowing that, all by themselves, they formulated the key concept or the linchpin idea in the research plan, is a description of a set of cognitive operations, or trains of thought, or deductions from theory. As an example, they might say that they have a strong feeling that they generated the idea themselves because they remember deducing a rather clever application of a theory they had been reading about.

What the reality monitoring framework reveals about remembering is that attributing source in this way is a metacognitive process where decisions about phenomenal characteristics are used to make inferences about what must have occurred. The alternate view – that remembering involves directly accessing an internal representation of an experience – is inconsistent with this framework.

Experimental studies

Demonstrating unconscious plagiarism in the laboratory has proved surprisingly difficult, and, we argue here, has yet to be done convincingly. If we are to accurately model unconscious plagiarism as seen in the real world, the following are necessary:

1 When asked to generate new ideas, participants actually produce ideas that have been previously experienced (e.g. when producing a melody, people produce melodies that they have heard before);
2 The production of these ideas can be traced uniquely to the prior experience, though this is not the attribution people themselves make (e.g. they could only have generated that melody if they had heard it before);
3 Participants really believe that the idea is their own (e.g. that however the question is asked, they stand by the claim that the tune is theirs).

None of the research to date has met all three criteria. So far, the focus has largely been on points 1 and 2. Many of the limited number of studies that have been carried out on unconscious plagiarism have been conducted by Marsh and his colleagues. We argue that often these studies fail to satisfy criteria 2 and (where this is tested) 3. As an example, Marsh and Bower (1993) investigated participants' rate of unconscious plagiarism using a word-puzzle task. The paradigm they used is typical of most of the research in this area. They first asked participants to solve word puzzles (based on the game "Boggle") with a computer partner. After a delay, participants were asked to recall their previous solutions, and to generate novel solutions. Unconscious plagiarism was defined as generation of solutions previously offered by the computer partner during the first session. Significant numbers of these were claimed as the participant's own solutions. As we will show below, criterion 2 is not safely satisfied in this study.

The same paradigm has been used by others to show plagiarism of novel solutions to problems (Marsh, Landau, and Hicks,1997; Bink, Marsh, Hicks, and Howard, 1999) and generation of category exemplars (Brown and Murphy, 1989; Linna and Gülgöz, 1994). In all these studies, plagiarism is established statistically by comparing the rate of generation of solutions that had previously been encountered against the base-rate likelihood of generation of those solutions in the absence of the prior experience. Whilst this establishes that for the population of items, prior exposure increases the likelihood of that solution being offered, it is unsatisfactory as a demonstration of plagiarism for a particular item, by a particular individual, and does not satisfy criterion 2. *This is because in every case it remains true that the person could have generated that particular solution without the prior exposure.* That is, the studies do not rule out the possibility that the participants themselves could really have generated a new word from Boggle, drawing on the existing words within their mental lexicon, despite the fact that the computer partner had already generated the same word. It is just possible that the repeated word was indeed self-generated and novel to the participant. In the same way, it is conceivable that the participants did indeed generate novel ways to reduce traffic accidents or novel category exemplars and did not remember that another member of the group had also produced the same response. What sort of evidence might we require to rule out the possibility of two independently arrived-at creative solutions? There is, in fact, no definitive way this possibility can be eliminated. However, a number of suggestions present themselves. Perhaps a prior experience which did not mean much to a person at the time of exposure, but which later came to have significance, would be more likely to be unconsciously plagiarized than would an event whose significance was immediately apparent. Perhaps one is more likely to unwittingly appropriate ideas if one acquires knowledge in a domain only after being exposed to the idea, and one does not unconsciously plagiarize what one does not fully understand. When people are initially novices in a knowledge domain the requisite knowledge is not part of the repertoire at the time of the prior experience. Thus exposure to others' ideas still does not allow them to be incorporated into and integrated with a knowledge base. Our suspicion, tested explicitly in our studies described below, is that this initial state of ignorance at prior exposure actually reduces the possibility that a person could have generated that particular solution without the prior exposure. If the person later acquires expertise in the knowledge domain through formal training, this development of expertise increases the likelihood that unconscious plagiarism of others' ideas will occur. What could not initially be incorporated into a person's knowledge base now can be accommodated.

A further serious inadequacy in the studies to date is that none has really addressed criterion 3 above, concerning the level of belief that unconscious plagiarists profess about the source of the target ideas or solutions. Given that the existing literature on unconscious plagiarism fails to demonstrate the level of belief we have experienced in our students – or seen in high profile court cases – we believe that new paradigms need to be developed that address this issue. In fact, to the contrary, the laboratory research to date clearly indicates that participants who plagiarize are *not* really convinced that the plagiarized ideas are their own, and various experimental manipulations demonstrate this. A number of studies have shown that the stringency of the decision criterion, and hence the willingness of people to claim that they believe to a greater or lesser extent that they are plagiarizing, depends greatly on the type of memory test, the experimental conditions, and the type of instructions used, among other things.

For instance, Marsh et al. (1997) used a similar paradigm to that of Marsh and Bower (1993), except that they used creative problem solving as the task, instead of word puzzles (they asked groups of participants to generate ideas about how their university could be improved). During a second session one week later, participants were asked either to generate entirely novel solutions, or to state the source of previously generated solutions. They replicated Marsh and Bower's finding that participants tended to generate previously suggested solutions to a problem, even though instructed to generate entirely novel solutions. However, when asked to judge the source of solutions in a *recognition* version of the task, participants were much less likely to claim that someone else's idea was their own. The recognition task uses a more stringent criterion than the generation task. Furthermore, when similar rigorous conditions were introduced, such as increasing the likelihood that people would focus on the origin of the ideas during generation, or emphasizing that plagiarism must be avoided, the same reduction in plagiarism ensued. Conversely, conditions which reduced the subject's ability to adequately monitor the source of ideas, such as setting a time limit on the generation of ideas, had the effect of increasing plagiarism. Thus Marsh et al. suggested that unconscious plagiarism in the problem-solving paradigm is due to inefficient source monitoring when generating solutions. They argue that the resources required to think of new solutions mean that people are less careful about monitoring the source of the material. When they dedicate their resources appropriately (as in a recognition-plus-source-decision task), then plagiarism occurs much less frequently.

In similar vein, Bink, Marsh, Hicks, and Howard (1999) found that highly credible sources are plagiarized to a greater extent than are less credible sources, even though explicit memory for ideas from each source (as measured by free recall and source monitoring) was just the same. However, even the effect of credibility of source can be eliminated by having subjects elaborate on, and draw implications from, the ideas that were presented by each source. Presumably this activity refocuses the subjects' attention back to the source of the idea, and makes its origin explicit.

Studies have also shown that time delays between the initial generation of responses and the later generation of novel responses make it more likely that unconscious plagiarism will occur. Increases have been noted over one-week delays (Brown and Halliday, 1991; Marsh, Landau, and Hicks, 1997), as has participants forgetting the source of their responses. We also know that unconscious plagiarism is unrelated to either source-forgetting or -recognition, suggesting that it is separable from conscious recollection (Brown and Halliday, 1991).

The point about laxity or stringency of criteria in source monitoring is nicely illustrated in a study by Landau and Marsh (1997) where an emphasis is put on the analysis of task components in source monitoring. The initial *generation* of a solution to a puzzle in a dyad, or the later generation of novel solutions, are tasks quite different in their source-monitoring requirements to the phase of the experiment in which the subjects try to *recall* their own solutions. In the former, subjects may rely on nonanalytic information – what others have termed "familiarity" – and lax decision criteria. In the recall task a stricter, analytic, criterion for source monitoring is necessary. This was confirmed by Landau and Marsh when they manipulated factors known to influence source monitoring. Plagiarism increased and decreased with difficulty or ease of the discrimination in the task requiring high differentiation of sources (i.e., recall), but tasks requiring lax criteria were not affected.

What should not be forgotten is that, as noted by Johnson et al. (1993), source monitoring itself, as a metacognitive judgment, involves attributions varying in deliberateness. These judgments evaluate information according to flexible criteria and are subject to error and disruption.

The paradigm described in the above studies – which is really the only one that has been used to study unconscious plagiarism – struck us as problematic because it does not really mimic real-life plagiarism such as was seen in the George Harrison case, or as in our experiences with our students. In the former case, Harrison was so convinced that the work was his that he was prepared to go to court. In our students' case, they were so convinced that they were prepared to challenge their supervisors – a stressful undertaking for a Ph.D. student. Whichever way the question was put, whatever evidence was offered to the contrary, our students remain convinced that they were the creators of the idea. Satisfying criterion 3 is problematical for any studies in this area; at the very least, we suggest that methodological variations are important in establishing subjects' convictions.

Cryptic crossword studies

The literature on reality monitoring suggests a number of as-yet-untested hypotheses concerning unconscious plagiarism in real life. In our laboratory we attempted to ensure that some of the shortcomings of previous studies were addressed. We wanted to be more confident than could the authors of the studies above that when people unconsciously plagiarized in the laboratory, they really were unlikely to have generated the idea themselves. We also wanted to replicate the sorts of conditions that lead the subject to be convinced that they generated the idea; that is, we wanted to induce a strong belief that resembles the everyday experience. Although we believe that we have satisfied criterion 2 reasonably convincingly in the studies reported below, we are less confident that we have satisfied criterion 3. Evidence that induction of a strong belief in the ownership of the idea has occurred might require there to be important consequences for being mistaken. As eyewitness studies show us, there are sometimes drastic mismatches between the laboratory and the real world when the consequences of decisions differ.

Our intuition was that in order to replicate these real-world situations where postgraduate students appropriated their supervisors' ideas, we needed to design studies in which the participants could be convinced that they *could* have an ownership of the ideas, that it was entirely plausible that they could have generated them. A set of experiences needed to be created in which a subject would struggle with, and put resources into, a task. A similar sort of notion has been articulated by Wicklund (1989): it is that *acting on* an idea results in the appropriation of that idea, that the idea becomes internalized and translated into one's own language, calling into question yet again the sharp distinction between plagiarism and more unconscious influences on behavior, such as the concept of internalization conveys.

What postgraduate students do is to invest a great deal of time and effort into acquiring a body of knowledge of which they were previously relatively ignorant. In the course of this acquisition the student will indeed generate a number of research hypotheses and ideas, some of which are no doubt original. Our intuitions about effort and resources invested into a task suggested that one factor which increases the likelihood that unconscious plagiarism will occur is the development of expertise in a knowledge domain. New experts in a field are more likely to inadvertently plagiarize others' ideas than are those who lack such expertise.

People who do not know how to perform some task (such as how to solve anagrams) are more likely to later recollect the source of their attempts at performing the task (that they themselves tried to solve an anagram) than are people who learn how to solve anagrams after initial exposure to unsolved anagrams. For this latter group, familiarity, but not recollection, is likely to ensue. This hypothesis follows from well-established findings by Jacoby and Whitehouse (1989), Lindsay and Kelley (1996), and Whittlesea (1993), who found that when people are oriented to the past, they tend to attribute the facilitating influence of prior experiences to memory, but when they are oriented to other judgments, they may misattribute such memory influences to parameters relevant to those judgments, such as their knowledge of how to do anagrams. The person who lacks expertise in a domain should experience more source-specific episodic memories of tasks attempted than the expert, simply because the novice is more likely to be oriented to the past, while the expert is more likely to be oriented to what they know. Source-specifying memory – and hence recollection – is primarily available when the person is oriented to the past at study. On the other hand, a sense of familiarity will characterize the expert's judgment. When asked "Who solved this anagram?" the degree of salience of the person's knowledge base will affect the accuracy of the attribution. Under some circumstances, the person may ask whether his own expertise could explain the feeling of familiarity, especially if he has recently become an expert at solving problems of this type.

In our studies, then, we look at situations in which novices are initially required to work on problems, the solutions to which are highly unlikely to occur without training. One half of the group then receives training in subsequent sessions, and develops some expertise in problem solving. The development of a knowledge base is intended to encourage unconscious plagiarism, or misattribution of others' solutions to problems to oneself. The general paradigm is as follows: volunteers, usually university students, are asked to try to solve some cryptic clues, without any knowledge of cryptic crossword solution. Cryptic crosswords are word puzzles – superficially like ordinary crosswords – which require specialized knowledge for solution. This knowledge consists of a mixture of conventions which can be explicitly taught, and ingenuity in problem solving (e.g. solving anagrams) which is less easily taught. Inevitably, subjects feel very inadequate and baffled by what they are required to do. On some items, "assistance" is given; i.e., the experimenter provides a hint to the answer, though not the answer itself. On other items, the actual answer is provided. Finally, there is a group of items which have neither hints nor answers provided.

In subsequent sessions, the trained group participants became skilled in solving such puzzles, following formal instruction in the conventions used. A control group received no such training. Two weeks later, both groups were asked to work on and try to solve the same clues they had initially encountered (i.e., before any participant had knowledge of how to do the task). These included items that had been presented alone, with hints, or with answers. The trained group thus encountered old problems after being equipped with new knowledge, and, as suggested above, we expected that the salience of the person's knowledge base would affect the accuracy of the attribution. The question of interest was whether the trained group would be more likely than the control group to believe that they had solved an old problem themselves. Increasing rates of misattribution of external sources to internal sources – or unconscious plagiarism – relative to the control group could then only be a consequence of the new knowledge. Even more compelling evidence of this would come from a relatively greater tendency of the trained group to attribute to their own ability solutions that had actually been provided by the experimenter. So we expected that unconscious plagiarism would occur for information initially encountered prior to the development of expertise in a domain. Source misattributions of this type probably reflect an inferential process which renders self-generation of ideas a plausible option. After all, part of the training itself involved solving similar sorts of cryptic clues.

In our first experiment, all subjects were presented with cryptic crossword clues in session 1, and asked to try to solve these (e.g. "Mad save to get pot (4)" or "This one-eyed sealord sound like Nellie's boy (6)." For some of these clues, the *actual* answers ("VASE" or "NELSON") or *hints* about the answers ("an anagram of SAVE" or "abbreviate Nellie to Nel, and it sounds like Nel's son") were provided by the experimenter, while other clues were simply provided alone, with no help or answer. However, our naive subjects were unable to take advantage of these clues to solve the puzzles, since they did not understand the cryptic crossword solution process. They were then assigned at random to two groups: a control and an expertise group. The expertise group was given about an hour's training in solving cryptic crosswords; the control group was dismissed.

In session 2, which occurred some days later, both groups returned to the laboratory and commenced the solution of a set of clues. For each clue solved, the subjects had to indicate whether: (a) they were guessing the answer; (b) they had solved the clue themselves; (c) they were remembering the answer from being shown it in session 1; or (d) they obtained the answer from the hints shown in session 1. The clues presented in session 2 were the old clues from session 1 (which had been shown alone, with answers, or with hints) along with new clues never shown before.

Overall, the development of expertise through training produced more correct solutions, as might be expected. Analyses were conducted on the additional solutions that were achieved at the second test session, i.e., if the person actually managed to solve the clue at time 1, this was not scored. (Despite initial screening for subjects who were not able to do cryptic crosswords, some clues were solved in session 1, perhaps due to guessing.) We found that, as might be expected, subjects who now had some training in cryptic crossword solution solved more clues when compared to those who lacked the training. More importantly, they were more likely to claim to have solved them themselves. With regards to the proportion of unconsciously plagiarized responses, an interesting pattern emerged: the control group subjects were sensitive to the type of initial exposure they had had to the items. They claimed self-solution for 70 percent of control items, 60 percent of hint items, and 33 percent of answer items. That is, without training, participants acknowledged that different amounts of information had been available at the original test. However, the expertise group were not sensitive in their source judgments: they claimed self-solution for 70 to 75 percent of items, irrespective of the original exposure. Even though they had seen the answer previously for one third of the trials, on three quarters of those trials the expertise group believed they had solved the clue themselves. Thus, it appears that developing additional expertise in a domain causes participants to fail to acknowledge that the solution had been available previously. This compares to a rate of 33 percent in the control group for the same items. Thus, the data suggest that the development of expertise tends to lead people to unconsciously plagiarize, i.e., to fail to discriminate between material generated by themselves and material provided externally.

Unfortunately, however, there was a puzzling outcome in the proportions of correct answers given. Higher accuracy in solving clues was found for those old items that had been presented alone than for those that had been associated with hints and answers. A possible explanation for this unexpected and contradictory finding was that answers presented alone were those that the subjects had worked hardest on in the time available. The presence of hints and answers may even have been a hindrance to working on the solutions themselves.

We rectified this problem in a further experiment in which we (a) increased the amount of training given; and (b) equated the initial time spent on solution for the three conditions (control, hint, answer). In this new experiment, in session 1, prior to the training in cryptic crossword solution, all subjects worked for the same amount of time on each clue alone. After 20 seconds of such work, the clues or answers were provided for some of the items, and in all three conditions (clues, answers, control questions) an extra 15 seconds of work time was allotted. Thus, now we could ensure that all clues were properly read and worked on for a period free of the distraction of the hints and answers.

In this experiment, our assessment of unconscious plagiarism employed a more sensitive dependent measure than merely the categories of : "solved it myself," "was provided with the answer," and so on. We asked subjects to use a rating scale from 1: "worked it out entirely by myself" to 7: "I am remembering information given to me in session 1." Our findings were, firstly, that all subjects improved from session 1 to session 2 (probably as a result of practice at the task), but the trained group solved more in session 2 than did the control group. So our training manipulation was effective, even though the training was still only about 2 hours in total. (It is extremely difficult to get subjects motivated enough to spend more time learning to do an activity that may not be of great interest to them!) Did we obtain unconscious plagiarism in this study? Yes, but the detectable effect was more subtle because of the more sensitive question that we asked. When we considered previously unsolved items that were correctly solved in the second session, we found the following. For "hint" questions (i.e., where the solution had been partially provided in session 1), the trained group solved significantly more new items than the control group. Of greater interest was the fact that they were also significantly more confident that they had themselves generated the solution than were the control group; the mean confidence ratings were 5.3 for controls and 3.6 for the trained group. But this finding was not replicated for clues with answers provided. For "answer" questions (i.e., where the actual answer had been provided by the experimenter in session 1), the trained group solved more of these sorts of questions, but they were *not* more confident that they had generated the answer themselves; the mean confidence rating for controls was 5.4 and that for the trained group was 5.0. This finding is not what we expected: the new "experts" were fairly sure that they were remembering information given to them in the first session. Finally, considering the "no assistance" questions that had been presented to them without either hints and answers, the participants who had been trained solved more new questions than the control group, but they were also no more confident (mean confidence rating of 2.5) than the control group (mean confidence rating of 3.1) that they had generated the solution themselves (as indeed both groups had). This same general pattern of results was evident whether we measured only items newly solved in session 2 or all correctly solved items: unconscious plagiarism only emerges for the trained group for questions provided with hints, not for questions provided with answers. Consistent with the plagiarism results, the trained group was more likely than the control group to say that they had not previously seen hint questions in session 1 (13 percent of total responses compared to 5 percent of total responses). There were no differences for answer questions (12 percent for trained and 14 percent for controls) nor for no-assistance questions (19 percent for the trained group and 20 percent for the control group).

In an effort to explore this outcome more thoroughly, we wondered if perhaps we could distinguish the unconscious plagiarism rate of those subjects who seemed to have benefited more from training and those who seemed to have benefited less. Would there be a stronger belief from the "greater experts" that they had generated the solutions themselves? When we divided the trained group into those who improved by more than the median number of new solutions and those who fell below this standard, we did not find a greater susceptibility by the former group to unconscious plagiarism.

How to interpret these results? In both experiments, we found unconscious plagiarism increased as expertise developed. Methodologically, the second experiment was stronger than the first. Its outcome showed us that unconscious plagiarism is an effect that is experimentally demonstrable only under specific conditions. Our hypothesis was that cognitive elaboration, the development of expertise, creates a richer data base from which to draw inferences about the source of one's knowledge. From the viewpoint of the source monitoring framework, the external sources of information dominate what the untrained group remembers, but for the trained, there are both internal and external sources of information which become richly integrated. Cognitive operations brought about by increases in the knowledge base, and sensory and supporting data are incorporated into a more unified source of knowledge. When hints are given for cryptic clues, there exist optimal conditions for confidence that one generated the solution alone, since the external knowledge provided is only partial, and the subject did indeed supply some of the newly learned appropriate cognitive operations in reaching the solution. The use of these operations is monitored and contributes to the unconscious plagiarism. However, when the actual answer is provided, the external knowledge provided is complete, and the subject may rely on this alone, rather than supplying cognitive operations, to reach the solution. The provision of solutions may be less forgettable, and more associated with an external source, than in the hints condition.

Such an account is consistent with the functionalist account of memory (cf. Gruppuso, Lindsay, and Kelley, 1997): some information contributes to automatic uses of memory and is not sufficient to accomplish the task of source identification, and some information contributes to task accomplishment (i.e., identifying source) and is recollected. The information whose source is most likely to be forgotten is that which is partly externally and partly internally generated, rather than wholly external or wholly internal.

Our demonstration that the development of expertise increases the likelihood of unconscious plagiarism compared to a control condition suggests that misattributions about source are based heavily on metacognitive processes such as plausibility and other bases for decision making. The fact that the trained group was no more likely to give belief ratings indicating that they themselves had solved the problems presented alone and the problems presented with answers than the untrained group, shows the subtle recruitment of the newly gained knowledge in the hint problems. The experiment is analogous to our postgraduate students' unconscious plagiarism: discussions with supervisors will probably canvass a number of half-formed or suggestive, rather than fully-operationalized, "finished" ideas. It is this combination of external initial and subsequent internal sources that provides a most powerful condition to observe unconscious plagiarism. Beliefs about ownership of others' ideas are memory illusions, which may arise from miscombining parts of previously experienced stimuli, much as Reinitz, Verfaellie, and Milberg (1996) found for amnesics who suffer from a selective inability to intentionally remember how stimulus parts are interrelated. So rather than looking at unconscious plagiarism solely in terms of old items claimed as new, research could focus instead on old, new, recombined, and partially new productions. A relevant study here which needs further exploration is that by Tenpenny et al. (1998), who found that inadvertent plagiarism rarely occurs when people attempt to produce truly original material, not just material that is novel in a particular context. In their study, when subjects generated both real and fictitious category exemplars, they did not later inadvertently plagiarize their own fictitious category examples as they did the real examples. As we suggested above, entirely new products may be quite easily recollected in their correct context, because they are uniquely contextualized.

At this point it is appropriate to review the improvements in methodology that our studies represent when compared with those of Marsh and his colleagues. Both our studies and others' successfully meet criterion 1 above, in that people are producing ideas that they have previously experienced when asked to generate new ones. The particular strength of our studies is in satisfying criterion 2: the production of these ideas can be traced uniquely to the prior experience. We know this because our untrained group could not have generated previously unsolved clues from knowledge they had previously acquired. They lacked the necessary knowledge both at the initial session and at the later session; yet they claimed that some solutions were generated by themselves. Criterion 3 is harder, and perhaps impossible, to satisfy in the light of what we know about the external and internal sources of information which contribute to memory decisions. It is most likely, however, whenever circumstances make internal sources of information salient, the person has a greater sense of conviction about the self-generation of the idea.

Other considerations

We have considered some conditions which lead to unconscious plagiarism in naturalistic settings, in particular the development of expertise in a domain. Although any conditions which do not emphasize the source of information are likely to result in misappropriation of others' ideas, our studies showed that this is much more likely to occur when external sources of information are interwoven with internal input. There are, of course, other mechanisms which have been proposed to contribute to the misattribution of external to internal information. One such mechanism is the average difference in memory strength that might ensue from studying two classes of items (Marsh and Bower, 1993; Marsh and Landau, 1995), with plagiarized items being more available compared with items that were not later plagiarized. Others have suggested that the plagiarized and unplagiarized items involve different weightings of source monitoring decision criteria (Bink, Marsh, and Hicks, 1999), similar to those we have suggested above. As we stated, plagiarized items which are believed to have been self-generated may have different phenomenological characteristics than do unplagiarized items.

The view we are espousing – that inadvertent plagiarism is a special case of source monitoring failure – means that any impediments to efficient source monitoring arising from manipulations of contextual factors will increase the likelihood of unconscious plagiarism. Indeed, support for our view has been obtained by Macrae, Bodenhausen, and Calvini (1999), who found just that: unconscious plagiarism increased as perceptual similarity increased; cognitive distraction and retrieval context increased the difficulty of discriminating. Other circumstances associated with disruptions to efficient source monitoring such as confabulation, amnesia, and aging should all affect the likelihood of unconscious plagiarism (Johnson et al., 1993).

Our interest in translating the everyday experience of our colleagues' postgraduate students' plagiarism into the laboratory does not stop at simulating the naturalistic situation of exposure to a new body of knowledge. We intend to explore other everyday phenomena that we suspect strongly influence the likelihood of unconscious plagiarism, and the degree of belief in the plagiarized ideas. For instance, the result of repeated expenditure of cognitive effort on a topic is that the mode of expression of a particular idea will change to fit the person's own style. Thus, whilst a supervisor might present an idea in their style, the student takes away the idea and works on it. The result is an idea that becomes expressed in the student's own language. Later, the student might come to believe that the idea is theirs because the mode of expression feels more naturally theirs than their tutor's. We believe that stylistic familiarity may be one metacognitive heuristic that people employ to identify the source of ideas. Thus, ideas that become translated into one's own mode of expression are more likely to be attributed to oneself. Similarly, having subjects work on others' ideas may achieve the same outcome, internalizing and personalizing the ideas in ways that make them stylistically familiar.

Observations from everyday life also suggest that unconscious plagiarism will increase if there are multiple (irrelevant) exposures to the source of the original idea. In real life, unlike the typical laboratory paradigm, pairs or groups of individuals discuss topics over a number of meetings, with a particular idea arising only at one meeting. Such circumstances are likely to increase the rates of plagiarism since the availability of any one source will be reduced by the repetition of similar experiences. Thus, the experimental literature to date may seriously underestimate the prevalence of unconscious plagiarism in the real world because the paradigm commonly used has employed only a single prior exposure to the context, which is uniquely associated with the content. That is, in previous studies, topic X (discussion of ecology, say) is uniquely associated with person Y (the confederate in the experiment). However, in real life, such as in the Ph.D. example, the topic of interest will have been raised often, either as discussions with several people, or as internal thoughts. Likewise, the context may have been experienced often. The student may have had many discussions with the supervisor at which the critical topic was not raised. Thus, remembering the occasion on which a particular topic was discussed with a particular person may be problematic because both content and context are associated with different objects.

A further possible implication of our results (pointed out to us by Bennett Schwartz, personal communication, November 2000) is that true expertise is associated with less likelihood of plagiarism than developing expertise. So that while the postgraduate student might be at risk of unconsciously plagiarizing, the professor is much less likely to do so. Without having the necessary empirical data available, the following is speculation. However, if our view is correct, i.e., that unconscious plagiarism is likely to occur when external sources of information are interwoven with internal input, and that this state of affairs characterizes the process of developing expertise, this would logically imply that the postgraduate student is indeed more susceptible.

Summary

The everyday experience of our academic colleagues is that on several occasions their postgraduate students have unconsciously plagiarized their ideas. We have begun to explore in our laboratory several key conditions that characterize the real-life experience of a student who acquires expertise in a domain of which they were previously ignorant. Of particular interest to us was the integration of external and internal information that occurs under these circumstances, which presents the person with a difficult source monitoring task. Our studies confirmed other studies' results showing that plagiarism of "neatly packaged" finished solutions is prevalent under these circumstances. But beliefs about the ownership of ideas were stronger when the idea contained elements of internal and external processing. While we agree with most researchers that the source monitoring framework is the most appropriate model for explaining unconscious plagiarism, we believe that not enough attention has been paid to the importance of belief about the ownership of ideas, nor to the joint influence of external and internal sources of information. Finally, we reiterate that the phenomenon of unconscious plagiarism is an example of metacognitive activity in everyday life. Like all metacognitive activity, it involves a decision about the state of one's memory, inferences about the circumstances which led to that state, and guidance about how to act on that state.

REFERENCES

Bink, M. L., Marsh, R. L., and Hicks, J. L. (1999). An alternative conceptualization to memory "strength" in reality monitoring. *Journal of Experimental Psychology: Learning, Memory, and Cognition*, 25, 804–809.

Bink, M. L., Marsh, R. L., Hicks, J. L., and Howard, J. D. (1999). The credibility of a source influences the rate of unconscious plagiarism. *Memory*, 7, 293–908.

Brown, A. S., and Halliday, H. E. (1991). Cryptomnesia and source memory difficulties. *American Journal of Psychology*, 104, 475–490.

Brown, A. S., and Murphy, D. R. (1989). Cryptomnesia: delineating inadvertant plagiarism. *Journal of Experimental Psychology: Learning, Memory, and Cognition*, 15, 432–442.

Garry, M., Manning, C. G., Loftus, E. F., and Sherman, S. J. (1996). Imagination inflation: imagining a childhood event inflates confidence that it occurred. *Psychonomic Bulletin and Review*, 3, 208–214.

Gruppuso, V., Lindsay, D. S., and Kelley, C. M. (1997). The process-dissociation procedure and similarity: defining and estimating recollection and familiarity in recognition memory. *Journal of Experimental Psychology: Learning, Memory, and Cognition*, 23, 259–278.

Hyman, I. E., and Pentland, J. (1996). The role of mental imagery in the creation of false childhood memories. *Journal of Memory and Language*, 35, 101–117.

Jacoby, L. L., and Whitehouse, K. (1989). An illusion of memory: false recognition influenced by unconscious perception. *Journal of Experimental Psychology: General*, 118, 126–135.

Johnson, M. K. (1988). Reality monitoring: an experimental phenomenological approach. *Journal of Experimental Psychology: General*, 117, 390–394.

Johnson, M. K., and Raye, C. L. (1981). Reality monitoring. *Psychological Review*, 88, 67–85.

Johnson, M. K., Hashtroudi, S., and Lindsay, D. S. (1993). Source monitoring. *Psychological Bulletin*, 114, 3–28.

Landau, J. D., and Marsh, R. L. (1997) Monitoring source in an unconscious plagiarism paradigm. *Psychonomic Bulletin and Review*, 4, 265–270.

Lindsay, D. S., and Kelley, C. M. (1996). Creating illusions of familiarity in a cued recall remember/know paradigm. *Journal of Memory and Language*, 35, 197–211.

Linna, D. E., and Gülgöz, S. (1994). Effect of random response generation on crytomnesia. *Psychological Reports*, 74, 387–392.

Macrae, C. N., Bodenhausen, G. V., and Calvini, C. (1999) Contexts of cryptomnesia: may the source be with you. *Social Cognition*, 17, 273–297.

Marsh, R. L., and Bower, G. H. (1993). Eliciting cryptomnesia: unconscious plagiarism in a puzzle task. *Journal of Experimental Psychology: Learning, Memory, and Cognition*, 19, 673–688.

Marsh, R. L., and Landau, J. D. (1995). Item availability in cryptomnesia: assessing its role in two paradigms of unconscious plagiarism. *Journal of Experimental Psychology: Learning, Memory, and Cognition*, 21, 1568–1582.

Marsh, R. L., Landau, J. D., and Hicks, J. L. (1997). Contributions of inadequate source monitoring to unconscious plagiarism during idea generation.

Journal of Experimental Psychology: Learning, Memory, and Cognition, 23, 886–897.

Mazzoni, G., and Loftus, E. F. (1996). When dreams become reality. *Consciousness and Cognition: An International Journal,* 5, 442–462.

Pennycook, A. (1998). Borrowing others' words: text, ownership, memory, and plagiarism. In V. Zamel and R. Spack (eds.), *Negotiating academic literacies: teaching and learning across languages and cultures,* pp. 265–292. Mahwah, NJ: Lawrence Erlbaum Associates.

Reinitz, M. T., Verfaellie, M., and Milberg, W. P. (1996). Memory conjunction errors in normal and amnesic subjects. *Journal of Memory and Language,* 35, 286–299.

Roen, S. N., and McNenny, L. F. (1992). Collaboration as plagiarism – cheating is in the eye of the beholder. Paper presented at the 43rd Annual Meeting of the Conference on College Composition and Communication. Cincinnati, OH.

Roig, M. (1997). When college students' attempts at paraphrasing become instances of potential plagiarism. *Psychological Reports,* 84, 973–982.

Stein, M. J. (1986). Teaching plagiarism. Paper presented at the 37th Annual Meeting of the Conference on College Composition and Communication. New Orleans, LA.

Tenpenny, P. L., Keriazakos, M. S., Lew, G. S., and Phelan, T. P. (1998). In search of inadvertent plagiarism. *American Journal of Psychology.* 111, 529–559.

Whittlesea, B. W. (1993). Illusions of familiarity. *Journal of Experimental Psychology: Learning, Memory, and Cognition,* 19, 1235–1253.

Wicklund, R. A. (1989). The appropriation of ideas. In P. B. Paulus (ed.), *Psychology of group influence* (2nd edition), pp. 393–423. Hillsdale, NJ: Lawrence Erlbaum Associates.

Part 3

Metacognition in different populations

8 Metacognition in older adults: implications for application

Christopher Hertzog

Metacognition is a construct that has received considerable attention in developmental psychology, including psychological gerontology – the science of aging. As I treat it here, metacognition is a broad umbrella term that covers several related constructs: knowledge about cognition, beliefs (both about oneself and about cognition in general), and monitoring (Hertzog and Hultsch, 2000). Much of the emphasis in studies of aging and metacognition has been placed on the role of beliefs about memory and aging, both in oneself and others, and how those beliefs may influence beliefs about one's own cognitive functioning. Traditionally, beliefs have played less of a role in research by experimental psychologists interested in metacognition. This line of theory and research has typically focused on processes of awareness and judgment concerning the status of the cognitive system, concentrating on the constructs of monitoring and control achieved via utilization of monitoring (e.g. Nelson, 1996). This state of affairs seems to be changing, as scientists interested in metacognition have begun to consider the potential importance of constructs such as causal attributions in explaining the accuracy or inaccuracy of measures of monitoring (e.g. Koriat, Goldsmith, and Pansky, 2000).

The construct of metacognition has appeared in a wide variety of theoretical treatments of cognition, including theories of intelligence and problem solving (e.g. Davidson and Sternberg, 1998). For the purposes of this chapter, I focus more narrowly on the domains of learning and memory. Scientists interested in applied aspects of memory and cognition have given considerable attention to self-reports of memory functioning (e.g. Herrmann, 1982; Rabbitt and Abson, 1990). One critical question is whether older adults can accurately assess their current ability to re-member information in everyday contexts. In clinical settings, adults of all ages often present themselves complaining of poor memory. To what extent are such complaints accurate? Do they have predictive validity for actual memory impairment, as assessed by standardized neuropsycholog-ical evaluation? What are the variables that influence accuracy of memory self-reports?

169

In this chapter I treat some of the applied implications of age differences and similarities in both metacognitive beliefs and metacognitive monitoring. The chapter is divided into two major parts. The first part considers aspects of beliefs about memory, aging, and the self. First, I selectively review the literature on memory beliefs in adulthood, arguing that the available data suggest that subjective beliefs about memory can be reliably and validly assessed, and that several interesting conclusions can be drawn about the nature of such beliefs. Second, the problem of accuracy of these beliefs is reviewed in the context of a number of methodological issues that must be addressed, such as the nature of the criterion tasks used to assess the accuracy of memory complaints. Third, I review the results of a recent study (Hertzog, Park, Morrell, and Martin, 2000) that casts much of the earlier literature in a different light. Finally, I consider the implications of recent findings for applied issues and for future research on the topic of older adults and memory beliefs.

The second part of the chapter focuses on the applied implications of a fascinating feature of aging and memory monitoring. The accuracy of online monitoring of encoding and retrieval processes seems to be spared by aging, even though learning and memory are impaired (e.g. Hertzog, Kidder, Powell-Moman, and Dunlosky, 2002). John Dunlosky, myself, and colleagues have begun to translate the implications of this sparing into a new program of research on memory training programs for older adults. First, I describe the empirical literature that supports the argument of relative sparing of metacognitive monitoring, and contrast it to research results that suggest some aspects of monitoring may be impaired with aging. Second, I provide a brief description of aspects of our training program and describe some preliminary results from that program.

Beliefs about memory and aging

Adults of all ages believe that memory declines during adulthood, for themselves and for others (see Hertzog and Hultsch, 2000, for a review). The pioneering work of McFarland, Ross, and Giltrow (1992) and of Ellen Ryan and colleagues (e.g. Ryan and Kwong See, 1993) established empirical evidence that individuals hold a stereotype of declining memory and cognition as a dominant feature of aging (Heckhausen, Dixon, and Baltes, 1989; Hummert, 1990). As noted by McFarland et al. (1992), these beliefs form an implicit theory about aging and memory that can operate without explicit awareness to influence one's perception of self and others, and that can also influence behaviors in everyday life (Langer, 1989).

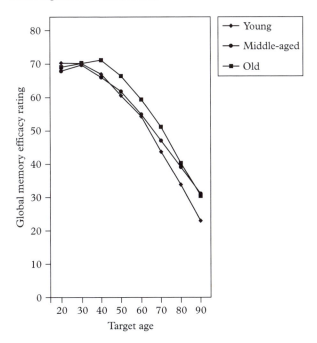

Figure 8.1 Implicit theory functions for the Global Memory Efficacy scale from the GBMI for young, middle-aged, and older adults. From Lineweaver and Hertzog (1998). © Swets and Zeitlinger. Reprinted with permission.

Lineweaver and Hertzog (1998) used a new technique to quantify implicit theories about memory and aging, using an instrument called the General Beliefs About Memory (GBMI) scale. Individuals were asked to rate the level of memory ability (generally and specific to particular aspects of memory, such as memory for names and faces). They also rated control over memory functioning, now and in the future. Respondents' implicit theories about memory change were scaled by having them rate the average adult at different age decades (from age 20 through age 90). Figure 8.1 shows the resulting data for ratings of global memory functioning for three groups of adult raters (young, middle-aged, and old). The respondents clearly perceived memory decline over the adult lifespan, one that accelerated in rate after age 50. For the most part, adults of all ages believed in substantial memory decline for the average adult. Nevertheless, there were significant age differences, with older adults believing in a longer period of relative maintenance in early adulthood. Similar patterns were also obtained for specific aspects of memory functioning. The pattern of ratings for different aspects of memory suggested

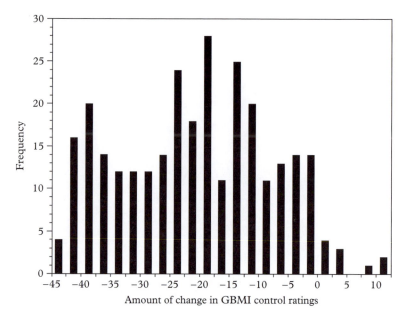

Figure 8.2 Frequency histogram of GBMI change scores for the Control over Memory rating from the GBMI. A negative score indicates perceived decline from age 20 to age 90. From Hertzog et al. (1999). © Academic Press. Reprinted with permission.

some variations that supported the construct validity of the rating method (see Lineweaver and Hertzog, 1998, for additional details). For example, individuals rated memory for names as declining more precipitously than memory for faces (consistent with familiar stereotypes) and perceived less decline in remote memory (facts learned long ago) than new episodic memories (information just learned).

There were also individual differences in ratings of change in memory and in control over memory. Figure 8.2 shows a frequency distribution of perceived changes in control over memory from age 20 to age 90. Clearly the respondents in our study varied in the magnitude of rated decline in control over memory, but decline perceptions were far more common than perceptions of stability.

The patterns shown in Figures 8.1 and 8.2 have been replicated in my laboratory (see Hertzog, Lineweaver, and McGuire, 1999). In a recent investigation, Hertzog, York, and Baldi (2001) produced virtually identical GBMI curves in a sample of young college students and a sample of community-dwelling older adults. We also used a new measure of implicit theories inspired by the GBMI. The goal was to establish convergent evidence for the implicit theory with an alternative method, while also assessing more directly the possibility that people may believe in normative decline but may preserve the possibility of memory stability or even improvement as an atypical but achievable outcome of lifespan development. Individuals were shown idealized age curves like the one depicted in Figure 8.1, and asked to rate its typicality (on a 1–7 Likert scale) and to estimate the percentage of the population that conformed to this curve. Eight different curves, or profiles, were rated, showing either some type of decline, improvement, or stability. For example, the continuous-decrement profile graphed linear decline from age 20 to 90, while the late-decrement profile looked much like Figure 8.1, except that the profile showed stability from age 20 to age 50 and decline thereafter, and an early improvement profile showed linear increment until age 50, and stability thereafter.

As hypothesized, younger and older adults both rated the three decline profiles as more typical, and estimated that the highest percentage of persons in the population conformed to either a continuous-decrement or late-decrement profile. Thus, there was general agreement between the two methods of scaling implicit theories. However, older adults had significantly higher typicality ratings and percentage estimates for the stability profile and the three improvement profiles. For example, older adults estimated that continuous improvement over the adult lifespan characterized 18 percent of the population, compared to younger adults' estimate of 8 percent. Both types of implicit theory questionnaires therefore indicate that older and younger adults believe in age-related memory decline, but that older adults perceive somewhat later onset of decline or are more likely to believe in the possibility of memory improvement. Although older adults may be somewhat more positive about memory aging than younger adults, the fact that most older adults believe in memory decline places them at risk for negative effects of those beliefs in memory-demanding situations.

Implicit theories are not inert, but instead can exert powerful influences on other beliefs and behavior. For example, Carol Dweck and colleagues have shown that two different implicit theories of academic performance exist, one that treats performance as a reflection of innate ability, the other treating performance as a reflection of skill acquisition through learning and effort (Dweck, 1999). Individuals who believe that performance reflects innate ability are more prone to test anxiety, less likely to exert effort effectively to master new material, and more avoidant of assessment situations when they are uncertain about the likelihood of success. Elliott and Lachman (1989) have suggested that older adults are in a similar bind. Societally shared beliefs about the decline of memory for the average adult are apparently internalized to apply to oneself as well. Those older adults who have an implicit theory of inevitable age decrements in memory differ from older adults who believe that memory is a skill that can be maintained over the adult lifespan. Older adults who believe in inevitable decline are more likely to attribute their own good or bad memory performance to ability, perceive aging to be the cause of their own poor performance, and are less likely to exert effort and utilize effective strategies to learn and remember (Devolder and Pressley, 1992; Lachman, Steinberg, and Trotter, 1987). Data from my laboratory suggests that attributions of memory performance to strategy and effort are associated with use of superior relational strategies to organize material at study for a free recall test (Hertzog, McGuire, and Lineweaver, 1998). Moreover, these attributions are associated with less perceived decline in implicit theories of control over memory, as measured by the GBMI (Hertzog et al., 1999).

Hertzog, York, and Baldi (2001) provided additional evidence about the link of implicit theories to causal attributions. Respondents made causal attribution ratings, on a 1–7 scale, for the importance of controllable causes (skill, effort, and importance of task) and uncontrollable causes (age, ability, heredity, and luck) for each of the different developmental profiles discussed earlier. Both younger and older adults were more likely to attribute decline profiles to uncontrollable causes than to controllable ones. However, older adults were more likely than younger adults to rate improvement profiles as being caused by uncontrollable causes. After several other rating tasks, participants received a forty-word free recall test. Correlations between the degree of emphasis on controllable causes (computed as the difference between mean controllable cause ratings and mean uncontrollable cause ratings) and free recall performance were computed. Attributional emphasis on control was unrelated to free recall in younger adults. For older adults, the controllable emphasis for the stability profile correlated 0.22 with free recall, and the controllable emphasis for the improvement profiles correlated 0.32 with free recall. This evidence suggests that, for older adults, an implicit theory of memory that promotes beliefs in the inherent controllability of positive trajectories for memory development over the lifespan promotes behaviors that enhance memory task performance.

Lachman, Bandura, Weaver, and Elliott (1995) developed the Memory Controllability Inventory (MCI) to measure whether individuals believe that decline in their own memory functioning is inevitable because of the aging process. For example, one of their Inevitable Decrement scale items states, "No matter how much I use my memory, it is bound to get worse as I get older." They compared and contrasted these beliefs with other

MCI scales, including risk for Alzheimer's disease, the expectation for dependence on others for remembering (Independence), and the belief that memory is a skill which can be practiced and maintained even in old age (Effort Utility). Individuals varied in their responses, and, as expected, internalization of negative age stereotypes was negatively correlated with the implicit theory of memory as a controllable skill.

Middle-aged individuals often report deep concern about the possibility of contracting Alzheimer's disease (Cutler and Hodgson, 1996) and are anxious about aging, in part due to deficits thought to emerge in old age (Lynch, 2000). Likewise, studies of self-rated anxiety about memory suggest that older adults may report more anxiety in memory-demanding situations (Cavanaugh, Grady, and Perlmutter, 1983; Davidson, Dixon, and Hultsch, 1991), possibly because their negative implicit theories about aging and memory heighten their sense of risk for cognitive failure and its possible implications regarding onset of chronic cognitive impairment.

Our study of implicit theories of memory (Hertzog, York, and Baldi, 2001) also included Lachman et al.'s (1995) MCI. For older adults, controllable emphasis in attributions for the stability profile correlated -0.25 with the MCI Inevitable Decrement scale and 0.27 with the MCI Independence scale. For younger adults, comparable correlations were obtained (-0.29, 0.25, respectively). Thus, adults of all ages show small but significant relationships of internalized implicit theories, as measured by the MCI, and causal attributions for successful patterns of memory aging.

Lineweaver and Hertzog (1998) provided a more explicit link between implicit theories about memory and aging and beliefs about one's own memory. They created the Personal Beliefs About Memory (PBMI) instrument that contains self-rating scales that are analogs of the rating scales used to measure general beliefs in the GBMI. Individuals rated their own memory and control over memory. Lineweaver and Hertzog showed that the age curves generated by the participants had a high degree of consistency with personal beliefs. They did so by computing a predicted score for each individual, in which the person's own age was substituted into a regression equation that described each individual's sets of ratings for persons from ages 20 to 90. In essence, the predicted score represented the rated memory level of the average individual who is the same age as the respondent. Predicted scores for different types of memory functioning were summed to create a scale measuring expected personal memory beliefs, given one's implicit theory about memory and aging. This scale correlated 0.55 with the actual personal memory beliefs. Predicted scores for control over memory, computed with the same technique, correlated 0.42

with ratings of personal control over memory. These robust relationships of implicit theories and personal memory ratings have been replicated in subsequent studies (e.g. Hertzog, York, and Baldi, 2001).

These findings suggest that people's implicit theories of memory change in adulthood may have an important influence on their current perceptions of their own memory functioning. Indeed, they raise the question of whether individuals actually access specific information about their own experiences with remembering and forgetting when they complete self-rating scales (see below). In a similar vein, McFarland et al. (1992) suggested that perceptions of change in one's own memory over the life-span are strongly influenced by one's implicit theory of change. Consistent with Ross' (1989) theory about processes of retrospection, McFarland et al. argued that individuals construct judgments about personal change by starting with the current level of perceived functioning and then working backwards in time, based upon their implicit theory about change over this time interval. This hypothesis can be contrasted with alternative hypotheses that individuals either sample episodes from their past to form the retrospective judgment or store current self-evaluations as they are formed, creating a set of temporally graded beliefs that can be accessed to construct a judgment about personal change. In essence, the idea is that individuals' retrospective judgments of personal change are not actually based on monitoring personal changes, but instead represent yet another manifestation of implicit theories of aging and change.

Hertzog, Lineweaver, and Powell-Moman (2001) found evidence consistent with this hypothesis. Personal ratings of memory change over the past ten years were strongly predicted by the amount of change the average adult was believed to experience over that same ten-year age interval. This relationship was statistically significant when controlling for ratings of one's own current level of memory functioning. Such outcomes are consistent with longitudinal findings that actual changes in level of memory performance are not strongly correlated with perceptions of memory change over that same interval (McDonald-Miszczak, Hertzog, and Hultsch, 1995; but see Lane and Zelinski, in press). In all likelihood, perceptions of change are influenced by actual experiences of remembering and forgetting, but these experiences are filtered through the lens of an implicit theory that helps determine the significance and generality attributed to such events.

Limited predictive validity of memory beliefs questionnaires

It has been known for some time that individuals' beliefs about their own current levels of memory function do not necessarily correspond to information gained from testing their memory (e.g. Sunderland et al., 1986). Subjective memory complaints or rated memory ability correlate weakly, if at all, with individual differences in memory task performance (Hertzog and Hultsch, 2000; Rabbitt et al., 1995). In fact, it is often the case that subjective memory complaints correlate more highly with depressive affect than they do with objectively measured memory performance (e.g. Bolla et al., 1991; Niederehe and Yoder, 1989). The problem is not limited to questionnaires; initial predictions of memory task performance (e.g. responses to the question "How many words will you recall in this free recall task?") often have weak correlations with performance, although individuals' predictions become more accurate after task experience (Dunlosky and Hertzog, 2000; Hertzog, Dixon, and Hultsch, 1990).

Herrmann (1982), in reviewing the early literature on memory self-reports, suggested that the weak correlations might indicate poor reliability and validity of questionnaires designed to measure beliefs about memory. However, two decades of research have consistently shown that these scales have good internal consistency and reasonable factorial validity (e.g. Hertzog, Hultsch, and Dixon, 1989). Thus, the weak relationships between subjective beliefs about one's own memory and actual memory performance cannot necessarily be attributed to poor measurement properties in the beliefs questionnaires. The scales measure something, consistently and coherently. Whether what they measure is actually the construct of interest is, of course, another matter.

The memory beliefs data summarized in the preceding section provide a possible explanation of the limited predictive validity of memory beliefs for memory performance. The current generation of memory questionnaires may tap underlying systems of beliefs that are more influenced by implicit theories about memory, aging, and age-related decline than they are by accurate monitoring of memory successes and failures (see Cavanaugh, Feldman, and Hertzog, 1998). Just as perceptions of memory change may reflect beliefs about change rather than monitoring of change, perceptions of one's current level of memory functioning may be influenced by beliefs about how persons of one's own age function. This does not necessarily imply that individuals cannot make accurate assessments of their own memory function. Indeed, social cognitive theory suggests that individuals may, in principle, be able to access different aspects of stored representations in memory, depending upon instructions, priming manipulations, explicit retrieval cues, and other factors (Wyer and Srull, 1986; Cavanaugh et al., 1998). Thus, it could be the case that individuals will generally tend to respond to memory questionnaires on the basis of rapidly accessible schemas about oneself or other persons, but that different sources of information could be interrogated, given an optimal retrieval context and sufficient motivation to spend the time and effort required for such retrieval searches.

It may be possible to design questionnaires differently so as to mitigate the influence of variables that limit validity of responses about one's own memory. Moreover, it is important that scientists question their own assumptions about the proper criteria for establishing validity of beliefs questionnaires. It is an open question whether one should expect that beliefs about one's own memory will be calibrated to differences in memory functioning between individuals. Individuals may vary in the extent to which they make social comparisons regarding memory, and they may also be differentially influenced by the strength of affective responses to memory failures when they occur. Certainly, one major issue with metamemory questionnaires is that respondents are implicitly required to construct their own standards for evaluating whether their memory is good or excellent, whether their memory problems are serious or benign, and so on. Variable criteria for rating scale thresholds could also attenuate the correlations.

Rabbitt et al. (1995) provide a good general review of a number of other possible causes of the limited predictive validity phenomenon. In many cases, self-report questionnaires require individuals to estimate the frequency of experienced memory problems or cognitive failures in everyday life (see Gilewski and Zelinski, 1986). Rabbitt et al. pointed out that older adults often report fewer cognitive lapses than younger adults in self-assessment questionnaires, and suggested that one explanation is that "as people age the demands that their environments make upon them may wane faster than their abilities, so that they may actually make fewer lapses than they once did" (p. S135). Individual differences in lifespan changes in such environmental demands could also constrain correlations between self-reports and memory performance, as could forgetting of forgetting incidents, or individual differences in optimism regarding the importance of everyday cognitive failures.

Hertzog, Park, Morrell, and Martin (2000) reviewed in detail three alternative hypotheses that could account for the limited predictive validity of memory beliefs scales. One possible explanation of the limited correlations is the practice of creating aggregate memory complaint scales that combine responses across multiple types, or domains, of memory (Rabbitt and Abson, 1990). Memory beliefs questionnaires typically sum responses over multiple items so as to increase the reliability of the beliefs scales. For example, the Memory Functioning Questionnaire (MFQ; Gilewski, Zelinski, and Schaie, 1990) queries frequency of memory problems during the past week across a wide variety of domains (e.g. remembering names, faces, phone numbers, and appointments) and then aggregates these responses into an overall Frequency of Forgetting scale. The *domain-specificity hypothesis* states that individuals' ratings vary over domains of memory, and that predictive validity will be highest when the domain of the memory task matches the domain of the self-reports. In essence, the problem of limited correlations in the aggregate is one of throwing out the baby with the bath water in the aggregation process. That is, predictive validity for specific memory tasks is diluted by summing responses over multiple memory domains (Rabbitt et al., 1995).

The second hypothesis is based on questions about whether the proper criterion variables are being used. The *ecological validity hypothesis* states that the limited predictive validity derives from the fact that subjective beliefs about memory arise in the context of everyday uses of memory, and that these aspects of everyday memory are inadequately sampled by standard laboratory tasks such as free recall of word lists (Bruce, 1985; Gruneberg, Morris, and Sykes, 1991). Indeed, Larrabee and West (1991) found somewhat higher correlations of memory complaints to memory tasks designed to have higher ecological validity (e.g. face–name learning, telephone number memory, grocery list recall). The idea, then, is that the fault lies in the disconnection between ecologically embedded beliefs and decontextualized memory tasks. As such, this hypothesis has been offered as a justification for the need for practical memory research (e.g. Herrmann et al., 1996).

Hertzog, Park, Morrell, and Martin (2000) offered a different kind of ecologically based hypothesis about predictive validity of memory beliefs scales. They termed it the *behavioral specificity hypothesis*. It states that individuals are capable of accurately reporting memory-related problems in everyday life, and that predictive validity will be maximized when the questions are specific to observable behaviors. Although this hypothesis sounds much like the ecological validity hypothesis, it differs from it because the root cause of the limited predictive validity is seen as a property of both (a) the questions included in instruments like the Memory Functioning Questionnaire (questions not specific to actual behaviors); and (b) the criterion variable employed (task performance, rather than actual behaviors). Memory-related behaviors differ from memory tasks, no matter whether the content of the tasks shows face validity. Memory operates in specific environmental contexts that may have a major influence on effective everyday memory functioning (Cohen, 1993). To the extent that individuals are aware of their successes and failures in specific situations, their self-assessments of memory-related behaviors should be more accurate than context-free self-ratings obtained by the questionnaires. However, this accuracy would only be manifested when the actual behaviors themselves were measured.

To be more concrete, consider the everyday prospective memory problem of taking medications on a schedule, as prescribed. This behavior is generically termed "medication adherence." It is only in part an issue of memory per se, because in everyday life individuals develop routines and external aids to support "remembering." In effect, people often use strategies to reduce their reliance on retrieving the intention to take their medicines (e.g. Intons-Peterson and Fournier, 1986). Individuals who distrust their memory may create the best support structure for adherence behavior – paradoxically, those who have high confidence in their memory may be at greatest risk of forgetting. The larger point is that individuals are able to monitor their memory successes and failures (e.g. Dunlosky and Hertzog, 2000), and they are presumably also able to monitor the effectiveness of their strategies for supporting adherence. Hence, individuals' reports of whether they are having difficulties remembering to take their medications as prescribed need not necessarily have a strong relationship to self-ratings of "problems with remembering appointments" or other facets of prospective memory in everyday life. More important, their ratings of the specific behaviors in question may have much better predictive validity for future problems with that behavior than their ratings of their memory in general, or their self-ratings aggregated over multiple types of memory.

From the behavioral specificity perspective, it should be possible to produce valid reports of problems with remembering to take medications, provided that (a) the questions focus on the specific behavior and guide retrieval of information about it; and (b) the specific behavior itself (in this case, actual medication adherence in everyday life) is measured as the criterion variable. With respect to the first point, the questions must provide a retrieval context that cues remembering of the behaviors of interest (and that avoids responses based on self-schemas, internalized stereotypes of decline, and so forth). With respect to the second point, it may not be sufficient to simulate the actual behavior with a laboratory task. Instead, it may be necessary to engage in naturalistic observation of the behavior in context, even though this can be practically difficult to achieve. Perhaps for this reason, the behavioral specificity hypothesis has not been previously evaluated.

Behavioral specificity in self-reported medication adherence

Hertzog, Park, Morrell, and Martin (2000) reported data relevant to the three hypotheses. The study involved the assessment of medication adherence in a sample of 121 rheumatoid arthritis patients, ages 35 to 84 (see also Park et al., 1999). Each participant filled out an extensive set of questionnaires (including the MFQ), completed a battery of cognitive tasks (including tests of episodic memory), and was interviewed about medication usage. At the time of the interview, all their prescription medications were transferred into bottles provided by the experimenter. These bottles contained special caps with a microelectronic chip that recorded the date and time the bottle was opened. In this way, their medication adherence could be unobtrusively monitored. After a one-month observation period, the bottle caps were collected and the adherence data were downloaded and processed for analysis. Thus, a critical feature of the study was its measurement of the actual behavior of interest, medication usage.

Another critical feature of the study was the nature of the medication interview. The participant had been asked to bring all prescription drugs to the interview. As each bottle was produced, the interviewer asked a series of questions about the nature of the prescription, whether the bottle label accurately described the prescription regimen, and so on. A critical question, similar to the MFQ Frequency of Forgetting scale items, asked "How often over the last month did you forget to take this medicine as prescribed?" Arguably, the physical presence of the pill bottle and the interview context established a set of effective retrieval cues that decreased the likelihood that individuals would base responses solely on self-schemas or memory stereotypes. A frequency rating was obtained for each medication, and an overall medication nonadherence variable was computed by taking the mean rating across all medications.

We correlated adherence errors in the third and fourth weeks of monitoring medication usage with the measure of forgetting to take medications, as reported during the interview. The subjective forgetting measure correlated 0.35 and 0.42 with later nonadherence ($p < 0.01$). Conversely, this measure did not correlate appreciably with any of the cognitive tasks in the measurement battery. Two trials of free recall correlated -0.06 and -0.09 with the subjective forgetting ratings, and a prospective memory task (telephoning the laboratory on a schedule provided to participants) correlated 0.02 with subjective forgetting.

Items from the MFQ Frequency of Forgetting scale were divided into three sets, reflecting three domains: retrospective memory, prospective memory, and working memory. All three of these subscales correlated between 0.20 and 0.35 with the different cognitive measures, and the pattern of correlations refuted the domain-specificity hypothesis. There was no tendency for the subscales to have higher correlations with tasks measuring their own domain of memory. For example, the (retrospective) free recall tasks had equivalent correlations with all three subscales.

However, correlations of the MFQ Frequency of Forgetting subscales with the cognitive tasks were higher than the correlations of these subscales with actual medication adherence errors. This outcome was

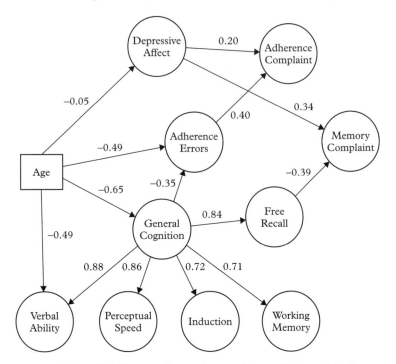

Figure 8.3 Structural equation model predicting subjective memory complaints and complaints about medication adherence from other variables. From Hertzog, Park, Morrell, and Martin (2000). © John Wiley and Sons Limited. Reprinted with permission.

inconsistent with the ecological validity hypothesis, as traditionally stated. The MFQ Frequency of Forgetting scale was more highly correlated with laboratory memory tasks than with actual medication adherence in everyday life.

We computed a structural equation model that summarized the data, and that simultaneously evaluated the influence of depressive affect and age on medication adherence errors, adherence complaints, and subjective memory functioning as measured by the MFQ (see Hertzog, Park, Morrell, and Martin, 2000, for details). Figure 8.3 shows the structural regression parameter estimates. A General Cognition factor was successfully modeled as accounting for correlations among different cognitive variables, including Perceptual Speed, Verbal Ability, and Free Recall. However, Free Recall (the latent variable formed from multiple recall tasks that measured retrospective or episodic memory) had the strongest relationship to Memory Complaint (defined by the three

MFQ subscales). The key feature of the model, however, was that Adherence Complaints were predicted by actual Adherence Errors, whereas Memory Complaints were predicted by Free Recall. This dissociation is exactly what is expected from the behavioral specificity hypothesis. Furthermore, this relationship was statistically independent of Depressive Affect. Hence one cannot argue that the relationship is an artifact of depressive affect increasing errors and elevating complaints. Finally, an interesting feature of the results was that age was *positively* related to adherence (i.e., negatively associated with adherence errors). Older adults were more adherent than middle-aged adults, even though they performed worse on the standardized measures of cognitive ability and had lower levels of subjective memory, as measured by the MFQ (see Park et al., 1999, for further discussion of this unexpected outcome).

Applied implications: aging and memory beliefs

The emerging data on memory beliefs and aging have some potentially important implications. First, the fact that middle-aged and older adults may have internalized stereotypes of decline, even when these beliefs are not necessarily accurate, suggests that they may be prone to reactive depression if critical episodes of forgetting are construed as diagnostic of impending Alzheimer's disease or memory dysfunction (Cutler and Hodgson, 1996). Moreover, these internalizations can create a self-fulfilling prophecy, in which expectations of poor memory lead to heightened anxiety and negative affect that constrain effective functioning in specific contexts (see also Levy, 1996). As a society we have succeeded in raising awareness that Alzheimer's disease is precisely that, a disease that does not afflict all older adults. Yet, knowing that "senility" is not universal in old age is cold comfort for those who may overestimate the prevalence of memory disorders and who believe, for whatever reason, that they are specifically at risk. From an applied perspective, restructuring of beliefs about the nature of memory and aging may be important for protecting the mental health of older adults, and can have practical benefits for improving memory performance in the laboratory and everyday life (Lachman et al., 1992).

Second, the pervasive implicit theory that memory declines with age can have important consequences for how older adults are evaluated and treated in today's society. Erber and her colleagues have shown that older adults' memory lapses are more likely to be attributed to aging and lower memory ability, whereas the same lapses in younger adults are attributed to factors such as motivation and effort (see Erber and

Prager, 1999, for a review). This aging double-standard can have practical consequences. For example, Kwong See, Hoffman, and Wood (2001) showed that age stereotypes about memory loss can cause older eyewitnesses to be perceived as less believable, and make mock jurors more susceptible to misinformation from younger witnesses than older ones! More generally, interviewers of older adults need to attend to the ways in which their internalized stereotypes about older adults' cognition and memory may have adverse impact on the nature of the information they receive and on the older adult whom they interview (Kwong See and Ryan, 1999).

Third, the limited predictive validity of self-reports about memory have potential consequences for how memory complaints are regarded in clinical settings. The DSM-IV (American Psychiatric Association, 1994) diagnostic category of age-associated memory impairment includes as one of its criteria subjective complaints of memory problems (e.g. Rediess and Caine, 1996). Studies suggesting that subjective memory complaints have limited predictive validity for actual memory functioning have led some to question whether subjective complaints have any utility whatsoever in clinical settings (e.g. Rabbitt and Abson, 1990). The results from Hertzog, Park, Morrell, and Martin (2000) regarding the behavioral specificity hypothesis place this literature in a somewhat different light. Questionnaires that ask individuals to rapidly rate themselves on a variety of memory domains may not have much clinical utility, given low correlations of complaints with deficiencies in memory function, as assessed by standardized tests. However, the behavioral specificity effects suggest that asking individuals about the specific behaviors that are the basis of their complaints could increase the validity of the self-reports to a degree that would make them clinically useful. Of course, this is mere speculation based on a single study, but further work validating the behavioral specificity principle and testing its possible clinical implications is certainly encouraged by our initial findings.

Finally, the studies reviewed here suggest that individuals will often answer questions about their memory based on self-schemas rather than on other mechanisms, such as a careful reconstruction of relevant past events and outcomes. Such findings are completely consistent with results from survey research (e.g. Jobe and Mingay, 1991) and with the cognitive interview (e.g. Fisher and Geiselman, 1992) suggesting that how a survey or interview constructs a retrieval context can have a dramatic impact on the validity of the responses. These outcomes suggest that new methods for constructing memory beliefs questionnaires may be needed in order to maximize their practical relevance and utility for assessing older adults' memory beliefs.

Aging and memory monitoring

One of the earliest arguments for evaluating aging and metacognition centered on the hypothesis that age-related deficits in monitoring encoding
and retrieval processes could account for age-related variance in episodic
memory (e.g. Lachman, Lachman, and Thronesbery, 1979; Perlmutter,
1978). Indeed, this hypothesis, in different forms, still persists today.
For example, Bieman-Copland and Charness (1994) argued that older
adults have deficient acquired knowledge of strategy effectiveness because
they lack the cognitive resources to monitor differential effects of variation in encoding processes on performance. Certainly, it appears that
in at least some respects older adults may experience difficulties with
source monitoring (Chalfonte and Johnson, 1996; Henkel, Johnson, and
DeLeonardis, 1998) and with discriminating between veridical memories
and gist-consistent lures (Jacoby, 1999). Such effects may reflect quali-
tatitive age differences in the kinds of information that are accessible at retrieval. However, a fairly substantial body of evidence suggests that older
adults can monitor strategic effectiveness (e.g. Dunlosky and Hertzog,
2000) and that the accuracy of their monitoring of elementary encoding
and retrieval processes remains intact, even when the memory processes
themselves are impaired (Allen-Burge and Storandt, 2000; Butterfield,
Nelson, and Peck, 1988; Connor, Dunlosky, and Hertzog, 1997; see
Hertzog and Hultsch, 2000; Lovelace, 1990, for reviews). Boundary
conditions under which age differences emerge probably exist, however.
For example, feeling-of-knowing accuracy may be deficient when older
adults lack self-efficacy or experience in a particular knowledge domain
(Marquié and Huet, 2000).

Hertzog et al. (2002) provided new additional evidence favoring the
hypothesis of age-invariance in the monitoring of encoding processes during associative learning. Older and younger adults were presented with a
list of paired associates. Their ability to monitor learning processes was
assessed by asking them, immediately after finishing study of an item,
to rate their confidence that that item would be remembered in a recall
test. These kinds of item-by-item ratings, termed judgments of learning
(JOLs), will vary between items, presumably as a function of information (or cues) that can be accessed and evaluated about probability of
item recall (see Koriat, 1997; Nelson, 1996). In order to obtain JOLs,
the stimulus–response (S–R) paired-associate item is studied, and then
the JOL is typically obtained by presenting the stimulus and requiring a
rating of the probability of response recall at a later test. For example,
after studying the S–R pair "tick–spoon" the JOL would be obtained
by presenting "tick–" and asking for a rating of subjective confidence in

later recall. This rating can be made on a number of different scales, although recent work often requests a subjective confidence on a 0 to 100 percent confidence scale (e.g. Hertzog et al., 2002; Koriat, 1997).

To the extent that an individual can effectively monitor learning, variations in JOLs between items should correlate with item recall outcomes. JOLs will also vary as a function of measurable item properties, such as word concreteness or pre-existing associations between words, as well as according to other factors that may influence degree of learning (Dunlosky and Matvey, 2001; Koriat, 1997). On the other hand, JOL accuracy is often limited because JOLs are influenced by cues that are not diagnostic of learning, such as retrieval fluency (Benjamin, Bjork, and Schwartz, 1998).

Hertzog et al. (2002) manipulated associative relatedness by randomly presenting related (e.g. king–crown) or unrelated (e.g. tick–spoon) items. Consistent with earlier work (Rabinowitz et al., 1982), older adults' JOLs were highly influenced by associative relatedness. Because relatedness was also strongly related to paired-associate learning, individuals' JOLs correlated about 0.5 (Goodman–Kruskal gamma correlations), on average, with item recall. These correlations measure relative accuracy of the judgments, ignoring the issue of calibration of scale in subjective confidence to the actual probability of item recall. There were no reliable age differences in relative accuracy within relatedness item classes (related or unrelated) when continuous JOL rating scales (0 to 100 percent confidence) were employed. Relative accuracy was relatively low within relatedness classes, however. For example, gamma correlations for unrelated items (see Hertzog et al., 2002, Experiment 3) were approximately 0.3.

A number of studies have shown that relative JOL accuracy for paired associates can be boosted by providing delayed JOLs, in which the rating is delayed until a few seconds after initial item encoding (Nelson and Dunlosky, 1991). The most plausible explanation for this effect is that the delay changes the nature of the cues accessed at the time the judgment is made. After a delay, the individual must initiate a retrieval search in secondary (or long-term) memory for the associate. Successful retrieval of the item or partial information about the item is highly correlated with probability of retrieval at a later recall test. This account is rendered more plausible by the fact that methods of obtaining delayed judgments that do not initiate a retrieval search do not produce higher relative JOL accuracy. Instances of delayed-JOL tasks that are not associated with high relative accuracy, including presentation of both elements of the S–R pair in the JOL (Dunlosky and Nelson, 1992), delayed category-level JOLs for taxonomic groups of items (Kelemen, 2000), or delayed aggregate

JOLs about information contained in prose passages (Maki, 1998), do not produce higher relative JOL accuracy. What is most important for our purposes is that there is compelling evidence that older adults also show a strong delayed-JOL effect in paired-associate learning, indicating that they can effectively use retrieval monitoring to produce accurate forecasts of later recall performance (Connor et al., 1997; Dunlosky and Connor, 1997).

The accuracy of delayed-JOLs has potential benefits for educational applications based on multitrial learning and regulation of study behavior (e.g. Thiede, 1999). Indeed, a procedure long advocated in educational research to enhance learning – self-testing – can be seen as analogous to a learning mechanism that utilizes JOLs to guide additional study behavior (Dunlosky and Hertzog, 1998). The self-testing procedure involves optimizing learning by having individuals attempt to retrieve items from memory, given a cue. For example, if one is learning a list of foreign language vocabulary, such as German, one might use cue cards that contain the English word on one side and the German word on the other side. Individuals would then self-test by showing themselves the English word (e.g. "potato") and determining whether they can retrieve its German equivalent (e.g. "Kartoffel"). Words that have already been learned (i.e., can be retrieved) would be set aside, and additional study would be allocated to words that had not yet been learned.

A large body of research suggests that learning is maximized when individuals use additional study trials to focus on items that have the lowest level of prior learning. By and large, younger adults appear to use metacognitive monitoring to allocate study time in such a normatively effective manner, although other variables influence study behavior (Son and Metcalfe, 2000; Thiede and Dunlosky, 1999). Fisher (1996), relying on quantitative models for paired-associate learning, suggested that older adults' associative learning can be optimized by tailoring how study trials and rehearsal are paced and spaced to match an older learner's acquisition and forgetting rates. It seems obvious to this author that, for this tailoring to be regulated by the older adult, rather than by an experimenter, effective metacognitive monitoring and utilization by the older learner will be required.

In some experiments, older adults have exhibited study behavior that appears to be equivalent to younger adults'. For example, both age groups are more likely, under standard paired-associate conditions, to choose items that had not been recalled at Trial N for additional study at Trial N + 1 (Dunlosky and Hertzog, 1997). However, in at least some cases older adults have appeared deficient in their utilization of monitoring to control learning. An important series of early studies in this regard was conducted by Murphy and colleagues (Murphy et al., 1981; Murphy et al., 1987). Older adults were less accurate at utilizing monitoring to determine recall readiness in a serial recall task. Murphy and his colleagues did not directly measure monitoring of recall readiness through metacognitive judgments. Murphy et al. (1987) did, however, use a think-aloud procedure and observational techniques to measure rehearsal behavior. Under standard conditions, older adults rehearsed less and performed more poorly on serial recall of supraspan lists. Forcing older adults to spend additional rehearsal time led to improvements in recall, but did not lead to more self-testing. However, instructing older adults about the potential importance of self-testing increased rehearsal, self-testing behavior, and recall performance. These results suggest that older adults can benefit from instructions to utilize monitoring to guide study behavior.

Dunlosky and Connor (1997) studied the relationship of monitoring and recall outcomes at Trial N to study time allocation at Trial N + 1. Retrieval monitoring was guided by having individuals make delayed JOLs for all items in a trial prior to a recall test. Optimal utilization of monitoring would be reflected in negative correlations of JOLs with study time of items at the next trial, because individuals should allocate more time and effort to learning items they had not previously mastered. Although older adults showed equivalent relative accuracy of delayed JOLs, their study time allocation had a significantly lower correlation with subsequent study time. Older adults could have been engaged in more maintenance rehearsal, given concerns about an increased probability of item forgetting over trials. Older adults are generally more prone to forgetting or interference in paired-associate learning than are younger adults (see Kausler, 1994), and they may have some degree of accurate metacognitive knowledge or belief regarding the possibility of item forgetting without maintenance rehearsal.

Nevertheless, the results of Dunlosky and Connor (1997), along with earlier work, suggest the possibility that older adults do not optimally utilize monitoring to guide learning. Note that the state of affairs may be even worse than indicated by these studies. The very act of measuring monitoring behavior through measuring JOLs may increase the probability of utilization of that monitoring. Age differences in spontaneous utilization of monitoring, as in self-testing behavior, may be even more profound.

Metacognitive monitoring and control: applied implications

The foregoing review of the literature on metacognition and aging has important potential impact for the design of memory training procedures for older adults (Dunlosky and Hertzog, 1998). Typically, memory training with older adults has focused on strategy training (e.g. Schmitt, Murphy, and Sanders, 1981; Yesavage and Rose, 1984), beliefs restructuring (Caprio-Prevette and Fry, 1996; Lachman et al., 1992), anxiety reduction (e.g. Hill, Sheikh, and Yesavage, 1988), or a combination of techniques (e.g. Best, Hamlett, and Davis, 1992; Stigsdotter and Bäckman, 1989). Combinations of training approaches may be optimal for achieving long-lasting training effects (Stigsdotter Neely and Bäckman, 1993). However, explicit training in the use of metacognitive monitoring to achieve self-regulation has been conspicuously absent in gerontological training research.

Recently, Dunlosky and colleagues have begun an investigation of the extent to which adding training in self-testing can enhance strategy training and other multimodal training approaches. The rationale for this approach is that training self-testing and other metacognitively based approaches will enable the learner to be more flexible in adapting learning strategies to achieve the desired level of mastery, through such techniques as selective restudy, spaced retrieval practice, and the like (see Dunlosky and Hertzog, 1998). Camp and associates have demonstrated that even memory-impaired older adults can benefit from training in simple techniques, such as spaced retrieval, that enhance everyday memory functioning (e.g. Camp et al., 1996). Arguably, metacognitive enhancement techniques like self-testing are easier to master than complex mnemonics, and may have greater applicability in everyday life.

In a first demonstration project, McGuire (2001) trained paired-associate learning. Her procedure included a pretraining procedure (targeted at dysfunctional beliefs and creating a positive attitude toward learning). Pretraining was followed by either (a) self-testing training; (b) strategy training (generation of imagery and sentence mediators); (c) a combination of the two; or (d) a practice-only control. The design also included a test–retest control with no intervening contact. A small number of approximately twenty older participants was included in each group, and the training component was relatively brief (approximately six hours of total training). McGuire detected no statistically robust training effects, but both the self-testing group and the strategy group showed an improvement in sample means on a paired-associate recall test after training. The combination group (which had the total amount of training held constant, and hence half the training in self-testing compared to the self-testing group) did not show the same level of training enhancement. However, the combination group did show significant transfer effects to a name–face associative learning task. McGuire's results suggested that self-testing training might be beneficial for older adults, but that more training (especially with combined strategy and self-testing training) would probably be needed to achieve robust training effects. Furthermore, McGuire's pre-test and post-test study were experimenter-paced. There is reason to believe that self-paced study will allow for a greater opportunity to benefit from self-testing and allocation of additional study time and effort (Dunlosky and Hertzog, 1998).

Dunlosky and associates (Dunlosky, Kubat-Silman, and Hertzog, 2002) recently carried out a larger training study at the University of North Carolina at Greensboro that also targets associative learning. In this case, more training in both self-testing and mediator strategy use was provided, in part through extensive homework practice exercises between experimenter-led sessions. The research design includes a test–retest control group, a strategy training group, and a combined strategy/self-testing training group. Experimenter-paced study conditions did not show any significant training effects on paired-associate recall. For self-paced study, the control group showed relatively stable performance between pre-test and post-test, but recall improved by about 10 percent for the standard strategy group and about 25 percent for the combined strategy and self-testing training group. Training of self-testing may be an important additional component for multimodal training programs to enhance learning and memory of older adults.

Conclusions

Research on metacognition with older adults holds great promise for enhancing the everyday functioning of older adults. Culturally determined implicit theories about memory and aging can be assessed using new techniques that measure these beliefs at the level of individuals. Self-report techniques can be enhanced so as to maximize the validity of the self-reports for indicating everyday memory problems. Through such techniques, older individuals at risk for harmful negative self-evaluation or early cognitive decline may be identified and, perhaps, assisted. Likewise, memory training programs for older adults that have had mixed success, in terms of achieving practical benefits for memory enhancement, may be improved through the adoption of a model of self-regulation based on metacognitive theory, and through the implementation of metacognitively oriented control procedures, such as self-testing.

NOTE

Research described in this chapter was supported by grants from the National Institute on Aging, one of the National Institutes of Health, to C. Hertzog (R37 AG13148) and to D. C. Park (R01 AG09868).

REFERENCES

Allen-Burge, R., and Storandt, M. (2000). Age equivalence in feeling-of-knowing experiences. *Journal of Gerontology: Psychological Sciences*, 55B, P214–P223.

American Psychiatric Association (1994). *Diagnostic and statistical manual of mental disorders (4th edition)*. Washington, DC: American Psychiatric Association.

Benjamin, A. S., Bjork, R. A., and Schwartz, B. L. (1998). The mismeasure of memory: when retrieval fluency is misleading as a metamnemonic index. *Journal of Experimental Psychology: General*, 127, 55–68.

Best, D. L., Hamlett, K. W., and Davis, S. W. (1992). Memory complaint and memory performance in the elderly: the effects of memory-skills training and expectancy change. *Applied Cognitive Psychology*, 6, 405–416.

Bieman-Copland, S., and Charness, N. (1994). Memory knowledge and memory monitoring in adulthood. *Psychology and Aging*, 9, 287–302.

Bolla, K. I., Lindgren, K. N., Bonaccorsy, C., and Bleeker, M. L. (1991). Memory complaints in older adults: fact or fiction? *Archives of Neurology*, 48, 61–64.

Bruce, D. (1985). The how and why of ecological memory. *Journal of Experimental Psychology: General*, 114, 78–90.

Butterfield, E. C., Nelson, T. O., and Peck, V. (1988). Developmental aspects of the feeling of knowing. *Developmental Psychology*, 24, 654–663.

Camp, C. J., Foss, J. W., O'Hanlon, A. M., and Stevens, A. B. (1996). Memory interventions for persons with dementia. *Applied Cognitive Psychology*, 10, 193–210.

Caprio-Prevette, M. D., and Fry, P. S. (1996). Memory enhancement program for community-based older adults: development and evaluation. *Experimental Aging Research*, 22, 281–303.

Cavanaugh, J. C., Feldman, J., and Hertzog, C. (1998). Memory beliefs as social cognition: a reconceptualization of what memory questionnaires assess. *Review of General Psychology*, 2, 48–65.

Cavanaugh, J. C., Grady, J., and Perlmutter, M. (1983). Forgetting and use of memory aids in 20- and 70-year olds' everyday life. *International Journal of Aging and Human Development*, 17, 113–122.

Chalfonte, B. L., and Johnson, M. K. (1996). Feature memory and binding in young and older adults. *Memory and Cognition*, 24, 403–416.

Cohen, G. (1993). Memory and aging. In G. M. Davies and R. H. Logie (eds.), *Memory in everyday life*, pp. 419–438. Amsterdam: Elsevier.

Connor, L. T., Dunlosky, J., and Hertzog, C. (1997). Age-related differences in absolute but not relative metamemory accuracy. *Psychology and Aging*, 12, 50–71.

Cutler, S. J., and Hodgson, L. G. (1996). Anticipatory dementia: a link between memory appraisals and concerns about developing Alzheimer's disease. *The Gerontologist*, 36, 657–664.

Davidson, H. A., Dixon, R. A., and Hultsch, D. F. (1991). Memory anxiety and memory performance in adulthood. *Applied Cognitive Psychology*, 5, 423–434.

Davidson, J. E., and Sternberg, R. J. (1998). Smart problem solving: how metacognition helps. In D. J. Hacker, J. Dunlosky, and A. C. Graesser (eds.), *Metacognition in educational theory and practice*, pp. 47–68. Mahwah, NJ: Lawrence Erlbaum Associates.

Devolder, P. A., and Pressley, M. (1992). Causal attributions and strategy use in relation to memory performance differences in younger and older adults. *Applied Cognitive Psychology*, 6, 629–642.

Dunlosky, J., and Connor, L. T. (1997). Age differences in the allocation of study time account for age differences in memory performance. *Memory and Cognition*, 25, 691–700.

Dunlosky, J., and Hertzog, C. (1997). Older and younger adults use a functionally identical algorithm to select items for restudy during multi-trial learning. *Journal of Gerontology: Psychological Sciences*, 52, 178–186.

(1998). Training programs to improve learning in later adulthood: helping older adults educate themselves. In D. J. Hacker, J. Dunlosky, and A. C. Graesser (eds.), *Metacognition in educational theory and practice*, pp. 249–275. Mahwah, NJ: Lawrence Erlbaum Associates.

(2000). Updating knowledge about strategy effectiveness: a componential analysis of learning about strategy effectiveness from task experience. *Psychology and Aging*, 15, 462–474.

Dunlosky, J., Kubat-Silman, A., and Hertzog, C. (2002). *Training metacognitive skills improves older adults' associative learning*. Unpublished manuscript.

Dunlosky, J., and Matvey, G. (2001). Empirical analysis of the intrinsic–extrinsic distinction of judgments of learning (JOLs): effects of relatedness and serial position on JOLs. *Journal of Experimental Psychology: Learning, Memory, and Cognition*, 27, 1180–1191.

Dunlosky, J., and Nelson, T. O. (1992). Importance of the kind of cue for judgments of learning (JOL) and the delayed-JOL effect. *Memory and Cognition*, 20, 374–380.

Dweck, C. S. (1999). *Self-theories: their role in motivation, personality, and development*. Philadelphia, PA: Psychology Press.

Elliott, E., and Lachman, M. E. (1989). Enhancing memory by modifying control beliefs, attributions, and performance goals in the elderly. In P. S. Fry (ed.), *Psychological perspective of helplessness and control in the elderly*, pp. 339–367. Amsterdam: North Holland.

Erber, J. T., and Prager, I. G. (1999). Age and memory: perceptions of forgetful young and older adults. In T. M. Hess and F. Blanchard-Fields (eds.), *Social cognition and aging*, pp. 197–217. New York: Academic Press.

Fisher, D. L. (1996). State models of paired associate learning: the general acquisition, decrement, and training hypotheses. In W. A. Rogers, A. D. Fisk, and N. Walker (eds.), *Aging and skilled performance: advances in theory and applications*, pp. 17–43. Mahwah, NJ: Lawrence Erlbaum Associates.

Fisher, R. P., and Geiselman, R. E. (1992). *Memory enhancing techniques for investigative interviewing: the cognitive interview*. Springfield, IL: Charles Thomas.

Gilewski, M. J., and Zelinski, E. M. (1986). Questionnaire assessment of memory complaints. In L. W. Poon, T. Crook, K. L. Davis, C. Eisdorfer, B. J. Gurland, A. W. Kaszniak, and L. W. Thompson (eds.), *Handbook for clinical memory assessment of older adults*, pp. 93–107. Washington, DC: American Psychological Association.

Gilewski, M. J., Zelinski, E. M., and Schaie, K. W. (1990). The Memory Functioning Questionnaire for assessment of memory complaints in adulthood and old age. *Psychology and Aging*, 5, 482–490.

Gruneberg, M. M., Morris, P. E., and Sykes, R. N. (1991). The obituary on every-day memory and its practical application is premature. *American Psychologist*, 46, 76–78.

Heckhausen, J., Dixon, R. A., and Baltes, P. B. (1989). Gains and losses in development throughout adulthood as perceived by different adult age groups. *Developmental Psychology*, 25, 109–121.

Henkel, L. A., Johnson, M. K., and DeLeonardis, D. M. (1998). Aging and source monitoring: cognitive processes and neuropsychological correlates. *Journal of Experimental Psychology: General*, 127, 251–268.

Herrmann, D. J. (1982). Know thy memory: the use of questionnaires to assess and study memory. *Psychological Bulletin*, 92, 434–452.

Herrmann, D., Johnson, M., McEvoy, C., Hertzog, C., and Hertel, P. (eds.) (1996). *Basic and applied memory: theory in context*. Hillsdale, NJ: Lawrence Erlbaum Associates.

Hertzog, C., Dixon, R. A., and Hultsch, D. F. (1990). Relationships between metamemory, memory predictions, and memory task performance in adults. *Psychology and Aging*, 5, 215–227.

Hertzog, C., and Hultsch, D. F. (2000). Metacognition in adulthood and aging. In T. Salthouse and F. I. M. Craik (eds.), *Handbook of aging and cognition*, 2nd edition, pp. 417–466. Mahwah, NJ: Lawrence Erlbaum Associates.

Hertzog, C., Hultsch, D. F., and Dixon, R. A. (1989). Evidence for the convergent validity of two self-report metamemory questionnaires. *Developmental Psychology*, 25, 687–700.

Hertzog, C., Kidder, D. P., Powell-Moman, A., and Dunlosky, J. (2002). Aging and monitoring associative learning: is monitoring accuracy spared or impaired? *Psychology and Aging*, 17, 209–225.

Hertzog, C., McGuire, C. L., and Lineweaver, T. T. (1998). Aging, attributions, perceived control, and strategy use in a free recall task. *Aging, Neuropsychology, and Cognition*, 5, 85–106.

(1999). Beliefs about memory and aging. In F. Blanchard-Fields and T. M. Hess (eds.), *Social cognition and aging*, pp. 43–68. New York: Academic Press.

Hertzog, C., Lineweaver, T. T., and Powell-Moman, A. (2001). *Implicit theories of aging and memory: a potent influence on beliefs about changes in one's own memory?* Unpublished manuscript.

Hertzog, C., Park, D. C., Morrell, R. W., and Martin, M. (2000). Ask and ye shall receive: behavioral specificity in the accuracy of subjective memory complaints. *Applied Cognitive Psychology*, 14, 257–275.

Hertzog, C., York, A. R., and Baldi, R. A. (2001). New measures of implicit theories about memory and aging. Paper presented at the 13th Annual American Psychological Society Conference, Toronto, Ontario.

Hill, R. D., Sheikh, J. I., and Yesavage, J. A. (1988). Pretraining enhances mnemonic training in elderly adults. *Experimental Aging Research*, 14, 207–211.

Hummert, M. L. (1990). Multiple stereotypes of elderly and young adults: a comparison of structure and evaluations. *Psychology and Aging*, 5, 183–193.

Intons-Peterson, M. J., and Fournier, J. (1986). External and internal memory aids: when and how often do we use them? *Journal of Experimental Psychology: General*, 115, 267–280.

Jacoby, L. L. (1999). Ironic effects of repetition: measuring age-related differences in memory. *Journal of Experimental Psychology: Learning, Memory, and Cognition,* 25, 3–22.

Jobe, J., and Mingay, D. J. (1991). Cognition and survey measurement: history and overview. *Applied Cognitive Psychology,* 5, 175–192.

Kausler, D. H. (1994). *Learning and memory in normal aging.* San Diego, CA: Academic Press.

Kelemen, W. L. (2000). Metamemory cues and monitoring accuracy: judging what you know and what you will know. *Journal of Educational Psychology,* 92, 800–810.

Koriat, A. (1997). Monitoring one's own knowledge during study: a cued-utilization approach to judgments of learning. *Journal of Experimental Psychology: General,* 126, 349–370.

Koriat, A., Goldsmith, M., and Pansky, A. (2000). Toward a psychology of memory accuracy. *Annual Review of Psychology,* 51, 481–537.

Kwong See, S. T., Hoffman, H. G., and Wood, T. L. (2001). Perceptions of an old female eyewitness: is the older eyewitness believable? *Psychology and Aging,* 16, 346–350.

Kwong See, S. T., and Ryan, E. B. (1999). Intergenerational communication: the survey interview as a social exchange. In N. Schwarz, D. Park, B. Knäuper, and S. Sudman (eds.), *Cognition, aging, and self-reports,* pp. 245–262. Philadelphia, PA: Psychology Press.

Lachman, J. L., Lachman, R., and Thronesbery, C. (1979). Metamemory through the adult lifespan. *Developmental Psychology,* 15, 543–551.

Lachman, M. E., Bandura, M., Weaver, S. L., and Elliott, E. (1995). Assessing memory control beliefs: the Memory Controllability Inventory. *Aging and Cognition,* 2, 67–84.

Lachman, M. E., Steinberg, E. S., and Trotter, S. D. (1987). Effects of control beliefs and attributions on memory self-assessments and performance. *Psychology and Aging,* 2, 266–271.

Lachman, M. E., Weaver, S. L., Bandura, M., Elliott, E., and Lewkowicz, C. J. (1992). Improving memory and control beliefs through cognitive restructuring and self-generated strategies. *Journal of Gerontology: Psychological Sciences,* 47, P293–P299.

Lane, C. J., and Zelinski, E. M. (in press). Longitudinal hierarchical linear models of the memory functioning questionnaire. *Psychology and Aging.*

Langer, E. (1989). *Mindfulness.* Reading, MA: Addison-Wesley.

Larrabee, G. J., and West, R. L. (1991). The association of memory complaint with computer-simulated everyday memory performance. *Journal of Clinical and Experimental Neuropsychology,* 13, 466–478.

Levy, B. (1996). Improving memory in old age through implicit self-stereotyping. *Journal of Personality and Social Psychology,* 71, 1092–1107.

Lineweaver, T. T., and Hertzog, C. (1998). Adults' efficacy and control beliefs regarding memory and aging: separating general from personal beliefs. *Aging, Neuropsychology, and Cognition,* 5, 264–296.

Lovelace, E. A. (1990). Aging and metacognitions concerning memory function. In E. A. Lovelace (ed.), *Aging and cognition: mental processes, self awareness, and interventions,* pp. 157–188. Amsterdam: North Holland.

Lynch, S. M. (2000). Measurement and prediction of aging anxiety. *Research on Aging*, 22, 533–558.

Maki, R. H. (1998). Predicting performance on text: delayed versus immediate predictions and tests. *Memory and Cognition*, 26, 959–964.

Marquié, J. C., and Huet, N. (2000). Age differences in feeling-of-knowing and confidence judgments as a function of knowledge domain. *Psychology and Aging*, 15, 451–461.

McDonald-Miszczak, L., Hertzog, C., and Hultsch, D. F. (1995). Stability and accuracy of metamemory in adulthood and aging: a longitudinal analysis. *Psychology and Aging*, 10, 553–564.

McFarland, C., Ross, M., and Giltrow, M. (1992). Biased recollections in older adults: the role of implicit theories of aging. *Journal of Personality and Social Psychology*, 62, 837–850.

McGuire, C. L. (2001). *Memory monitoring intervention for healthy older adults.* Unpublished doctoral dissertation, Georgia Institute of Technology.

Murphy, M. D., Sanders, R. E., Gabriesheski, A. S., and Schmitt, F. A. (1981). Metamemory in the aged. *Journal of Gerontology*, 36, 185–193.

Murphy, M. D., Schmitt, F. A., Caruso, M. J., and Sanders, R. E. (1987). Metamemory in older adults: the role of monitoring in serial recall. *Psychology and Aging*, 2, 331–339.

Nelson, T. O. (1996). Consciousness and metacognition. *American Psychologist*, 51, 102–116.

Nelson, T. O., and Dunlosky, J. (1991). When people's judgments of learning (JOLs) are extremely accurate at predicting subsequent recall: the "delayed-JOL effect." *Psychological Science*, 2, 267–270.

Niederehe, G., and Yoder, C. (1989). Metamemory perceptions in depressions of older and younger adults. *Journal of Nervous and Mental Disease*, 177, 4–14.

Park, D. C., Hertzog, C., Leventhal, H., Morrell, R. W., Leventhal, E., Birchmore, D., Martin, M., and Bennett, J. (1999). Medication adherence in rheumatoid arthritis patients: older is wiser. *Journal of the American Geriatric Society*, 47, 172–183.

Perlmutter, M. (1978). What is memory aging the aging of? *Developmental Psychology*, 14, 330–345.

Rabbitt, P. M. A., and Abson, V. (1990). "Lost and found": some logical and methodological limitations of self-report questionnaires as tools to study cognitive aging. *British Journal of Psychology*, 81, 1–16.

Rabbitt, P., Maylor, E., McInnes, L., Bent, N., and Moore, B. (1995). What goods can self-assessment questionnaires deliver for cognitive gerontology? *Applied Cognitive Psychology*, 9, S127–S152.

Rabinowitz, J. C., Craik, F. I. M., Ackerman, B. P., and Hinchley, J. L. (1982). Aging and metamemory: the roles of relatedness and imagery. *Journal of Gerontology*, 37, 688–695.

Rediess, S., and Caine, E. D. (1996). Aging, cognition, and DSM-IV. *Aging, Neuropsychology, and Cognition*, 3, 105–117.

Ross, M. (1989). Relation of implicit theories to the construction of personal histories. *Psychological Review*, 96, 341–357.

Ryan, E. B., and Kwong See, S. T. (1993). Age-based beliefs about memory changes for self and others across adulthood. *Journal of Gerontology: Psychological Sciences*, 48, P108–P118.

Schmitt, F. A., Murphy, M. D., and Sanders, R. E. (1981). Training older adult free recall rehearsal strategies. *Journal of Gerontology*, 36, 329–337.

Son, L. K., and Metcalfe, J. (2000). Metacognitive and control strategies in study-time allocation. *Journal of Experimental Psychology: Learning, Memory, and Cognition*, 26, 204–221.

Stigsdotter, A., and Bäckman, L. (1989). Multifactorial memory training with older adults: how to foster maintenance of improved performance. *Gerontology*, 35, 260–267.

Stigsdotter Neely, A., and Bäckman, L. (1993). Long-term maintenance of gains from memory training in older adults: two 3½-year follow-up studies. *Journal of Gerontology: Psychological Sciences*, 48, P233–P237.

Sunderland, A., Watts, K., Baddeley, A. D., and Harris, J. E. (1986). Subjective memory assessment and test performance in elderly adults. *Journal of Gerontology*, 41, 376–384.

Thiede, K. W. (1999). The importance of monitoring and self-regulation during multitrial learning. *Psychonomic Bulletin and Review*, 6, 662–667.

Thiede, K. W., and Dunlosky, J. (1999). Toward a general model of self-regulated study: an analysis of selection of items for study and self-paced study time. *Journal of Experimental Psychology: Learning, Memory, and Cognition*, 25, 1024–1037.

Wyer, R. S. Jr., and Srull, T. K. (1986). Human cognition in its social context. *Psychological Review*, 93, 322–359.

Yesavage, J. L., and Rose, T. L. (1984). Semantic elaboration and the method of loci: a new trip for older learners. *Experimental Aging Research*, 10, 155–159.

9 Sense and sensitivity: metacognition in Alzheimer's disease

Chris Moulin

> Everyone complains of his memory,
> and no one complains of his judgement.
> *François Duc de La Rochefoucauld,*
> *(1613–1680)*

Consider two presentations of patients that are typical of people attending memory clinics for neuropsychological assessment. Patient A was referred by her family doctor, after her husband had insisted that she had a professional opinion on her memory problems. She presented with a marked memory impairment, but enjoyed the testing session and joked about her memory not being as good as it used to be, but she was confident that she was scoring well in the formal assessments of memory. She could give no examples of her memory difficulties, and denied it was having any impact on her life. And yet, just the day before she had been upset that she could not remember her grandchildren's names, or recognise her sister. Patient B self-referred to see a community-based screening team and harangued his family doctor for a referral for formal memory assessment. He did not joke about his problems, but complained constantly that his memory was failing him. He gave detailed vignettes of recent memory failures, such as failing to lock up the house, but his scores on a range of memory assessments were well within the normal range. Detailed testing, history, and medical examination suggested that Patient A had Alzheimer's disease, and that Patient B was one of the group of clients called the "worried well."

Both of these patients clearly had opinions about their memory that did not relate well to their standing relative to the population norm. Patient A was unaware of her memory problem, and Patient B believed he had a memory deficit when he did not. If the clinician were to have diagnosed on the basis of these self-assessments, the wrong patient would have received medical support for their memory condition. But is there anything diagnostic about a person's awareness of memory function? Would it be possible to develop a test that measured awareness of memory processes

197

that might be diagnostic of conditions such as Alzheimer's disease? Is it that Patient A is cognitively impaired just because she is unaware?

In this chapter I describe how I have applied a metacognitive framework to research the memory processing of people with Alzheimer's disease (AD). The eventual aim is to inform clinicians of the types of task that can be used both to detect significant memory impairment in AD and to ameliorate memory loss. A metacognitive approach to memory dysfunction mostly concerns the application of strategies and mnemonics to help someone overcome their memory impairment. The keystone for the appropriateness of behavioral interventions is proficient metacognitive processing. One facet of metacognition is memory awareness – the cognizance of memory ability. If a person has no awareness of their memory deficit, how can they compensate for it in their memory-related behaviors?

Here I outline a set of studies that ascertain the status of metacognition in Alzheimer's disease, the most prevalent form of dementia. I briefly describe the cognitive profile of AD and review the literature on metacognition with list-based and item-based paradigms in AD. The main aim of the chapter is to describe a rationale my colleagues and I have used successfully to explore metacognition in memory-impaired groups: the sensitivity approach. This approach stemmed from a need to understand whether there is a contribution of metacognitive processes to the episodic deficit in AD. Its advantage is that it is not as susceptible to floor effects in recall as the traditional accuracy-based approaches to metacognition. I review the findings of some studies using this emphasis on sensitivity, discuss its strengths and weaknesses and present some novel data. With this approach, my colleagues and I find that there is little evidence that a metacognitive deficit contributes to episodic dysfunction in AD.

Alzheimer's disease

AD is a form of dementia characterized by a progressive degeneration of cognitive abilities. The Alzheimer brain develops senile plaques and neurofibrillary tangles, which are the chief neuropathological markers of the disease. These are caused by agglomerations of dead cell matter – AD patients suffer from increased cell death compared to healthy older adults. Most atrophy is in the temporoparietal and anterior frontal regions (Cummings and Benson, 1992), and plaques and tangles tend to cluster around regions that are important for memory functioning, especially the hippocampus (Arriagada, Marzloff, and Hyman, 1992). There is also a reduction in the neuro-transmitter, acetylcholine (ACh) in AD

(Corkin, 1981). The major function of ACh is as part of an arousal system involved in attention and memory.

Impaired learning and episodic memory are the behavioral hallmarks of AD, with memory impairment being a virtually universal presenting symptom. In particular, research suggests that the problem in AD is deficient encoding processes. Evidence for this comes from several sources. Firstly, studies that describe the performance of AD patients suggest they do not benefit from factors that operate at encoding to the same degree as controls. For repeatedly presented items on multiple trial learning tasks, AD patients typically show a shallower learning curve than controls (e.g. Woodward, Dunlosky, and Salthouse, 1999). Also, AD patients show little or no benefit to recall from more study time or the use of category cues at encoding (Almkvist et al., 1999) and recall is equally poor for organizable or semantically related word-lists (Herlitz and Viitanen, 1991). Secondly, studies have shown that by making up for inadequacies at encoding it is possible to equate AD patients' and controls' memory, for example by increasing presentation times in the AD group (Kopelman, 1985). Finally, AD patients do not show the typical qualities of episodic memory in their task performance: they appear over-reliant on primary memory when recalling a word list (Greene, Baddeley, and Hodges, 1996) and they show a reduction in the epiphenomena of episodic memory, for example they have source monitoring deficits (Multhaup and Balota, 1997).

In addition to a clear memory dysfunction, AD patients also show executive deficits on a range of tasks: verbal fluency (Storandt, Botwinick, and Danziger, 1986), sustained attention (Della Sala, Logie, and Spinnler, 1992), and abstraction and judgment (Moss and Albert, 1988). Because of these two facets of the disease (memory and executive function), AD has been conceptualized as a combined amnesic and executive deficit (Baddeley 1986, 1997; Becker 1987).

The premise for the present research into metacognition in AD was that the episodic memory deficit in Alzheimer's disease would have characteristics that are a function of the executive deficit. By definition, metacognitive functions surrounding memory must be 'executive' and one would expect to find clear-cut deficits in metamemory. Evidence for the role of the executive function in metacognition comes from neuropsychological studies that consider the role of the executive disorders in isolation. Executive disorders produce deficiencies in episodic memory, even though the patient is not amnesic. For example, isolated damage to the frontal lobes can impair attention, memory for temporal order, and encoding processes (Shimamura, 1994). In general, frontal deficits affect memory through poor organization and the inability to use effective strategies. Studies with head injury patients have indicated that there is a relationship between executive function and general deficit awareness: people who perform badly on tests of executive function are also likely to be unaware of their cognitive deficits (Stuss, 1991).

The rationale for the work described here was straightforward. There is evidence that metacognition and deficit awareness are executive in nature and that the cognitive profile of AD is, in part, dysexecutive. It is conceivable that impaired metacognition is one aspect of the executive deficit in AD. Specifically, my colleagues and I were interested in applying a metacognitive framework to the episodic dysfunction in AD, in an attempt to explain and ultimately remedy the memory impairment found in AD. Given that the most debilitating part of the disease is deficient episodic memory, and that this seems mostly to be due to a failure during encoding, these areas were the foci of the research reported here.

Metacognitive accuracy and metacognitive sensitivity

Most studies of metacognition in memory-impaired groups use an accuracy-based methodology, where a participant's metacognitive assessment of performance is compared with their actual performance.[1] That is, subjective assessments (e.g. a prediction of recall following study) are compared with objective data (e.g. recall of an item). Following convention, a group or an individual is metacognitively impaired when their assessment does not accurately correspond with their actual performance. This approach is sufficient for comparing different types of metacognitive judgments in normal populations. For example, Dunlosky and Nelson (1992) showed that predictions of future performance were much more accurate after a delay than immediately. (For a review of empirical measures associated with the control and monitoring framework see Nelson and Narens [1990]; and see Schwartz and Metcalfe [1994] for comparison of different paradigms.) It is this emphasis on the accuracy of predictions that has characterized previous research into metacognition

---

[1] Accuracy is described as either relative or absolute (cf. micro- versus macroprediction, Schwartz and Metcalfe, 1994). Absolute accuracy refers to whether a judgment is calibrated to actual memory performance (i.e., whether 20 percent of items assigned to the 20 percent confidence bin are recalled, and 80 percent of the 80 percent confidence items are recalled). Relative accuracy is independent of the overall levels of prediction and performance. It considers whether an item with 20 percent confidence is less likely to be recalled than an 80 percent item. Here I group the relative and absolute measures together because they both consider how accurate judgments are in whether they relate to performance or not. In contrast, our sensitivity approach is ultimately unconnected to memory performance.

in AD. Almost without exception, these previous studies show a poor relation between AD patients' assessment of performance and how they actually perform (for a review of the AD metacognition literature see below).

My colleagues and I argued that there are logical difficulties in concluding that people with AD have impaired metacognition on this kind of evidence. It is inferred that metamemory is inaccurate when participants' predictions of performance fail to relate to how they actually perform: a word that has been recalled should have been predicted as being more likely to be recalled than a word that was not recalled. Problems arise with this approach when testing participants who have an episodic memory impairment, because their likelihood of remembering *any* item is at floor. Memory performance is often so poor that it makes statistical comparisons of groups' metacognitive abilities impossible, or at least difficult to interpret.

In addition, the reason that metamemory judgments lack predictive power at test may be because of processes that occur after encoding. AD participants could be making appropriate predictions of recall during study that would be predictive were it not for the separate episodic memory deficit. That is, participants may accurately monitor the difficulty of different items to be learned, and may take appropriate steps to control their encoding to achieve learning. Using accuracy-based measures of metacognition does not allow one to focus on what occurred during study. Given that the episodic dysfunction in AD is likely to result from an encoding deficit, it would be advantageous to understand metacognitive processes during encoding.

The sensitivity approach is best summarized by taking an extreme analogy. The accuracy approach would not be very useful in memory experiments on undergraduates with very long intervals (e.g. one year). Judgments of learning would not predict future performance very well, but it would not be inferred from this that accurate metacognition was absent at encoding. In this way, sensitivity considers the appropriateness of judgments made at encoding regardless of subsequent performance.

My colleagues and I adopted Nelson and Narens' (1990) framework where metacognition is conceptualized as flows of information from the object level to the meta level (monitoring) and from the meta level to the object level (control). A to-be-remembered stimulus forms the object level and a representation of that stimulus forms the meta level. In this framework, memory is a reflective process: monitoring involves the assessment of the registration of a stimulus in memory and controlling entails the manipulation of the stimulus or processing to achieve optimum performance. Through feedback, control and monitoring ensures efficient memory processing. Monitoring evaluates the registration of an item and control is applied until the processing is sufficient. Such a model is pertinent to memory impairment: does an inability to control and monitor memory contribute to the memory impairment in AD? Moreover, because learning can be thought of as a reflective process dependent on this system, then evaluation of control and monitoring is central to the successful application of behavioral interventions in AD. If control and monitoring of memory is deficient in AD then the introduction of strategies and mnemonics to compensate for inadequacies in encoding in AD seems futile. However, if a deficit in either control or monitoring in isolation was part of the cognitive dysfunction in AD then practitioners could better target behavioral interventions.

I review some studies of sensitivity during encoding. The reasoning is simple; if metacognition is intact at encoding in AD, then memory monitoring and control by participants with AD should be as sensitive as normals to differences at the object level. In the experiments reported here, participants study words or lists that have been selected on the basis of objective measures or 'normative' assessments of difficulty. Participants make predictions of future performance or allocate study time for these words. Following convention, predicting future recall is a measure of memory monitoring, whereas recall readiness is a measure of memory control. Traditionally, measures of metacognitive accuracy examine whether the ratings and study times of the AD patients are predictive of the performance measure.

Here I present work from two separate fields: global judgments and item judgments. Both sections start with a consideration of previous research into AD and metacognition. Global judgments are assessments of performance for a whole set of items (e.g. predicting the level of recall for a ten-item list). Item judgments consider performance for individual stimuli (e.g. assessing the certainty that a particular word will be recalled). For global judgments I examined the shift in predictions between a prediction made before study and a prediction made after study. For item judgments I examined predictions made for items that have various objective properties. In all of the studies reported here, I recruited participants with a diagnosis of AD made by an independent clinician. Participants with a history of stroke or depression were excluded from the study. The mean mini-mental state examination scores (Folstein, Folstein, and McHugh, 1975) ranged from 15 to 22, indicating that these participants were relatively early in the disease process: all participants were living independently in the community and were able to give their own consent to the study. The control groups were of a similar background, age, and level of education.

Metacognition in Alzheimer's disease: global judgments and midpoint anchoring

Much research into a possible metacognitive deficit in AD stems from a clinical interest in a deficit in disease awareness (anosognosia). Studies of awareness are simple: they ask people whether they think they are cognitively impaired, or diseased, and then compare these ratings to objective measures. From this sort of study, there is strong evidence for anosognosia in early AD (Joynt and Shoulson, 1985; McGlynn and Kaszniak, 1991; Reisberg et al., 1985; Schneck, Reisberg, and Ferris, 1982).

Most studies use a more memory-orientated task to assess awareness in AD, and make claims specific to memory impairment. The most prevalent method has been a global judgment approach, where participants are asked to predict performance on a whole list of items. Within a memory task, participants predict the number of items they will remember, and this is compared with the number of items they subsequently recall. McGlynn and Kaszniak (1991) examined the discrepancy between predicted and actual performance on a variety of tasks in this manner. They found that there were significant differences in AD patients' and controls' discrepancies between performance and prediction for immediate and delayed word recall, immediate and delayed picture recall, delayed picture recognition, digit span, verbal span, and verbal fluency. There were no significant differences (i.e., patients were not significantly more discrepant than controls) for other tasks: immediate and delayed word recognition, immediate picture recognition, and spatial span. A cogent feature of this study is that it establishes that the metacognitive deficit found in AD is not merely an inability to estimate performance in general using a global judgment. McGlynn and Kaszniak found that AD patients are not impaired at predicting other people's performance even though they are impaired at predicting their own. The most compelling evidence for a metacognitive deficit in AD is that participants can be unaware of their own poor performance, whilst they remain aware of the cognitive functioning of their spouses (e.g. Reisberg et al., 1985).

Global predictions of performance vary according to the point at which they are made. Some studies use predictions, i.e., estimations of performance before test (e.g. Schacter et al., 1986; McGlynn and Kaszniak, 1991), whereas others use postdictions, i.e., estimates of performance after test (e.g. Lopez et al., 1994). Regardless of when the judgment is made, studies assessing the accuracy of predictive and postdictive predictions have identified, without exception, that AD patients overestimate their actual performance. From this evidence, researchers concluded that metacognition is impaired in AD (e.g. Schacter et al., 1986; Correa, Graves, and Costa, 1996; McGlynn and Kaszniak, 1991).

My colleagues and I argued that one aspect of memory monitoring was overlooked in these previous studies of global judgments in AD: the relative pattern of participants' judgments. Although the AD group overestimates their performance, they may still be monitoring memory proficiently. AD patients could be making judgments that are sensitive to their cognitive processes at encoding, but which are poorly calibrated with regards to final recall. To assess this possibility, predictions made before and after study were compared in AD patients. According to Nelson and Narens' (1990) framework, participants who alter their predictions according to exposure to the to-be-remembered list must be basing their judgments on memory monitoring. There is evidence that both the young and old became more accurate at predicting performance between a prediction made before study, and a prediction made after study (Connor, Dunlosky, and Hertzog, 1997). Would AD participants show the same sensitivity to factors operating during encoding – would they show a shift between predictions before and after study?

There was some evidence that despite overestimating performance, AD participants do monitor performance, which led to the expectation that AD patients would be sensitive during encoding. Lopez et al. (1994) investigated anosognosia in AD. Before testing, 44 percent of patients denied that they had any memory problems. After standardized neuropsychological assessment the number of participants who reported unawareness was reduced to 23 percent. Therefore, in Lopez et al.'s study, participants are more likely to be aware of their deficit having completed cognitive testing.

Further evidence that AD patients are monitoring memory comes from findings that AD patients' judgments are sensitive to the task at hand. McGlynn and Kaszniak (1991) found that the AD group's postdictions were significantly more discrepant than controls for some tasks (word recall, picture recall, delayed picture recognition, digit span, verbal span, and verbal fluency). However, there were no differences between groups on other – arguably easier – tasks (word recognition, immediate picture recognition, and spatial span). Although it is difficult to interpret this data because no information is given on the relative levels of recall, it does suggest that AD patients are predicting different levels of performance for different types of task. This suggests the AD group is taking into consideration the task when predicting future performance.

In a series of experiments, my colleagues and I examined the predictions made before and after study for recall of ten word lists (Moulin, Perfect, and Jones, 2000b, Experiment 1) and yes/no recognition of ten

Table 9.1. *Means (and standard deviations) of the number of items (maximum ten) for prestudy and poststudy predictions of performance and actual memory performance for AD and older adult control (OAC) groups*

	List 1			List 2		
	Prestudy	Poststudy	Memory[a]	Prestudy	Poststudy	Memory[a]
Recall (Moulin et al., 2000b)						
AD	5.13 (1.20)	1.88 (3.01)	0.75 (1.13)	3.75 (1.77)	2.50 (2.00)	1.13 (1.36)
OAC	5.94 (1.44)	5.38 (1.86)	4.81 (1.72)	4.75 (1.00)	4.81 (1.38)	4.50 (1.15)
Recognition (Moulin, 1999)						
AD	5.50 (1.83)	4.25 (2.18)	6.13 (2.75)	5.31 (1.74)	5.25 (2.08)	5.25 (1.98)
OAC	5.56 (1.90)	7.44 (1.97)	9.13 (1.02)	7.19 (2.01)	7.75 (1.69)	8.88 (1.63)

[a] Memory: Actual recall performance was measured as the number of items correctly recalled, whereas actual recognition performance was measured as the number of correct hits minus the number of false positives.

word lists (Moulin, 1999). In these experiments, sixteen AD patients were compared to sixteen older adult controls.

The predictions and actual performance from these experiments are shown in Table 9.1. Consider first the data from the studies where recall was the test measure. It is clear that there are two effects in the AD sample. Firstly, the AD group significantly revises its estimates from the prestudy prediction to the poststudy prediction. The poststudy prediction is much lower than the prestudy condition, indicating a shift to a more realistic judgment of performance. Based on the sensitivity rationale, it was argued that this shift was as a result of feedback from memory monitoring. The AD group revises its estimates downwards because it is sensitive to factors that operate during encoding. Secondly, the prestudy prediction on the second to-be-remembered list is lower than the prestudy prediction on the first. Again, it was argued that this shift was due to the fact that the study-test procedure provides information on which participants can base their prediction of performance.

These observations were supported by formal analysis of both groups' non-directional discrepancies between performance and predictions. There was only a significant group difference for the discrepancy of predictions for the first prestudy judgment. Moreover, these patterns were confirmed when participants studied four lists of to-be-remembered words (Moulin et al., 2000b, Experiment 2). That is, using non-directional discrepancies, AD patients are as accurate as controls at predicting performance after study. The only point at which the two groups differ is for the prestudy predictions made on the first list, where in support of the literature, the AD group is less accurate and overestimates their performance. The general pattern is that AD patients become more able to accurately predict their performance across exposure to the study-recall procedure.

The findings for the study where the subsequent test is recognition (lower panel of Table 9.1) were a little less easy to interpret, perhaps because people were unsure of the demands of a recognition test.[2] In any case, it is clear that there is the same tendency for the AD group to shift their predictions between prestudy and poststudy for the first list, and the means clearly show that both groups are more accurate at predicting memory performance on the second list. On the first study-recognition list, the AD group initially predicted memory at about 50 percent of performance, but they revised this estimate downward after study. On the second study-recognition list, the AD group predicted at about 50 percent again, but did not revise their estimates downward. In fact, the mean poststudy prediction for the AD group was the same as their actual performance. The older adult control group predicted recognition at a level similar to the AD group on the prestudy prediction of the first list, but revised this upward after study. On the second list, their prestudy prediction was higher than for the first list, and both the mean prediction before and after study was comparable for the recognition performance on list 2. It was inferred that the study-test procedure of list 1 aids memory monitoring on list 2 through metacognitive feedback.

The most important point is that the comparison of the recall and recognition predictions made in separate experiments indicate that AD participants are sensitive to the test requirements. The predictions made for recognition are clearly higher than the predictions made for recall. Moreover, this sensitivity is wholly appropriate given the memory performance in each of the experiments.

In summary, I proposed that asking participants to make two judgments at different stages of the procedure enables the examination of the sensitivity to factors that operate during encoding. Importantly, the AD groups showed a substantial shift in their predictions as a result of having had an opportunity to study the list, even though the initial list 1 prediction was woefully inaccurate. This shift in judgments, or sensitivity, is based upon metamemory monitoring.

---

[2] Schwartz and Metcalfe (1994) claim that predictions of recognition are counterintuitive, probably due to the Frequency Paradox (Mandler, Goodman, and Wilkesgibbs, 1982), whereby although high frequency words are more likely to be recalled than low frequency words, it is low frequency words that are more likely to be correctly recognized.

It was therefore concluded that global predictions in AD are reflective of ongoing cognitive processes but are poorly calibrated, especially with regards to the first prestudy prediction. What was driving this poor calibration? One explanation was that the AD patients initially made their predictions on a "rule of thumb," based on their stored representation of what memory performance ought to be. As they enter the dementing process, patients do not update their representation of memory beliefs – i.e., they forget that they forget! This interpretation was supported by evidence from the aging literature. Connor et al. (1997) present a review of previous research into global predictions in aging. Older adults have been observed to overestimate memory performance in the predictions that they make (e.g. Bruce, Coyne, and Botwinick, 1982; Coyne, 1985), although sometimes they underestimate it (e.g. McDonald-Miszczak, Hunter, and Hultsch, 1994). Connor et al. (1997) proposed that this inconsistency could be due to the use of the midpoint of the scale. They suggested that individuals 'anchor' their predictions near the midpoint of the possible range of performance – treating it as an "intuitively plausible performance level" (p. 51); they know little about the memory task they are about to undertake. In their review of global judgment predictions in the young and old, they show that of fourteen experiments, seven give mean predictions in the range 45–55 percent of performance in the young group, whereas in the old, twelve of the fourteen studies give mean predictions in the same range.

In a brief task, I explored this midpoint anchoring effect in individuals with AD, and young and older adult controls. Twenty-four participants in each group were asked to predict recall performance (expecting a subsequent test) for six different lists. Participants were not told what the form of the test would be, the mode of presentation, or the type of materials. Participants made predictions for lists with two, three, four, ten, twenty, and thirty items in a counterbalanced order. They reported verbally the level of performance as the number of items for that list that they thought they would recall. Recall performance was not actually measured and the participants were debriefed. Of interest was whether the groups showed the same midpoint bias, or whether there was any sensitivity to list length that set the groups apart. Because AD participants have intact primary memory (Greene et al., 1996), one would expect recall for two to four items in the AD group to be as good as controls. In fact, a 50 percent prediction would be inappropriate for all groups for the shorter lists, where recall would be expected to be at ceiling, even in the older adult and AD groups. However, on the basis of the findings above and those of Connor et al., I expected that all the groups would predict performance at the midpoint of the maximum level of performance, consistent with the use of a rule of thumb, for the longer, episodic memory-mediated lists.

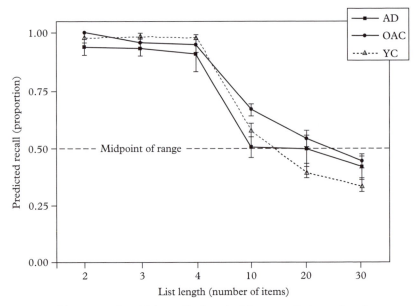

Figure 9.1 Sensitivity to list length. Mean predictions of performance (as a proportion) for lists of different lengths for AD, OAC, and YC participants.
Note: Error bars = 1 standard error.

Figure 9.1 shows the results of this experiment. The predictions of items recalled were converted into a proportion of list length. For clarity, I compared just the AD and older adult groups. A repeated measures 2 × 6 (group × list length) ANOVA indicated that the older adult and AD groups predicted significantly different levels of recall: $F(1, 45) = 5.70$, $MSe = 0.06$, $p < 0.05$, with the older adults predicting higher recall overall (76 percent versus 69 percent). There was also a main effect of list length: $F(1, 45) = 268.37$, $MSe = 0.05$, $p < 0.001$, indicating that participants predict different levels of recall (as a proportion) for different list lengths. This in itself suggests that for the list lengths presented here there is more than a simple midpoint anchoring effect. There was no significant interaction, $F < 1$; suggesting that the AD and older adult groups do not differ in how they predict performance according to list length. This is borne out in the shape of the curves in Figure 9.1, with OAC and AD being clearly very similar.

The most notable aspect of Figure 9.1 is the apparent primary/secondary memory split, with predictions near 100 percent for the shorter lists, and 50 percent for the subsequent lists. This graph shows that if midpoint anchoring is influencing predictions of performance, it is clearly only at longer list lengths (ten and twenty items), and in any case, does not vary significantly between groups. Although there is only partial support for midpoint anchoring in this study, it is nonetheless clear that the predictions of AD participants are (a) significantly lower than an older adult control groups'; and (b) as sensitive to list length as controls. However, the modal values of the predictions were 5/10, 10/20 and 15/30 in the AD group. These are probably gross overestimations of recall performance. This study indicated that AD predictions are in keeping with premorbid experience and expectations, and this is what makes them initially inaccurate. This line of research needs more exploration, but taken at face value with the global sensitivity measures described above, it indicates that there is very little attenuation of memory performance expectations in AD, but that during encoding of to-be-remembered stimuli, there is appropriate and sensitive memory monitoring. Patient A was typical of this pattern. She was inappropriate in her initial appraisal of performance, but during testing made remarks about her memory difficulties that suggested some awareness. Moreover, she had forgotten the episodes from her recent life that were indicative of her memory problem.

Metacognition in AD: item judgments

There has been less focus on item judgments as a means of measuring metacognition in AD. Item judgments are evaluations of metamemory for individual stimuli, usually to-be-remembered words. They differ according to what stage they are made at (e.g. before or after test; before, during, or after acquisition); whether they are estimates of recall or recognition performance; and also whether the task is semantic (e.g. general knowledge) or episodic.

Most previous research into memory monitoring in AD has utilized the feeling-of-knowing (FOK) paradigm. This requires a participant to predict future memory performance of an item that is currently non-recallable. FOK judgments are not impaired in AD for general knowledge materials (Bäckman and Lipinska, 1993; Lipinska and Bäckman, 1996). The results of these studies for semantic memory do not favor a deficit in memory monitoring as part of the episodic memory deficit in AD. However, there is evidence that episodic memory monitoring in normal populations is distinct from general knowledge monitoring, and is less accurate (e.g. Schwartz and Metcalfe, 1994; Perfect and Hollins, 1999). Therefore, it is not clear whether intact metacognition for general knowledge would have any bearing on episodic memory functioning.

Pappas et al. (1992) examined FOK episodic memory accuracy in AD. This study is more directly relevant to the present work because they studied metamemory judgments in episodic memory with recall and recognition tasks. For the recall task, they were unable to draw conclusions about the predictive accuracy of metamemory judgments because of floor effects in the recall of the AD group and a lack of range in the prediction ratings. However, for the recognition task, with performance off floor, they found that AD patients do not predict recognition as accurately as controls.

Although the focus of this work is processes that operate during encoding, the previous research into judgments made after test (i.e., confidence in recalled answer) is of interest, because they show no deficit in AD. Researchers have often asked participants to ascribe confidence judgments to retrieved answers as a part of the FOK test. For confidence in recognition for general knowledge items (Bäckman and Lipinska, 1993; Lipinska and Bäckman, 1996) and confidence in recall for both episodic and semantic materials (Pappas et al., 1992) there is no difference between controls and patients in the accuracy of their judgements. AD patients seem perfectly able to judge the veracity of a retrieved answer.

All these previous studies are limited in their ability to address metamemory function at encoding because they examine metamemory judgments made after encoding and before retrieval. Moreover, two studies use general knowledge materials rather than assessing performance on a memory task that includes an encoding phase. The previous research into item judgments in AD was therefore equivocal. There is evidence that metacognition is intact for tests of general knowledge, but some evidence that predictive accuracy is impaired on episodic memory tests. However, the work is unclear, because it is plagued by floor effects, which makes it difficult to compare evaluations of encoding with subsequent performance.

With the global judgments, there was evidence that Alzheimer's patients were monitoring their memory performance during encoding; at least, they revised their predictions away from an inaccurate first prediction in response to studying the to-be-remembered list. My colleagues and I were interested in whether AD patients would make item judgments that were reflective of objective factors that are known to influence recall. As an objective measure, the item's recallability (Rubin and Friendly, 1986) was used. This is based on the normative probability of recall in a memory test. Words with known recallability values were presented and the effect of the items' characteristics on participants' item judgments was examined. This was carried out for judgments of learning (JOLs; e.g. Nelson and Narens, 1990), a prediction of subsequent performance made after

Table 9.2. *Means (and standard deviations) of judgments of learning (JOLs) for objectively easy and difficult words*

| | Metacognitive sensitivity JOLs | | Metacognitive accuracy recall gamma |
	Easy words	Difficult words	
AD	4.04 (0.75)	2.83 (0.60)	0.14 (0.71)[a]
OAC	4.15 (0.74)	3.45 (0.98)	0.54 (0.55)

Source: Moulin, Perfect, and Jones (2000a)
[a] Number of participants = 10 for recall gamma in the AD group.

study. If the AD group was metacognitively competent, they would be able to make JOLs that reflected differences in the stimuli from an appraisal of the object level during encoding. That is, they would judge an objectively difficult to recall word as less likely to be recalled than an easy word.

In Moulin, Perfect, and Jones (2000a, Experiment 1) we describe an item sensitivity procedure. The to-be-remembered stimuli were five easy-to-recall words (e.g. sky) and five difficult-to-recall words (e.g. hint). Participants were presented with these items to study at a rate of one word every 2 seconds. After each word had been presented, participants were asked to make a JOL rating on a scale of 1 to 5. The mean JOLs for the sample of sixteen older adults and sixteen AD patients are given in Table 9.2. The mean JOLs show no group differences in magnitude, but do demonstrate an effect of item type (with easier words being judged as more likely to be recalled) and no interaction. That is, both groups respond appropriately to objective difficulty in their relative JOLs. It was argued that these JOLs are made on the basis of memory monitoring that is in operation during encoding of the to-be-remembered items. For completeness, subsequent recall of the items was recorded for both groups and Table 9.2 also shows the recall gammas for each group, a measure of metamemory accuracy. A gamma correlation closer to one indicates that the group is more accurate in predicting which items they will recall in the JOLs that they make. Although there are differences in the two groups' gammas, this difference failed to reach significance. This is probably due to the sample being reduced to ten in the AD group because of zero recall for six of the participants.

My colleagues and I also looked at metacognitive sensitivity for single items using a ranking procedure (Moulin et al., 2000a, Experiment 2), arguing that if AD patients ranked a range of words as appropriately as controls, this would be further evidence of intact metacognitive processing.

Controls and AD patients ranked ten words at study according to how likely they thought they were to recall each of the words. This procedure was carried out twice on the same list of words by each participant – once ranking from easiest to most difficult, and once from most difficult to easiest. A non-parametric correlation was used to assess the relation between each participant's subjective rank and the rank of probability of recall based on normative performance (Rubin and Friendly, 1986). There were no group differences in the mean correlation coefficients. The mean correlations for the AD group were 0.52 and 0.55 for trials 1 and 2 respectively, whereas for the control group they were 0.59 and 0.44. The lack of any group differences and the strong positive correlations suggest that both groups were capable of making predictions based on the normative qualities of the words. The accuracy measure again contributed very little to the assessment of metacognitive function: there were no significant differences in recall for participants' top-five words and bottom-five words, and there was no interaction.

Thus the data from item judgments were in agreement with those from global judgments: AD patients made appropriate and sensitive metamemory judgements. I argued that these sensitive predictions were based on intact underlying metacognitive processes.

Discussion: sense and sensitivity

The experiments described in this chapter take measures that are independent of AD participants' poor levels of recall, but that are nonetheless reflective of metamemory processes that operate during encoding. For global and item judgments I showed that in an episodic memory task, AD patients' judgments are as sensitive to objective factors operating at encoding as controls'. Whereas the accuracy approach has often produced equivocal results in AD, I demonstrated that metamemory processes are intact in this memory-impaired sample if one takes into account sensitivity. Such a conclusion would not have been possible with accuracy measures.

Of course, the accuracy approach is not always fruitless. It is adequate for assessing metacognitive processes at test (especially where recognition methodology excludes troublesome floor effects), or for stimuli where there is not such a marked memory deficit (e.g. general knowledge materials, Bäckman and Lipinska, 1993; Lipinska and Bäckman, 1996). Thus, where recognition measures and judgments at test have been studied, there is very little evidence for a metacognitive deficit in AD. For example, my own work (Moulin, 1999) found that AD patients were as accurate as controls at assigning post-test confidence ratings in a two-alternative forced-choice episodic memory task: AD gamma = 0.58, OAC gamma = 0.64. There was no difference ($F < 1$) in the groups' accuracy, and the level of the gammas show that the groups are both accurate. However, there were significant differences in the groups' recognition memory performance (AD: 65 percent of items correctly recognised; OAC: 92 percent). A Pearson's bivariate correlation showed no relation between metamemory accuracy and memory performance between subjects for the sixteen AD participants, $r = 0.02$. This suggested that AD does not cause a deficit in metacognition at test, and that metacognitive accuracy is not related to the episodic deficit.

Another area where the accuracy approach is more appropriate is when researchers are interested in comparing two different memory-impaired groups. For compelling evidence from neuropsychological studies of metacognitive accuracy, one has to turn to work such as Shimamura and Squire (1986). Using the FOK procedure, they found a deficit in predictive accuracy for a Korsakoff's group relative to another memory-impaired group (non-Korsakoff's amnesia), despite equally poor memory in the two groups. This is an important study – it shows that metacognitive failure is not a necessary part of a memory deficit. Even so, a deficit in metamemory accuracy in this case does not illuminate the understanding of encoding processes in memory-impaired groups.

There are some possible shortcomings of the sensitivity approach. The first is that despite being an appropriate gauge of factors that are important at study, the sensitivity measures do not necessarily reflect participants' awareness of their memory processes. Participants might simply be sensitive to the objective differences on the basis of the normative characteristics of the words rather than their registration in memory.

A number of researchers have discussed the basis on which predictions of performance can be made. Lovelace (1984) suggested that monitoring could be based on normative or idiosyncratic awareness.[3] Normative awareness includes item difficulty – the surface characteristics of stimuli that are available before study (e.g. familiarity, pronouncability, word length). These contrast with idiosyncratic or privileged access components of metacognition that are based on the participant's own awareness of their memory system (e.g. an evaluation of how meaningful that word is personally, or an awareness of the amount of time devoted to studying it). These two contrasting means of predicting performance may capture

---

[3] Similarly, Hertzog and Dixon (1994) propose that metaknowledge can fall into three different conceptual categories: declarative knowledge about memory processing, awareness of online memory processing, and subjective beliefs about the memory system.

the differences between the AD and control groups' predictions. The AD group may be sensitive but not accurate because they are relying on normative characteristics and not idiosyncratic characteristics. This could explain why their JOLs relate to norms of recall performance, but not to their actual performance.

Koriat (1997) put forward a framework by which to classify the basis on which people assessed learning proficiency during study. Koriat suggests that assessments of how well an item has been learned can be based on intrinsic, extrinsic, or mnemonic cues. Intrinsic cues are taken from the qualities of the to-be-remembered stimulus itself, such as an awareness of word familiarity or pronouncability. Extrinsic cues are derived from the awareness of processes operating at encoding, such as the number of presentations or the time available at study. Mnemonic cues ensue from the learner's subjective experience of learning and their privileged access to their memory system. Mnemonic cues rely not on the mere appraisal of an item or the conditions under which it was encountered, but a bona fide awareness of whether an item has been sufficiently learnt. Intrinsic and extrinsic cues can be accessed directly during a learning episode – they are a knowledge-based heuristic that can infer an item's registration in memory – whereas mnemonic cues give rise to a 'feeling of knowing' that can be used to assess memory processes and subsequent performance.

These considerations of the basis of metacognitive judgments are pertinent to the research presented here, since my colleagues and I argued that sensitivity is reflective of underlying metacognitive operations. Clearly, in presenting participants with stimuli with clear objective differences we may be emphasizing the normative or intrinsic elements of their memory awareness. It is conceivable that we have demonstrated that AD patients are sensitive to objective qualities of stimuli – they can base their predictions on intrinsic cues as well as controls can. It could be argued that for metacognition to be of mnemonic use, it should have a mnemonic basis. It is not clear whether the appropriate sensitivity observed in the studies here arises from (a) an awareness of the memory trace which has been affected by the objective factor (Figure 9.2a); or (b) an awareness of the objective factor which incidentally and independently affects memory performance (Figure 9.2b). For instance, consider that a word such as "brassiere" is easier to recall than "impropriety." AD participants and controls have shown an ability to allocate JOLs at encoding that is appropriate given what is known about the recallability of the two words. An idiosyncratic or mnemonic metacognition hypothesis (Figure 9.2a) would be that the characteristics of "brassiere" (e.g. imagability, word frequency, pleasantness) influence the memory trace (and/or associative processes, episodic tags, specific recollections) which affects the likelihood of recall.

(a) Sensitivity to online processes; aware of memory processing.
Sensitivity based on mnemonic cues.

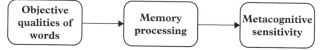

(b) Sensitivity to objective qualities; not aware of memory processing.
Sensitivity based on intrinsic or extrinsic cues.

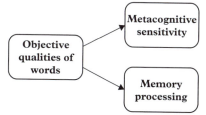

Figure 9.2 Sensitivity to metacognitive processes or cognitive processes?

Memory monitoring taps into all this activity at the object level, and bases the JOL on it. A so-what hypothesis (Figure 9.2b) would be that recall is contingent upon the objective (or intrinsic) qualities of "brassiere" and the JOLs are just an assessment of those objective qualities – *not* their affect on the memory system.

This is important for the application of metacognition to AD. If practitioners were to implement strategies that can help people's memory performance, it would be most desirable to base that work on a true mnemonic (or idiosyncratic) appraisal of performance. In some ways, an overuse of normative or stored metacognitions may even exacerbate the memory deficit in AD. If an AD patient is merely considering the surface characteristics of "brassiere" without acknowledging that it is very poorly encoded, they will not devote the control strategies appropriate to provide proficient learning. Perhaps the normative appraisal of items, without awareness of the patient's extreme memory deficit, would seduce the patient into underestimating the effort needed to learn the item sufficiently.

A second shortcoming of the sensitivity approach is that participants might not be considering future performance in their JOLs. This idea is captured in the difference between ease-of-learning (EOL) and JOL measures, two measures reported in normal populations in the metacognition literature. EOLs are defined as metamemory judgments made before the memory item has been mastered (i.e., during presentation and before prolonged study), rather than the JOLs made after the item has been presented (as reported here). Nelson and Narens (1990) suggest that because EOL judgments occur prior to encoding, they cannot tap memory processes but can only tap item difficulty. It is hypothesized that, in contrast, JOLs, made after an item has been learned, can tap metaknowledge about how well that item is stored in memory. JOLs are a much more accurate predictor of subsequent performance than EOLs. For example, Leonesio and Nelson (1990) found that subsequent recall is predicted much better by JOLs (gamma = 0.31) than by EOLs (gamma = 0.12). Also, they found that EOLs are a relatively poor measure of monitoring performance, in that EOLs did not correlate with the number of trials required to learn the various items in a constant-study-time situation.

It is possible that the sensitivity approach overemphasizes the surface characteristics of the to-be-remembered items, and AD participants make predictions akin to an EOL rather than a JOL. To explore metacognition more fully, the differences in surface characteristics could be removed and instead participants could make sensitivity judgments based on other factors that increase recall. This may enable the measurement of idiosyncratic elements of metacognition.

These two shortcomings were the reasoning behind some research into repetition and JOLs in Alzheimer's disease (Moulin, Perfect, and Fitch, in press; Moulin, Perfect, and Jones, 2000c). Basically, my colleagues and I were interested in whether we could display sensitivity to extrinsic or mnemonic factors. In two experiments, participants made sensitivity judgments based on item repetition, an extrinsic cue (Koriat, 1997). I hoped that this would address whether sensitivity in the AD group is based on surface characteristics alone (Figure 9.2b) or an evaluation of memory processes (Figure 9.2a). Sensitivity in this case would at least rely on the JOLs reflecting the awareness of repetition, and the effect that can have on memory. To summarize the procedure, AD participants and controls were presented with a set of equally recallable items that were presented either once, twice, or three times. Participants were instructed to study the item until recall readiness, and following that make a JOL in the standard manner. It was found that whereas the control group was sensitive to repetition in its study time, JOLs, and memory performance, the AD group was only sensitive in its allocation of study time and its memory performance. The AD participants showed no sensitivity to repetition in the JOLs they made: unlike controls they did not rate words as getting any more likely to be recalled with increasing presentations. In a subsequent experiment, this pattern of performance was not changed if study time was kept constant: older adults' JOLs were sensitive to repetition and AD patients' were not. It is unclear whether this is evidence of a deficit in metacognition since the allocation of study time was appropriate in AD. Because study time allocation (metacognitive control) is reliant upon memory monitoring (as measured by JOLs in this case), it is clear that on some level the memory processes are being monitored. Because the control and monitoring framework (Nelson and Narens, 1990) posits that proficient control is reliant upon monitoring of memory, this was described as evidence of a dissociation between control and monitoring in AD. However, it is not possible to conclude that the control of memory can be sensitive to repetition whereas monitoring is not, since without some monitoring of repetition, the study times would not be appropriate. To reconcile this problem my colleagues and I suggested that some aspects of memory monitoring cannot be captured in self-report, and the monitoring of repetition that enables the appropriate allocation of study time in AD is not measured in self-report JOLs in the AD group. From this, it would appear that the control group is sensitive to idiosyncratic or extrinsic factors that can only be reported in JOLs through an evaluation of the memory trace. In the AD group it is possible that this sort of monitoring is absent, or is swamped by the evaluation of normative or intrinsic factors.

There are no other clear-cut findings in the literature where monitoring can be separated from control in this way. Modest but reliable associations between study time and monitoring measures are usually found (the "monitoring effects control" hypothesis; Nelson, 1993). Both FOKs and EOLs are related to study time in normal populations (Nelson and Leonesio, 1988), although there is evidence that the aging process affects the relationship between memory monitoring and memory control as measured by JOLs and recall readiness (Dunlosky and Connor, 1997). However, the idea that monitoring can be insensitive to changes in memory performance (as shown by the AD group's lack of discrimination for repetition in their JOLs) receives some support from experiments on normal populations. For example, memory can be improved by factors that do not influence metacognitive judgments, such as priming (Jameson et al., 1990; Mazzoni and Nelson, 1995). Therefore, memory performance can be improved by factors that are not consciously available for self-report at the object level, for example priming influences memory performance but not the magnitude of metamemory judgments (Jameson et al. 1990).

The results of these studies into repetition and metacognition are problematic for the understanding of sensitivity and the JOLs made to items with objective difficulties. My colleagues and I found that AD patients' JOLs are sensitive to objective difficulty (e.g. recallability), but not repetition. Because the sensitivity to repetition work exposes a specific defect in AD patients' ability to make appropriate JOLs, it seems more likely that the JOLs made by the AD patients are not tapping the sort of process shown in Figure 9.2a, but rather the sort of relationship in Figure 9.2b. However, studies need to be designed to address this issue directly. I believe that AD patients may be an interesting population in which to explore these theoretical issues. The dissociation shown between control and monitoring found in the work discussed here on metacognition in AD is an example of the benefits of applying metacognition to a clinical population.

As well as examining sensitivity to repeats, my colleagues and I aim to look at other manipulations with objective properties but that operate as extrinsic or mnemonic cues, for example level of processing, generation effect, retention intervals, and so on. This way, it could be assessed whether metamemory judgments are sensitive to other factors that affect recall, which are not related to the surface features of the to-be-remembered items. This is an example of how this work naturally leads into therapeutic uses of metacognition since in these proposed experiments we will be considering what improves memory function in AD and what their appreciation of this is.

The work reported here is an important first step in attempting to assess whether a metacognitive deficit does contribute to the episodic deficit in AD. There is clear evidence that AD patients respond appropriately to the objective qualities of to-be-remembered materials. However, in the case of sensitivity to repetition there is some evidence that self-report of memory monitoring may be impaired in AD (although metamemory control is still appropriate and must therefore be based on some sort of feedback from memory monitoring).

In conclusion, I believe the sensitivity approach shows that AD patients are as capable as controls at making predictions of performance that are related to factors operating at encoding; there is little evidence here that a metacognitive deficit is a major component of the episodic failure in AD. The sensitivity approach with patients has also exposed some interesting differences in normative and idiosyncratic (or intrinsic and extrinsic) bases for metacognition. Moreover, the novel empirical work presented in this chapter demonstrates a tendency for global predictions to be fixed at premorbid levels.

Because of the apparent lack of a marked monitoring deficit in AD, it should be possible to design interventions to help people with memory loss in AD. Because I argued that monitoring must influence control behavior (even if this is not consciously reportable) then it is clearly problematic that AD patients initially overestimate their performance on a list of items. However, my colleagues and I have demonstrated that through exposure to test and study, AD participants build a more realistic appreciation of their abilities. If a more realistic appreciation of future performance is central to the appropriate effort and control of the object level at encoding, then it should be possible to 'train' memory awareness in AD, and see benefits in performance. If AD patients can update their perceptions of performance in the long term as they can in the laboratory for shorter time periods, then there may be a reduction in negative memory-related affect, and an improvement in memory performance. This self-empowering aspect of memory awareness should be the ultimate goal of research into the metacognitive abilities of neuropsychological populations.

I return to the vignettes of two patients presented at the start of the chapter. An assessment of memory beliefs and awareness may be diagnostic in cases such as these. I have shown that it is unlikely that a person with dementia will underestimate their memory performance (e.g. Patient A overestimates her performance). In cases where patients are inaccurate and underestimate their performance (such as Patient B), the clinician might want to use this information to contribute to their diagnosis, and identify a suitable intervention. Thus metacognitive assessment could have applications in differential diagnosis, because an underestimate of performance may indicate memory-related anxiety and an overestimate, memory impairment. The awareness of memory function could potentially be used to differentiate different dementia types. For instance, it might be expected that there is a more isolated and severe metacognitive impairment in those dementias where frontal neuropathology is more prominent than in AD (e.g. fronto-temporal dementia).

In addition to this diagnostic use, future research should focus on the use of metacognitive sensitivity as a clinical instrument. With advances in drug treatments for dementia, metacognitive assessment could measure the extent to which patients can reflect on their cognitive abilities, and thus gauge for themselves the efficacy of their treatment. Thus, metacognitive assessment would be a central part of validating the person's subjective experience of dementia, and tailoring their treatment to their perceived needs.

ACKNOWLEDGMENTS

This work was supported by a charitable grant from the Research Institute for the Care of the Elderly (RICE) to the author. I am very grateful for the testing carried out by Fiona Fitch and Alice North, and the helpful comments of Niamh James. This work would not have been possible without the kind co-operation of the staff and patients of the RICE memory disorders clinic, St. Martin's Hospital, Bath, UK, and especially the Institute's director, Roy Jones.

REFERENCES

Almkvist, O., Fratiglioni, L., Aguero-Torres, H., Viitanen, M., and Backmän, L. (1999). Cognitive support at episodic encoding and retrieval: similar patterns of utilization in community-based samples of Alzheimer's disease and vascular dementia patients. *Journal of Clinical and Experimental Neuropsychology*, 21, 816–830.

Arriagada, P. V., Marzloff, K., and Hyman, B. T. (1992). Distribution of Alzheimer-type pathologic changes in nondemented elderly individuals matches the pattern in Alzheimer's disease. *Neurology*, 42, 1681–1688.

Bäckman, L., and Lipinska, B. (1993). Monitoring of general knowledge: evidence for preservation in early Alzheimer's disease. *Neuropsychologia*, 31, 335–345.

Baddeley, A. D. (1986). *Working memory*. Oxford: Oxford University Press.

(1997). *Human memory: theory and practice*. Hove, UK: Psychology Press.

Becker, J. T. (1987). A two-component model of memory deficit in Alzheimer's disease. In R. J. Wurtman, S. H. Corkin, and J. H. Growdon (eds.), *Alzheimer's disease: advances in basic research and therapies*, pp. 343–348. Cambridge, MA: Center for Brain Sciences and Metabolism Charitable Trust.

Bruce, P. R., Coyne, A., and Botwinick, J. (1982). Adult age differences in metamemory. *Journal of Gerontology*, 37, 354–357.

Connor, L. T., Dunlosky, J., and Hertzog, C. (1997). Age-related differences in absolute but not relative metamemory accuracy. *Psychology and Aging*, 12, 50–71.

Corkin, S. (1981). Acetylcholine, aging and Alzheimer's disease: implications for treatment. *Trends in Neuroscience*, 4, 287–290.

Correa, D. D., Graves, R. E., and Costa, L. (1996). Awareness of memory deficit in Alzheimer's disease patients and memory impaired older adults. *Aging, Neuropsychology and Cognition*, 3, 215–228.

Coyne, A. C. (1985). Adult age, presentation time, and memory performance. *Experimental Aging Research*, 11, 147–149.

Cummings, J. L., and Benson, D. F. (1992). *Dementia: a clinical approach*. Boston, MA: Butterworth's.

Della Sala, S., Logie, R. H., and Spinnler, H. (1992). Is primary memory deficit of Alzheimer patients due to a "central executive" impairment? *Journal of Neurolinguistics*, 7, 325–346.

Dunlosky, J., and Connor, L. T. (1997). Age differences in the allocation of study time account for age differences in memory performance. *Memory and Cognition*, 25, 691–700.

Dunlosky, J., and Nelson, T. O. (1992). Importance of the kind of cue for judgments of learning (JOL) and the delayed JOL effect. *Memory and Cognition*, 20, 374–380.

Folstein, M. F., Folstein, S. E., and McHugh, P. R. (1975). Mini-mental state: a practical method for grading the cognitive state of the patient for the clinician. *Journal of Psychiatric Research*, 12, 189–198.

Greene, J. D. W., Baddeley, A. D., and Hodges, J. R. (1996). Analysis of the episodic memory deficit in early Alzheimer's disease: evidence from the doors and people test. *Neuropsychologia*, 34, 537–551.

Herlitz, A., and Viitanen, M. (1991). Semantic organization and verbal episodic memory in patients with mild and moderate Alzheimer's disease. *Journal of Clinical and Experimental Neuropsychology*, 13, 559–574.

Hertzog, C., and Dixon, R. A. (1994). Metacognitive development in adulthood and old age. In J. Metcalfe and A. P. Shimamura (eds.), *Metacognition: knowing about knowing*, pp. 227–251. Cambridge, MA: MIT Press.

Jameson, K. A., Narens, L., Goldfarb, K., and Nelson, T. O. (1990). The influence of near-threshold priming on metamemory and recall. *Acta Psychologica*, 73, 55–68.

Joynt, R. J., and Shoulson, I. (1985). Dementia. In K. M. Heilman and E. Valenstein (eds.), *Clinical neuropsychology*. New York: Oxford University Press.

Kopelman, M. D. (1985). Rates of forgetting in Alzheimer-type dementia and Korsakoff's syndrome. *Neuropsychologia*, 15, 527–541.

Koriat, A. (1997). Monitoring one's own knowledge during study: a cue utilization approach to judgments of learning. *Journal of Experimental Psychology: General*, 126, 349–370.

Leonesio, R. J., and Nelson, T. O. (1990). Do different metamemory judgements tap the same underlying aspects of memory? *Journal of Experimental Psychology: Learning, Memory, and Cognition*, 16, 464–470.

Lipinska, B., and Bäckman, L. (1996). Feeling of knowing in fact retrieval: further evidence for preservation in early Alzheimer's disease. *Journal of the International Neuropsychological Society*, 2, 350–358.

Lopez, O. L., Becker, J. T., Somsak, D., Dew, M. D., and DeKosky, S. T. (1994). Awareness of cognitive deficits and anosognosia in probable Alzheimer's disease. *European Journal of Neurology*, 34, 277–282.

Lovelace, E. A. (1984). Metamemory: monitoring future recallability during study. *Journal of Experimental Psychology: Learning, Memory, and Cognition*, 10, 756–766.

Mandler, G., Goodman, G. O., and Wilkesgibbs, D. L. (1982). The word frequency paradox in recognition. *Memory and Cognition*, 10, 33–42.

Mazzoni, G., and Nelson, T. O. (1995). Judgments of learning are affected by the kind of encoding in ways that cannot be attributed to the level of recall. *Journal of Experimental Psychology: Learning, Memory, and Cognition*, 21, 1263–1274.

McDonald-Miszczak, L., Hunter, M. A., and Hultsch, D. F. (1994). Adult age differences in predicting memory performance: the effects of normative information and task experience. *Canadian Journal of Experimental Psychology*, 48, 95–118.

McGlynn, S. M., and Kaszniak, A. W. (1991). When metacognition fails: impaired awareness of deficit in Alzheimer's disease. *Journal of Cognitive Neuroscience*, 3, 183–189.

Moss, M. B., and Albert, M. S. (1988). Alzheimer's disease and other dementing disorders. In M. S. Albert and M. B. Moss (eds.), *Geriatric neuropsychology*, pp. 293–303. New York: The Guildford Press.

Moulin, C. J. A. (1999). *Does a metacognitive deficit contribute to the memory impairment in Alzheimer's disease?* Unpublished Ph.D. thesis, Bristol University.

Moulin, C. J. A., Perfect, T. J., and Fitch, F. (in press). Judgments of learning, study time and item repetition in Alzheimer's disease. In P. Chambres, M. Izaute, and P.-J. Marescaux (eds.), *Metacognition: process, function, and use.* Dordrecht, Netherlands: Kluwer Academic Press.

Moulin, C. J. A., Perfect, T. J., and Jones, R. W. (2000a). Evidence for intact memory monitoring in Alzheimer's disease: metamemory sensitivity at encoding. *Neuropsychologia*, 38, 1242–1250.

(2000b). Global predictions of memory in Alzheimer's disease: evidence for preserved metamemory monitoring. *Aging, Neuropsychology and Cognition*, 7, 230–244.

(2000c). The effects of repetition on allocation of study time and judgements of learning in Alzheimer's disease. *Neuropsychologia*, 38, 748–756.

Multhaup, K. S., and Balota, D. A. (1997). Generation effects and source memory in healthy older adults and in adults with dementia of the Alzheimer type. *Neuropsychology*, 11, 382–391.

Nelson, T. O. (1993). Judgments of learning and the allocation of study time. *Journal of Experimental Psychology: General*, 122, 269–273.

Nelson, T. O., and Leonesio, R. J. (1988). Allocation of self-paced study time and the labor in vain effect. *Journal of Experimental Psychology: Learning, Memory, and Cognition*, 14, 676–686.

Nelson, T. O., and Narens, L. (1990). Metamemory: a theoretical framework and some new findings. In G. H. Bower (ed.), *The psychology of learning and motivation, Volume 26*, pp. 125–173. San Diego, CA: Academic Press.

Pappas, B. A., Sunderland, T., Weingartner, H. M., Vitiello, B., Martinson, H., and Putnam, K. (1992). Alzheimer's disease and feeling of knowing for knowledge and episodic memory. *Journal of Gerontology: Psychological Sciences*, 47, 159–164.

Perfect, T. J., and Hollins, T. S. (1999). Feeling of knowing judgments do not predict subsequent recognition performance for eyewitness memory. *Journal of Experimental Psychology: Applied*, 5, 250–264.

Reisberg, B., Gordon, B., McCarthy, M., and Ferris, S. H. (1985). Clinical symptoms accompanying progressive cognitive decline in Alzheimer's disease. In V. L. Melnick and N. N. Dubler (eds.), *Alzheimer's dementia*, pp. 19–39. Clifton, NJ: Humana Press.

Rubin, D. C., and Friendly, M. (1986). Predicting which words get recalled: measures of free recall, availability, goodness, emotionality, and pronounceability for 925 nouns. *Memory and Cognition*, 14, 79–94.

Schacter, D. L., McLachlan, D. R., Moscovitch, M., and Tulving, E. (1986). Monitoring of recall performance by memory disorders patients. *Journal of Clinical and Experimental Neuropsychology*, 8, 130.

Schneck, M. K., Reisberg, B., and Ferris, S. H. (1982). An overview of the current concepts of Alzheimer's disease. *American Journal of Psychiatry*, 139, 165–173.

Schwartz, B. L., and Metcalfe, J. (1994). Methodological problems and pitfalls in the study of human metacognition. In J. Metcalfe and A. P. Shimamura (eds.), *Metacognition: knowing about knowing*, pp. 93–113. Cambridge, MA: MIT Press.

Shimamura, A. P. (1994). The neuropsychology of metacognition. In J. Metcalfe and A. P. Shimamura (eds.), *Metacognition: knowing about knowing*, pp. 253–276. Cambridge, MA: MIT Press.

Shimamura, A. P., and Squire, L. R. (1986). Memory and metamemory: a study of feeling-of-knowing phenomenon in amnesic patients. *Journal of Experimental Psychology: Learning, Memory, and Cognition*, 12, 452–460.

Storandt, M., Botwinick, J., and Danziger, W. L. (1986). Longitudinal changes: patients with mild SDAT and matched healthy controls. In L. W. Poon (ed.), *Clinical memory assessment of older adults*, pp. 277–284. Washington, DC: American Psychological Association.

Stuss, D. T. (1991). Disturbance of self awareness after frontal system damage. In G. P. Prigatano and D. L. Schacter (eds.), *Awareness of deficits after brain injury: clinical and theoretical issues*, pp. 63–83. New York: Oxford University Press.

Woodward, J. L., Dunlosky, J., and Salthouse, T. A. (1999). Task decomposition analysis of inter-trial free recall performance on the Rey Auditory Verbal Learning test in normal aging and Alzheimer's disease. *Journal of Clinical and Experimental Neuropsychology*, 21, 666–676.

10 The development of metacognitive knowledge in children and adolescents

Wolfgang Schneider and Kathrin Lockl

Historically, research on the development of metacognition, that is, knowledge about cognition, dates back to the work of Jean Piaget and his claim that young children do not know that there are such things as conceptual, perceptual, and emotional perspectives of points of view. Piaget and his colleagues used the concept of egocentrism to interpret the findings of their developmental studies on a wide variety of social-cognitive topics such as perceptual perspective taking, and understanding of thoughts, dreams, or intentions. Although there is broad agreement today that young children are not as egocentric as Piaget believed them to be, his claim that perspective-taking abilities and related psychological knowledge develop quickly over time has been confirmed in numerous studies (see Flavell, 2000).

A second line of research on metacognitive development was initiated in the early 1970s by Brown, Flavell, and their colleagues (for reviews, see Brown et al., 1983; Flavell, Miller, and Miller, 1993). At the very beginning, research focused on knowledge about memory, which was coined "metamemory" by Flavell (1971). Later on, the concept was broadened and termed "metacognition" (Flavell, 1979). Metacognition was defined as any knowledge or cognitive activity that takes as its cognitive object, or that regulates, any aspect of any cognitive activity (Flavell et al., 1993, p. 150). Obviously, this is a very broad conceptualization that includes people's knowledge of their own information-processing skills, as well as knowledge about the nature of cognitive tasks, and about strategies for coping with such tasks. Moreover, it includes executive skills related to monitoring and self-regulation of one's own cognitive activities. Although most developmental studies classified as "metacognitive" have explored children's metamemory, that is, their knowledge about memory, the term has also been applied to studies investigating children's comprehension, communication, and problem-solving skills (Flavell, 2000; Schneider and Pressley, 1997).

In the early 1980s, a third wave of studies focused on young children's knowledge about the mental world, better known as "theory-of-mind" research. This wave is still very much in motion and may have produced more than 800 publications within the last fifteen years or so. It deals with very young children's understanding of mental life and age-related changes in this understanding, for instance their knowledge that mental representations of events need not correspond to reality. In retrospect, it appears that this paradigm emerged from two initially independent lines of inquiry. One line was directly linked to research on metacognitive development, assessing children's understanding of mental verbs such as "knowing" or "forgetting" (Johnson and Wellman, 1980; Wellman, 1985). Wellman and colleagues conceptualized young children's developing metacognitive knowledge and their understanding of mental verbs as the development of a "theory of mind." The other line of developmental research was mainly stimulated by a philosophical discussion (see Premack and Woodruff, 1978) on the issue of whether chimpanzees have a theory of mind, that is, possess the concept of belief. In a now classic study, Wimmer and Perner (1983) transferred this issue to the human species. They tested young children's understanding of false belief, confirming the assumption that children below the age of about four find it impossible to believe that another person could hold an assertion that the child knows to be false. A little later, beginning at about age four, children come to recognize assertions as the expression of someone's belief that is not necessarily true. Subsequent theory-of-mind research has addressed young children's understanding of mental states such as desires, intentions, emotions, attention, consciousness, etc.

Given that this chapter focuses on the development of metacognitive knowledge, predominantly in the area of memory, it seems important to elaborate on the differences between this older research paradigm and more recent theory-of-mind research (for a more detailed discussion see Flavell, 2000; Kuhn, 1999, 2000). Although researchers in both traditions share the same general objective, that is, explore children's knowledge about and understanding of mental phenomena, the research literatures have been distinct and unconnected because they focused on different developments. For instance, whereas theory-of-mind researchers have investigated children's initial knowledge about the existence of various mental states such as desires and intentions, metacognitive researchers have focused more on task-related mental processes such as strategies for improving performance on various tasks or attempts to monitor improvements. Flavell (2000) conceives of this approach as "problem centered," and suggests that it may be labeled "applied theory-of-mind."

A second distinction between the two research paradigms concerns the age groups under study. Because theory-of-mind researchers are mainly interested in the origins of knowledge about mental states, they predominantly study infants and young children. On the other hand, metacognitive researchers investigate knowledge components and skills that already require some understanding of mental states, and thus mainly test older children and adolescents. A further distinction concerns the fact that developmental research on metacognition deals with what a child knows about his or her own mind rather than somebody else's. As noted by Flavell (2000), how and how often other people use their minds in similar situations is not of primary interest. In contrast, it is the participant's understanding of some other person's mind that is usually of central concern in theory-of-mind studies.

Kuhn (1999, 2000) recently developed a conceptual framework to connect the theory-of-mind paradigm to related theoretical constructs such as metacognition. She chose the heading of "metaknowing" as an umbrella term to encompass any cognition that has cognition – either one's own or others' – as its object. The dichotomy between procedural knowing (knowing how) and declarative knowing (knowing that) was used to distinguish between types of "meta-knowing." Knowing about declarative knowledge (as a product) was labeled "metacognitive knowing," whereas knowing about procedural knowing (knowing how) was addressed under the heading of "metastrategic knowing." In Kuhn's framework, the metacognitive knowing component addresses young children's understanding of mental states and thus refers to theory-of-mind research, whereas metastrategic knowing refers to what children know about their cognitive processes and what impact this has on performance, an issue typically addressed in research on metacognitive development such as metamemory. Although the labels chosen by Kuhn seem debatable (e.g. metamemory comprises more than knowledge about strategies, see below), the idea of linking the two research lines in a common framework is important and deserves further attention.

In the following, empirical findings regarding the development of metamemory in childhood and adolescence will be discussed in some detail. Given that we are dealing with a complex and fuzzy construct, different conceptualizations and taxonomies of metamemory as well as methodological issues are briefly summarized before we proceed to the main findings.

Conceptualizations of metamemory

As already noted above, the term "metamemory" refers to knowledge about memory processes and contents. Flavell and Wellman (1977) came up with a taxonomy of metamemory that distinguished between two main categories, "sensitivity" and "variables." The sensitivity category included knowledge of when memory activity is necessary, for instance awareness that a particular task in a particular setting requires the use of memory strategies. This category corresponds to the procedural knowledge component mentioned above and indicates mostly implicit and unconscious memory activities. In contrast, the variables category corresponds to the declarative knowledge component and refers to explicit, conscious, factual knowledge that performance in a memory task is influenced by a number of different factors or variables. In their taxonomy of metamemory, Flavell and Wellman focused on the latter category and argued that metamemory encompasses at least three different areas: person, task, and strategy knowledge. An example of a person variable is the child's mnemonic self-concept, including clear ideas about his or her memory strengths and weaknesses. The task variable refers to knowledge about characteristics of a memory task that make it easier (e.g. familiar materials, high inter-item associations) or harder (e.g. long item lists, short study time). Finally, strategy knowledge encompasses knowledge about the use of encoding and retrieval strategies in memory tasks, and of the benefit of such use for performance. Flavell and Wellman assumed that most declarative metacognitive knowledge is actually a combination of several subcategories, and that the categories should be conceived of as overlapping and interactive.

The taxonomy of metamemory was not intended to be exhaustive. A number of other theorists have since contributed to the development of metamemory theory (for useful reviews and critiques, see Joyner and Kurtz-Costes, 1997; Schneider, 1999; Schneider and Pressley, 1997; Wellman, 1985). For instance, Paris and colleagues (e.g. Paris and Lindauer, 1982; Paris and Oka, 1986) introduced a component called "conditional metacognitive knowledge" that referred to children's ability to justify or explain their decisions concerning memory actions. Whereas declarative knowledge, as defined by Flavell and colleagues, focuses on "knowing that," the component added by Paris and colleagues deals with "knowing why" information.

Subsequent research also focused on the procedural knowledge component that was not sufficiently described in Flavell and Wellman's taxonomy. Brown and her colleagues (Brown, 1978; Brown et al., 1983) elaborated on Flavell and Wellman's work. Brown's frame of reference was the competent information processor, one possessing an efficient "executive" that regulated cognitive behaviors. In her view, this regulatory component is responsible for selecting and implementing strategies, monitoring their usefulness, and modifying them when necessary. It was assumed that children do not monitor and regulate their performance well, as compared to metacognitively mature adults. Overall, Brown et al. took the perspective that memory-monitoring and regulation processes play a large role in complex cognitive tasks such as comprehending and memorizing text materials. They also argued that the two aspects of metamemory (i.e., the declarative and procedural components) complicate its definition (see also Joyner and Kurtz-Costes, 1997). That is, they are not only closely related but also fundamentally different in nature. Whereas the declarative knowledge component is primarily statable, stable, and late developing, the procedural knowledge component is not necessarily statable, rather unstable, relatively age-independent, and dependent on the specific task or situation.

Pressley, Borkowski, and their colleagues (e.g. Pressley, Borkowski, and Schneider, 1987, 1989) have proposed an elaborate model of metacognition, the Good Information Processor Model, that not only includes aspects of procedural and declarative metacognitive knowledge but also links these concepts to other features of successful information processing. According to this model, sophisticated metamemory is closely related to the learner's strategy use, motivational orientation, general knowledge about the world, and automated use of efficient learning procedures. All of these components are assumed to interact. For instance, specific strategy knowledge influences the adequate application of memory strategies, which in turn affects knowledge. As the strategies are carried out, they are monitored and evaluated, which leads to expansion and refinement of specific strategy knowledge.

Although the fuzziness and vagueness of the metamemory concept has repeatedly been criticized (e.g. Cavanaugh and Perlmutter, 1982), the basic distinction between declarative and procedural metacognitive knowledge seems widely accepted in the developmental literature (cf. Alexander, Carr, and Schwanenflugel, 1995; Schneider and Bjorklund, 1998). It should be noted, however, that another conceptualization of (declarative) metamemory has recently been developed by O'Sullivan and Howe (1995, 1998). These authors believe that the traditional conceptualization described above is overly restrictive, in that it focuses on accurate knowledge and its development over time. O'Sullivan and Howe prefer a more comprehensive view of metamemory, namely children's naive beliefs about memory. According to these authors, the advantages of such an approach include the possibility of relating developmental changes in children's beliefs about memory to their assumptions about other aspects of the mind, thus linking metamemory research to research on children's theory of mind. Moreover, young children's naive beliefs about the functions of memory can be compared with older children's assumptions, thus filling a gap in the traditional developmental metamemory literature. Finally, metamemory assessments can be conducted in areas where we are not sure about the correct answers (e.g. research on long-term retention). Although this view seems well founded and interesting, the question remains whether the assessment of naive memory beliefs as recommended by O'Sullivan and Howe (1998) is indeed qualitatively different from assessment procedures used in "traditional" metamemory interview studies (e.g. Kreutzer, Leonard, and Flavell, 1975), and whether a conceptualization of metamemory that comprises both accurate knowledge and naive beliefs represents true progress regarding the terminology issue.

Clarification of the terminology issue seems important. Figure 10.1 contains an overview of various theoretical perspectives popular in the field of developmental psychology, making links between the various taxonomies and terminologies that were used by different research lines. It should be noted that conceptualizations of metacognitive knowledge in other fields of psychology such as gerontology and general cognitive psychology are narrower in scope. For example, several questionnaires assessing declarative metamemory in adults and the elderly focus on participants' beliefs about their memory and thus restrict the concept to the person variable of Flavell and Wellman's taxonomy (e.g. Dixon and Hertzog, 1988; Herrmann, 1982). In contrast, conceptualizations of metamemory in the field of cognitive psychology exclusively elaborate on the procedural knowledge component (e.g. Metcalfe and Shimamura, 1994; Nelson, 1996; Nelson and Narens, 1990, 1994). In fact, as noted by Joyner and Kurtz-Costes, most of the current work on metamemory comes from cognitive psychologists who focus on monitoring and self-regulation processes in adults. Given that the focus of this chapter is on developmental issues, we will rely on the broader conceptualization of metamemory, describing developmental differences in both declarative and procedural knowledge components.

Development of declarative metamory

In general, children's declarative metamemory increases with age and is correlated with age-related improvements in memory behavior (see Joyner and Kurtz-Costes, 1997; Schneider, 1999; Schneider and Pressley, 1997, for recent reviews). Although it is widely believed that young children do not know much about memory, and that metamemory does not develop before the elementary school years, some qualifications seem in order here.

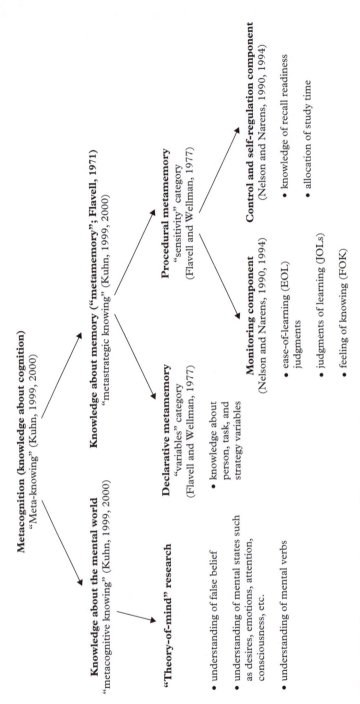

Figure 10.1 Taxonomy of metacognition components.

When do children know the relevant mental verbs?

A basic precondition for the development of declarative metamemory is understanding of mental verbs such as "thinking," "forgetting," or "knowing." Misciones et al. (1978), as well as Wellman and Johnson (1979; Johnson and Wellman, 1980), found that although four-year-olds understood mental verbs much better than did three-year-olds, children's competent use of mental verbs was highly constrained. Subsequent work in the theory-of-mind tradition (e.g. Astington and Olson, 1990; Lyon and Flavell, 1993; Schwanenflugel, Fabricius, and Alexander, 1994) confirmed that knowledge of mental verbs is a long-term development, with children's understanding being limited compared to adults' understanding, including for verbs such as remembering versus understanding, recalling versus recognizing, planning and comparing. On the other hand, the work by Johnson and Wellman (1980) showed that mental verbs can be correctly applied to mental states from the age of four years on. Thus, even though preschoolers and kindergarteners appear to have a limited understanding of the concept of memory, they can handle the basic terminology. Accordingly, it makes sense to ask young children what they know about their memory.

The development of knowledge about person, task, and strategy variables

The earliest interview study on children's metamemory was published by Kreutzer et al. (1975). Children in kindergarten, grades 1, 3, and 5, were asked about person, task, and strategy variables. For example, children were asked if they ever forgot things, if it was easier to remember the gist of a story than to recall it verbatim, and if learning pairs of opposites (e.g. "boy–girl") was easier or harder than learning pairs of unrelated words (e.g. "Mary–walk"). Other questions were more demanding. For instance, children's knowledge of retrieval strategies was tested by asking them to think of all the things they could do to try to find a jacket they had lost while at school.

Overall, the results of this study and related assessments (e.g. Myers and Paris, 1978; Schneider et al., 1986; Weinert and Schneider, 1999) indicated substantial improvements on most of the variables as a function of age. For example, 70 percent of the six-year-old children did not realize that remembering pairs of opposites would be easier than remembering unrelated pairs of words. By age eleven, 100 percent of the children said that the opposites would be easier to learn. Large age differences were consistently found for most interview items. Regarding person variables, only the older school children realized that memory skills vary from person to person and from situation to situation. Six- and seven-year-old children were convinced that they always remembered well and that they were better at remembering than their friends. This finding is consistent with other demonstrations that the memory-related self-concept of young children is overly optimistic (e.g. Yussen and Levy, 1975; Schneider, 1998a).

This does not mean, however, that young children do not possess any adequate knowledge about memory. Even the kindergarteners in the Kreutzer et al. (1975) study knew that remembering many items is more difficult than remembering just a few, and a majority of the kindergarten children knew that using external devices (e.g. writing telephone numbers down) helps in remembering information. Other studies using even younger samples of children found that preschoolers possess accurate, though rudimentary, ideas about the usefulness of a strategic approach to remembering. When asked about the importance of external retrieval cues in the context of a hide-and-seek task, even four-year-olds understood that a retrieval cue should be associated with the target (e.g. Beal, 1985; Justice, 1989; Schneider and Sodian, 1988). Another aspect of metamemory that young children do understand is the effect of effort on remembering. O'Sullivan (1993) investigated four-year-olds' knowledge about the effects of effort and incentives on recall. Results indicated that the majority of children believed that an increase in effort or incentive would yield increases in recall.

Although these interview studies demonstrated that young children do have a basic understanding of memory, more sophisticated knowledge does not appear until later. Factual knowledge about the importance of task characteristics and memory strategies develops rapidly once children enter school. Whereas young elementary school children do not have a clear understanding of the effects of task difficulty and strategy use on memory performance, this pattern changes during the next few years. For instance, only the nine- and ten-year-olds but not the seven-year-olds studied by Moynahan (1978) knew that taxonomically organized items are easier to recall than conceptually unrelated items (see also Schneider, 1986). Knowledge about the usefulness of memory strategies was tapped in several studies that focused on organizational strategies (e.g. Justice, 1985, 1986; Schneider, 1986; Sodian, Schneider, and Perlmutter, 1986). As a main result, these studies reported a major shift in knowledge between kindergarten and grade 6. For instance, Sodian et al. (1986) assessed four- and six-year-old children's understanding of organizational strategies. Children were presented videotaped memory strategies such as sorting items by category, by color, or simply looking at the items. They were then asked to make pairwise comparisons between these strategies. It was shown that both preschoolers and kindergarten children did not make a difference between taxonomic sorting and color sorting, even though sorting by category was judged more positively by the older children. Overall, the "looking at" strategy was also positively evaluated (O'Sullivan [1993] confirmed that preschoolers have great faith in this strategy, even though it is ineffective). Studies that focused on school children and included other strategies such as naming and rehearsal revealed interesting developmental trends (Justice, 1985, 1986; Schneider, 1986). Whereas four-year-olds preferred the looking strategy over all other options, six-year-olds were more likely to view all four strategies as equally effective. Eight- and ten-year-olds preferred taxonomic sorting and rehearsal, but did not differentiate between these two. By the age of twelve there is a clear understanding that taxonomic sorting is superior to rehearsal in tasks that require recall of items that can be grouped into semantic categories. Overall, it appears that younger children are able to judge the greater effectiveness of a strategy in a paired comparison task only when the two strategies under consideration produce substantially different levels of performance. In contrast, older children are able to make more subtle judgments about the effectiveness of the various strategies (Justice, 1985; Justice et al., 1997).

Similar age trends were observed when the interaction of memory variables was considered. Wellman (1978) presented memory problems to five- and ten-year-olds. Each problem consisted of ranking three picture cards, each of which contained a memorizing scenario. For instance, one set consisted of pictures of three boys, each of whom was supposed to remember a certain number of items (either three, nine, or eighteen items). This was a simple problem tapping a single task variable. A more complicated interaction problem (item by strategy) was depicted with the following three cards: (a) boy A who was to remember eighteen items simply by looking; (b) boy B who just looked at three items; and (c) boy C who wrote down the names of three items. Whereas all of the children solved the simple memory problem, substantial developmental differences were found for the complex memory problems, which were solved by almost all of the school children (i.e., those aged seven upwards) but only by a smaller proportion of the kindergarteners (i.e., five- to six-year-olds). Although these findings seem to indicate that young children have problems with considering and comparing different features of memory problems at the same time, this does not mean that they are generally unable to solve such problems. When the task was to predict memory performance based on information about the number of items and the effort invested, even kindergarteners succeeded in combining these two factors, although the role of effort was overestimated. Overall, then, it appears that knowledge about the interaction of memory variables develops very slowly, continuing well into adolescence.

Taken together, the empirical evidence illustrates that some declarative metamemory is already there in preschool children and develops steadily over the elementary school years. Knowledge of most facts about memory is already impressive by eleven or twelve years of age. Nonetheless, declarative metamemory is not complete by the end of childhood. For instance, several studies on knowledge about text processing have shown that understanding the relative importance of text elements and the effectiveness of different reading strategies continues to develop, as does understanding of task and person variable interactions that determine memory (see Baker and Brown, 1984; Brown et al., 1983; Schneider and Pressley, 1997). Even adolescents and young adults lack knowledge about some powerful and important memory strategies when the task is to read, comprehend, and memorize complex text materials (see Garner, 1987; Pressley and Afflerbach, 1995).

Development of procedural metamemory

According to Nelson and Narens (1990, 1994), self-monitoring and self-regulation correspond to two different levels of metacognitive processing that interact very closely. Self-monitoring refers to keeping track of where you are with your goal of understanding and remembering (a bottom-up process). In comparison, self-regulation or control refers to central executive activities and includes planning, directing, and evaluating your behavior (a top-down process).

The most studied type of procedural metamemory is that of self-monitoring: evaluating how well one is progressing (e.g. Borkowski, Milstead, and Hale, 1988; Brown et al., 1983; Schneider, 1998b). The developmental literature has focused on monitoring components such as ease-of-learning (EOL) judgments, judgments of learning (JOL), and feeling-of-knowing (FOK) judgments, and also explored some aspects of control and self-regulation such as allocation of study time and termination of study.

EOL judgments occur in advance of the learning process, are largely inferential, and refer to items that have not yet been learned (Nelson and Narens, 1994). The corresponding memory paradigm is performance prediction. A form of performance prediction, first introduced by Flavell, Friedrichs, and Hoyt (1970) and subsequently often used in developmental research, is prediction of one's own memory span. Individuals are presented incrementally longer lists of materials to be learned, such as pictures, words, or figures, and are asked to indicate whether they could still recall a list that long. Children's memory is then tapped using the same lists. Comparisons of the predictor value with actual memory span yields the metamemory indicator. Performance prediction accuracy can be measured for a variety of memory tasks, including list-learning paradigms and text-learning tasks (see Schneider, Körkel, and Weinert, 1990).

Of the studies on EOL judgments that used list-learning paradigms, most have found that preschool and kindergarten children overestimate their memory performance, whereas elementary school children are much more accurate (e.g. Schneider et al., 1986; Worden and Sladewski-Awig, 1982; Yussen and Levy, 1975). Although this phenomenon has been repeatedly observed, the underlying mechanisms are not yet clear. Several studies have tried to identify young children's difficulties in making accurate performance predictions. It was found that their predictions tended to be more accurate in familiar than in unfamiliar, laboratory-type situations (Justice and Bray, 1979; Schneider, 1998a; Wippich, 1980). Moreover, young children's predictions were more accurate when they were tested using nonverbal as opposed to more traditional verbal measures (e.g. Cunningham and Weaver, 1989). Also, preschoolers and kindergarteners were found to be more accurate in predicting other children's performance than their own (Schneider, 1998a; Stipek, 1984).

Overall, more recent work on this issue does not support the original assumption that young children's overestimations of future performance are due to metacognitive deficiencies (Schneider, 1998a; Visé and Schneider, 2000). For instance, the study by Visé and Schneider explored possible reasons for young children's unrealistic predictions. In particular, the study examined whether overestimation in performance prediction is due to deficits in metacognitive monitoring or to motivational factors, for example wishful thinking. Four-, six-, and nine-year-old children were asked to predict their own performance in motor tasks (ball throwing and jumping) and memory tasks (memory span and hide-and-seek task). Children in the "wish condition" were asked to declare which performance they wished to achieve in the next trial, children in the "expectation condition" were asked to indicate which scores they expected to achieve in the next trial. A comparison of children's performance and their postdictions (i.e., their estimates of performance assessed after completion of the task) indicated that all children were well able to monitor their performance, regardless of task, even though they did not use this knowledge for further predictions. Accordingly, the memory monitoring deficiency hypothesis could not account for the overestimation phenomenon. Furthermore, four- and six-year-old children did not differentiate between their wishes and their expectations, thus replicating and extending the findings by motivational researchers (e.g. Stipek, 1984; Wellman, 1985). However, even for nine-year-old children, significant differences between estimate conditions (wish versus expectation) were only found for the jumping task. Taken together, findings gave at least partial support for the wishful thinking hypothesis and also clear evidence that overestimation in preschoolers and kindergarteners was linked to their belief (causal attribution) that effort has a powerful effect on performance. However, because such motivational processes are not similarly influential in school children, performance on EOL tasks indeed reflects memory monitoring in this population. Although EOL judgments can already be accurate in young elementary school children, there are subtle improvements over the elementary school years (see Pressley and Ghatala, 1990; Schneider et al., 1990).

Whereas numerous developmental studies have addressed differences in memory performance prediction, only a few studies have dealt with *judgments of learning (JOL)* that occur during or soon after acquisition of memory materials and are predictions about future test performance on recently studied (and probably still recallable) items. Some studies evaluated children's postdictions (Bisanz, Vesonder, and Voss, 1978; Pressley, Levin, Ghatala, and Ahmad, 1987). For instance, Pressley et al. compared seven- and ten-year-olds' postdictions for entire word lists and individual items. There were two major findings: (a) although rather accurate postdictions were found even for the younger age group, the older children were significantly better; and (b) those children who were most accurate with regard to estimating performance on individual items were not necessarily similarly accurate when asked to postdict performance on the entire list, and vice versa.

In a more recent study, Schneider et al. (2000) used a paired-associate learning task to assess developmental trends in six-, eight-, and ten-year-olds' JOL judgments. A major goal of the study was to explore whether children's delayed JOLs (given about 30 seconds after the learning process) would correspond more closely with actual learning outcomes than judgments provided immediately after learning the item pairs (i.e., immediate JOLs). The so-called "delayed-JOL effect" has been repeatedly confirmed in the adult literature (e.g. Mazzoni and Nelson, 1995; Nelson and Dunlosky, 1991). A second goal of the study was to compare individual-item JOLs with aggregate JOLs based on all items of a given list. As a main result, findings indicated that the delayed-JOL effect typically observed for adults also operated in children, regardless of age. That is, individual-item JOLs were much more accurate when obtained after a delay of about 30 seconds than immediately after study. Secondly, overconfidence was typically larger for item-by-item JOLs than for aggregate-item JOLs for all age groups, thus replicating the aggregation effect obtained with adults. As a matter of fact, the pattern of findings for the older school children was very similar to that found for adults. In accord with the findings reported by Pressley, Levin, Ghatala, and Ahmad (1987), however, only low to moderate correlations were found between the two estimation procedures, which leads one to assume that they are tapping different aspects of the estimation process (see also Mazzoni and Nelson, 1995; Nelson and Narens, 1994).

Overall, these findings support the assumption that children's ability to judge their own memory performance after study of test materials seems to increase over the elementary school years. However, even young children are able to monitor their performance quite accurately when judgments are given not immediately after study but are somewhat delayed. According to Nelson and Narens (1994), the difference in accuracy between immediate and delayed judgments could be due to the fact that immediate judgments are based on analyses tapping working memory, whereas delayed judgements are based on search processes addressing the contents of the long-term store.

A number of studies have explored children's *feeling-of-knowing (FOK) accuracy* (e.g. Cultice, Somerville, and Wellman, 1983; DeLoache and Brown, 1984; Wellman, 1977). FOK judgments occur either during or after a learning procedure and are judgments about whether a currently unrecallable item will be remembered at a subsequent retention test. Typically, children are shown a series of items and asked to name them. When children cannot recall the name of an object given its picture, they are asked to indicate whether the name could be recognized if the experimenter provided it. These FOK ratings are then related to subsequent performance on the recognition test.

Overall, most of the available evidence on FOK judgments suggests that FOK accuracy improves continuously across childhood and adolescence (e.g. Wellman, 1977; Zabrucky and Ratner, 1986). However, the pattern of developmental trends is not entirely clear. In a study that avoided a methodological problem apparent in previous research on FOK judgments, Butterfield, Nelson, and Peck (1988) showed that six-year-olds' FOK judgments were actually more accurate than those of ten- and eighteen-year-olds. Obviously, this finding did not square well with the results of previous research.

A recent study by Lockl and Schneider (in press) was based on a methodologically improved design similar to that used by Butterfield et al. (1988) but included different age groups (i.e., seven-, eight-, nine-, and ten-year-olds). Although the major goal of this study was to replicate the findings by Butterfield and colleagues, another aim was to explore the basis of FOK judgments by comparing the traditional "trace-based" view with the "trace accessibility" model developed by Koriat (1993). Whereas the former assumes a two-stage process of monitoring and retrieval, the latter proposes that FOK judgments are based on retrieval attempts and determined by the amount of information that can be spontaneously generated, regardless of its correctness. A prediction derived from the trace accessibility view is that FOK judgments for correctly recalled items and incorrect answers (commission errors) should be comparably high and also considerably higher than FOK judgments for omission errors. As a main result regarding the first question, no developmental trends in the accuracy of FOK judgments were found. Overall, FOK accuracy was low but significantly above chance for all age groups. The main difference between these findings and those by Butterfield and colleagues concerned the performance of the youngest age group (i.e., first graders). Whereas FOK accuracy was rather high for the American first graders, it was lower in the case of the German first graders. Although there is no truly convincing reason for the differences between both studies regarding their youngest age groups, the findings suggest that there are no significant developmental trends in FOK accuracy over the course of the elementary school years. However, given the inconsistency in findings for the young elementary school children, more research is needed here.

Furthermore, Lockl and Schneider's findings provided support for the "trace accessibility" view and the assumption that feeling of knowing can be dissociated from knowing. That is, the magnitude of FOK judgments given after commission errors did not differ much from that of FOK judgments provided after correct recall. In comparison, FOK judgments were considerably higher after commission than after omission errors. This contrasts sharply with the finding that recognition performance was comparable in the case of commission and omission errors (about 50 percent correct), whereas it was nearly perfect when items had been already correctly recalled before.

Several developmental studies addressed aspects of children's *control and self-regulation processes* such as termination of study and allocation of study time. One example of self-regulation concerns knowledge of *recall readiness*. Recall readiness assessments are made after material has been studied at least once. Typically, participants are asked to continue studying until their memory of the materials to be learned is perfect. For instance, Flavell et al. (1970) found that kindergarten children are often too optimistic about their readiness for a test and have low levels of recall after they say they are ready. By comparison, elementary school children were found to be considerably more accurate. Flavell et al. concluded from this that older children's more accurate assessments were due to their greater self-testing during study.

One problem with this interpretation is that relatively short lists of items corresponding to each child's memory span were used in this study. In subsequent studies that included memory tasks other than serial recall (e.g. free recall, memory for text), older elementary school children were not very good at determining when they had studied items long enough to master the material (e.g. Gettinger, 1985; Leal, Crays, and Moely, 1985). Self-testing strategies were rarely observed in these studies. Apparently, most grade-school children do not spontaneously use task-relevant regulation strategies in recall readiness tasks. Although self-testing occurs more frequently as a function of increasing age, there is still room for improvement in this skill during adolescence and young adulthood.

Another example of self-regulation concerns the *allocation of study time*. Research on study time allocation observes how learners deploy their attention and effort. As already noted by Brown et al. (1983), the ability to attend selectively to relevant aspects of a memory task is a traditional index of the learner's understanding of the task. Developmental studies on the allocation of study time examined whether school children and adults were more likely to spend more time on less well-learned material. In a classic experiment, Masur, McIntyre, and Flavell (1973) asked seven-year-olds, nine-year-olds, and college students to learn a list of pictures for free recall. After the first study and first free recall trial, participants were instructed to select half of the pictures for additional study. Although all of the participants could distinguish between recalled and unrecalled items, the older children and adults were more likely to select previously unrecalled items for further study (for similar findings, see Bisanz et al., 1978).

One problem with the studies by Masur et al. (1973) and Bisanz et al. (1978) is that participants were forced to be selective. Thus it remains unclear how young children may behave in a more spontaneous study situation. Spontaneous allocation of study time was assessed by Dufresne and Kobasigawa (1989). In this study, six-, eight-, ten-, and twelve-year-old children were asked to study booklets containing either "easy" (highly related) or "hard" (unrelated) paired-associate items until they were sure they could remember all pairs perfectly. As a main result, it was demonstrated that the younger participants (six- and eight-year-olds) spent about the same amount of time on easy pairs as they spent on hard pairs. In contrast, participants in the two older age groups devoted considerably more time to studying the hard items than the easy ones. These findings are in accord with those of previous studies, in that cognitive self-regulation can be observed in older but not younger school children (e.g. Bisanz et al., 1978). Dufresne and Kobasigawa (1989) noted that the younger children in their study were well able to discriminate between easy and hard pairs. Accordingly, it appears that the major difference between the younger and older school children in their sample concerned the monitoring–self-regulation link. That is, accurate monitoring lead to appropriate self-regulation in the older subsample but not in the group of younger children. Although a more recent study by Kobasigawa and Metcalf-Haggert (1993) indicates that even six-year-old children can allocate study time differentially when differences in item difficulty are particularly salient, this seems more of an exception than a rule.

To explore the transition from inappropriate to appropriate study time allocation in more detail, Lockl and Schneider (2002) recruited samples of children aged seven, nine, and ten years. Children were presented with a series of paired-associated pictures (e.g. pictures of an apple and a pear, which is an easy-to-remember item-pair; pictures of a carrot and a book, which is a hard-to-remember item-pair). Children were told that they had to study the pictures until they were sure they could remember all pairs perfectly. In order to overcome certain methodological problems of previous studies (Dufresne and Kobasigawa, 1989; Kobasigawa and Metcalf-Haggert, 1993), the items were presented via computer which allowed study times to be measured more precisely. Moreover, the order of "easy" and "difficult" item-pairs was randomly determined for every child by the computer. As a main result, the outcomes of previous studies were confirmed: whereas young school children spent about the same amount of time on easy pairs as they spent on hard pairs, older school children devoted more time to studying the hard items than the easy ones. Accordingly, signs of effective self-regulation were observed in advanced elementary school children but were absent in younger children. In accord with the findings of Dufresne and Kobasigawa (1989), even young children were able to distinguish between hard and easy pairs.

One problem with the paradigm of the allocation of study time is that it may not only tap metacognitive processes but may also be influenced by motivational variables. Le Ny, Denhière, and Le Taillanter (1972) assumed that "the process of studying a particular item is dependent upon the motivation state induced through instructions; these determine a 'norm of study' to be reached" (p. 281). In fact, several studies confirmed the "norm-affects-allocation hypothesis" in the adult literature (e.g. Dunlosky and Thiede, 1998; Nelson and Leonesio, 1988). That is, self-paced study time was affected by instructions provided to the participants. However, the question remains whether young children are also sensitive to changes in the norm of study. Possibly, young children could demonstrate more effective self-regulation skills when a higher norm of study is induced.

To explore this issue further, Lockl and Schneider (in preparation) conducted a study which investigated the effects of incentives and instructions on children's learning. Half of the seven- and nine-year-olds involved in the experiment were told that each correct answer would result in five cents being added to a book gift certificate for their class. Following the procedure by Dunlosky and Thiede (1998) one group was instructed to study until they were absolutely certain that they remember each pair ("accuracy-emphasized instructions"), and the other group was told to spend only as much time as was needed to learn each item ("speed-emphasized instructions"). Overall, the results confirm the findings obtained in previous studies, with older children differentiating more between easy and difficult pairs. Regarding the effects of instructions, the study revealed that the children studied all pairs longer when they were told to study until they were absolutely certain that they remember each pair. Moreover, this instruction also increased the difference of the study times between easy- and hard-to-remember pairs. That is, the children tended to spend more time on hard materials than on easy materials when the importance of mastery was emphasized. However, the accuracy-emphasized instruction had a smaller effect on younger children than on older children. Regarding the impact of incentives, no differences in study time were found between those children who received five cents for every correct answer and children who did not receive anything. Accordingly, these findings indicate that young children cannot be prompted easily to spend more time on studying hard material. Further research is needed to investigate whether stronger or more engaging incentives may lead to a more effective regulation of study time in young children.

Taken together, the available evidence on the development of self-regulation skills shows that there are clear increases from middle childhood to adolescence. Effective self-regulation occurs only in highly constrained situations during the elementary school years and continues well into adolescence. In contrast, the literature on the development of monitoring skills yields a less consistent pattern. Although most studies indicated age-related increases, others showed no developmental trend at all. More developmental research based on sophisticated methodologies is needed to solve this puzzle.

Metamemory–memory relationships

From the beginning, one main reason for studying metamemory was because of the presumed relationship to memory performance. Many researchers believed that there was a reciprocal relationship between knowing about memory and memory behaviors (e.g. Flavell and Wellman, 1977; Weinert, 1986). However, the same researchers also emphasized the fact that one cannot always expect strong links between metamemory and memory behavior. For one thing, the learner might not be motivated enough to exert the effort necessary to use a memory strategy, or may be too tired to carry out the strategy. Another possibility is that there may not be sufficient time to use the procedure.

Correlational evidence for the metamory–memory performance relationship

In view of these theoretical problems, it came as no surprise that the first series of empirical studies on the metamemory–memory link yielded only weak support for such a relationship (cf. the reviews by Brown et al., 1983; Cavanaugh and Perlmutter, 1982). In view of only low to moderate correlations, Cavanaugh and Perlmutter came to a very pessimistic conclusion and assumed that the study of metamemory had little value.

In contrast to Cavanaugh and Perlmutter's (1982) discouraging analysis, subsequent reviews of the literature developed a more optimistic view (see Schneider, 1985; Wellman, 1983). In a first statistical meta-analysis of empirical studies addressing the metamemory–memory relationship issue, Schneider (1985) reported an overall correlation of 0.41, which was based on twenty-seven studies and a total of 2,231 participants. A second meta-analysis carried out a few years later and based on a considerably larger sample (sixty studies and more than 7,000 participants) replicated the 0.41 correlation. Correlations were also calculated separately for memory monitoring (laboratory tasks, text processing, and training studies), and declarative metamemory (in particular, knowledge about memory strategies; see Schneider and Pressley, 1997, for more details). As a main result, clear-cut age-related increases were found for the correlation between metacognitive knowledge about strategy use and memory performance. The memory monitoring data were less consistent, indicating that, depending on the specific task requirements, correlations between monitoring and memory performance could be substantial even for young school children, and typically did not increase much as a function of age.

Overall, then, there is no doubt that there is a reliable statistical association between metamemory and memory. Even though caution is required in evaluating the age trends due to small numbers of correlations in some of the categories, the data are generally homogeneous from grade 4 (nine to ten years) on. For instance, the correlations for monitoring observed in laboratory tasks are greater than those for organizational strategies at the younger age levels but not for older school children. The size of correlations depended on several factors such as the type of task (e.g. organizational strategies versus EOL judgments), age of the child, task difficulty, and presentation of the metamemory assessment (before or after the memory task). The relation seems generally stronger for older than for younger children, and after experience with a memory task than before.

For example, studies looking at metamemory–memory behavior relationships in semantic categorization and elaboration tasks did not yield strong connections between the two factors until the elementary school years (e.g. Lange, Guttentag, and Nida, 1990; Schneider, 1986), and not consistently until age ten (Hasselhorn, 1992, 1995). Indeed, the "strategy emergence theory" advanced by Hasselhorn (1995) assumes that strategic knowledge is acquired between ages eight and ten, mainly due to important changes in the children's knowledge base occurring at the start of elementary school. However, although the metamemory–memory behavior link typically increases as a function of age, its quality and size are affected by the type of task. For instance, metamemory–memory relationships are far from perfect when performance on complex text comprehension tasks is analyzed (e.g. Körkel and Schneider, 1992). On the other hand, when the task is simple and familiar, as in the case of the hide-and-seek tasks described above, substantial metamemory–memory relationships can be found even for preschool children (e.g. Schneider and Sodian, 1988).

Causal modeling approaches

In general, the research evidence based on numerous correlational studies points to a bidirectional relationship between metamemory and memory behavior (Borkowski et al., 1988; Brown, 1978; Schneider, 1985). Metamemory can influence behavior, which in turn leads to enhanced metamemory. Several studies (e.g. Fabricius and Hagen, 1984; Hasselhorn, 1986; Kurtz and Weinert, 1989; Schneider, Körkel, and Weinert, 1987) have used multivariate causal modeling procedures to examine the causal interplay among metamemory, memory behavior, and memory performance. These analyses permit the conclusion that even relatively young elementary school children possess knowledge that has direct impact on strategic behaviors, which in turn adds to their task-specific metamemory.

In one recent study, Schneider, Schlagmüller, and Visé (1998) first constructed a comprehensive metamemory battery that was repeatedly administered to a large sample of more than 600 nine-, and ten-year-olds. The battery assessed both general memory knowledge and task-specific knowledge, that is, knowledge about categorization strategies.

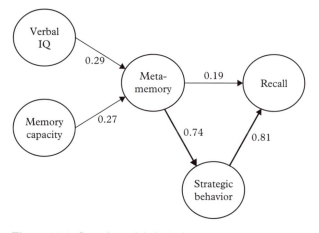

Figure 10.2 Causal model depicting metamemory–memory relationships (modified after Schneider, Schlagmüller, and Visé, 1998).

A subsample of these children were then given a sort–recall task, memory span and articulation speed tasks, and also an intelligence test. Results of a LISREL (linear structural equation modeling) causal modeling procedure revealed that both IQ and memory capacity had a moderate direct impact on metamemory (see Figure 10.2). Moreover, metamemory had a substantial indirect effect of about 0.6 on recall (via strategy use). There was also a very strong direct link between strategy use and recall. Consequently, individual differences in metamemory explained a large proportion of the variance in the recall data (see Körkel and Schneider, 1992, for similar patterns of findings regarding text recall).

Findings from training studies

Several investigations of the relationship between metamemory and strategy use have been in training studies, which attempted to move beyond simple correlations in order to understand the causal relationship among metamemory, strategy use, and memory performance (i.e., amount of recall). In most of these studies, children were first given baseline metamemory and memory assessments, before they were instructed in the use of one or more memory strategies. In a last step, metamemory and memory were assessed in a post-test session. Several researchers used so-called "transfer" tasks in the post-test session to assess the flexibility of strategy use in a situation that was similar but not identical to the one experienced during the training sessions. The idea behind this was that "metamnemonically sophisticated" children would have greater facility than their peers in learning new strategies and transferring these strategies to new task settings (see Borkowski, 1985; Brown et al., 1983).

For instance, Carr et al. (1989) instructed young American and German elementary school children in how to use organizational strategies. The training procedure took several sessions and was aimed at improving children's conditional metacognitive knowledge ("knowing why"). Children were not only taught the organizational strategy but also informed about the strategy's particular advantage regarding long-term retention of items. They were given feedback about performance changes as a function of practice, and also explicitly told that improvement was due to strategy use. Furthermore, children learned to distinguish situations where strategy use was appropriate from those where it was not.

As a main result, most of the children in both samples acquired the organizational strategy very quickly and considerably improved their declarative knowledge about memory strategies. Interestingly, in a transfer task given several months later, success was positively correlated with task-specific metamemory. This finding is in accord with those obtained from large-scale studies conducted by Paris and colleagues (e.g. Paris and Oka, 1986) that used such an "informed strategy approach" in the area of reading comprehension.

Researchers focusing on the strategy instruction approach repeatedly emphasized that simply teaching a student how to carry out a strategy does not ensure that the student understands how the strategy benefits performance (e.g. Pressley, Borkowski, and O'Sullivan, 1985; Pressley and McCormick, 1995). Obviously, such understanding is critical for a student to use a strategy after instruction. An important series of studies carried out by these researchers dealt with children's monitoring abilities when a decision between competing strategies had to be made. These studies were motivated by the idea that even though most children (and many adults) do not effectively monitor the effectiveness of strategies spontaneously, they may be able to do so after specific instruction. For instance, Ghatala, Levin, Pressley, and their colleagues (e.g. Ghatala, 1986; Ghatala, Levin, Pressley, and Goodwin, 1986) conducted several studies that focused on monitoring strategy effectiveness. In most of these studies, young elementary school children practiced two strategies, one of which was more appropriate than the other for the given memory task. Then children were required to select one of the two strategies on a maintenance trial. It was shown that in order for monitoring training to be effective in young elementary school children, it had to be very explicit, repeatedly illustrating the advantages of the better strategy and reminding children to keep track of their performance as a function of strategy use. By comparison, even though older children and adolescents did not always spontaneously monitor strategy effectiveness, rather subtle reminders were sufficient to establish monitoring in these groups.

Recent trends and future directions

As noted above, much of the current work on metamemory comes from cognitive psychologists who focus on monitoring and self-regulation processes in adults. Nonetheless, research on developmental issues in the field of metamemory is still active, particularly in more applied settings. In the final section of this chapter, we summarize recent developments.

Metamemory in educational settings

During the last fifteen years or so, several attempts have been made to apply metacognitive theory to educational settings (cf. Moely et al., 1986; Moely, Santulli, and Obach, 1995; Palincsar, 1986; Paris and Oka, 1986; Pressley, 1995; Pressley, Goodchild, Fleet, and Zajchowski, 1989).

One interesting and effective approach to teaching knowledge about strategies was developed by Palinscar and Brown (1984). Here, teachers and students take turns executing reading strategies that are being taught with instruction occurring in true dialogue. Strategic processes are made very overt, with plenty of exposure to modeling of strategies and opportunities to practice these techniques over the course of a number of lessons. The goal is that children discover the utility of reading strategies, and that teachers convey strategy-utility information as well as information about when and where to use particular strategies. Teachers using reciprocal instruction assume more responsibility for strategy implementation early in instruction, gradually transferring control over to the student (see Palincsar, 1986, for an extensive description of the implementation of reciprocal instruction; see Rosenshine and Meister, 1994, for a realistic appraisal of its benefits).

Another more large-scale approach concerns the implementation of comprehensive evaluation programs that aim to assess the systematic instruction of metacognitive knowledge in schools. As emphasized by Joyner and Kurtz-Costes (1997), both Moely and Pressley, with their colleagues, have conducted very ambitious programs of evaluating effective instruction in public school systems. For instance, Pressley and colleagues found that effective teachers regularly incorporated strategy instruction and metacognitive information about effective strategy selection and modification as a part of daily instruction. It seems important to note that strategy instruction was not carried out in isolation but integrated in the curriculum and taught as part of language, arts, mathematics, science, and social studies. In accord with the assumption of the Good Information Processor Model outlined above (Pressley, Borkowski, and Schneider, 1989), effective teachers did not emphasize the use of single strategies but taught the flexible use of a range of procedures that corresponded to subject matter, time constraints, and other task demands. On most occasions, strategy instruction occurred in groups, with the teachers modeling appropriate strategy use. By comparison, the work by Moely and colleagues illustrated that the effective teaching process described by Pressley and colleagues does not necessarily constitute the rule, and that effective teachers may represent a minority group in elementary school classrooms. That is, Moely's observations of teaching methods in regular classrooms revealed that, in general, teachers did not support metacognitive processing very much, and that there was much room for improvement. Taken together, the careful documentations of instructional procedures carried out by Pressley, Moely, and their research groups have shown that there is a lot of potential for metacognitively guided instructional processes in children's everyday learning.

Other researchers have focused on the relationship between measures of metamemory and children's school performance. For instance, Geary, Klosterman, and Adrales (1990) explored the relationship between declarative metamemory and academic performance in second and fourth graders. The sample not only included "normal" elementary school children but also learning-disabled children. Not surprisingly, Geary et al. found that fourth graders performed better than second graders on the metamemory battery, and that metamemory–memory relationships increased with age, even though the link was moderate at best. Contrary to expectations, however, children with learning disabilities did not perform differently from academically normal children.

A similarly unexpected finding was presented by Farrant, Boucher, and Blades (1999), who compared metamemory abilities in children with autism, age- and language-matched mentally retarded children, and language-matched young normal controls. Children's ages in the various experiments ranged from five to nine years. The metamemory tests used in these studies included items derived from the Kreutzer et al. (1975) battery and also false-belief tasks. It was hypothesized that children with autism should show impairments of metacognitive knowledge because their concepts of self and others are less well developed compared to those of normal children, and because their executive functions may be impaired. Surprisingly, these predictions were not supported. The children with autism were not impaired on any of the metamemory tasks, although they were less likely than controls to make spontaneous use of memory strategies involving other people. Also, unexpectedly few of the children failed the false-belief tasks. Although the autistic children in the study by Farrant et al. (1999) were somewhat special in that they also performed rather well on standard tests of intelligence, the fact that both their metacognitive knowledge and their performance on false-belief tasks was unimpaired represents something of a mystery and is not compatible with current theories of the psychological causes of autism. In particular, the findings challenge those theories that suggest that people with autism have impaired acquisition of concepts and understandings of self and others.

Memory monitoring and eyewitness memory

The importance of memory monitoring and control processes for children's and adults' testimony has been demonstrated in several recent studies by Koriat, Goldsmith, and their colleagues. Koriat and Goldsmith (1994, 1996) developed a framework for the strategic regulation of memory accuracy which was based on eyewitness reports of adults. The underlying assumption was that in recounting past events, people do not simply report all that comes to mind, but attempt to control their memory reporting in accordance with a variety of personal and situational goals. One particular means of strategic control is what Koriat and Goldsmith called *report option*, that is, the option to choose which pieces of information to report and which to withhold. When a premium is placed on accurate reporting, as for example in eyewitness testimony, adult rememberers attempt to enhance the accuracy of the information that they provide by selectively screening out answers that are likely to be incorrect. As shown by Koriat and Goldsmith (1994, 1996), the accuracy of adults' testimony can be further increased when incentives are given in that correct answers are reinforced by monetary rewards.

In a recent study, Koriat et al. (in press) used the experimental approach developed by Koriat and Goldsmith (1994) to investigate whether report option plays a similar role in children's eyewitness testimony. Koriat et al. (in press) presented children of ages eight to thirteen with a computerized slide show which depicted an incident in the life of a family. Next, several versions of a metamemory questionnaire were provided that orthogonally manipulated test format (i.e., recall versus recognition) and report option (i.e., free versus forced report). That is, in addition to the standard methods of free recall and forced recognition, Koriat et al. also included two uncommon procedures, forced recall, in which children were required to provide an answer to all questions, and free recognition, in which they had the option of skipping over multiple-choice items. The same motivation for accurate reporting was maintained for all conditions (through monetary payoff).

As a main result, Koriat et al. found that children of all ages could enhance the accuracy of their testimony by screening out wrong answers under free-report conditions. However, in addition to age differences in memory quantity, there were also age differences in the accuracy of information provided under free-report conditions in that the older children outperformed the younger ones. Interestingly, these age differences were also obtained in retesting after one year, even in the high-incentive condition. Nevertheless, despite the observed age differences, it seems important to note that the absolute levels of accuracy demonstrated by the youngest participants (i.e., eight-year-olds) achieved in immediate testing were rather high. Thus the findings of this study indicate that young children can regulate their memory reporting to produce a more accurate record of past events when they are allowed to screen out wrong answers and when they are explicitly motivated to do so. Undoubtedly, this finding has important practical implications for forensic interviewing.

In a related study, Roebers, Moga, and Schneider (2001) assessed recall accuracy of even younger children (six- to eight-year-olds) and adults using a similar scenario. Participants were shown a video film about a conflict between two groups of children. Three weeks later, they were asked a set of unbiased specific questions about the video. Participants' accuracy motivation was manipulated across three conditions: they were either forced to provide an answer to each question (low-accuracy motivation), or initially instructed to withhold answers when they were not sure about their correctness (medium-accuracy motivation), or instructed to withhold answers *and* rewarded for each correct answer (high-accuracy motivation). Overall, results revealed the expected age trends regarding quantity and quality of recall. However, when motivation for accuracy was high, even the youngest children in the sample performed very well. It seems impressive that no age differences in accuracy were found in this condition (free report plus incentive), even though adults were included in the sample.

Taken together, studies exploring metamemory in applied settings have shown that the concept is highly relevant in explaining performance differences in school or at court. Although we have learned a lot about the development of metacognitive knowledge in childhood and adolescence, there is still more to explore. Despite its fuzziness, the metamemory construct has managed to maintain its importance over a period of thirty years. We predict that it will continue to do so for some time to come.

REFERENCES

Alexander, J. M., Carr, M., and Schwanenflugel, P. J. (1995). Development of metacognition in gifted children: directions for future research. *Developmental Review*, 15, 1–37.

Astington, J. W., and Olson, D. R. (1990). Metacognitive and metalinguistic language: learning to talk about thought. *Applied Psychology: An International Review*, 39, 77–87.

Baker, L., and Brown, A. L. (1984). Metacognitive skills and reading. In P. D. Pearson (ed.), *Handbook of reading research*, pp. 353–394. New York: Longman.

Beal, C. R. (1985). Development of knowledge about the use of cues to aid prospective retrieval. *Child Development*, 56, 631–642.

Bisanz, G. L., Vesonder, G. T., and Voss, J. F. (1978). Knowledge of one's own responding and the relation of such knowledge to learning. *Journal of Experimental Child Psychology*, 25, 116–128.

Borkowski, J. G. (1985). Signs of intelligence: strategy generalization and metacognition. In S. R. Yussen (ed.), *The growth of reflection in children*, pp. 105–144. Orlando: Academic Press.

Borkowski, J. G., Milstead, M., and Hale, C. (1988). Components of children's metamemory: implications for strategy generalization. In F. E. Weinert and M. Perlmutter (eds.), *Memory development: universal changes and individual differences*, pp. 73–100. Hillsdale, NJ: Lawrence Erlbaum Associates.

Brown, A. L. (1978). Knowing when, where and how to remember: a problem of metacognition. In R. Glaser (ed.), *Advances in instructional psychology, Volume 1*, pp. 77–165. Hillsdale, NJ: Lawrence Erlbaum Associates.

Brown, A. L., Bransford, J. D., Ferrara, R. A., and Campione, J. C. (1983). Learning, remembering, and understanding. In J. H. Flavell and E. M. Markham (eds.), *Handbook of child psychology: Volume III. Cognitive development*, pp. 77–166. New York: Wiley.

Butterfield, E. C., Nelson, T. O., and Peck, V. (1988). Developmental aspects of the feeling of knowing. *Developmental Psychology*, 24, 654–663.

Carr, M., Kurtz, B. E., Schneider, W., Turner, L. A., and Borkowski, J. G. (1989). Strategy acquisition and transfer among American and German children: environmental influences on metacognitive development. *Developmental Psychology*, 25, 765–771.

Cavanaugh, J. C., and Perlmutter, M. (1982). Metamemory: a critical examination. *Child Development*, 53, 11–28.

Cultice, J. C., Somerville, S. C., and Wellman, H. M. (1983). Preschoolers' memory monitoring: feeling-of-knowing judgments. *Child Development*, 54, 1480–1486.

Cunningham, J. G., and Weaver, S. L. (1989). Young children's knowledge of their memory span: effects of task and experience. *Journal of Experimental Child Psychology*, 48, 32–44.

DeLoache, J. S., and Brown, A. L. (1984). Where do I go next? Intelligent searching by very young children. *Developmental Psychology*, 20, 37–44.

Dixon, R. A., and Hertzog, C. (1988). A functional approach to memory and metamemory development in adulthood. In F. E. Weinert and M. Perlmutter (eds.), *Memory development: universal changes and individual differences*, pp. 293–330. Hillsdale, NJ: Lawrence Erlbaum Associates.

Dufresne, A., and Kobasigawa, A. (1989). Children's spontaneous allocation of study time: differential and sufficient aspects. *Journal of Experimental Child Psychology*, 47, 274–296.

Dunlosky, J., and Thiede, K. W. (1998). What makes people study more? An evaluation of factors that affect self-paced study. *Acta Psychologica*, 98, 37–56.

Fabricius, W. V., and Hagen, J. W. (1984). The use of causal attributions about recall performance to assess metamemory and predict strategic memory behavior in young children. *Developmental Psychology*, 20, 975–987.

Farrant, A., Boucher, J., and Blades, M. (1999). Metamemory in children with autism. *Child Development*, 70, 107–131.

Flavell, J. H. (1971). First discussant's comments: what is memory development the development of? *Human Development*, 14, 272–278.

　(1979). Metacognition and cognitive monitoring. A new area of cognitive-developmental inquiry. *American Psychologist*, 34, 906–911.

　(2000). Development of children's knowledge about the mental world. *International Journal of Behavioral Development*, 24, 15–23.

Flavell, J. H., Friedrichs, A. G., and Hoyt, J. D. (1970). Developmental changes in memorization processes. *Cognitive Psychology*, 1, 324–340.

Flavell, J. H., Miller, P. H., and Miller, S. A. (1993). *Cognitive development*. Englewood Cliffs, NJ: Prentice-Hall.

Flavell, J. H., and Wellman, H. M. (1977). Metamemory. In R. V. Kail and J. W. Hagen (eds.), *Perspectives on the development of memory and cognition*, pp. 3–33. Hillsdale, NJ: Lawrence Erlbaum Associates.

Garner, R. (1987). *Metacognition and reading comprehension*. Norwood, NJ: Ablex.

Geary, D. D., Klosterman, I. H., and Adrales, K. (1990). Metamemory and academic achievement: testing the validity of a group-administered metamemory battery. *Journal of Genetic Psychology*, 151, 439–450.

Gettinger, M. (1985). Time allocated and time spent relative to time needed for learning as determinants of achievement. *Journal of Educational Psychology*, 77, 3–11.

Ghatala, E. S. (1986). Strategy-monitoring training enables young learners to select effective strategies. *Educational Psychologist*, 21, 43–54.

Ghatala, E. S., Levin, J. R., Pressley, M., and Goodwin, D. (1986). A componential analysis of the effects of derived and supplied strategy-utility information on children's strategy selections. *Journal of Experimental Child Psychology*, 41, 76–92.

Hasselhorn, M. (1986). *Differentielle Bedingungsanalyse verbaler Gedächtnisleistungen bei Schulkindern*. Frankfurt a. Main: Peter Lang.

　(1992). Task dependency and the role of category typicality and metamemory in the development of an organizational strategy. *Child Development*, 63, 202–214.

　(1995). Beyond production deficiency and utilization inefficiency: mechanisms of the emergence of strategic categorization in episodic memory tasks. In F. E. Weinert and W. Schneider (eds.), *Memory performance and competencies: issues in growth and development*, pp. 141–159. Mahwah, NJ: Lawrence Erlbaum Associates.

Herrmann, D. J. (1982). Know the memory: the use of questionnaires to assess and study memory. *Psychological Bulletin*, 92, 434–452.

Johnson, C. N., and Wellman, H. M. (1980). Children's developing understanding of mental verbs: remember, know, and guess. *Child Development*, 51, 1095–1102.

Joyner, M. H., and Kurtz-Costes, B. (1997). Metamemory development. In N. Cowan (ed.), *The development of memory in childhood*, pp. 275–300. Hove, UK: Psychology Press.

Justice, E. M. (1985). Preschoolers' knowledge and use of behaviors varying in strategic effectiveness. *Merrill-Palmer Quarterly*, 35, 363–377.

(1986). Developmental changes in judgments of relative strategy effectiveness. *British Journal of Developmental Psychology*, 4, 75–81.

(1989). Preschoolers' knowledge and use of behaviors varying in strategic effectiveness. *Merrill-Palmer Quarterly*, 35, 363–377.

Justice, E. M., Baker-Ward, L., Gupta, S., and Jannings, L. R. (1997). Means to the goal of remembering: developmental changes in awareness of strategy use–performance relations. *Journal of Experimental Child Psychology*, 65, 293–314.

Justice, E. M. and Bray, N. W. (1979). *The effects of context and feedback on metamemory in young children*. Unpublished manuscript, Old Dominion University, Norfolk, VA.

Kobasigawa, A., and Metcalf-Haggert, A. (1993). Spontaneous allocation of study time by first- and third-grade children in a simple memory task. *Journal of Genetic Psychology*, 154, 223–235.

Koriat, A. (1993). How do we know what we know? The accessibility model of the feeling of knowing. *Psychological Review*, 100, 609–639.

Koriat, A., and Goldsmith, M. (1994). Memory in naturalistic and laboratory contexts: distinguishing the accuracy-oriented and quantity-oriented approaches to memory assessment. *Journal of Experimental Psychology: General*, 123, 297–315.

(1996). Memory metaphors and the real-life/laboratory controversy: correspondence versus storehouse conceptions of memory. *Behavioral and Brain Sciences*, 19, 167–228.

Koriat, A., Goldsmith, M., Schneider, W., and Nakash-Dura, M. (2001). The credibility of children's testimony: can children control the accuracy of their memory reports? *Journal of Experimental Child Psychology*, 79, 405–437.

Körkel, J., and Schneider, W. (1992). Domain-specific versus metacognitive knowledge effects on text recall and comprehension. In M. Carretero, M. Pope, R. J. Simons, and J. I. Pozo (eds.), *Learning and instruction: European research in an international context, Volume 3*, pp. 311–324. New York: Pergamon Press.

Kreutzer, M. A., Leonard, C., and Flavell, J. H. (1975). An interview study of children's knowledge about memory. *Monographs of the Society for Research in Child Development*, 40, no. 159.

Kuhn, D. (1999). Metacognitive development. In L. Balter and C. S. Tamis-LeMonda (eds.), *Child psychology: a handbook of contemporary issues*, pp. 259–286. Philadelphia, PA: Psychology Press.

(2000). Theory of mind, metacognition, and reasoning: a life-span perspective. In P. Mitchell and K. J. Riggs (eds.), *Children's reasoning and the mind*, pp. 301–326. Hove, UK: Psychology Press.

Kurtz, B. E., and Weinert, F. E. (1989). Metamemory, memory performance, and causal attributions in gifted and average children. *Journal of Experimental Child Psychology*, 48, 45–61.

Lange, G., Guttentag, R. E., and Nida, R. E. (1990). Relationships between study organization, retrieval organization, and general and strategy-specific memory knowledge in young children. *Journal of Experimental Child Psychology*, 49, 126–146.

Le Ny, J.-F., Denhière, G., and Le Taillanter, D. (1972). Regulation of study-time and interstimulus similarity in self-paced learning conditions. *Acta Psychologica*, 36, 280–289.

Leal, L., Crays, N., and Moely, B. E. (1985). Training children to use a self-monitoring study strategy in preparation for recall: maintenance and generalization effects. *Child Development*, 56, 643–653.

Lockl, K. and Schneider, W. (2002). Zur Entwicklung des selbstregulierten Lernens im Grundschulalter: Zusammenhänge zwischen Aufgabenschwierigkeit und Lernzeiteinteilung [The development of self-regulated learning in elementary school children: associations between task difficulty and allocation of study time]. *Psychologie in Erziehung und Unterricht*, 49, 3–16.

(in press). Developmental trends in children's feeling-of-knowing judgments. *International Journal of Behavioral Development*.

(in preparation). The effects of incentives and instructions on children's allocation of study time.

Lyon, T. D., and Flavell, J. H. (1993). Young children's understanding of forgetting over time. *Child Development*, 64, 789–800.

Masur, E. F., McIntyre, C. W., and Flavell, J. H. (1973). Developmental changes in apportionment of study time among items in a multitrial free recall task. *Journal of Experimental Child Psychology*, 15, 237–246.

Mazzoni, G., and Nelson, T. O. (1995). Judgments of learning are affected by the kind of encoding in ways that cannot be attributed to the level of recall. *Journal of Experimental Psychology: Learning, Memory, and Cognition*, 21, 1263–1274.

Metcalfe, J., and Shimamura, A. P. (1994). *Metacognition: knowing about knowing.* Cambridge, MA: MIT Press.

Misciones, J. L., Marvin, R. S., O'Brien, R. G., and Greenburg, J. T. (1978) A developmental study of preschool children's understanding of the words "know" and "guess." Child Development, 48, 1107–1113.

Moely, B. E., Hart, S. S., Santulli, K., Leal, L., Johnson, T., Rao, N., and Burney, L. (1986). How do teachers teach memory skills? *Educational Psychologist*, 21, 55–71.

Moely, B. E., Santulli, K. A., and Obach, M. S. (1995). Strategy instruction, metacognition, and motivation in the elementary school classroom. In F. E.

Weinert and W. Schneider (eds.), *Memory performance and competencies: issues in growth and development*, pp. 301–321. Mahwah, NJ: Lawrence Erlbaum Associates.

Moynahan, E. D. (1978). Assessment and selection of paired-associate strategies: a developmental study. *Journal of Experimental Child Psychology*, 26, 257–266.

Myers, M., and Paris, S. G. (1978). Children's metacognitive knowledge about reading. *Journal of Educational Psychology*, 70, 680–690.

Nelson, T. O. (1996). Consciousness and metacognition. *American Psychologist*, 51, 102–116.

Nelson, T. O., and Dunlosky, J. (1991). When people's judgments of learning (JOLs) are extremely accurate at predicting subsequent recall: the "delayed-JOL effect." *Psychological Science*, 2, 267–270.

Nelson, T. O., and Leonesio, R. J. (1988). Allocation of self-paced study time and the "labor-in-vain effect." *Journal of Experimental Psychology: Learning, Memory, and Cognition*, 14, 676–686.

Nelson, T. O., and Narens, L. (1990). Metamemory: a theoretical framework and new findings. In G. Bower (ed.), *The psychology of learning and motivation: advances in research and theory, Volume 26*, pp. 125–173. New York: Academic Press.

(1994). Why investigate metacognition? In J. Metcalfe and A. P. Shimamura (eds.), *Metacognition: knowing about knowing*, pp. 1–25. Cambridge, MA: MIT Press.

O'Sullivan, J. T. (1993). Applying cognitive developmental principles in classrooms. In R. Pasnak and M. L. Howe (eds.), *Emerging themes in cognitive development*, pp. 168–187. New York: Springer-Verlag.

O'Sullivan, J. T., and Howe, M. L. (1995). Metamemory and memory construction. *Consciousness and Cognition: An International Journal*, 4, 104–110.

(1998). A different view of metamemory with illustrations from children's beliefs about long-term retention. *European Journal of Psychology of Education*, 13, 9–28.

Palincsar, A. S. (1986). The role of dialogue in providing scaffolded instruction. *Educational Psychologist*, 21, 73–98.

Palinscar, A. S., and Brown, A. L. (1984). Reciprocal teaching of comprehension-fostering and comprehension-monitoring actitivities. *Cognition and Instruction*, 1, 117–175.

Paris, S. G., and Lindauer, B. K. (1982). The development of cognitive skills during childhood. In B. Wolman (ed.), *Handbook of developmental psychology* (pp. 33–349). Englewood Cliffs, NJ: Prentice Hall.

Paris, S. G., and Oka, E. R. (1986). Children's reading strategies, metacognition, and motivation. *Developmental Review*, 6, 25–56.

Premack, D., and Woodruff, G. (1978). Does the chimpanzee have a theory of mind? *Behavioral and Brain Sciences*, 1, 515–526.

Pressley, M. (1995). What is intellectual development about in the 1990s? In F. E. Weinert and W. Schneider (eds.), *Memory performance and competencies: issues in growth and development*, pp. 1–25. Hillsdale, NJ: Lawrence Erlbaum Associates.

Pressley, M., and Afflerbach, P. (1995). *Verbal protocols of reading: the nature of constructively responsive reading.* Hillsdale, NJ: Lawrence Erlbaum Associates.

Pressley, M., Borkowski, J. G., and O'Sullivan, J. T. (1985). Children's metamemory and the teaching of memory strategies. In D. L. Forrest-Pressley, G. E. MacKinnon, and T. G. Waller (eds.), *Metacognition, cognition, and human performance, Volume 1,* pp. 111–153. Orlando, FL: Academic Press.

Pressley, M., Borkowski, J. G., and Schneider, W. (1987). Cognitive strategies: good strategy users coordinate metacognition and knowledge. In R. Vasta and G. Whitehurst (eds.), *Annals of child development, Volume 5,* pp. 89–129. New York: JAI Press.

(1989). Good information processing: what it is and what education can do to promote it. *International Journal of Educational Research,* 13, 857–867.

Pressley, M., and Ghatala, E. S. (1990). Self-regulated learning: monitoring from text learning. *Educational Psychologist,* 25, 19–33.

Pressley, M., Goodchild, F., Fleet, J., and Zajchowski, R. (1989). The challenges of classroom strategy instruction. *Elementary School Journal,* 89, 301–342.

Pressley, M., Levin, J. R., Ghatala, E. S., and Ahmad, M. (1987). Test monitoring in young children. *Journal of Experimental Child Psychology,* 43, 96–111.

Pressley, M., and McCormick, C. (1995). *Advanced educational psychology for educators, researchers, and policymakers.* New York: HarperCollins.

Roebers, C., Moga, N., and Schneider, W. (2001). The role of accuracy motivation on children's and adults event recall. *Journal of Experimental Child Psychology,* 78, 313–329.

Rosenshine, B., and Meister, C. (1994). Reciprocal teaching: a review of the research. *Review of Educational Research,* 64, 479–530.

Schneider, W. (1985). Developmental trends in the metamemory–memory behavior relationship: an integrative review. In D. L. Forrest-Pressley, G. E. MacKinnon, and T. G. Waller (eds.), *Metacognition, cognition, and human performance, Volume 1,* pp. 57–109. New York: Academic Press.

(1986). The role of conceptual knowledge and metamemory in the development of organizational processes in memory. *Journal of Experimental Child Psychology,* 42, 218–236.

(1998a). Performance prediction in young children: effects of skill, metacognition and wishful thinking. *Developmental Science,* 1, 291–297.

(1998b). The development of procedural metamemory in childhood and adolescence. In G. Mazzoni and T. O. Nelson (eds.), *Monitoring and control processes in metacognition and cognitive neuropsychology,* pp. 1–21. Mahwah, NJ: Lawrence Erlbaum Associates.

(1999). The development of metamemory in children. In D. Gopher and A. Koriat (eds.), *Attention and performance XVII – cognitive regulation of performance: interaction of theory and application,* pp. 487–513. Cambridge, MA: MIT Press.

Schneider, W., and Bjorklund, D. F. (1998). Memory. In W. Damon, D. Kuhn, and R. S. Siegler (eds.), *Handbook of child psychology: cognition, perception and language, Volume 2,* pp. 467–521. New York: John Wiley and Sons.

Schneider, W., Borkowski, J. G., Kurtz, B. E., and Kerwin, K. (1986). Metamemory and motivation: a comparison of strategy use and performance in German and American children. *Journal of Cross-Cultural Psychology*, 17, 315–336.

Schneider, W., Körkel, J., and Weinert, F. E. (1987). The effects of intelligence, self-concept, and attributional style on metamemory and memory behavior. *International Journal of Behavioral Development*, 10, 281–299.

(1990). Expert knowledge, general abilities, and text processing. In W. Schneider and F. E. Weinert (eds.), *Interactions among aptitudes, strategies, and knowledge in cognitive performance*, pp. 235–251. New York: Springer.

Schneider, W., and Pressley, M. (1997). *Memory development between 2 and 20.* Hillsdale, NJ: Lawrence Erlbaum Associates.

Schneider, W., Schlagmüller, M., and Visé, M. (1998). The impact of metamemory and domain-specific knowledge on memory performance. *European Journal of Psychology of Education*, 13, 91–103.

Schneider, W., and Sodian, B. (1988). Metamemory–memory behavior relationships in young children: evidence from a memory-for-location task. *Journal of Experimental Child Psychology*, 45, 209–233.

Schneider, W., Visé, M., Lockl, K., and Nelson, T. O. (2000). Developmental trends in children's memory monitoring: evidence from a judgment-of-learning (JOL) task. *Cognitive Development*, 15, 115–134.

Schwanenflugel, P. J., Fabricius, W. V., and Alexander, J. (1994). Developing theories of mind: understanding concepts and relations between mental activities. *Child Development*, 65, 1546–1563.

Sodian, B., Schneider, W., and Perlmutter, M. (1986). Recall, clustering, and metamemory in young children. *Journal of Experimental Child Psychology*, 41, 395–410.

Stipek, D. J. (1984). Young children's performance expectations: logical analysis or wishful thinking? In J. G. Nicholls (ed.), *The development of achievement motivation*, pp. 121–142. Greenwich, CT: JAI Press.

Visé, M., and Schneider, W. (2000). Determinanten der Leistungsvorhersage bei Kindergarten- und Grundschulkindern: zur Bedeutung metakognitiver und motivationaler Einflussfaktoren [Determinants of performance prediction in kindergarten and school children: the importance of metacognitive and motivational factors]. *Zeitschrift für Entwicklungspsychologie und Pädagogische Psychologie*, 32, 51–58.

Weinert, F. E. (1986). Developmental variations of memory performance and memory related knowledge across the life-span. In A. Sorensen, F. E. Weinert, and L. R. Sherrod (eds.), *Human development: multidisciplinary perspectives*, pp. 535–554. Hillsdale, NJ: Lawrence Erlbaum Associates.

Weinert, F. E., and Schneider, W. (1999). *Individual development from 3 to 12: findings from the Munich longitudinal study.* Cambridge: Cambridge University Press.

Wellman, H. M. (1977). Preschoolers' understanding of memory-relevant variables. *Child Development*, 48, 1720–1723.

(1978). Knowledge of the interaction of memory variables: a developmental study of metamemory. *Developmental Psychology*, 14, 24–29.

(1983). Metamemory revisited. In M. T. H. Chi (ed.), *Trends in memory development research*, pp. 31–51. Basel: Karger.

(1985). A child's theory of mind: the development of conceptions of cognition. In S. R. Yussen (ed.), *The growth of reflection in children*, pp. 169–206. New York: Academic Press.

Wellman, H. M., and Johnson, C. N. (1979). Understanding of mental processes: a developmental study of "remember" and "forget." *Child Development*, 50, 79–88.

Wimmer, H., and Perner, J. (1983). Beliefs about beliefs: representation and constraining function of wrong beliefs in young children's understanding of deception. *Cognition*, 13, 103–128.

Wippich, W. (1980). Meta-Gedächtnis und Gedächtnis-Erfahrung. *Zeitschrift für Entwicklungspsychologie und Pädagogische Psychologie*, 12, 40–43.

Worden, P. E., and Sladewski-Awig, L. J. (1982). Children's awareness of memorability. *Journal of Educational Psychology*, 74 (3), 341–350.

Yussen, S. R., and Levy, V. M. (1975). Developmental changes in predicting one's own memory span of short-term memory. *Journal of Experimental Child Psychology*, 19, 502–508.

Zabrucky, K., and Ratner, H. H. (1986). Children's comprehension monitoring and recall of inconsistent stories. *Child Development*, 57, 1401–1418.

Conclusions

11   Metacognition research: an interim report

Asher Koriat

Recent years have witnessed a trend toward the establishment of metacognition as a field of investigation in its own right that pulls together researchers from a variety of areas. These areas include memory research, developmental psychology, judgment and decision-making, neuropsychology, reasoning and problem solving, social psychology, forensic psychology, educational testing, and consciousness. The few edited volumes that have appeared in recent years on metacognition illustrate the tendency of researchers from disparate areas of investigation to bring their research under the common umbrella of metacognition. This volume is also a witness to this tendency, which I expect to intensify in the years to come.

In this overview chapter, I will begin by pointing out the basic assumptions that seem to underlie much of the experimental work on metacognition. I will then outline several lines of research on metacognition, and show how the chapters in this volume actually reflect the converging influence of these different lines of research. In the main part of the chapter I will focus on the basic issues in metacognition, pointing out some of the contributions of the research reported in this book to the emerging unified field of metacognition.

Basic assumptions

Metacognition, narrowly defined, concerns people's cognitions and feelings about their cognitive states and cognitive processes. However, the term metacognition has been also used more broadly to refer to cognitions about cognition in general, as well as self-regulation processes that take cognitive processes as their object (see Schneider and Lockl, this volume).

Underlying much of the work on metacognition is a view of the person as an organism that actively monitors and regulates their cognitive processes towards the achievement of particular goals. Such a view has been dominant in social psychology ever since Heider's (1958) influential work, but has played a less prominent role in traditional information-processing models, in which cognition is sometimes conceived more like a medium through which information flows. The monitoring-and-control model that has been promoted by Nelson and his associates (Nelson, 1996; Nelson and Narens, 1990; see Son and Schwartz, this volume) assumes that in addition to an object level that is responsible for the processing of information, there exists a metalevel that monitors object-level processes, and regulates information processing and behavior accordingly. Thus, for example, during the study of new material, the degree of learning of different pieces of information is continuously monitored, and further learning resources are allocated until the learner's goal has been achieved.

The monitoring-and-control framework embodies two important metatheoretical assumptions (see Koriat, 2000). The first concerns the role of subjective experience. The assumption is that subjective beliefs and feelings play a supervisory, metalevel function. Phenomenal experience is relegated a critical role in the dynamics of the cognitive system: although many cognitive processes occur automatically and sometimes unconsciously, the assumption is that people generally monitor their ongoing mental processes, and the output of that monitoring is embodied in the form of subjective, phenomenal experience.

The second assumption concerns the causal role played by conscious, subjective experience. One of the reasons for the increased interest in metacognition lies in the belief that subjective experience is not a mere epiphenomenon, but actually affects and guides controlled cognitive processes and behavior (Son and Schwartz, this volume). Hence the interest in subjective reports is not only because such reports may mirror mental processes (as is generally the case when introspective reports are obtained). Rather, it is because subjective beliefs and feelings are assumed to play a *causal* role in affecting the regulation of cognitive processes and behavior (Koriat, 2000; Nelson, 1996).

The emphasis on subjective experience among students of metacognition coincides with the general emphasis on consciousness in models of memory (e.g. Tulving, 1985). The idea that different memory systems are associated with different types of consciousness implies that the subjective states of consciousness that accompany remembering represent an integral part of cognitive processes, and their assessment provides valuable cues regarding the nature of these processes. Indeed, some of the theoretical frameworks that have dominated the study of memory in recent years place a heavy emphasis on the quality of the subjective experience that accompanies remembering (Gardiner and Richardson-Klavehn, 2000; Jacoby and Kelley, 1987; Mitchell and Johnson, 2000; see Mazzoni and

Kirsch, this volume). The contributions of these theoretical frameworks should be integrated into the study of metacognition.

In sum, underlying metacognitive research is a view of the person as an active agent who has at their disposal an arsenal of cognitive strategies and devices that can be flexibly applied in order to reach certain goals. The choice of such strategies as well as their online regulation is based on the subjective monitoring of these processes.

Research traditions in metacognition

Historically, there have been several lines of research on metacognition, each with its own emphasis. The most systematic research has been conducted within two hitherto disparate areas – developmental psychology and cognitive psychology (see Koriat and Shitzer-Reichert, in press; Schneider and Lockl, this volume; Son and Schwartz, this volume). Each of these two traditions has contributed different experimental paradigms and different theoretical perspectives. In addition, research on various facets of metacognition has been conducted within other areas of psychology, such as judgment and decision-making, social psychology, and neuropsychology. I shall focus first on the developmental and cognitive research traditions, attempting to bring to the fore their different emphases.

The developmental and cognitive research traditions have much in common in terms of their basic assumption about the critical contribution of metacognition to cognitive performance. However, they differ in their methodological style and in their research goals. In the context of developmental psychology (see Schneider and Lockl, this volume), research on metacognition has been stimulated primarily by the work of Flavell and his associates (e.g. Flavell, 1971). Flavell emphasized the role that metacognitive skills play in the development of memory functioning in children, and proposed a conceptual framework that is much more extended than that which underlies cognitive-based research on metacognition (but see Mazzoni and Kirsch, this volume). The assumption that developmental changes in memory performance may reflect in part the development of metacognitive knowledge and metacognitive skills, has generated a great deal of research that attempts to specify the components of metacognitive abilities, their development with age, and their possible contribution to learning and memory performance. Developmental research has focused more on between-individual and between-group variation in different aspects of metacognitive knowledge, abilities, and strategies, rather than on the processes underlying metacognitive monitoring and control per se.

In contrast, the cognitive approach to metacognition has focused primarily on what developmental psychologists subsume under "procedural metamemory." That is, it tended to confine itself to the study of the processes and dynamics of metacognition, primarily in the context of memory processes. This line of research was influenced greatly by the classic work of Brown and McNeill (1966) on the tip-of-the-tongue (TOT) phenomenon, and by Hart's (1965) studies on the feeling of knowing (FOK). The focus of these pioneering investigations has been on the accuracy of partial knowledge and feelings of knowing when the retrieval of a memory target fails. Basic to their methodology is the focus on *within-individual* variation that can shed light on the working of metacognition. This focus is characteristic of a great deal of metacognition research in the context of cognitive psychology.

The difference in methodological styles between the developmental and cognitive approaches can be seen in the focus on cross-subject versus within-subject correlations (see Maki and McGuire, this volume). For example, in studying the memory–metamemory relationship, developmental psychologists typically focus on individual differences in measures of memory and metamemory, and base their conclusions on correlations across participants (e.g. Schneider and Pressley, 1997). It has been observed, for example, that such cross-individual correlations generally increase with age (see Schneider and Lockl, this volume). Cognitive students of metacognition, in contrast, typically focus on within-individual correlations, such as the correlation between FOK and recall or recognition memory (Schwartz and Metcalfe, 1994), between confidence and accuracy (Perfect, this volume), or between judgments of learning (JOL) and recall (Koriat, 1997).

The chapters in this book disclose a convergence between the two styles of research. For example, in the work reported in Hertzog (this volume) on metacognition and aging, some of the conclusions are based on the structure of inter-individual differences in memory and metamemory measures. Perfect's (this volume) research on the confidence–accuracy relationship was motivated primarily by findings involving cross-subject correlations. However, the research that he reported benefits greatly from the inclusion of measures of within-individual correlations. Maki and McGuire's chapter (this volume) also illustrates both methodologies: the accuracy of metacomprehension judgments can be evaluated by calculating the correlation between global measures of metacomprehension and actual test performance across subjects, or by calculating within-subject correlations between judgments made for several different texts with performance for these texts.

Further research still may be seen to represent a constructive merger between the two methodological approaches, focusing on inter-individual differences in intra-individual measures. For example, some of the experiments reported by Schneider and Lockl (this volume) borrow procedures from cognitive psychology to study age differences in monitoring and self-regulation as they reveal themselves through within-individual correlations. A similar effort underlies some of the work on metacognition in the elderly (e.g. Connor, Dunlosky, and Hertzog, 1997), as well as the work reported by Maki and McGuire (this volume) relating metacomprehension accuracy (as measured by within-subject correlations) to individual differences in verbal ability.

Apart from the developmental and cognitive traditions, several more restricted lines of research have also contributed to the study of metacognition. The first of these is within the area of decision-making. In fact, a great deal of the current work on metacognition can easily be classified under the rubric of judgment and decision-making (Koriat and Goldsmith, 1996b; see Mazzoni and Kirsch, this volume). At the same time, much of the extensive research initiated by Lichtenstein, Fischhoff, and Slovic (Keren, 1991; Lichtenstein, Fischhoff, and Phillips, 1982) on the calibration of subjective probabilities would certainly be classified as research on metacognition (e.g. Erev, Wallsten, and Budescu, 1994). Not only did that research contribute greatly to our understanding of the confidence–accuracy relationship, but it has also provided refined measures of that relationship that have since been applied to other metacognitive judgments (see Maki and McGuire, this volume); most important is the distinction between calibration (or bias) and resolution. In addition, the work on heuristics and biases of Tversky and Kahneman (see Kahneman, Slovic, and Tversky, 1982) has direct bearings on some of the central issues in metacognition such as the basis of metacognitive judgments (e.g. the availability heuristic, Tversky and Kahneman, 1973), or the reasons for illusions of knowing (e.g. hindsight and foresight biases; Fischhoff, 1982; Koriat and Bjork, 2001). The work by Gigerenzer and his group (e.g. Gigerenzer, Hoffrage, and Kleinbölting, 1991; Gigerenzer, Todd, and ABC Research Group, 1999) is also closely linked to issues discussed in metacognition.

A second line of research that is directly related to issues of metacognition is the current work on memory processes underlying memory accuracy and memory illusions (see Koriat, Goldsmith, and Pansky, 2000). This includes the work of Jacoby, Kelley, Whittlesea, and their associates on the subjective experience of remembering, and on illusions stemming from fluency misattributions (see Koriat et al., 2000). Jacoby's attributional view of memory embodies the idea that the very experience of remembering is the product of a metacognitive, attributional process. A similar assumption underlies Johnson's source-monitoring approach (see Mitchell and Johnson, 2000). This approach brings to the fore a variety of phenomenal cues that are used in deciding whether an event actually occurred or was just imagined (see Carroll and Perfect, this volume; Mazzoni and Kirsch, this volume). Recent work on false memory has also brought into attention the criticality of metacognitive processes in overcoming and escaping a variety of memory errors (Roediger and McDermott, 2000). A good example is Schacter's recent work on the distinctiveness heuristic (e.g. Dodson and Schacter, 2002).

A third line of research comes from social psychology (see Yzerbyt, Lories, and Dardenne, 1998). It goes without saying that many discussions in social cognition are about metacognitive processes. These include discussions of self-perception theory (Bem, 1972), attribution research (e.g. Jones et al., 1972; Ross, 1977) and dual-process theories (Chaiken and Trope, 1999). Of most interest to metacognitive researchers are the recent developments involving the role of subjective experience in social cognition. A rich body of research by Bless, Schwartz, Strack, Wänke, and others (see Bless and Forgas, 2000) has considered the informational value of cognitive and affective feelings, the effects of ease of retrieval and how these effects are modulated by mood, the contrast between informational and experiential factors that affect behavior, the judgmental adjustments that people make after recognizing that their judgments have been biased by contaminating influences, and many other issues with direct bearing on those discussed in this volume (see, for example, Mazzoni and Kirsch, this volume).

Finally, a fourth line of research is work in cognitive neuropsychology that attempts to specify possible correlates of "executive functions" such as those subsumed under metamemory (e.g. Burgess and Shallice, 1996). The general assumption is that impaired metacognitive processes are related to frontal-lobe damage (see Hertzog, this volume; Moulin, this volume).

As can be seen from this sketchy review, there is still much to be done in terms of pulling together the various threads of metacognitive research into a unified field. This volume, with its focus on applications, is a step in that direction. I shall now outline some of the major issues in metacognition as they are addressed in this volume: the bases of metacognitive judgments; the accuracy of these judgments and the factors that affect it; and the monitoring-based regulation of performance.

The monitoring of one's own knowledge

Much of the cognitive research on metacognition has concerned the monitoring of one's own knowledge, primarily the bases of monitoring and its accuracy. Let us begin by considering the basis of metacognitive judgments. Koriat and Levy-Sadot (1999) distinguished between experi-ence-based and information-based metacognitive judgments. The for-mer rely directly on a sheer feeling of knowing. For example, a person in the TOT state "feels" that the elusive name or word is about to emerge into consciousness (see Schwartz, 2001; Son and Schwartz, this volume). Similarly, a person who falls prey to unconscious plagiarism often experi-ences a firm conviction that the borrowed ideas are his / her own (Carroll and Perfect, this volume). Information-based or theory-based metacogni-tive judgments, in contrast, involve an explicit deduction from a variety of beliefs and memories. Such beliefs and memories clearly underlie many metacognitive predictions, perhaps giving rise to "judgments" of knowing rather than to "feelings" of knowing (Koriat, 1993).

Beliefs about memory

In this section we consider metacognitive beliefs, that is, beliefs about cognitive processes in general, including one's own. Such beliefs reflect one's "naive theory" about cognition, and may be explicit or implicit (see Mazzoni and Kirsch, this volume). The beliefs that people hold about cognition have received much more extended treatment by de-velopmental psychologists than by cognitive researchers (see Schneider and Lockl, this volume). Flavell's conceptualization, for example, places a heavy emphasis on metacognitive knowledge, that is, on what children explicitly know about cognitive functioning and limitations. Metacogni-tive knowledge includes beliefs about one's own memory, its strengths and weaknesses, about the conditions and variables that affect memory performance, and about different encoding and retrieval strategies and their effects on learning and remembering. Since Flavell's pioneering work, there has been a wealth of research in developmental psychology on children's beliefs about such matters as the limitations of short-term memory, the contribution of different task variables and learning strate-gies to memory performance, and so forth (e.g. Kreutzer, Leonard, and Flavell, 1975). In addition, there has been a great deal of work on chil-dren's theory of mind, and that research also touches upon some of the issues discussed in the context of metacognition (see Holland Joyner and Kurtz-Costes, 1997; Schneider and Bjorklund, 1998). Clearly, one's gen-eral beliefs about memory and the variables that affect it should contribute to one's metacognitive judgments in any given situation.

Much less research has been invested in the study of metacognitive be-liefs within the cognitive approach to metacognition. One reason for this neglect, perhaps, is that misconceptions about the working of memory are less prevalent among adults than among young children, and hence differences in people's theories about memory are less likely to play a critical role among adults than among children. Nevertheless, there has been some acknowledgment of the contribution of beliefs to adults' metacognitive judgments as well.

A good example comes from Perfect's chapter (this volume). According to the proposal advanced in that chapter, the reason why people's monitoring is less accurate for eyewitness memory than for general information is that people have greater insight into their relative expertise in areas of general knowledge than in eyewitnessing. People simply do not know how good they are in eyewitnessing. Indeed, feedback about one's memory performance in an eyewitness memory task in comparison to other people increased the confidence–accuracy correlation substantially.

Mazzoni and Kirsch (this volume) provide a general framework in which metacognitive beliefs play a prominent role in autobiographical reports. They propose a distinction between autobiographical beliefs and autobiographical memory. A person may report an autobiographical event with great confidence on the basis of a simple inference rather than on the basis of a recollective experience. In fact, it is possible to increase people's beliefs about the occurrence of an event without creating any specific memory of it.

Mazzoni and Kirsch's distinction parallels the distinction between information-based and experience-based metacognitive judgments. It is also reminiscent of Reder's (1987, 1988; Cary and Reder, in press) distinction between two strategies for making fact verifications about a studied story – plausibility and direct retrieval. The propensity of using each of these strategies was assumed to shift with retention interval towards greater use of the plausibility strategy. Mazzoni and Kirsch, however, proposed that people first check for recollective experience that affirms the occurrence of the stated episodic event, but the beliefs about the plausibility of the event can also determine how much recollective evidence it takes to classify that event as a memory.

Carroll and Perfect (this volume) advance a similar argument with regard to the contribution of beliefs to unconscious plagiarism. If participants have no expertise in an area, they will not be likely to attribute to themselves an idea to which they have been exposed. For unconscious plagiarism to occur, participants must be convinced that it was plausible that they had generated the ideas. Indeed, inadvertent plagiarism was found to increase as expertise developed. Glenberg and Epstein (1987) also showed that judgments of comprehension are closely related to beliefs about what one ought to know, that is, to perceived expertise in the particular domain.

Other analyses by cognitive students of metacognition have also invoked metacognitive beliefs as determinants of one's judgments and behavior. Several metacognitive biases have been assumed to result from people's misconceptions about the effects of various variables on memory performance. Such misconceptions include, for example, the belief that high-frequency words are better recognized than low-frequency words (Guttentag and Carroll, 1998), or that massed practice is more effective than spaced practice (Bjork, 1999). In Koriat's (1997) cue-utilization model of JOLs, a distinction was drawn between intrinsic and extrinsic cues that may contribute to JOLs, both of which may affect JOLs depending on one's beliefs. Intrinsic cues refer to inherent characteristics of the study materials (e.g. associative relatedness between paired associates). Extrinsic cues, on the other hand, pertain to the conditions of learning (e.g. number of presentations), or to the encoding operations applied by the learner (e.g. level of processing). Several results suggest that in making JOLs participants pay insufficient regard to the contribution of extrinsic factors relative to that of intrinsic factors (Koriat, Sheffer, and Ma'ayan, 2002; see also Carroll, Nelson, and Kirwan, 1997).

Global assessments of performance

The simplest measures of metacognitive monitoring are global or aggregate measures. For example, participants may be presented with a list of words and asked how many of them they are likely to recall. Of course, when global judgments are obtained before the study phase, participants' judgments should be heavily affected by their general beliefs about their own cognitive skills. When global judgments are obtained following the study phase, they might be affected in addition by feedback from one's encoding experience. Therefore we treat global metacognitive judgments as representing an intermediate category between theory-based and experience-based judgments. Maki and McGuire (this volume), however, note that global predictions and global postdictions of performance often yield different results in metacomprehension research.

Global metacognitive judgments are easy to obtain even with young children, and can be used to disclose over/underconfidence biases. Using such judgments, kindergarten children were found to be overly optimistic about their memory, believing that they would remember much of what they learn. Only during elementary school years do children become more realistic in their judgments. However, even young children's predictions tend to be accurate when the situation is familiar to them (see Schneider and Lockl, this volume). Schneider and Lockl note that it is not entirely clear that the inflated predictions of young children indeed reflect metacognitive deficiencies rather than motivational factors such as wishful thinking.

In several studies, participants were asked to make item-by-item JOLs during study, and in addition they were asked to provide a post-study aggregate judgment, that is, to estimate how many items they would recall. Similarly, after completing a forced-choice general-information questionnaire, participants have been asked to estimate how many items they had answered correctly. The general finding in these studies is that aggregate judgments typically yield an underconfidence bias even when the respective item-by-item judgments yield an overconfidence bias (Griffin and Tversky, 1992; Koriat et al., in press; Mazzoni and Nelson, 1995). It is interesting that children also display the pattern of stronger overconfidence bias in mean item-by-item JOLs than in aggregate judgments. The correlations, across subjects, between these two measures are rather low, suggesting that they may tap different aspects of monitoring (Schneider and Lockl, this volume).

In addition to global metacognitive judgments that are elicited in connection with a particular task, interest in practical aspects of memory has led to the development of self-report questionnaires about one's own memory functioning in general. These questionnaires, as discussed by Hertzog (this volume), have been used frequently with older adults, but also with brain-damaged patients. Self-reports about one's own memory are of interest in their own right, because they may have important implications for one's self-confidence and behavior. For example, as Hertzog describes, people's beliefs about the extent of memory decline in old age, and about the likelihood of contracting Alzheimer's disease are a major determinant of anxiety about aging. However, the accuracy of self-report measures is also of major interest. Moulin (this volume) refers specifically to the observation that Alzheimer's disease patients are generally unaware of their deficit, as evidenced by the discrepancy between their predicted and actual memory performance. Interestingly, as Moulin indicated, such discrepancies are not found when these patients predict other people's performance.

In sum, it is clear from this summary that metacognitive beliefs and theories as well as their effects have been mostly investigated in special populations such as young children, elderly adults, and brain-damaged patients.

Online measures of metacognitive judgments

An important contribution of the cognitive approach to metacognitive judgments concerns the bases of online metacognitive judgments. As discussed by Son and Schwartz (this volume), earlier approaches assumed that metacognitive judgments are based on direct access to memory traces. For example, Hart's (1965) conceptualization of FOK assumed a specialized internal monitor that directly detects the presence of the memory trace of the elusive target. A similar account has been proposed for JOLs: predictions of recall are based on direct read-out of the strength of the memory traces that are formed following study (Cohen, Sandler, and Keglevich, 1991). Some analyses of confidence judgments also implicitly assume that these judgments monitor the strength of memory traces.

In recent years, however, there has been a shift away from the trace-access view, although this view has not been entirely abandoned (see Metcalfe, 2000). More recent approaches assume that metacognitive feelings are based on the utilization of a variety of mnemonic cues. What these cues have in common is that they concern structural aspects of the processing of information rather than informational content (Koriat and Levy-Sadot, 1999). In the case of FOK judgments, the cues that have received some support are cue familiarity and accessibility (see Son and Schwartz, this volume). Recent findings suggest that these two cues contribute to FOK in a cascaded manner: whereas the effects of familiarity occur early, those of accessibility occur later, and only when cue familiarity is sufficiently high to drive the interrogation of memory for potential answers (Koriat and Levy-Sadot, 2001).

JOLs elicited during study have also been said to rely on fluency of processing (Begg et al., 1989; Benjamin and Bjork, 1996; Koriat, 1997), and in the case of delayed JOLs, perhaps on retrieval fluency as well (Nelson et al., 1998). Thus, delayed JOLs are substantially more accurate than immediate JOLs because they entail self-testing that provides feedback about retrieval fluency (see Dunlosky, Rawson, and McDonald, this volume). That is why the delayed-JOL advantage is most prominent for paired-associate learning when these JOLs are cued by the stimulus alone rather than by the entire cue-target pair.

Finally, subjective confidence in the correctness of retrieved information has also been claimed to rest on the ease with which information comes to mind (Kelley and Lindsay, 1993; Lindsay and Kelley, 1996).

Apart from perceptual and retrieval fluency, the source monitoring framework has brought to the fore a variety of phenomenal cues that are used to aid reality and source monitoring. Mazzoni and Kirsch (this volume) discuss the phenomenal quality of the content that comes to mind when a person is asked to decide whether a certain event occurred in their childhood. Such phenomenal characteristics as the vividness, richness, and amount of perceptual detail can help the person distinguish between memories and beliefs. In line with the work of Jacoby and Kelley (e.g. Jacoby and Kelley, 1987; Kelley and Jacoby, 2000), however, they also acknowledge the importance of processing fluency as an important basis of the subjective experience of memory. Carroll and Perfect (this volume) also make use of the source monitoring framework for analyzing unconscious plagiarism as representing a misattribution of external to internal sources. From the source monitoring framework, it follows that when people are required to justify their plagiarized ideas, the quality of their memory descriptions should be more similar to that characteristic of imagining (or beliefs, in Mazzoni and Kirsch's terms) than to that of external events.

The issue of accuracy

Central among the issues addressed in the study of metacognition is the question of accuracy. Since Hart's pioneering studies on the validity of FOK judgments, there has been a great deal of work on the correspondence between subjective and objective measures of memory performance. That work coincides with, in fact predates, the remarkable wave of accuracy-oriented research in memory (Koriat et al., 2000). As Koriat and Goldsmith (1996a) argued, there has been a shift in the study of memory from a storehouse metaphor, toward a correspondence metaphor. The storehouse metaphor has led laboratory-based research to focus almost exclusively on memory *quantity*, that is, on the amount of information (e.g. number of items) that can be recalled or recognized under different conditions. The emerging correspondence metaphor, in contrast, underlies the interest in memory *accuracy*, that is, in the extent to which memory reports can be trusted to be true. This interest has been motivated by many real-life memory phenomena, such as the question of the reliability of eyewitness testimony, the authenticity of memories of childhood sexual abuse, the observations demonstrating the malleability of memory such as those pertaining to the effects of post-event misinformation or imagination inflation, and so forth (see Mazzoni and Kirsch, this volume).

Of course, focus on correspondence and accuracy, is characteristic of a great deal of metacognitive research. The Brown and McNeill (1966) study on TOT, for example, was not concerned with the amount of partial information that people can retrieve about an elusive name or word. Rather it was concerned with the accuracy of that information. Of course, when it comes to metacognitive judgments, the first question generally addressed is "How accurate are these judgments?" This concern is central to the application of metacognitive research, and indeed figures prominently in most of the chapters in this volume.

The validity of metacognitive beliefs

When it comes to theory-based metacognitive judgments, a critical determinant of accuracy is the validity of one's naive theories and beliefs about one's own memory, and the factors that affect memory performance. Developmental psychologists have provided a great deal of information about the validity of children's metacognitive beliefs at different ages (see Schneider and Lockl, this volume). Among adults too, it is clear that people's metacognitive judgments are affected by their assumptions about how memory performance varies with different factors such as the passage of time, item difficulty, number of study trials, encoding strategies, and so on (e.g. Begg et al., 1989; Mazzoni and Cornoldi, 1993). Mazzoni and Kirsch (this volume) discuss how one's metacognitive beliefs can affect the decision whether an autobiographical event occurred. For example, because people believe in infantile amnesia, the lack of memory from early childhood would not be taken necessarily as evidence for nonoccurrence. However, the validity of such deductions depends, of course, on the accuracy of one's theories. As noted earlier, some of the wrong beliefs that people hold (see Bjork, 1999; Simon and Bjork, 2001) can result in illusions of knowing.

No less important are one's beliefs about the strengths and weaknesses of one's own memory. Hertzog (this volume) noted that among the elderly, self-reports about one's own memory are only mildly correlated with actual performance on memory tests. Among the explanations that he examined is the possibility that such reports do not mirror one's actual memory efficacy. Rather, they reflect one's beliefs about the functioning of memory in general (see Nisbett and Wilson, 1977). Moulin (this volume) proposed a similar explanation for the inflated global recall predictions given by patients with Alzheimer's disease before they have an opportunity to study the material. He argues that these predictions are based on preconceptions, because the patients actually decreased their predictions substantially following the first study trial.

The accuracy of online measures of metacognitive judgments

When item-by-item metacognitive measures are obtained, an important distinction is between calibration (or bias; see Maki and McGuire, this volume) and resolution. Calibration generally refers to the overall correspondence between mean predicted and mean actual memory performance. Resolution, or relative accuracy, refers to the discrimination between recalled and not-recalled items (in the case of FOK and JOL), or between correct and wrong answers (in the case of confidence judgments). It is generally estimated using a gamma correlation between judgments and performance across items (Nelson, 1984).

In order to obtain a valid measure of calibration, metacognitive judgments must be assessed using the same scale as that used to score performance. Not all of the studies on memory monitoring, however, have elicited metacognitive judgments in the form of assessed probabilities. This problem does not exist with regard to resolution.

As far as calibration is concerned, the results generally document an overconfidence bias in confidence judgments (see Lichtenstein et al., 1982). FOKs and JOLs, on the other hand, have generally been found to yield little overconfidence bias (Koriat, 1993, 1997).

As far as resolution is concerned, Son and Schwartz (this volume) note that by and large participants are generally accurate in their judgments. Nevertheless, there have been a number of reports in the literature that document strong dissociations between predicted and actual memory performance (e.g. Benjamin, Bjork, and Schwartz, 1998; Koriat, 1995; Simon and Bjork, 2001; see also Carroll and Perfect, this volume). What should be stressed is that these dissociations were deliberately generated by researchers as a vehicle for clarifying the mechanisms underlying metacognitive judgments, and do not mirror the ecological state of affairs.

The distinction between calibration and resolution, which is discussed in detail in Maki and McGuire's chapter, has important practical implications. In the case of JOLs, for example, calibration may affect a student's decision to continue studying for an exam or to stop, whereas resolution may guide the allocation of study time between different parts of the studied material. This distinction is also important for theoretical reasons: Koriat et al. (in press), for example, found that practice studying a list of paired associates improves resolution but impairs calibration (fostering increased underconfidence).

Variables that affect monitoring accuracy

What are the variables that increase or reduce monitoring accuracy? One factor that has been stressed is the degree of variability or homogeneity in the pool of items over which a within-person correlation is calculated. Koriat (1993) pointed out that changes in the characteristics of the items used can produce dramatic changes in the FOK–recall correlation. Perfect (this volume) made a similar point with regard to between-subject correlations: certain real-life factors may constraint the magnitude of the confidence–accuracy correlation by reducing inter-subject variability. For example, only eyewitnesses who have had a sufficient exposure to a crime are called to testify in court. Also, in psychological experiments, considerations of experimental control necessarily result in reduced variability between different eyewitnesses. Thus, the conditions that enhance experimental control reduce the likelihood of obtaining a high confidence–accuracy correlation.

Maki and McGuire (this volume) also stressed that the resolution of metacomprehension judgments depends on the discriminability between the items included in the study. They also reviewed other factors that affect metacomprehension accuracy. For example, whereas shallow processing of text generally leads to overconfidence, deeper processing leads to better calibrated predictions and postdictions. This effect bears some similarity to the hard–easy effect documented in the decision-making literature: the overconfidence bias observed when people indicate their confidence in their answers is reduced as the difficulty of the questions decreases (see, for example, Gigerenzer et al., 1991; Juslin, Winman, and Olsson, 2000). In fact, easy items tend to produce a certain degree of underconfidence (e.g. Griffin and Tversky, 1992). Indeed, a similar effect was observed by Maki (1998) for metacomprehension. Consistent with the hard–easy effect, Maki also found overconfidence to be higher among students who did poorly on the test.

Other results reviewed by Maki and McGuire indicate that as far as the resolution of metacomprehension judgments is concerned, it is medium difficulty texts that seem to yield the best resolution. Resolution also benefits from deeper processing as well as from rereading the texts (Rawson, Dunlosky, and Thiede, 2000). This latter effect parallels the observation that practice studying a list of paired associates improves resolution (see Koriat et al., in press).

Individual differences in monitoring accuracy

Is there a general metacognitive ability? Do people differ reliably in monitoring effectiveness and regulation skills, and if so, to what extent are these differences generalized across different domains and tasks? Some of the work in which metacognition is treated as a skill (for example, in developmental studies) actually implies that metacognition is indeed a reliable dimension of individual differences.

This question has been addressed in several different contexts. Maki and McGuire (this volume), for example, examined this question with regard to metacomprehension. The results of several studies indicate that there may exist stable and general individual differences in the over/underconfidence bias, but not in discrimination accuracy (resolution). The importance of individual differences in confidence judgments, that is, in over/underconfidence bias, is brought to the fore by Perfect (this volume). Perfect notes a pattern that has been consistently observed across a number of studies: whereas there was only a weak between-subject correlation between memory performance in a general-information task and in an eyewitness memory task (0.21), the respective correlation between mean confidence judgments in the two tasks was quite high (0.52). These results suggest that the reliable individual differences that have been observed in a number of studies in over/underconfidence bias reflect mostly reliable individual differences in confidence judgments alone. The individual differences in confidence, however, were not totally independent of performance because they yielded a relatively high correlation with performance on the general-information task (0.53).

By and large, the search for stable individual differences in discrimination accuracy (resolution) has been rather disappointing (Weaver and Kelemen, in press; see Maki and McGuire, this volume). It is rather surprising that systematic effects have been observed between different age groups in various aspects of metacognitive performance, but no reliable differences seem to exist within each group. Note, however, that resolution measures of memory accuracy have not yielded systematic age differences either (Schneider and Lockl, this volume).

Improving monitoring accuracy

An important practical challenge for metacognitive research is to find ways to train metacognition and help reduce metacognitive illusions. The need to develop techniques for the training of metacognition has been emphasized by Schneider and Lockl, by Maki and McGuire, and by Dunlosky et al. (this volume). Schneider and Lockl reviewed several attempts to train metacognition in children, most of which involve instructing children to apply specific cognitive strategies for learning and remembering. The results indicate some benefit from training under certain circumstances. Koriat et al. (2001) succeeded in enhancing the accuracy of children's reports by using a payoff schedule that encouraged children to volunteer all and only correct reports about a slide show. This procedure was found to improve children's memory accuracy even when they were tested a year later.

Several attempts have been made to reduce the overconfidence bias that is typically found in confidence judgments. Some of these were based on the assumption that overconfidence derives from a confirmation bias – a tendency to justify the choice that has already been made (Koriat, Lichtenstein, and Fischhoff, 1980).

More work has been carried out on the improvement of JOLs. Research on JOLs has indicated two variables that enhance the JOL–recall correlation markedly. The first is practice studying the same list of items: several studies indicated that resolution increases systematically from one study–test cycle to the next (e.g. King, Zechmeister, and Shaughnessy, 1980; Koriat, 1997; Koriat et al., in press). The second is delaying JOLs until shortly after study (see Dunlosky et al., this volume). As noted earlier, Dunlosky et al. present a convincing case for the argument that the delay-JOL effect derives from the opportunity that it offers for self-testing. It is argued that self-test will help enhance accuracy to the extent that the feedback from it rests on the same processes as those underlying performance in the criterion test.

A recent study (Koriat and Shitzer-Reichert, in press) suggests that the benefit that accrues from practice and delayed JOLs may rest on the same mechanism: when both manipulations were combined, the benefit for JOL resolution was not better than that found for each of them separately.

Monitoring-based self-regulation

As noted earlier, the interest in metacognition derives in part from the assumption that metacognitive judgments affect the strategic regulation of cognitive processes and behavioral responses. Indeed, as Son and Schwartz (this volume) note, there has been increased interest among cognitive students in the investigation of how people apply their metacognitive knowledge to optimize performance.

The interest in metacognitive regulation has been quite prominent among developmental psychologists, who have studied a variety of encoding and retrieval strategies as they develop with age. Research has attempted to specify what children at different ages know about the potential benefits of using these strategies, and the extent to which they make use of them (see Bjorklund and Douglas, 1997). The general conclusion (see Schneider and Lockl, this volume) is that there is a general increase from middle childhood to adolescence in self-regulation skills, and that during the elementary school years effective self-regulation occurs only in highly constrained situations.

An important distinction made by developmental psychologists is between metacognitive beliefs about the value of using a particular strategy, and the ability to actually use that strategy. For example, as discussed in Schneider and Lockl (this volume), both younger and older children can distinguish between easier and harder items in a study list. However, only the older children allocate more study time to the more difficult items (Dufresne and Kobasigawa, 1989). Thus, differences between younger and older children may sometimes lie not simply in the effectiveness of monitoring but in the ability to put the output of monitoring to use in the self-regulation of cognitive processes.

A seemingly reversed pattern is reported by Moulin (this volume) for patients with Alzheimer's disease: like control participants, they exhibited increased recall performance and reduced self-paced study time with repeated presentations of a list. However, unlike control participants, their JOLs showed no sensitivity to list repetition. Thus, regulation seems to demonstrate some sensitivity to repetition in the absence of a corresponding sensitivity in monitoring.

In comparison to the developmental approach to metacognition, only a restricted set of control processes has been investigated by cognitive psychologists (see Son and Schwartz, this volume). These include the selection of items for study or restudy during learning, and the time allocated to the study of different items in self-paced learning. The general finding is that learners choose the more difficult items for (re-)study unless the study goal is modest (e.g. to master six out of thirty items; Thiede and Dunlosky, 1999), in which case they choose the easier items. With regard to study time, more study time is allocated to the more difficult items, but the reverse is found when the overall amount of time available for study is too short relative to the difficulty of the material (Son and Metcalfe, 2000).

As far as the retrieval phase is concerned, the primary dependent variable has been the amount of time searching for a solicited target before the person gives up (see Son and Schwartz, this volume). People search longer for an elusive memory target when they experience a high FOK or when they are in a TOT state (Gruneberg, Monks, and Sykes, 1977; Nelson, Gerler, and Narens, 1984; Schwartz, 2001). Search time is also affected by the person's goals, for example, speed versus accuracy (Barnes et al., 1999). Reder and her associates (Reder, 1987; Reder and Ritter, 1992) also investigated more refined strategic choices, such as the choice to retrieve versus infer an answer or retrieve versus calculate a solution to an arithmetic problem.

As far as retrospective confidence judgments are concerned, people have been found to bet money on the correctness of their answer when they were confident about it even when their confidence judgments had little validity (Fischhoff, Slovic, and Lichtenstein, 1977). Koriat and Goldsmith (1996b) used a task that attempts to simulate that of a person on a witness stand who is sworn to tell "the whole truth and nothing but the truth" (see Mazzoni and Kirsch, this volume). They found that people generally enhance the accuracy of their reports by screening out pieces of information that they believe are likely to be wrong (i.e., answers endorsed with low confidence). Thus, under conditions that encourage memory accuracy, participants rely very heavily on their subjective confidence in the answer in deciding whether to volunteer or withhold it, and do so even when their confidence judgments have little validity. Children as young as eight years also rely on their confidence judgments in choosing which answers to report, thereby enhancing the accuracy of their reports in comparison to a situation in which they are forced to answer all questions (see Schneider and Lockl, this volume). Among adults, confidence judgments have also been found to affect the grain size of the memory report (e.g. reporting "the event took place in late afternoon" rather than "around 4:00–4:30 in the afternoon"). In general, people rely on their confidence judgments in choosing a level of generality for which their report is likely to be correct (Goldsmith, Koriat, and Weinberg-Eliezer, 2002). Of course, the degree of confidence that a person attaches to their report affects how much we (as well as judges) trust their report to be reliable (see Perfect, this volume).

Toward the application of metacognitive research

This brief overview illustrates the potential applications of metacognitive research in many different contexts. There have been several successful attempts to apply metacognitive theory and findings to real-life problems, but these attempts only scratch the surface of what is yet to be done. There is much to be accomplished in applying metacognitive theory to educational settings, and in incorporating monitoring and strategy instruction into the curriculum (Schneider and Lockl, this volume). The research on metacomprehension (Maki and McGuire, this volume) as well as that on JOLs (Dunlosky et al., this volume) illustrates some simple techniques by which the accuracy of one's metacognitive judgments can be markedly enhanced. On-the-job training programs have been shown to be susceptible to instilling an illusory sense of competence, and there are ways to avoid that (Bjork, 1999). Clearly, there are many ways in which metacognition research can be applied to optimize learning (Son and Schwartz, this volume). However, as some of the results suggest, effective monitoring skills and accurate metacognitive beliefs do not necessarily translate into effective self-regulation strategies (see Moulin, this volume; Schneider and Lockl, this volume).

Another area in which metacognition research has important implications is forensic psychology. There has been some acknowledgment on the part of the judicial system as well as law enforcement departments of the critical contribution of psychological theory to the improvement of current practices. An important task for metacognitive researchers is to educate the public about the malleability of memory (Mazzoni and Kirsch, this volume; Carroll and Perfect, this volume) and about ways in which the accuracy of memory reports can be enhanced (e.g. Koriat and Goldsmith, 1996b). The findings regarding the diagnosticity of confidence judgments in eyewitness testimony (Perfect, this volume) have important implications for the court. So have the findings documenting an overconfidence bias. In fact, the increased interest in the reliability and accuracy of memory has generated increased awareness of the metacognitive processes underlying several memory biases, and several proposals have been advanced of how metacognitive strategies can be used to help avoid or correct such biases.

Communication in its various forms is another domain in which metacognitive research can make important contributions. In everyday life not only do we have to monitor our learning and comprehension (Maki and McGuire, this volume), but we also have to monitor those of others. For example, teachers must monitor the comprehension of their pupils. They must assess the relative difficulty of different topics and regulate the amount of time spent teaching each of them. In lecturing or communicating with others, we must have an accurate knowledge about what the other knows or believes, and must assess online their degree of comprehension (Koriat and Bjork, 2001). Such knowledge is especially valuable when one has to take the perspective of the other (Nickerson, 1999; Schneider and Lockl, this volume).

Finally, metacognitive research has important implications in dealing with special populations. The results accumulated so far on metacognition in the elderly suggest that as far as the standard laboratory tasks are concerned, monitoring resolution is generally spared in old age (Hertzog, this volume). However, compared to younger adults, older people have been found to rely more heavily on gist, familiarity, or plausibility than on exact retrieval or recollection. This may result in impaired monitoring and control processes in old age. Studies linking metacognitive skills to frontal functions also suggest that memory deficits observed in some brain-damaged individuals may stem from impaired monitoring and control (see Moulin, this volume). Thus, metacognitive research can help not only in the development of diagnostic tools, but also in devising methods that alleviate some of the memory problems encountered in special populations.

It would seem that the goal of applying metacognitive research to real-word issues would be best served by further development and refinement of theories of metacognition. This goal, in turn, can benefit greatly by combining insights from the various lines of research and theorizing about metacognition.

REFERENCES

Barnes, A. E., Nelson, T. O., Dunlosky, J., Mazzoni, G., and Narens, L. (1999). An integrative system of metamemory components involved in retrieval. In D. Gopher and A. Koriat (eds.), *Attention and performance XVII – cognitive regulation of performance: interaction of theory and application*, pp. 287–313. Cambridge, MA: MIT Press.

Begg, I., Duft, S., Lalonde, P., Melnick, R., and Sanvito, J. (1989). Memory predictions are based on ease of processing. *Journal of Memory and Language*, 28, 610–632.

Bem, D. J. (1972). Self-perception theory. *Advances in Experimental Psychology*, 6, 1–59.

Benjamin, A. S., and Bjork, R. A. (1996). Retrieval fluency as a metacognitive index. In L. M. Reder (ed.), *Implicit memory and metacognition*, pp. 309–338. Hillsdale, NJ: Lawrence Erlbaum Associates.

Benjamin, A. S., Bjork, R. A., and Schwartz, B. L. (1998). The mismeasure of memory: when retrieval fluency is misleading as a metamnemonic index. *Journal of Experimental Psychology: General*, 127, 55–68.

Bjork, R. A. (1999). Assessing our own competence: heuristics and illusions. In D. Gopher and A. Koriat (eds.), *Attention and performance XVII – cognitive regulation of performance: interaction of theory and application*, pp. 435–459. Cambridge, MA: MIT Press.

Bjorklund, D. F., and Douglas, R. N. (1997). The development of memory strategies. In N. Cowan (ed.), *The development of memory in childhood*, pp. 201–246. Hove, UK: Psychology Press.

Bless, H., and Forgas, J. P. (2000). *The message within: the role of subjective experience in social cognition and behavior*. Hove, UK: Psychology Press.

Brown, R., and McNeill, D. (1966). The "tip of the tongue" phenomenon. *Journal of Verbal Learning and Verbal Behavior*, 5, 325–337.

Burgess, P. W., and Shallice, T. (1996). Confabulation and the control of recollection. *Memory*, 4, 359–411.

Carroll, M., Nelson, T. O., and Kirwan, A. (1997). Tradeoff of semantic relatedness and degree of overlearning: differential effects on metamemory and on long-term retention. *Acta Psychologica*, 95, 239–253.

Cary, M., and Reder, L. M. (in press). Metacognition in strategy selection: giving consciousness too much credit. In P. Chambres, M. Izaute, and P-J. Marescaux (eds.), *Metacognition: process, function, and use*. Dordrecht, The Netherlands: Kluwer.

Chaiken, S., and Trope, Y. (eds., 1999). *Dual process theories in social psychology*. New York: Guilford Publications.

Cohen, R. L., Sandler, S. P., and Keglevich, L. (1991). The failure of memory monitoring in a free recall task. *Canadian Journal of Psychology*, 45, 523–538.

Connor, L. T., Dunlosky, J., and Hertzog, C. (1997). Age-related differences in absolute but not relative metamemory accuracy. *Psychology and Aging*, 12, 50–71.

Dodson, C. S., and Schacter, D. L. (2002). When false recognition meets metacognition: The distinctiveness heuristic. *Journal of Memory and Language*, 46, 782–803.

Dufresne, A., and Kobasigawa, A. (1989). Children's spontaneous allocation of study time: differential and sufficient aspects. *Journal of Experimental Child Psychology*, 47, 274–296.

Erev, I., Wallsten, T. S., and Budescu, D. V. (1994). Simultaneous over- and underconfidence: the role of error in judgment processes. *Psychological Review*, 101, 519–527.

Fischhoff, B. (1982). For those condemned to study the past: heuristics and biases in hindsight. In D. Kahneman, P. Slovic, and A. Tversky (eds.), *Judgment under uncertainty: heuristics and biases*, pp. 335–351. Cambridge, UK: Cambridge University Press.

Fischhoff, B., Slovic, P., and Lichtenstein, S. (1977). Knowing with certainty: the appropriateness of extreme confidence. *Journal of Experimental Psychology: Human Perception and Performance*, 3, 552–564.

Flavell, J. H. (1971). First discussant's comments: what is memory development the development of? *Human Development*, 14, 272–278.

Gardiner, J. M., and Richardson-Klavehn, A. (2000). Remembering and knowing. In E. Tulving and F. I. M. Craik (eds.), *The Oxford handbook of memory*, pp. 229–244. Oxford, UK: Oxford University Press.

Gigerenzer, G., Hoffrage, U., and Kleinbölting, H. (1991). Probabilistic mental models: a Brunswikian theory of confidence. *Psychological Review*, 98, 506–528.

Gigerenzer, G., Todd, P. M., and ABC Research Group (1999). *Simple heuristics that make us smart*. New York: Oxford University Press.

Glenberg, A. M., and Epstein, W. (1987). Inexpert calibration of comprehension. *Memory and Cognition* 15, 84–93.

Goldsmith, M., Koriat, A., and Weinberg-Eliezer, A. (2002). The strategic regulation of grain size in memory reporting. *Journal of Experimental Psychology: General*, 131, 73–95.

Griffin, D. W., and Tversky, A. (1992). The weighing of evidence and the determinants of confidence. *Cognitive Psychology*, 24, 411–435.

Gruneberg, M. M., Monks, J., and Sykes, R. N. (1977). Some methodological problems with feeling of knowing studies. *Acta Pychologica*, 41, 365–371.

Guttentag, R., and Carroll, D. (1998). Memorability judgments for high- and low-frequency words. *Memory and Cognition*, 26, 951–958.

Hart, J. T. (1965). Memory and the feeling-of-knowing experience. *Journal of Educational Psychology*, 56, 208–216.

Heider, F. (1958). *The psychology of interpersonal relations*. New York: Wiley.

Holland Joyner, M., and Kurtz-Costes, B. (1997). Metamemory development. In N. Cowan (ed.), *The development of memory in children*, pp. 275–300. Hove, UK: Psychology Press.

Jacoby, L., and Kelley, C. M. (1987). Unconscious influences of memory for a prior event. *Personality and Social Psychology Bulletin*, 13, 314–336.

Jones, E. E., Kanouse, D. E., Kelley, H. H., Nisbett, R. E., Slavin, S., and Weiner, B. (1972), *Attribution: perceiving the causes of behavior.* Morristown, NJ: General Learning Press.

Juslin, P., Winman, A., and Olsson, H. (2000). Naive empiricism and dogmatism in confidence research: a critical examination of the hard–easy effect. *Psychological Review*, 107, 384–396.

Kahneman, D., Slovic, P., and Tversky, A. (1982). *Judgment under uncertainty: heuristics and biases.* Cambridge: Cambridge University Press.

Kelley, C. M., and Jacoby, L. (2000). Recollection and familiarity: process dissociation. In E. Tulving and F. I. M. Craik (eds.), *The Oxford handbook of memory*, pp. 215–228. Oxford, UK: Oxford University Press.

Kelley, C. M., and Lindsay, D. S. (1993). Remembering mistaken for knowing: ease of retrieval as a basis for confidence in answers to general knowledge questions. *Journal of Memory and Language*, 32, 1–24.

Keren, G. (1991). Calibration and probability judgments: conceptual and methodological issues. *Acta Psychologica*, 77, 217–273.

King, J. F., Zechmeister, E. B., and Shaughnessy, J. J. (1980). Judgments of knowing: the influence of retrieval practice. *American Journal of Psychology*, 93, 329–343.

Koriat, A. (1993). How do we know that we know? The accessibility model of the feeling of knowing. *Psychological Review*, 100, 609–639.

(1995). Dissociating knowing and the feeling of knowing: further evidence for the accessibility model. *Journal of Experimental Psychology: General*, 124, 311–333.

(1997). Monitoring one's own knowledge during study: a cue-utilization approach to judgments of learning. *Journal of Experimental Psychology: General*, 126, 349–370.

(2000). The feeling of knowing: some metatheoretical implications for consciousness and control. *Consciousness and Cognition*, 9, 149–171.

Koriat, A., and Bjork, R. A. (submitted). Illusions of competence in monitoring one's knowledge during study: the foresight bias.

Koriat, A., and Goldsmith, M. (1996a). Memory metaphors and the real-life/laboratory controversy: correspondence versus storehouse views of memory. *Behavioral and Brain Sciences*, 19, 167–188.

(1996b). Monitoring and control processes in the strategic regulation of memory accuracy. *Psychological Review*, 103, 490–517.

Koriat, A., Goldsmith, M., and Pansky, A. (2000). Toward a psychology of memory accuracy. *Annual Review of Psychology*, 51, 481–537.

Koriat, A., Goldsmith, M., Schneider, W., and Nakash-Dura, M. (2001). The credibility of children's testimony: can children control the accuracy of their memory reports? *Journal of Experimental Child Psychology*, 79, 405–437.

Koriat, A., and Levy-Sadot, R. (1999). Processes underlying metacognitive judgments: information-based and experience-based monitoring of one's own knowledge. In S. Chaiken and Y. Trope (eds.), *Dual process theories in social psychology*, pp. 483–502. New York: Guilford Publications.

(2001). The combined contributions of the cue-familiarity and the accessibility heuristics to feelings of knowing. *Journal of Experimental Psychology: Learning, Memory, and Cognition*, 27, 34–53.

Koriat, A., Lichtenstein, S., and Fischhoff, B. (1980). Reasons for confidence. *Journal of Experimental Psychology: Human Learning and Memory*, 6, 107–118.

Koriat, A., Sheffer, L., and Ma'ayan, H. (2002). Comparing objective and subjective learning curves: judgments of learning exhibit increased under-confidence with practice. *Journal of Experimental Psychology: General*, 131(2), 147–162.

Koriat, A., and Shitzer-Reichert, R. (in press). Metacognitive judgments and their accuracy: insights from the processes underlying judgments of learn-ing in children. In P. Chambres, M. Izaute, and P.-J. Marescaux (eds.), *Metacognition: process, function, and use*. New York: Kluwer.

Kreutzer, M. A., Leonard, C., and Flavell, J. H. (1975). An interview study of children's knowledge about memory. *Monographs of the Society for Research in Child Development*, 40 (1, Serial no. 159).

Lichtenstein, S., Fischhoff, B., and Phillips, L. D. (1982). Calibration of prob-abilities: the state of the art to 1980. In D. Kahneman, P. Slovic., and A. Tversky (eds.), *Judgment under uncertainty: heuristics and biases*, pp. 306–334. Cambridge: Cambridge University Press.

Lindsay, D. S., and Kelley, C. M. (1996). Creating illusions of familiarity in a cued recall remember/know paradigm. *Journal of Memory and Language*, 35, 197–211.

Maki, R. H. (1998). Metacomprehension of text: influence of absolute confidence level on bias and accuracy. In D. L. Medin (ed.), *The Psychology of learning and motivation, Volume 38*, pp. 223–248. San Diego, CA: Academic Press.

Mazzoni, G., and Cornoldi, C. (1993). Strategies in study time allocation: why is study time sometimes not effective? *Journal of Experimental Psychology: General*, 122, 47–60.

Mazzoni, G., and Nelson, T. O. (1995). Judgments of learning are affected by the kind of encoding in ways that cannot be attributed to the level of recall. *Journal of Experimental Psychology: Learning, Memory, and Cognition*, 21, 1263–1274.

Metcalfe, J. (2000). Feelings and judgement of knowing: is there a special noetic state? *Consciousness and Cognition*, 9, 178–186.

Mitchell, K. J., and Johnson, M. K. (2000). Source monitoring: attributing mental experiences. In E. Tulving and F. I. M. Craik (eds.), *The Oxford handbook of memory*, pp. 179–195. Oxford, UK: Oxford University Press.

Nelson, T. O. (1984). A comparison of current measures of the accuracy of feeling-of-knowing predictions. *Psychological Bulletin*, 95, 109–133.

Nelson, T. O. (1996). Consciousness and metacognition. *American Psychologist*, 51, 102–116.

Nelson, T. O., Gerler, D., and Narens, L. (1984). Accuracy of feeling-of-knowing judgments for predicting perceptual identification and relearning. *Journal of Experimental Psychology: General*, 113, 282–300.

Nelson, T. O., Graf, A., Dunlosky, J., Marlatt, A., Walker, D., and Luce, K. (1998). Effect of acute alcohol intoxication on recall and on judgments of learning during the acquisition of new information. In G. Mazzoni and T. O. Nelson (eds.), *Metacognition and cognitive neuropsychology: monitoring and control processes*, pp. 161–180. Mahwah, NJ: Lawrence Erlbaum Associates.

Nelson, T. O., and Narens, L. (1990). Metamemory: a theoretical framework and new findings. In G. H. Bower (ed.), *The psychology of learning and motivation: advances in research and theory, Volume 26*, pp. 125–173. San Diego, CA: Academic Press.

Nickerson, R. S. (1999). How we know – and sometimes misjudge – what others know: imputing one's own knowledge to others. *Psychological Bulletin*, 125, 737–759.

Nisbett, R. E., and Wilson, T. D. (1977). Telling more than we know: verbal reports on mental processes. *Psychological Review*, 84, 231–279.

Rawson, K. A., Dunlosky, J., and Thiede, K. W. (2000). The rereading effect: metacomprehension accuracy improves across reading trials. *Memory and Cognition*, 28, 1004–1010.

Reder, L. M. (1987). Strategy selection in question answering. *Cognitive Psychology*, 19, 90–138.

Reder, L. M. (1988). Strategic control of retrieval strategies. *The Psychology of Learning and Motivation*, 22, 227–259.

Reder, L. M., and Ritter, F. E. (1992). What determines initial feeling of knowing? Familiarity with question terms, not with the answer. *Journal of Experimental Psychology: Learning, Memory, and Cognition*, 18, 435–451.

Roediger, H. L., and McDermott, K. B. (2000). Distortions of memory. In E. Tulving and F. I. M. Craik (eds.), *The Oxford handbook of memory*, pp. 149–177. Oxford, UK: Oxford University Press.

Ross, L. (1977). The intuitive psychologist and his shortcomings: distortions in the attribution process. In L. Berkowitz (ed.), *Advances in experimental social psychology, Volume 10*, pp. 174–221. New York: Academic Press.

Schneider, W., and Bjorklund, D. F. (1998). Memory. In W. Damon, D. Kuhn, and R. S. Siegler (eds.), *Handbook of child psychology: cognition, perception, and language, Volume 2*, pp. 467–521. New York: Wiley.

Schneider, W., and Pressley, M. (1997). *Memory development between 2 and 20*. New York: Springer-Verlag.

Schwartz, B. L. (2001). The relation of tip-of-the-tongue states and retrieval time. *Memory and Cognition*, 29, 117–126.

Schwartz, B. L., and Metcalfe, J. (1994). Methodological problems and pitfalls in the study of human metacognition. In J. Metcalfe and A. P. Shimamura (eds.), *Metacognition: knowing about knowing*, pp. 115–135. Cambridge, MA: MIT Press.

Simon, D. A., and Bjork, R. A. (2001). Metacognition in motor learning. *Journal of Experimental Psychology: Learning, Memory, and Cognition*, 27, 907–912.

Son, L. K., and Metcalfe, J. (2000). Metacognitive and control strategies in study-time allocation. *Journal of Experimental Psychology: Learning, Memory, and Cognition*, 26, 204–221.

Thiede, K. W., and Dunlosky, J. (1999). Toward a general model of self-regulated study: an analysis of selection of items for study and self-paced study time. *Journal of Experimental Psychology: Learning, Memory, and Cognition*, 25, 1024–1037.

Tulving, E. (1985). How many memory systems are there? *American Psychologist*, 40, 85–398.

Tversky, A., and Kahneman, D. (1973). Availability: a heuristic for judging frequency and probability. *Cognitive Psychology*, 5, 207–232.

Weaver, C. A., and Kelemen, W. L. (in press). Comparing processing-based, stimulus-based, and subject-based factors in metacognition: evidence against a general metacognitive ability. In P. Chambres, M. Izaute, and P.-J. Marescaux (eds.), *Metacognition: process, function, and use*. New York: Kluwer.

Yzerbyt, V. Y., Lories, G., and Dardenne, B. (1998), *Metacognition: cognitive and social dimensions*. London, UK: Sage Publications.

Index

Note: page numbers in **bold type** refer to figures and tables; page numbers in *italic type* refer to passing mentions of an author or subject; personal names beginning with Mc are filed as Mac.